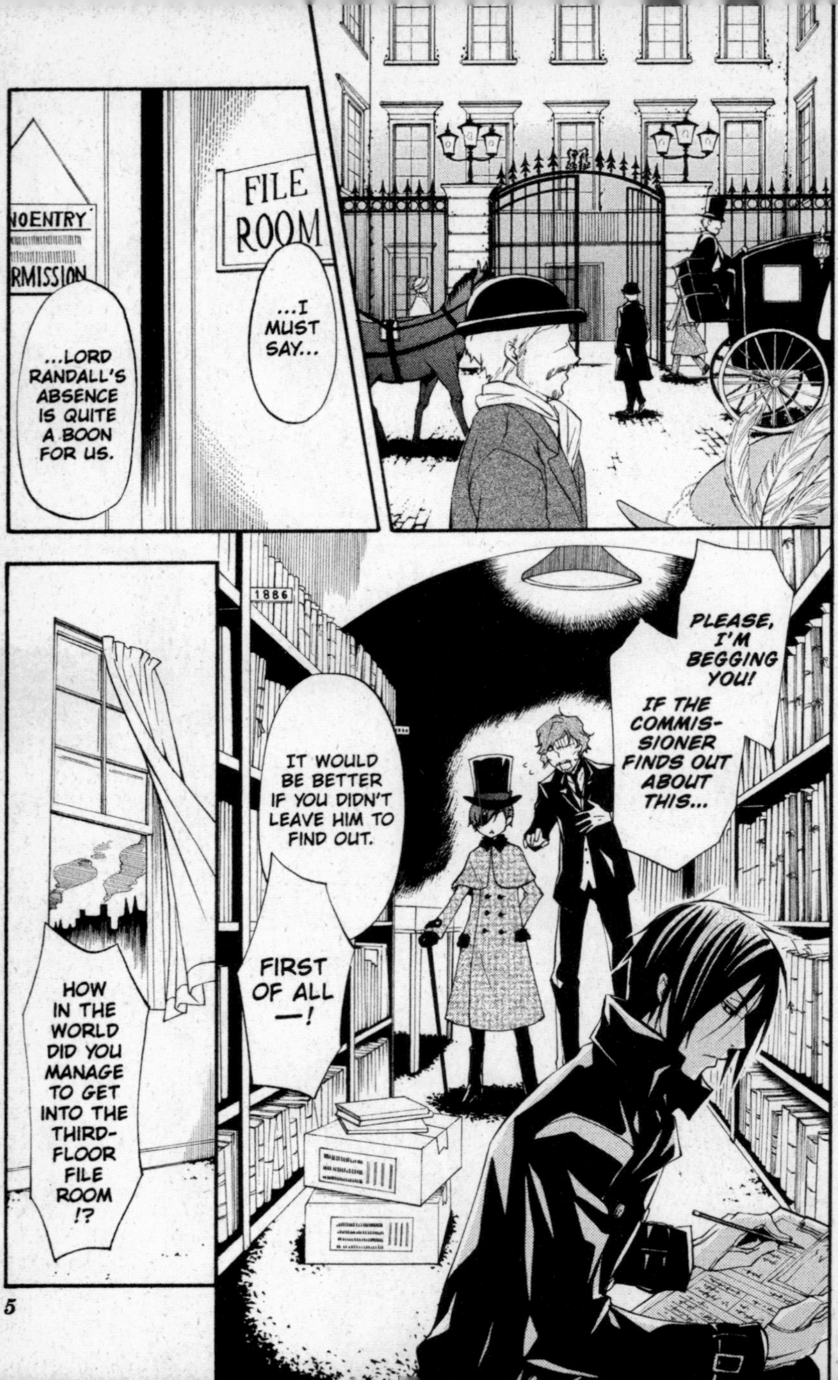
FILE ROOM
NOENTRY
RMISSION
...I MUST SAY...
...LORD RANDALL'S ABSENCE IS QUITE A BOON FOR US.
1886
PLEASE, I'M BEGGING YOU!
IF THE COMMISSIONER FINDS OUT ABOUT THIS...
IT WOULD BE BETTER IF YOU DIDN'T LEAVE HIM TO FIND OUT.
FIRST OF ALL—!
HOW IN THE WORLD DID YOU MANAGE TO GET INTO THE THIRD-FLOOR FILE ROOM!?

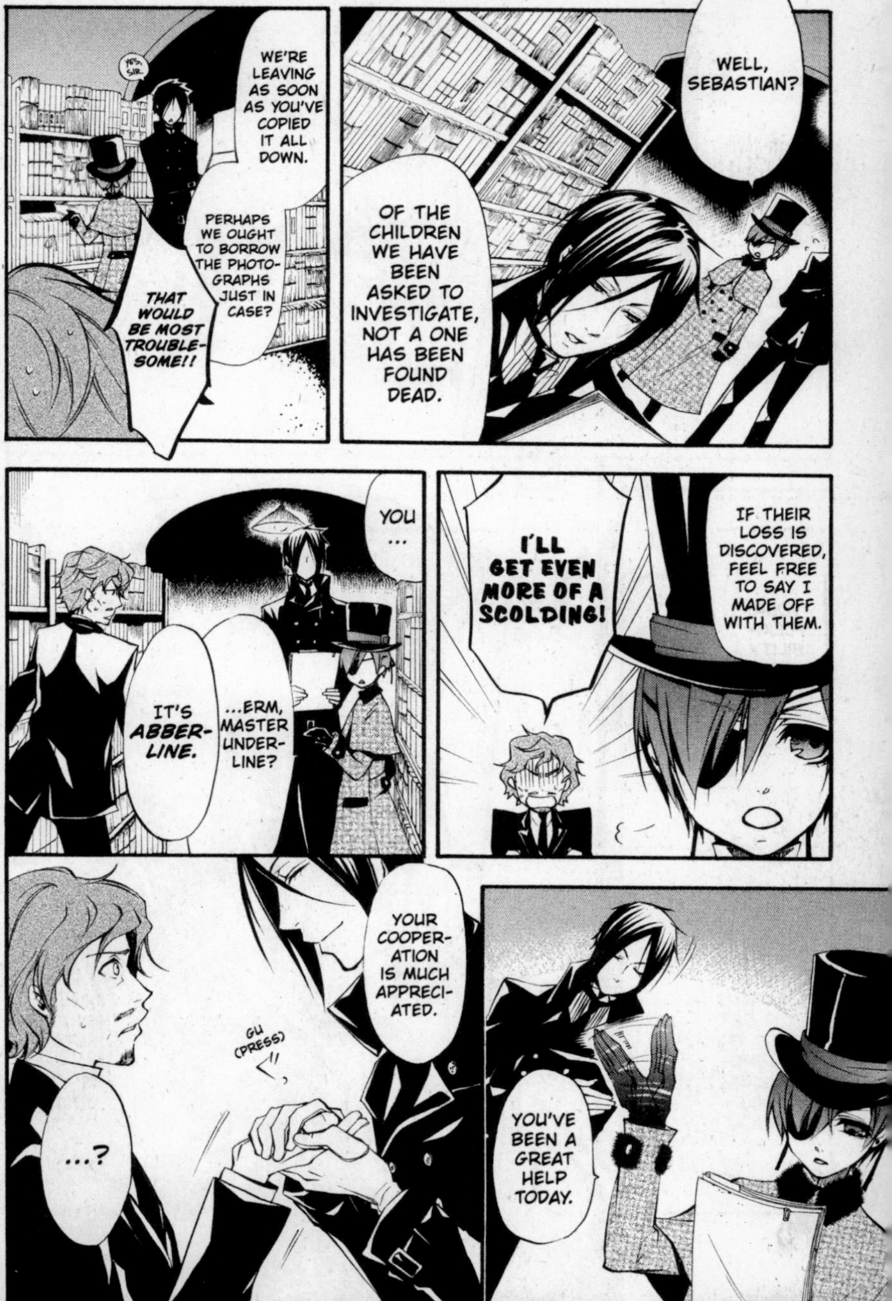
WELL, SEBASTIAN?
OF THE CHILDREN WE HAVE BEEN ASKED TO INVESTIGATE, NOT A ONE HAS BEEN FOUND DEAD.
WE'RE LEAVING AS SOON AS YOU'VE COPIED IT ALL DOWN.
YES, SIR.
PERHAPS WE OUGHT TO BORROW THE PHOTOGRAPHS JUST IN CASE?
THAT WOULD BE MOST TROUBLESOME!!
IF THEIR LOSS IS DISCOVERED, FEEL FREE TO SAY I MADE OFF WITH THEM.
I'LL GET EVEN MORE OF A SCOLDING!
YOU ...
...ERM, MASTER UNDERLINE?
IT'S ABBERLINE.
YOU'VE BEEN A GREAT HELP TODAY.
YOUR COOPERATION IS MUCH APPRECIATED.
GU (PRESS)
...?

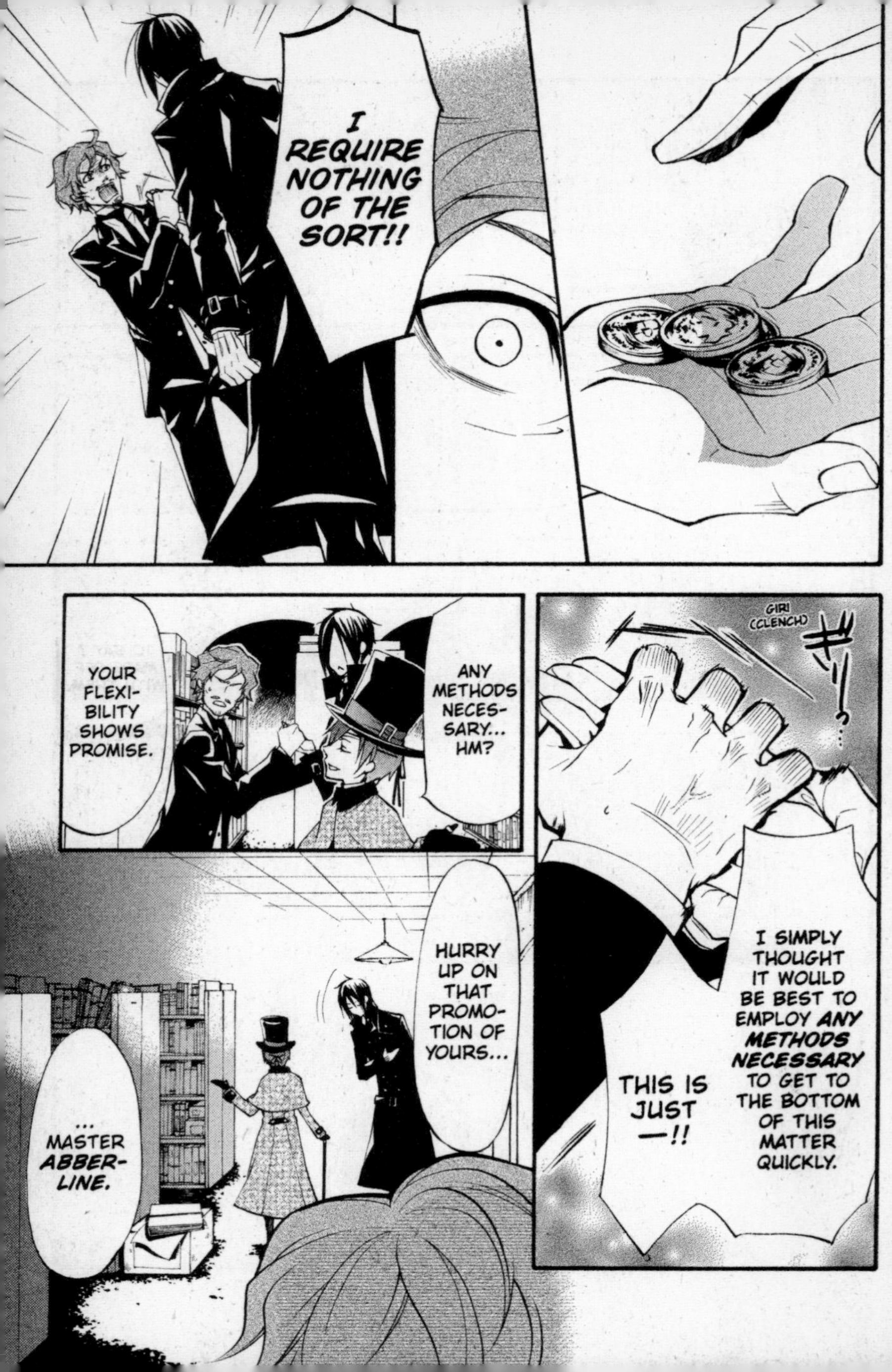
I REQUIRE NOTHING OF THE SORT!!
GIRI (CLENCH)
I SIMPLY THOUGHT IT WOULD BE BEST TO EMPLOY ***ANY METHODS NECESSARY*** TO GET TO THE BOTTOM OF THIS MATTER QUICKLY.
THIS IS JUST—!!
ANY METHODS NECESSARY... HM?
YOUR FLEXIBILITY SHOWS PROMISE.
HURRY UP ON THAT PROMOTION OF YOURS...
...MASTER ***ABBERLINE.***

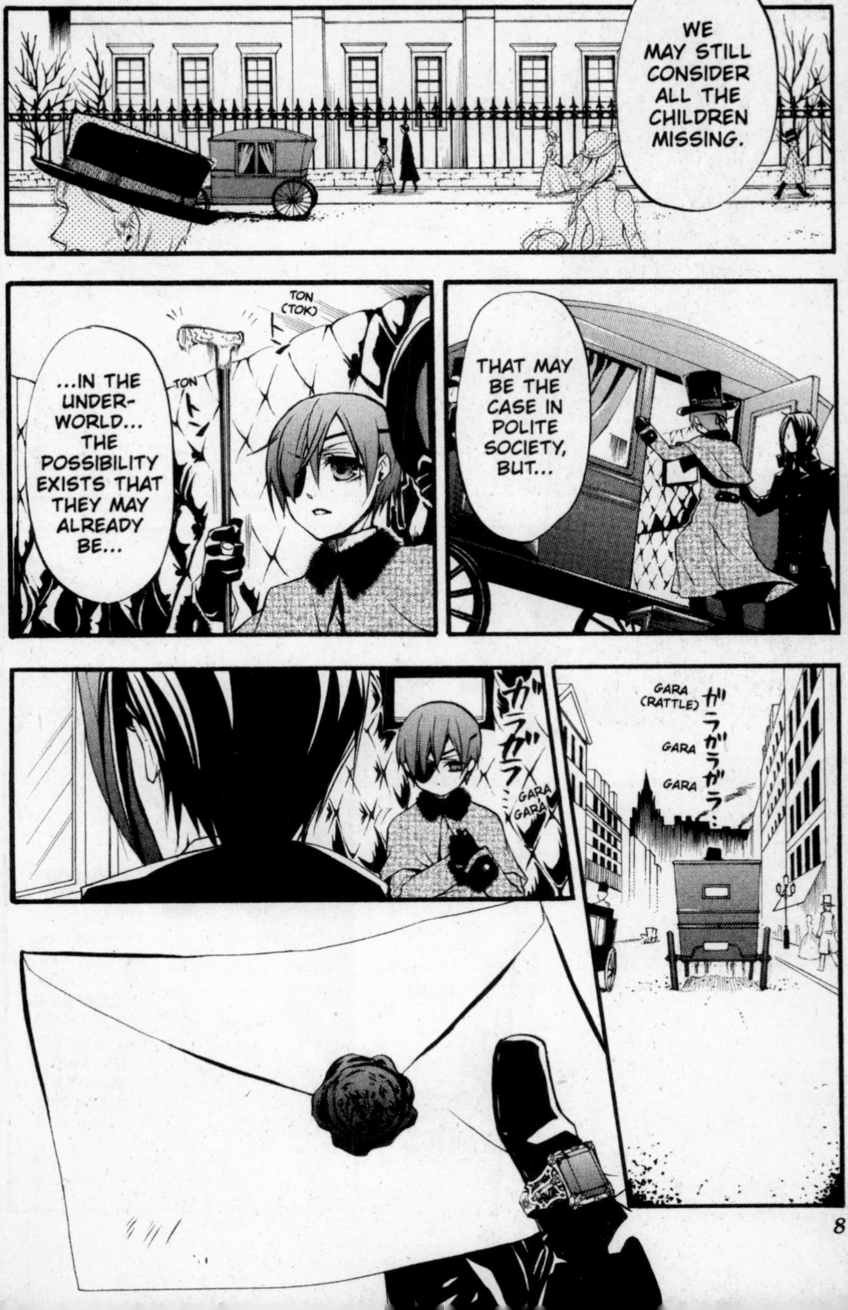
WE MAY STILL CONSIDER ALL THE CHILDREN MISSING.
THAT MAY BE THE CASE IN POLITE SOCIETY, BUT...
TON (TOK)
TON
...IN THE UNDER-WORLD... THE POSSIBILITY EXISTS THAT THEY MAY ALREADY BE...
GARA (RATTLE)
GARA
GARA
ガラガラガラ…
ガラガラ…
GARA GARA

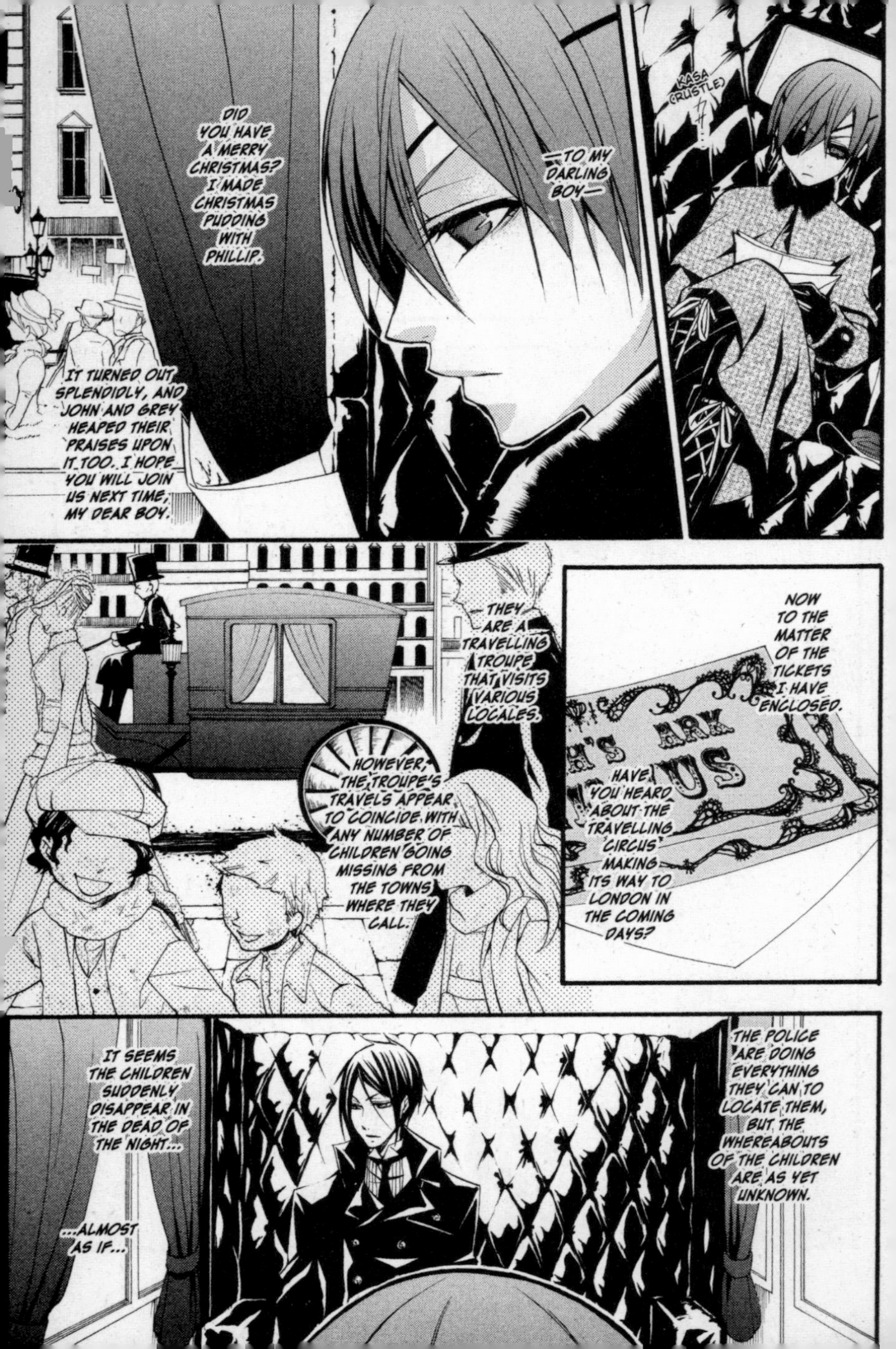
KASA (RUSTLE)
—TO MY DARLING BOY—
DID YOU HAVE A MERRY CHRISTMAS? I MADE CHRISTMAS PUDDING WITH PHILLIP.
IT TURNED OUT SPLENDIDLY, AND JOHN AND GREY HEAPED THEIR PRAISES UPON IT TOO. I HOPE YOU WILL JOIN US NEXT TIME, MY DEAR BOY.
NOW TO THE MATTER OF THE TICKETS I HAVE ENCLOSED.
HAVE YOU HEARD ABOUT THE TRAVELLING CIRCUS MAKING ITS WAY TO LONDON IN THE COMING DAYS?
THEY ARE A TRAVELLING TROUPE THAT VISITS VARIOUS LOCALES.
HOWEVER, THE TROUPE'S TRAVELS APPEAR TO COINCIDE WITH ANY NUMBER OF CHILDREN GOING MISSING FROM THE TOWNS WHERE THEY CALL.
THE POLICE ARE DOING EVERYTHING THEY CAN TO LOCATE THEM, BUT THE WHEREABOUTS OF THE CHILDREN ARE AS YET UNKNOWN.
IT SEEMS THE CHILDREN SUDDENLY DISAPPEAR IN THE DEAD OF THE NIGHT...
...ALMOST AS IF...

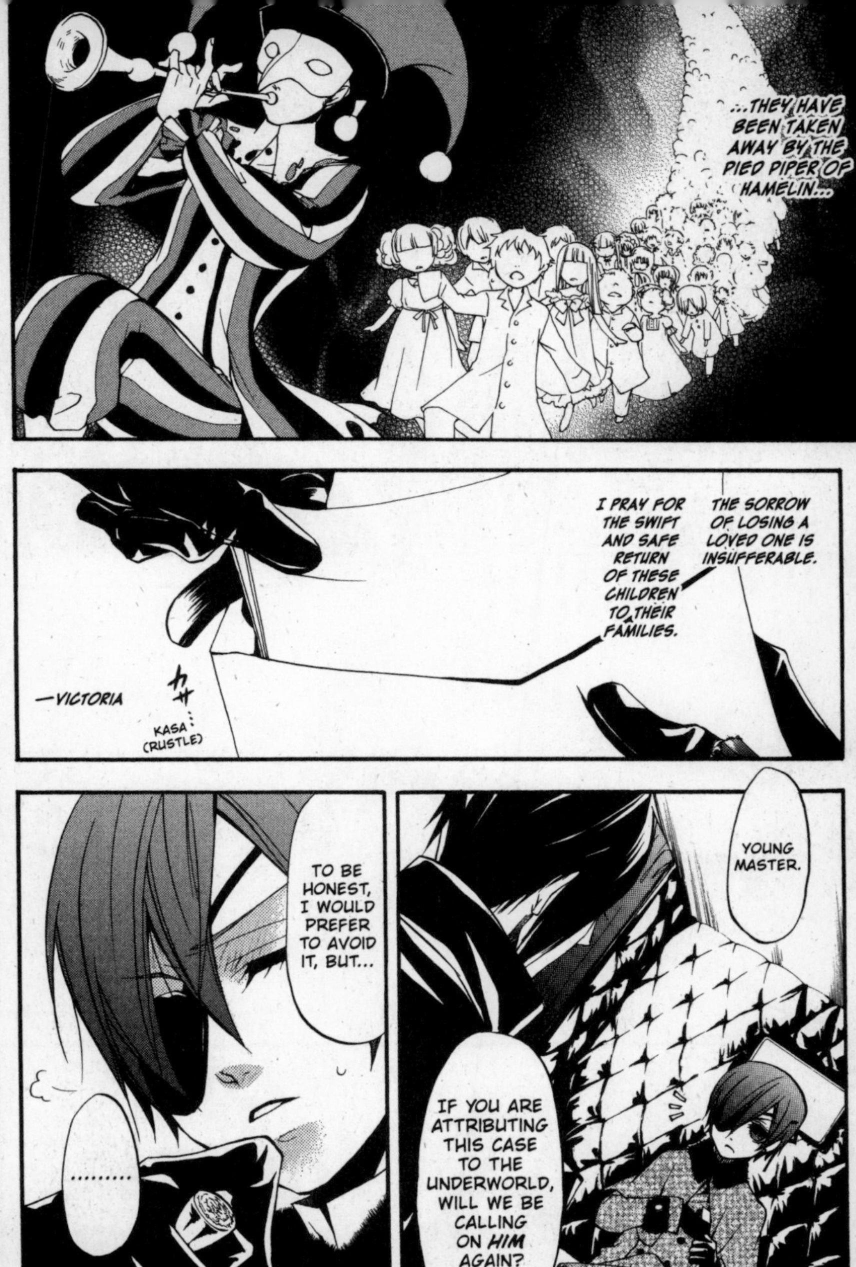
...THEY HAVE BEEN TAKEN AWAY BY THE PIED PIPER OF HAMELIN...
THE SORROW OF LOSING A LOVED ONE IS INSUFFERABLE.
I PRAY FOR THE SWIFT AND SAFE RETURN OF THESE CHILDREN TO THEIR FAMILIES.
—VICTORIA
KASA (RUSTLE)
YOUNG MASTER.
IF YOU ARE ATTRIBUTING THIS CASE TO THE UNDERWORLD, WILL WE BE CALLING ON *HIM* AGAIN?
TO BE HONEST, I WOULD PREFER TO AVOID IT, BUT...
....

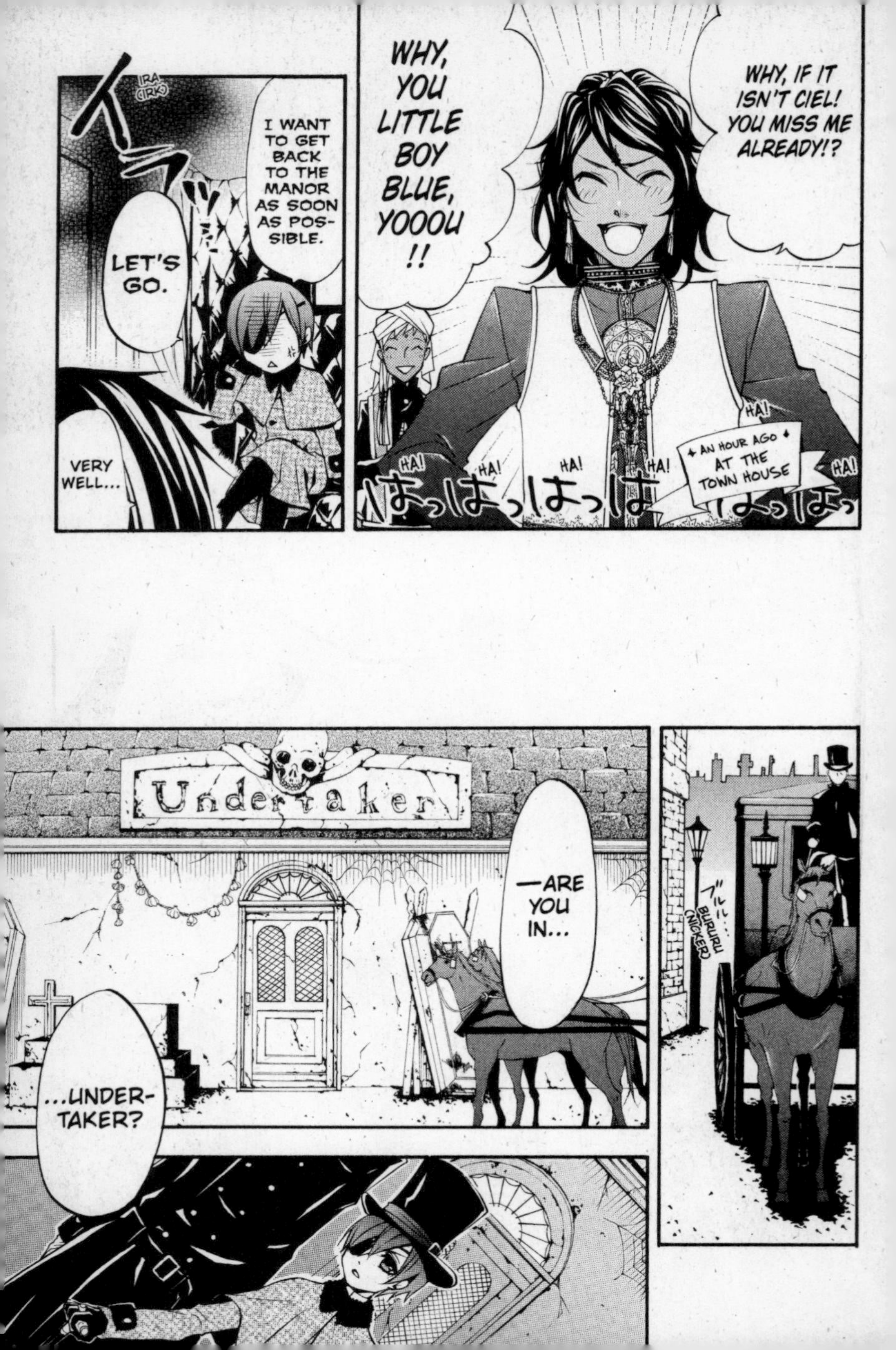

WHY, IF IT ISN'T CIEL! YOU MISS ME ALREADY!?
WHY, YOU LITTLE BOY BLUE, YOOOU!!
AN HOUR AGO AT THE TOWN HOUSE
HA! HA! HA! HA! HA! HA!
はっはっはっは
はっはっ
IRA (IRK)
I WANT TO GET BACK TO THE MANOR AS SOON AS POS-SIBLE.
LET'S GO.
VERY WELL...
ブルル… BURURU (NICKER)
Undertaker
—ARE YOU IN...
...UNDER-TAKER?

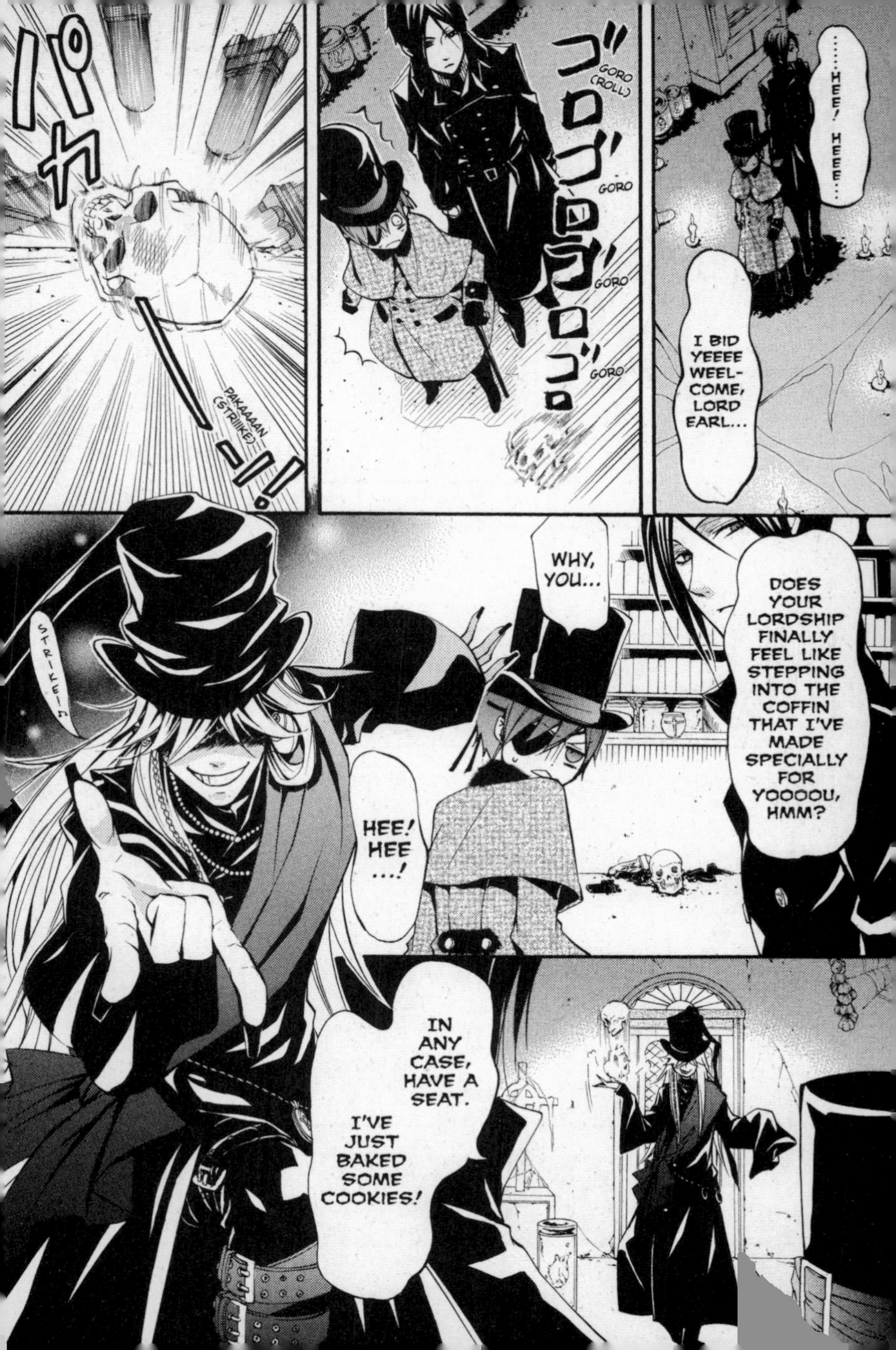
......HEE! HEEE...
I BID YEEEE WEEL-COME, LORD EARL...
ゴロゴロゴロゴロ
GORO (ROLL)
GORO
GORO
GORO
パカーン!!
PAKAAAAAN (STRIIKE)
DOES YOUR LORDSHIP FINALLY FEEL LIKE STEPPING INTO THE COFFIN THAT I'VE MADE SPECIALLY FOR YOOOOU, HMM?
WHY, YOU...
HEE! HEE ...!
IN ANY CASE, HAVE A SEAT.
I'VE JUST BAKED SOME COOKIES!
STRIKE!♪

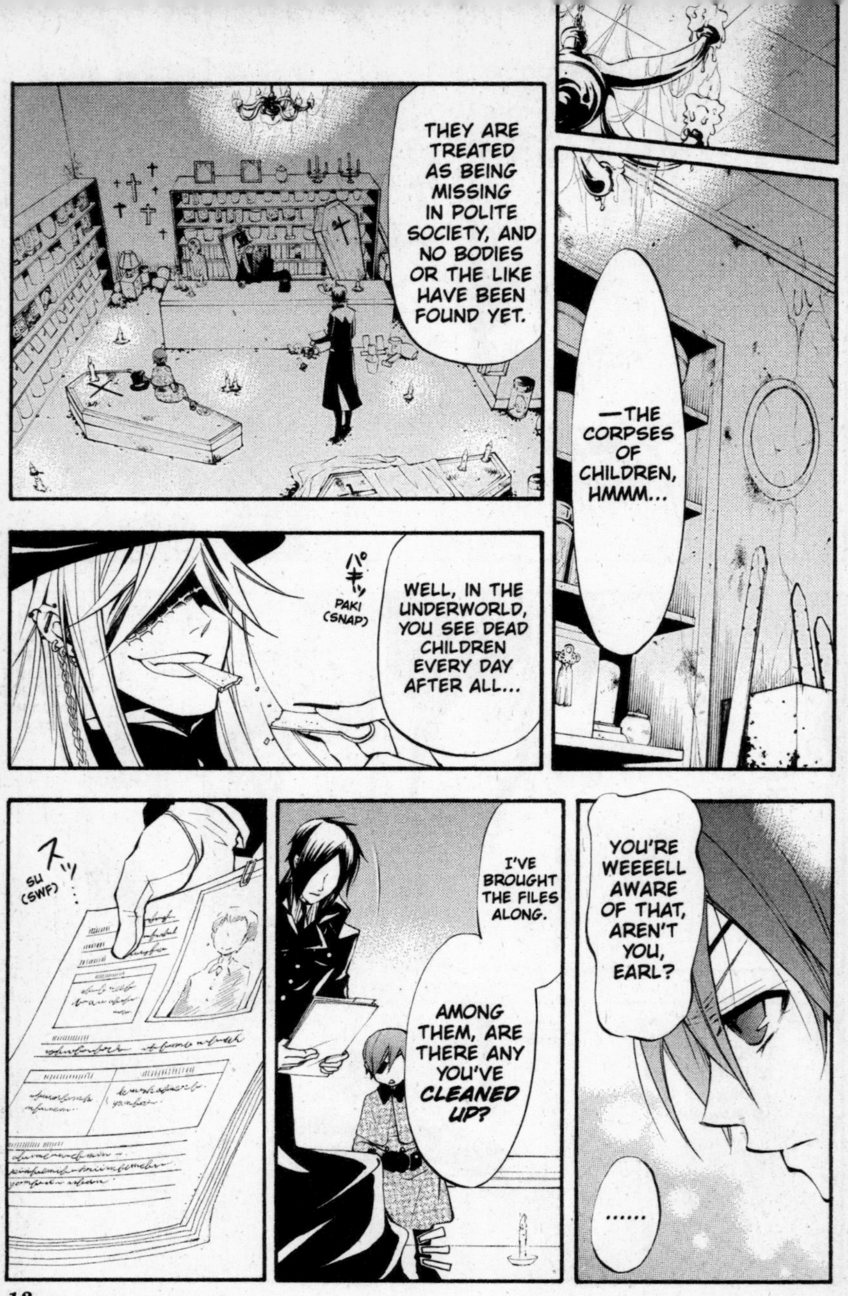

THEY ARE TREATED AS BEING MISSING IN POLITE SOCIETY, AND NO BODIES OR THE LIKE HAVE BEEN FOUND YET.
—THE CORPSES OF CHILDREN, HMMM...
PAKI (SNAP)
WELL, IN THE UNDERWORLD, YOU SEE DEAD CHILDREN EVERY DAY AFTER ALL...
YOU'RE WEEEELL AWARE OF THAT, AREN'T YOU, EARL?
......
I'VE BROUGHT THE FILES ALONG.
AMONG THEM, ARE THERE ANY YOU'VE CLEANED UP?
SU (SWF)

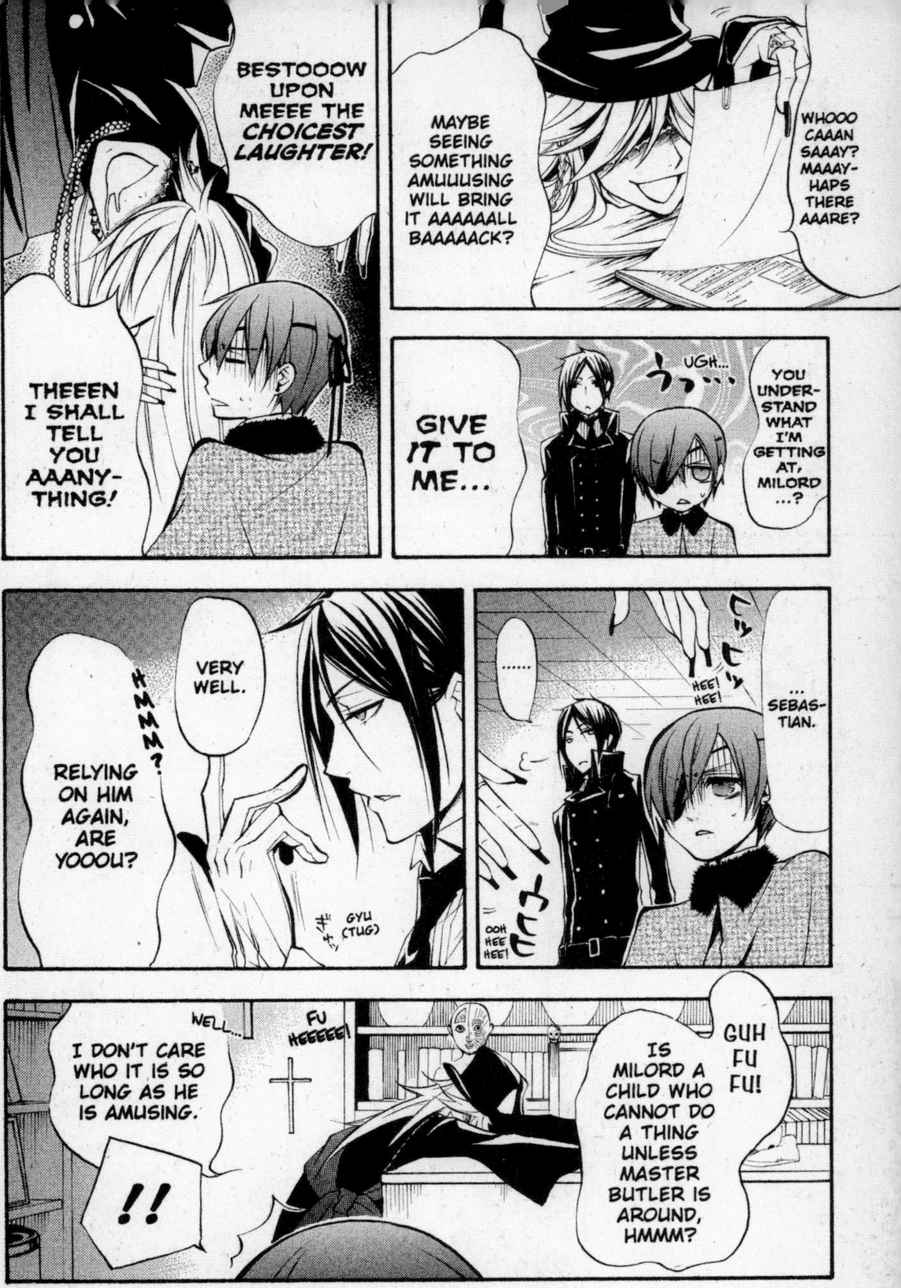
WHOOO CAAAN SAAAY? MAAAY-HAPS THERE AAARE?
MAYBE SEEING SOMETHING AMUUUSING WILL BRING IT AAAAAALL BAAAAACK?
YOU UNDER-STAND WHAT I'M GETTING AT, MILORD ...?
UGH...
GIVE *IT* TO ME...
BESTOOOW UPON MEEEE THE *CHOICEST LAUGHTER!*
THEEEN I SHALL TELL YOU AAANY-THING!
... SEBAS-TIAN.
HEE! HEE!
......
OOH HEE HEE!
VERY WELL.
HMMM?
RELYING ON HIM AGAIN, ARE YOOOU?
GYU (TUG)
GUH FU FU!
IS MILORD A CHILD WHO CANNOT DO A THING UNLESS MASTER BUTLER IS AROUND, HMMM?
FU HEEEEEE!
WELL...
I DON'T CARE WHO IT IS SO LONG AS HE IS AMUSING.
!!

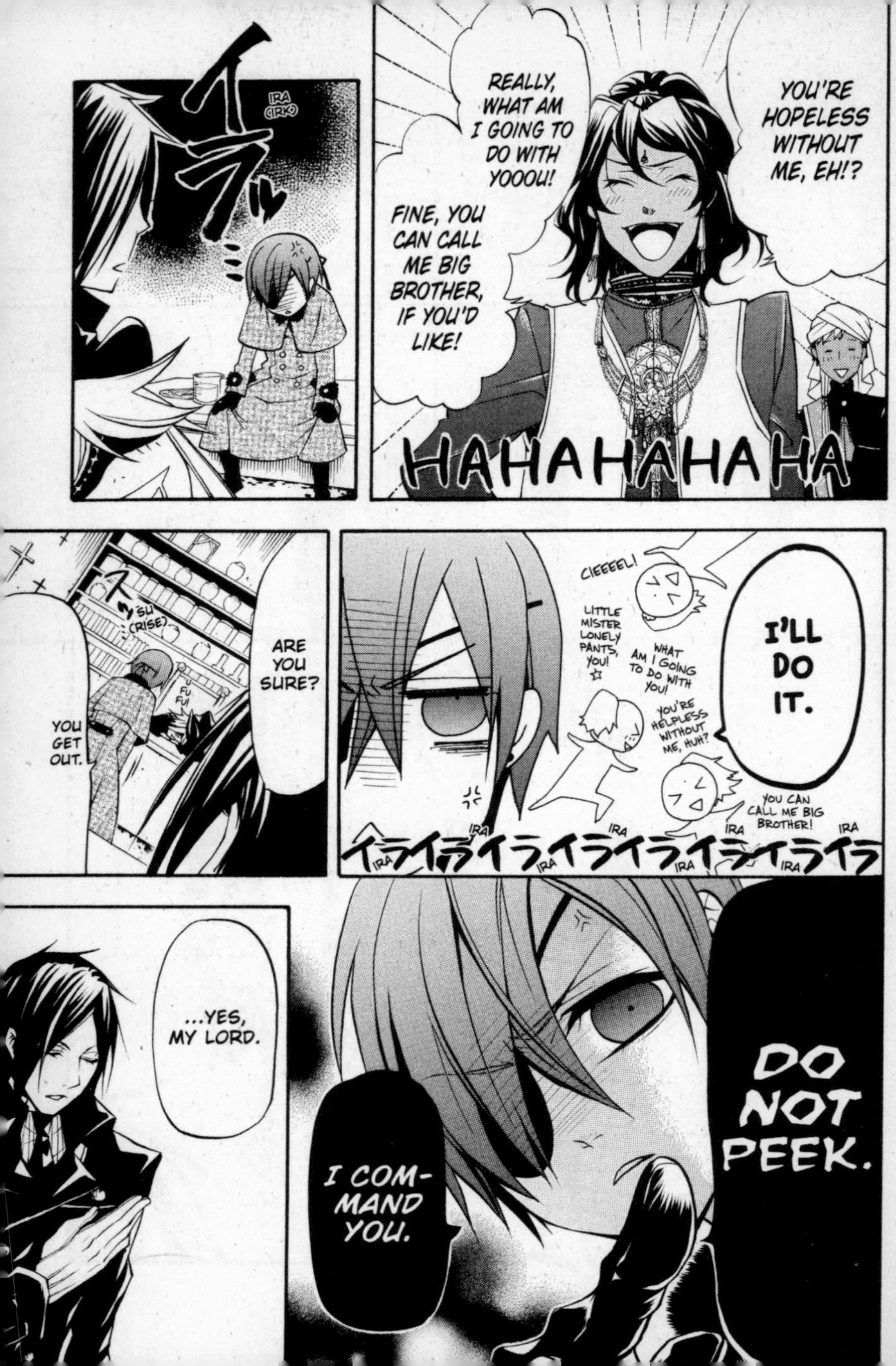
YOU'RE HOPELESS WITHOUT ME, EH!?
REALLY, WHAT AM I GOING TO DO WITH YOOOU!
FINE, YOU CAN CALL ME BIG BROTHER, IF YOU'D LIKE!
HAHAHAHAHAHA
IRA (IRK)
I'LL DO IT.
CIEEEEL!
LITTLE MISTER LONELY PANTS, YOU! ☆
WHAT AM I GOING TO DO WITH YOU!
YOU'RE HELPLESS WITHOUT ME, HUH?
YOU CAN CALL ME BIG BROTHER!
IRA IRA IRA IRA IRA IRA IRA IRA IRA IRA
ARE YOU SURE?
SU (RISE)
FU FU
YOU GET OUT.
DO NOT PEEK.
I COM-MAND YOU.
...YES, MY LORD.

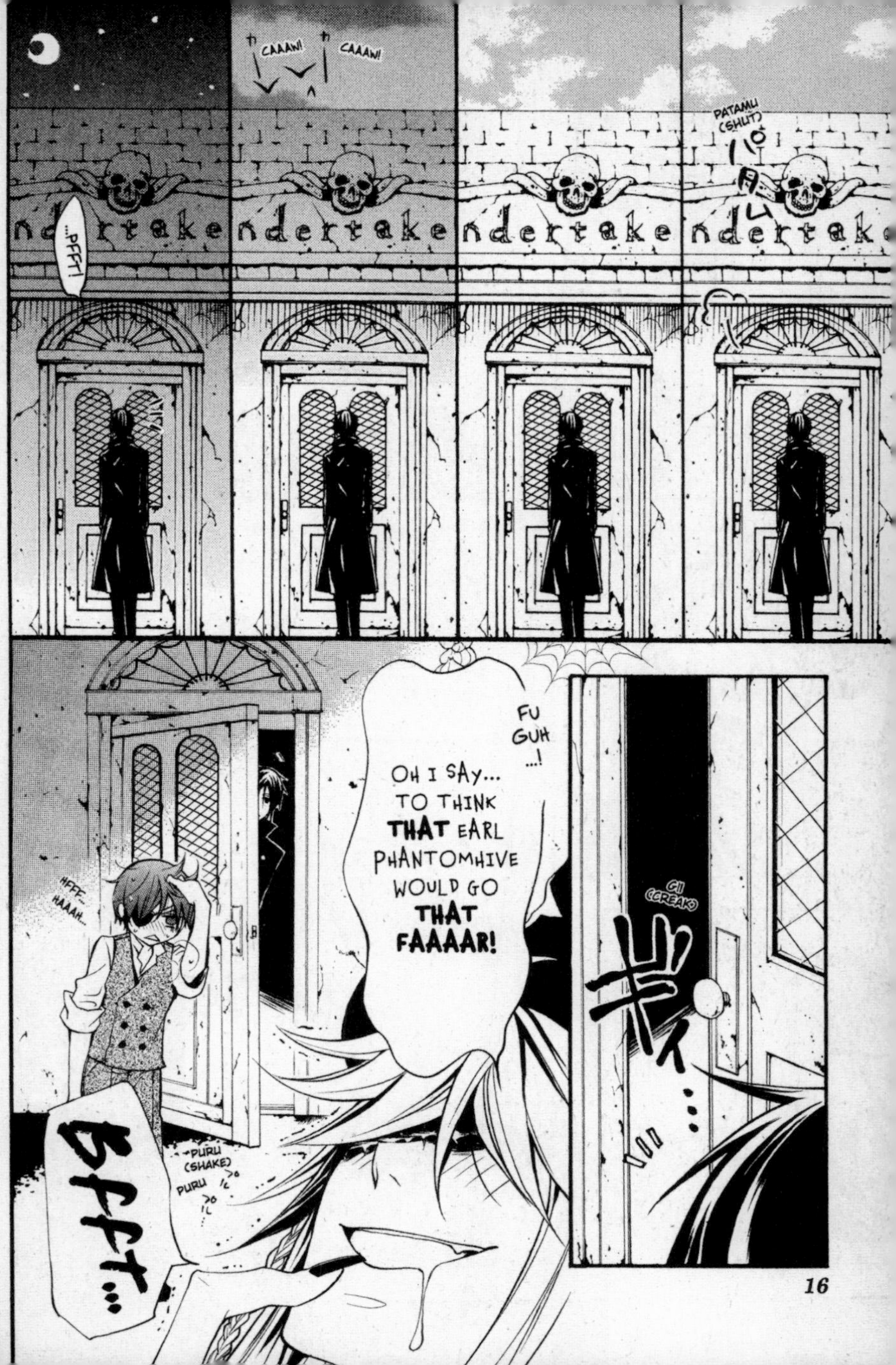
PATAMU (SHUT)
CAAAW!
CAAAW!
...PFFT!
GII (CREAK)
FU GUH ...!
OH I SAY... TO THINK THAT EARL PHANTOMHIVE WOULD GO THAT FAAAAR!
HFFF... HAAAH...
PURU (SHAKE)
PURU
BPFT...

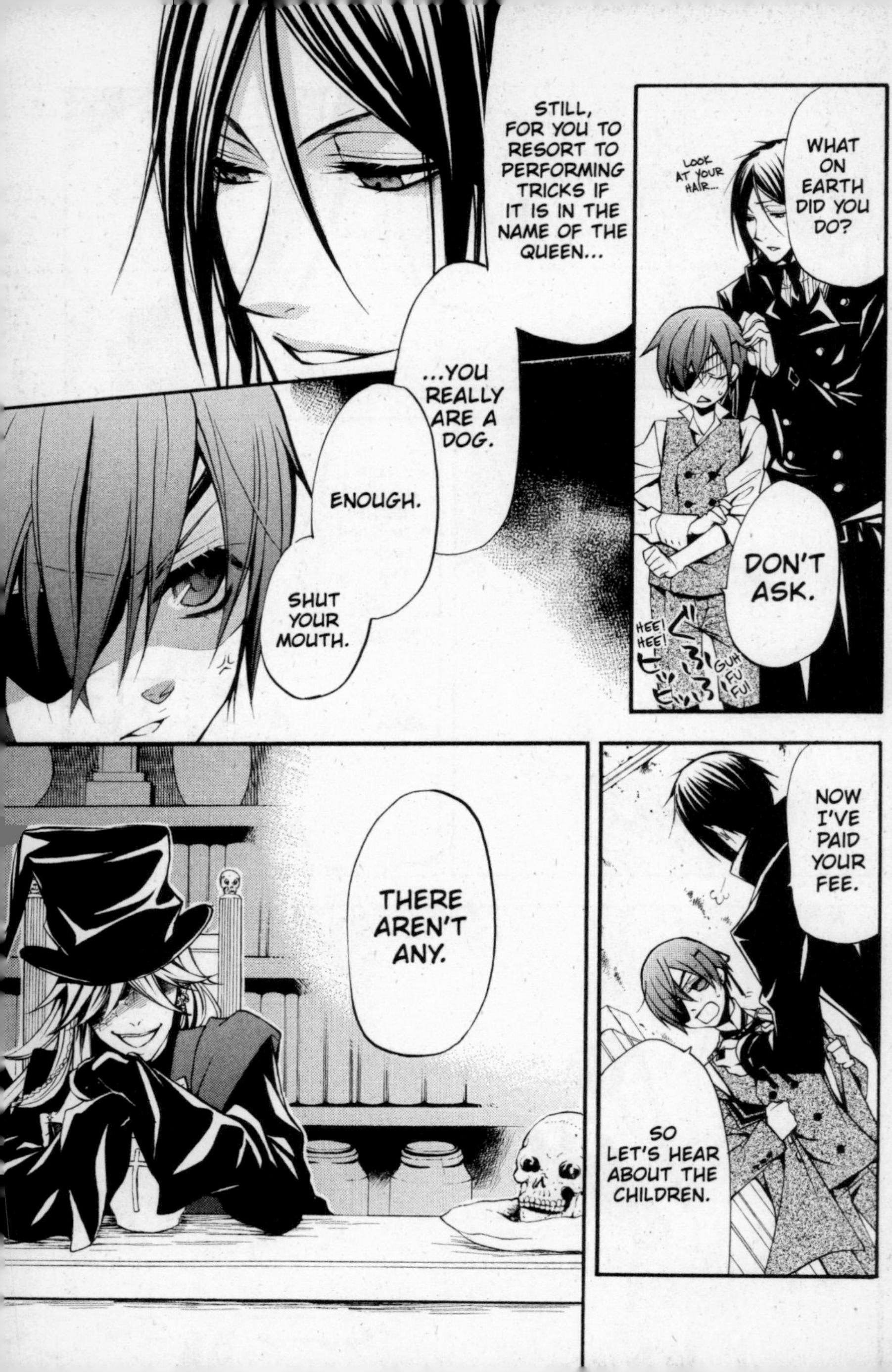
WHAT ON EARTH DID YOU DO?
LOOK AT YOUR HAIR...
DON'T ASK.
HEE! HEE!
GUH FU FU!
STILL, FOR YOU TO RESORT TO PERFORMING TRICKS IF IT IS IN THE NAME OF THE QUEEN...
...YOU REALLY ARE A DOG.
ENOUGH.
SHUT YOUR MOUTH.
NOW I'VE PAID YOUR FEE.
SO LET'S HEAR ABOUT THE CHILDREN.
THERE AREN'T ANY.

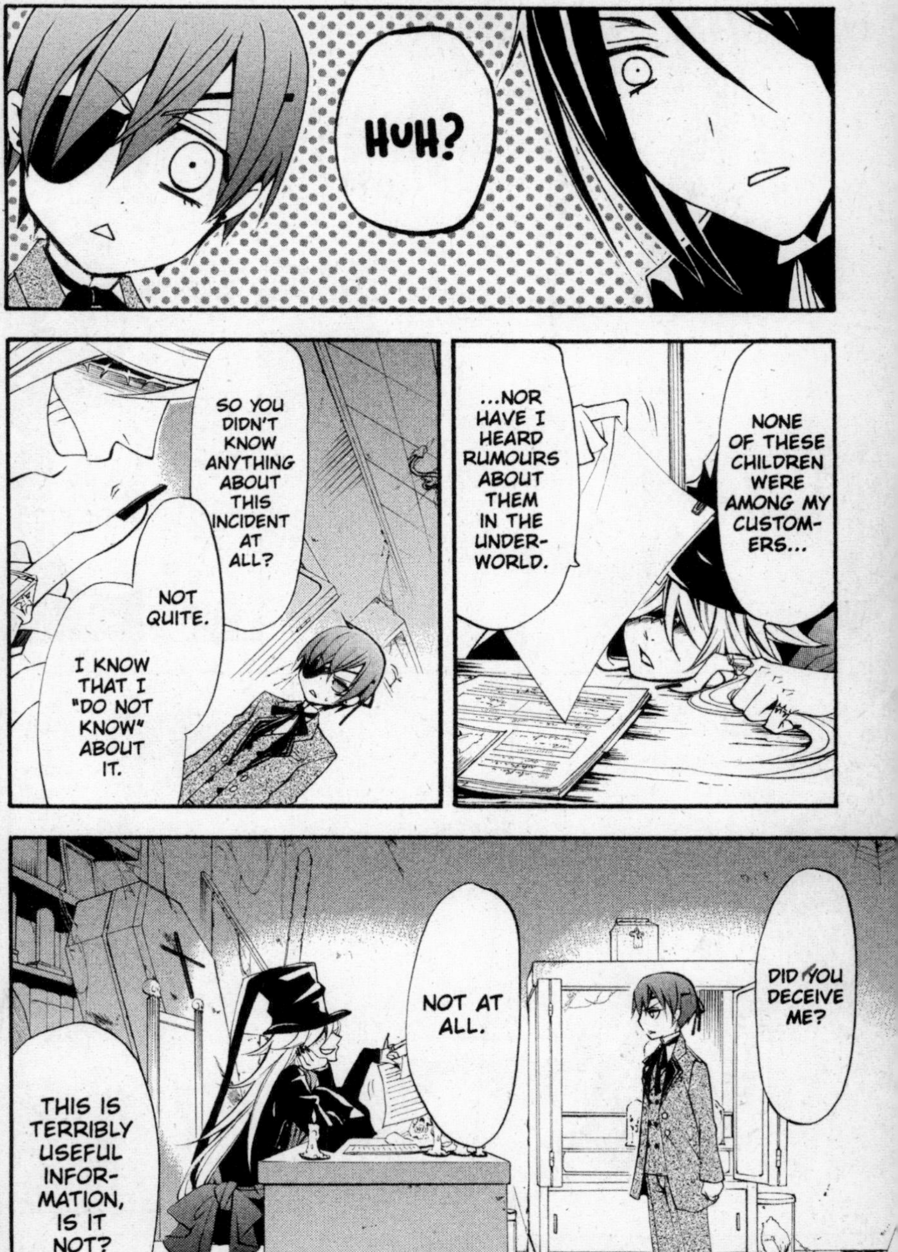
HUH?
NONE OF THESE CHILDREN WERE AMONG MY CUSTOMERS...
...NOR HAVE I HEARD RUMOURS ABOUT THEM IN THE UNDERWORLD.
SO YOU DIDN'T KNOW ANYTHING ABOUT THIS INCIDENT AT ALL?
NOT QUITE.
I KNOW THAT I "DO NOT KNOW" ABOUT IT.
DID YOU DECEIVE ME?
NOT AT ALL.
THIS IS TERRIBLY USEFUL INFORMATION, IS IT NOT?

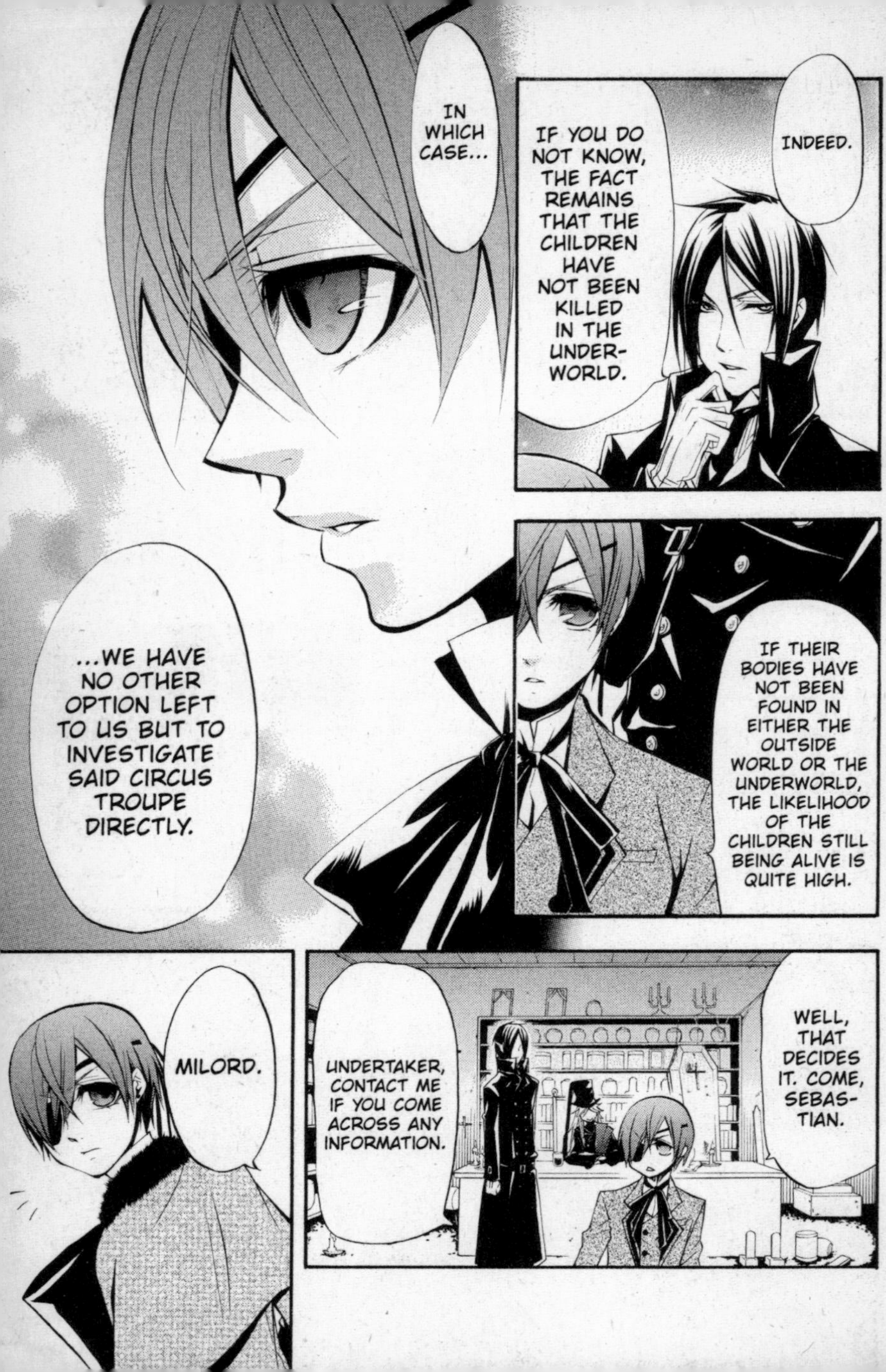
INDEED.
IF YOU DO NOT KNOW, THE FACT REMAINS THAT THE CHILDREN HAVE NOT BEEN KILLED IN THE UNDER-WORLD.
IF THEIR BODIES HAVE NOT BEEN FOUND IN EITHER THE OUTSIDE WORLD OR THE UNDERWORLD, THE LIKELIHOOD OF THE CHILDREN STILL BEING ALIVE IS QUITE HIGH.
IN WHICH CASE...
...WE HAVE NO OTHER OPTION LEFT TO US BUT TO INVESTIGATE SAID CIRCUS TROUPE DIRECTLY.
WELL, THAT DECIDES IT. COME, SEBAS-TIAN.
UNDERTAKER, CONTACT ME IF YOU COME ACROSS ANY INFORMATION.
MILORD.

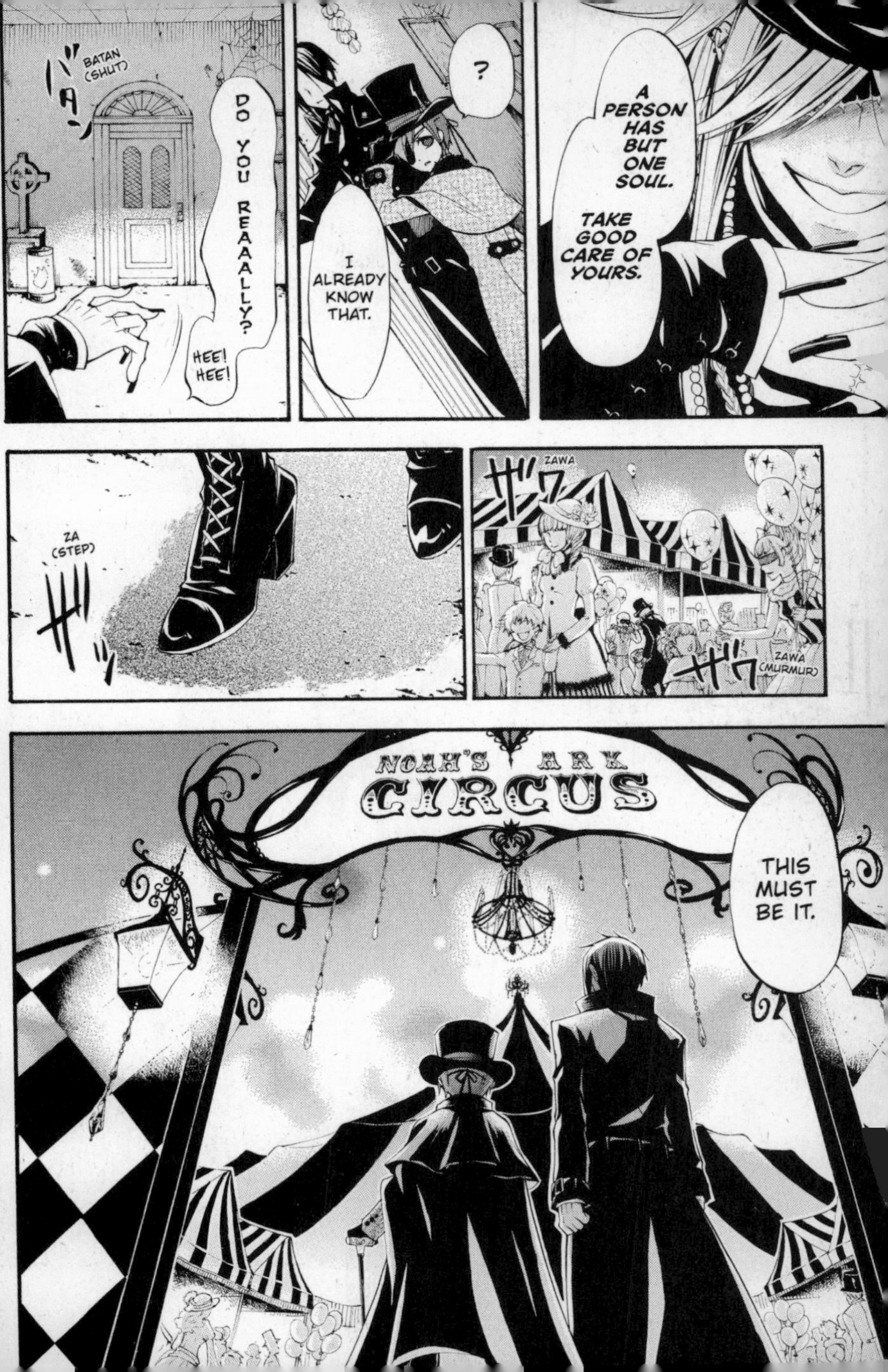

A PERSON HAS BUT ONE SOUL.
TAKE GOOD CARE OF YOURS.
?
I ALREADY KNOW THAT.
DO YOU REAAAALLY?
HEE! HEE!
バタン
BATAN (SHUT)
ザワ
ZAWA
ザワ
ZAWA (MURMUR)
ZA (STEP)
ザッ
NOAH'S ARK CIRCUS
THIS MUST BE IT.

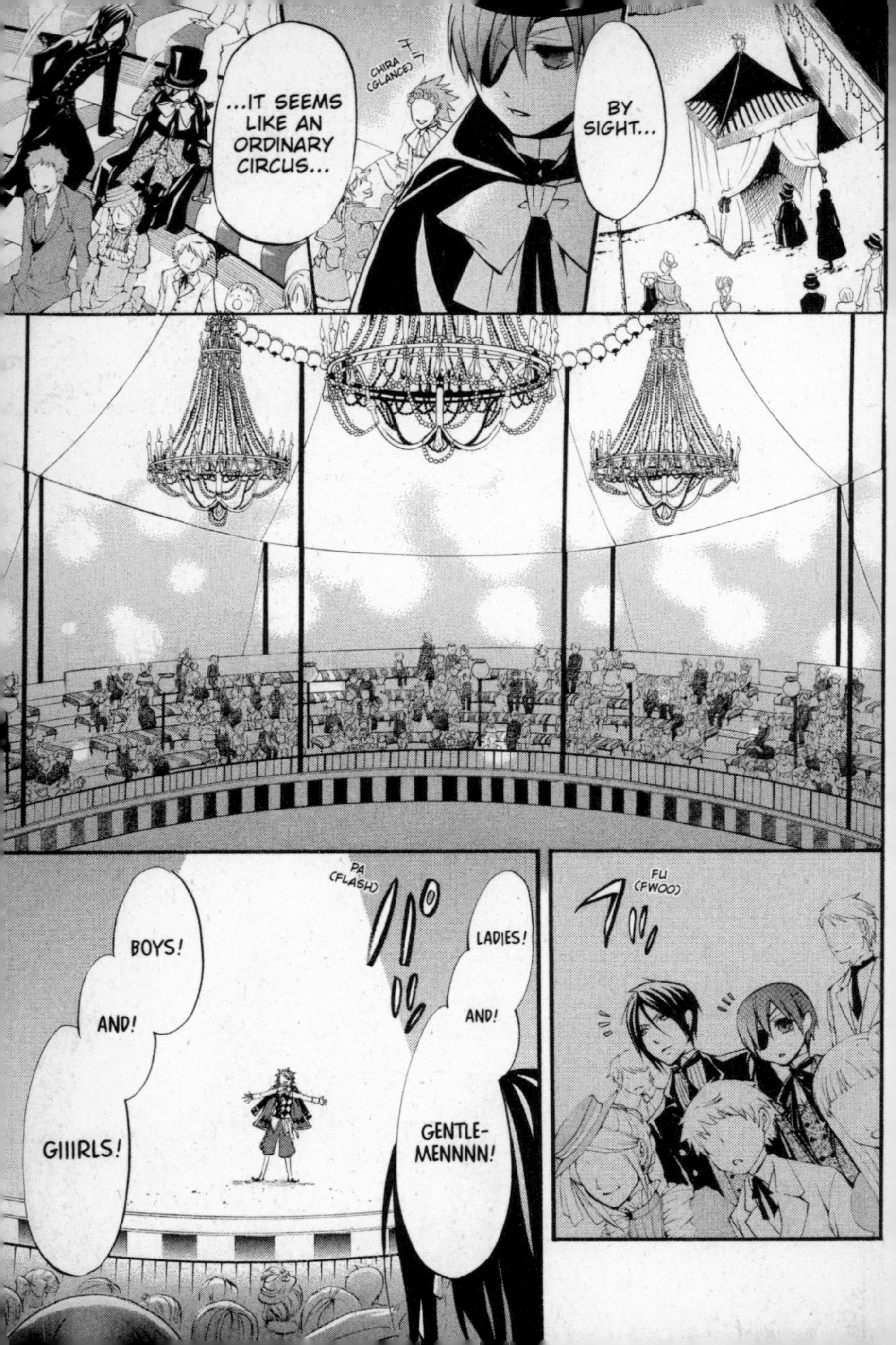
BY SIGHT...
チラ
CHIRA (GLANCE)
...IT SEEMS LIKE AN ORDINARY CIRCUS...
FU (FWOO)
PA (FLASH)
LADIES!
AND!
GENTLE-MENNNN!
BOYS!
AND!
GIIIRLS!

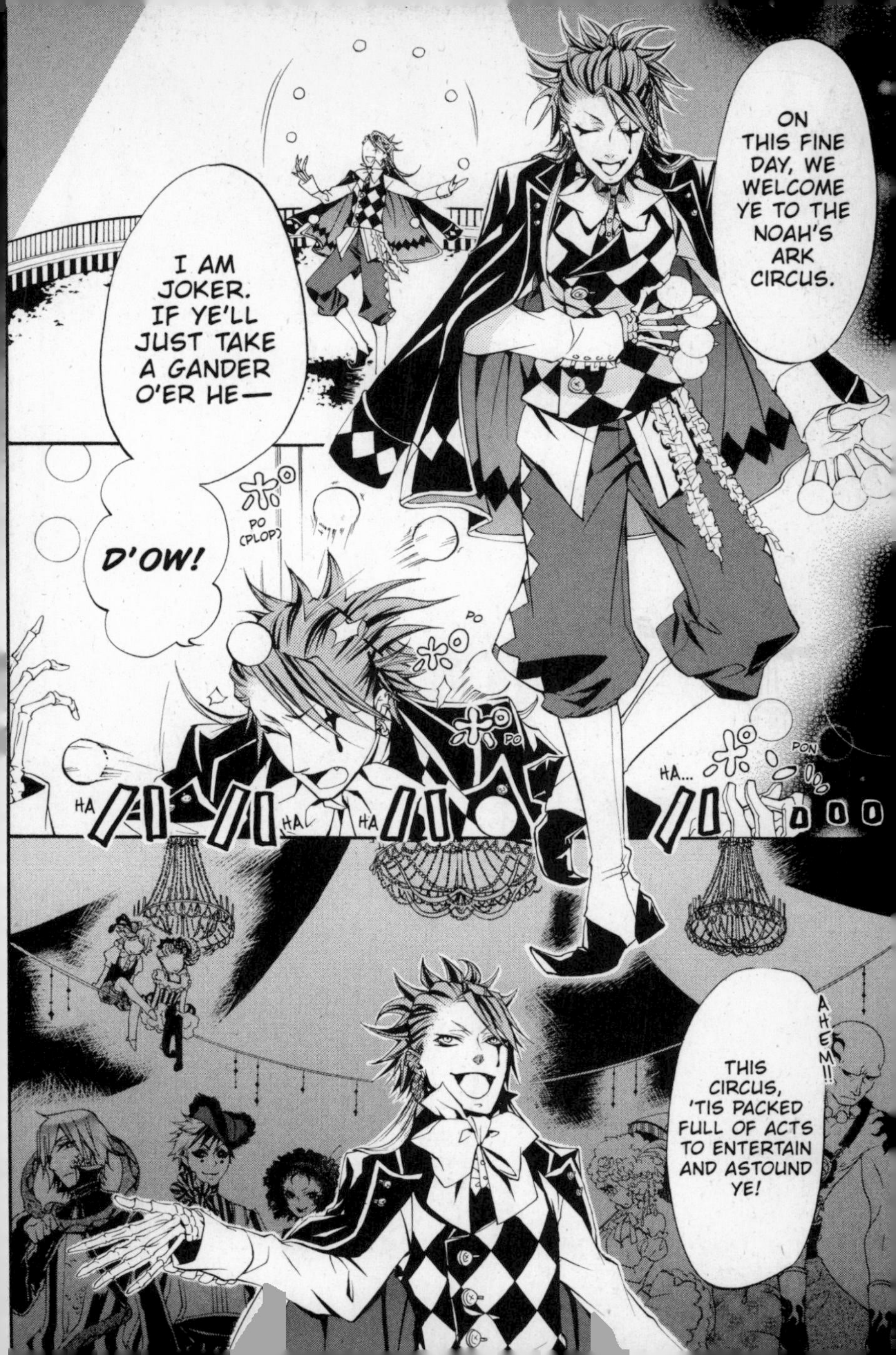
ON THIS FINE DAY, WE WELCOME YE TO THE NOAH'S ARK CIRCUS.
I AM JOKER. IF YE'LL JUST TAKE A GANDER O'ER HE—
PO (PLOP)
D'OW!
PON
HA...
PO
PO
HA
HA
HA
AHEM!!
THIS CIRCUS, 'TIS PACKED FULL OF ACTS TO ENTERTAIN AND ASTOUND YE!

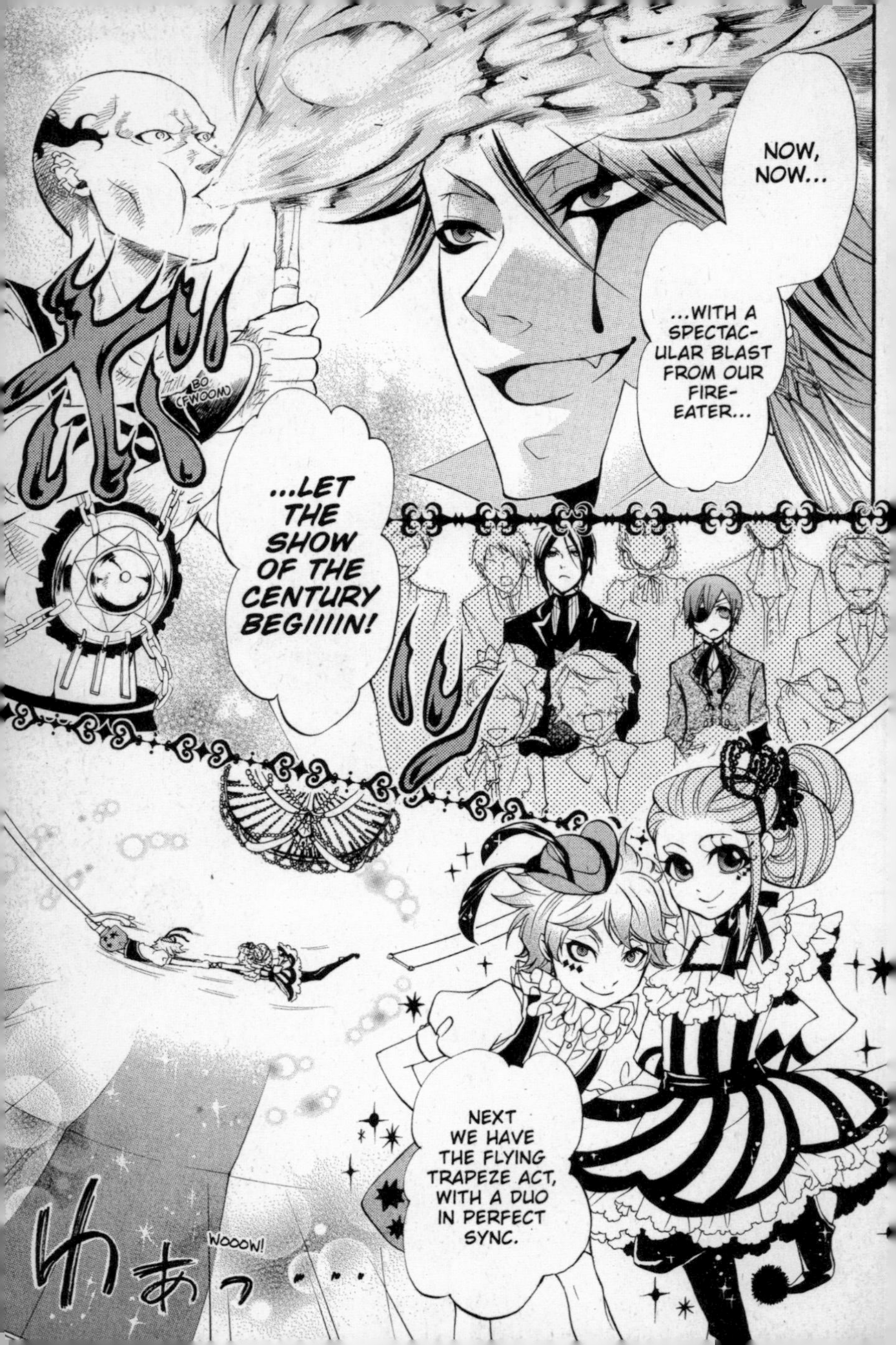
NOW, NOW...
...WITH A SPECTACULAR BLAST FROM OUR FIRE-EATER...
BO (FWOOM)
...LET THE SHOW OF THE CENTURY BEGIIIIN!
NEXT WE HAVE THE FLYING TRAPEZE ACT, WITH A DUO IN PERFECT SYNC.
WOOOW!

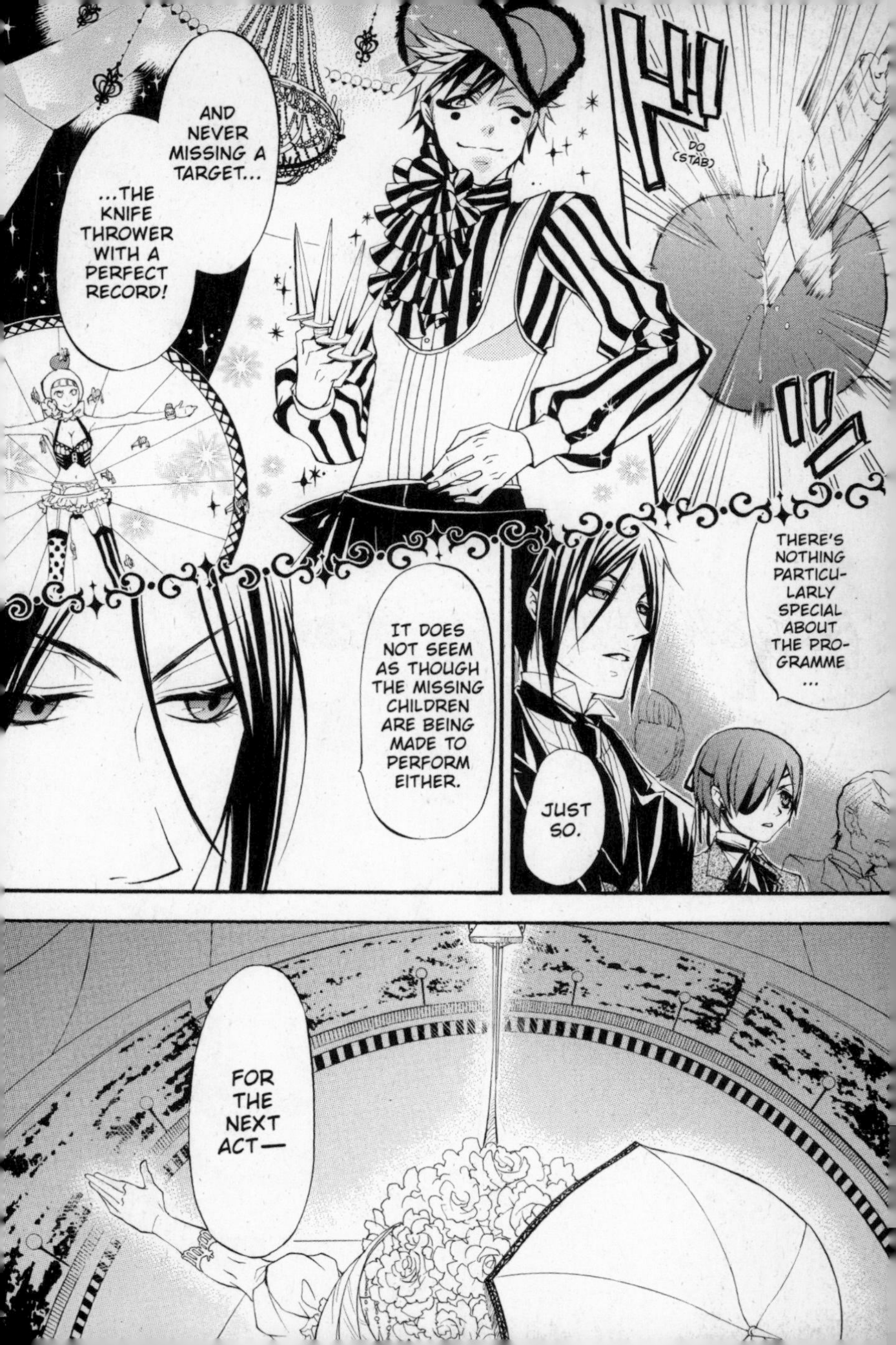

DO (STAB)
AND NEVER MISSING A TARGET...
...THE KNIFE THROWER WITH A PERFECT RECORD!
THERE'S NOTHING PARTICULARLY SPECIAL ABOUT THE PROGRAMME ...
JUST SO.
IT DOES NOT SEEM AS THOUGH THE MISSING CHILDREN ARE BEING MADE TO PERFORM EITHER.
FOR THE NEXT ACT—

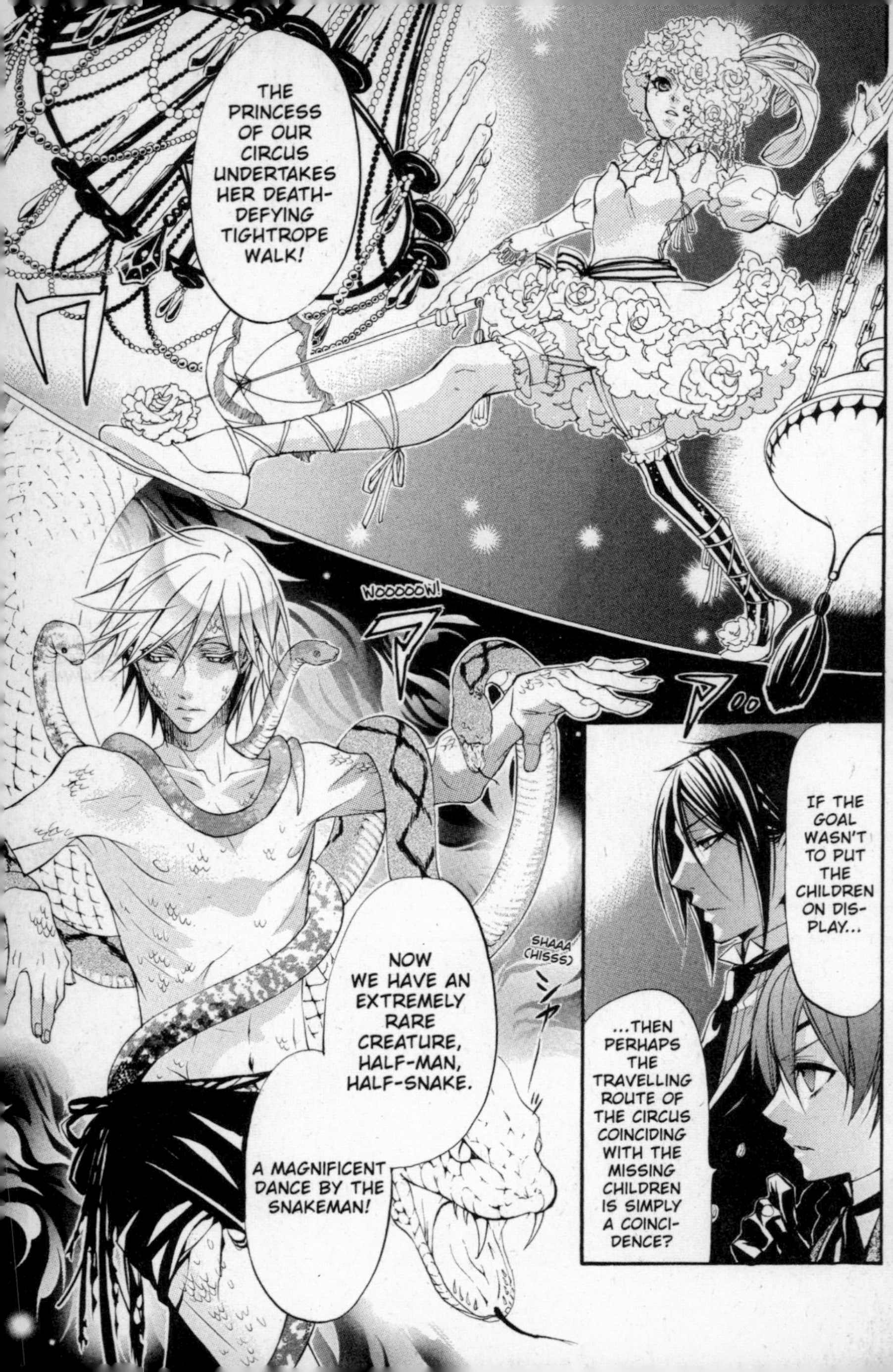
THE PRINCESS OF OUR CIRCUS UNDERTAKES HER DEATH-DEFYING TIGHTROPE WALK!
WOOOOOW!
IF THE GOAL WASN'T TO PUT THE CHILDREN ON DIS-PLAY...
...THEN PERHAPS THE TRAVELLING ROUTE OF THE CIRCUS COINCIDING WITH THE MISSING CHILDREN IS SIMPLY A COINCI-DENCE?
NOW WE HAVE AN EXTREMELY RARE CREATURE, HALF-MAN, HALF-SNAKE.
A MAGNIFICENT DANCE BY THE SNAKEMAN!
SHAAA (HISSS)

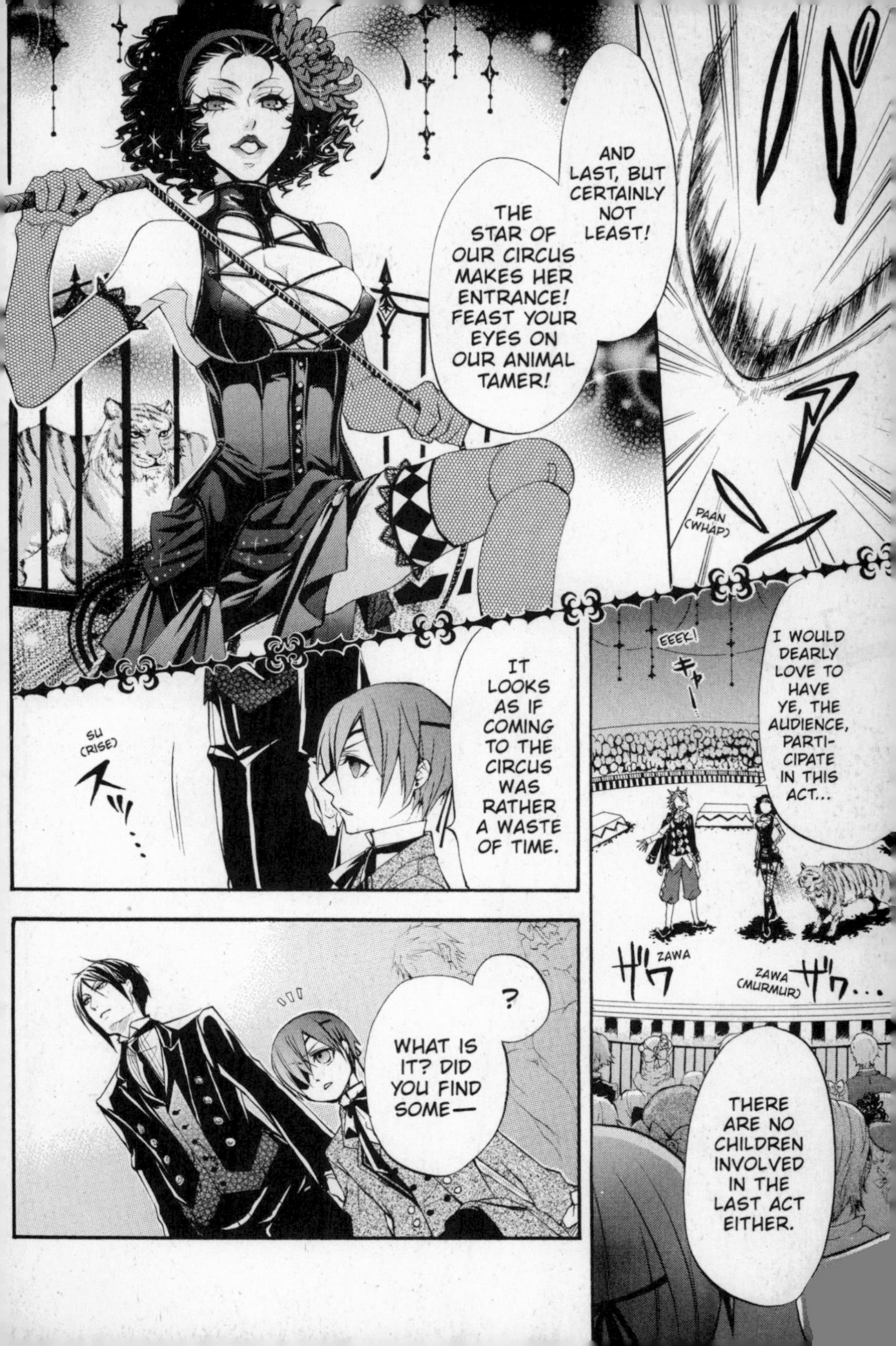
AND LAST, BUT CERTAINLY NOT LEAST!
THE STAR OF OUR CIRCUS MAKES HER ENTRANCE! FEAST YOUR EYES ON OUR ANIMAL TAMER!
PAAN (WHAP)
EEEK!
I WOULD DEARLY LOVE TO HAVE YE, THE AUDIENCE, PARTI-CIPATE IN THIS ACT...
ZAWA
ZAWA (MURMUR)
IT LOOKS AS IF COMING TO THE CIRCUS WAS RATHER A WASTE OF TIME.
SU (RISE)
THERE ARE NO CHILDREN INVOLVED IN THE LAST ACT EITHER.
?
WHAT IS IT? DID YOU FIND SOME—

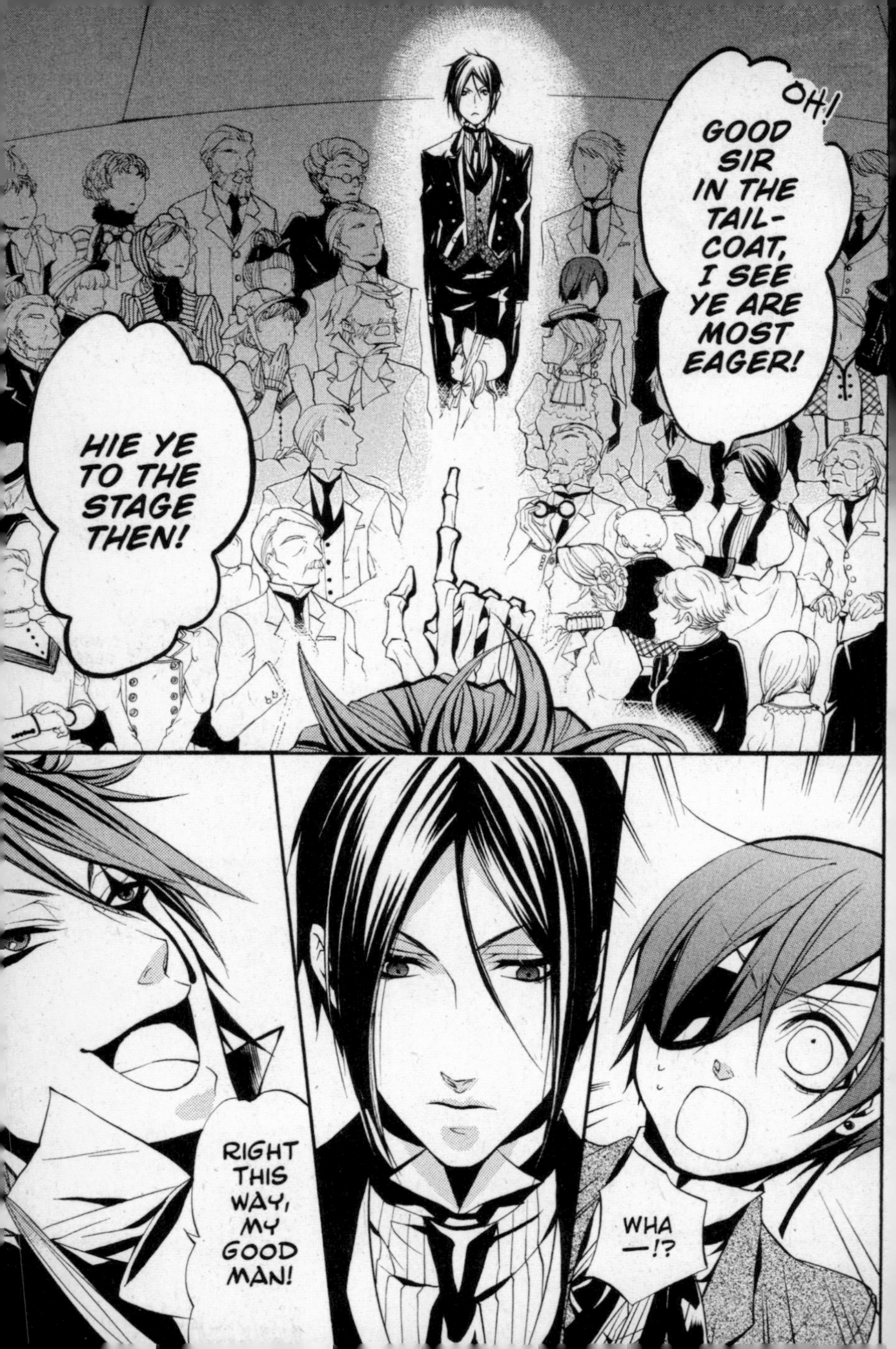
OH! GOOD SIR IN THE TAIL-COAT, I SEE YE ARE MOST EAGER!
HIE YE TO THE STAGE THEN!
WHA—!?
RIGHT THIS WAY, MY GOOD MAN!

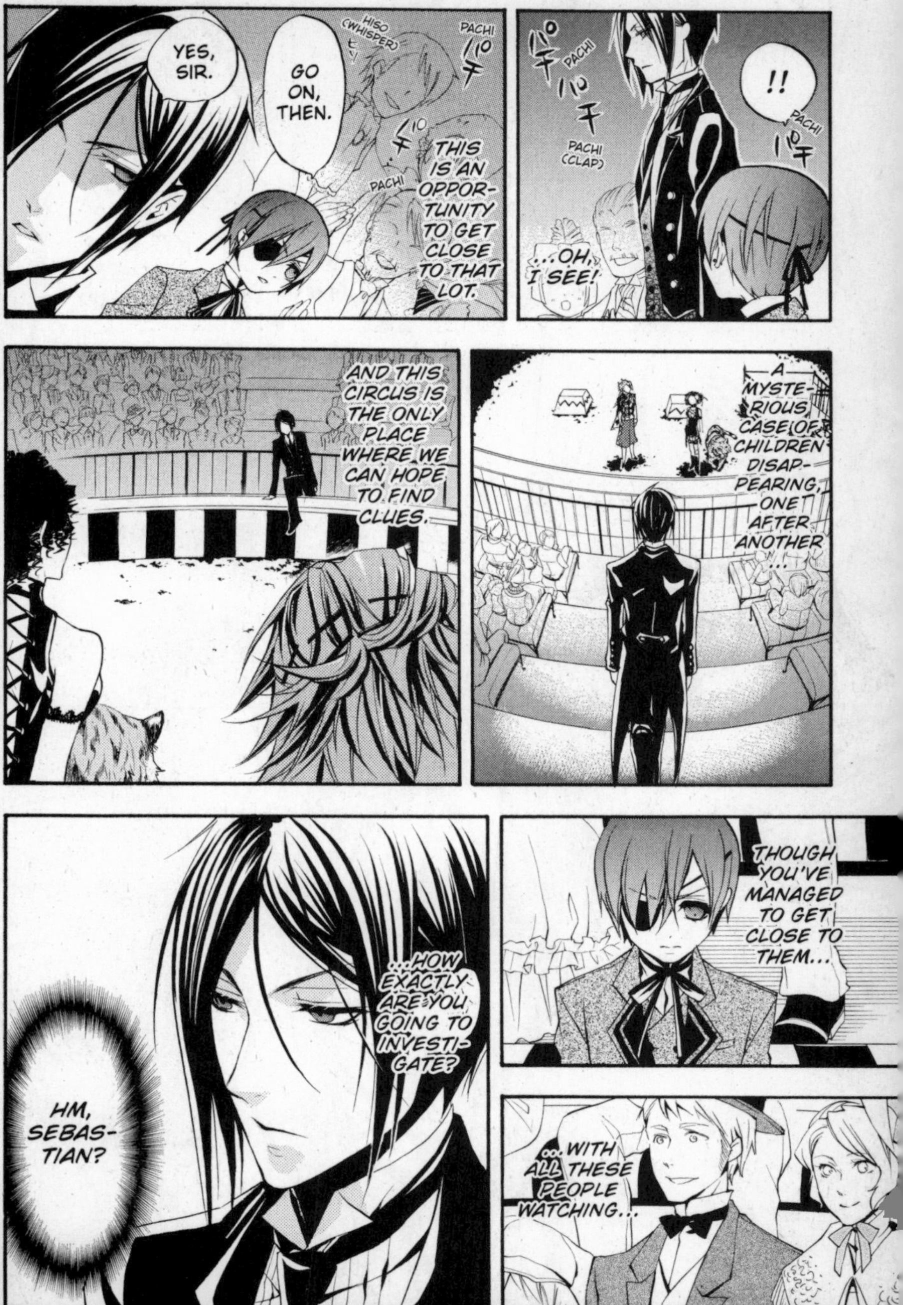
!!
PACHI
PACHI
PACHI
PACHI (CLAP)
...OH, I SEE!
HISO (WHISPER)
PACHI
GO ON, THEN.
THIS IS AN OPPORTUNITY TO GET CLOSE TO THAT LOT.
PACHI
YES, SIR.
A MYSTERIOUS CASE OF CHILDREN DISAPPEARING, ONE AFTER ANOTHER...
AND THIS CIRCUS IS THE ONLY PLACE WHERE WE CAN HOPE TO FIND CLUES.
THOUGH YOU'VE MANAGED TO GET CLOSE TO THEM...
...WITH ALL THESE PEOPLE WATCHING...
...HOW EXACTLY ARE YOU GOING TO INVESTIGATE?
HM, SEBASTIAN?

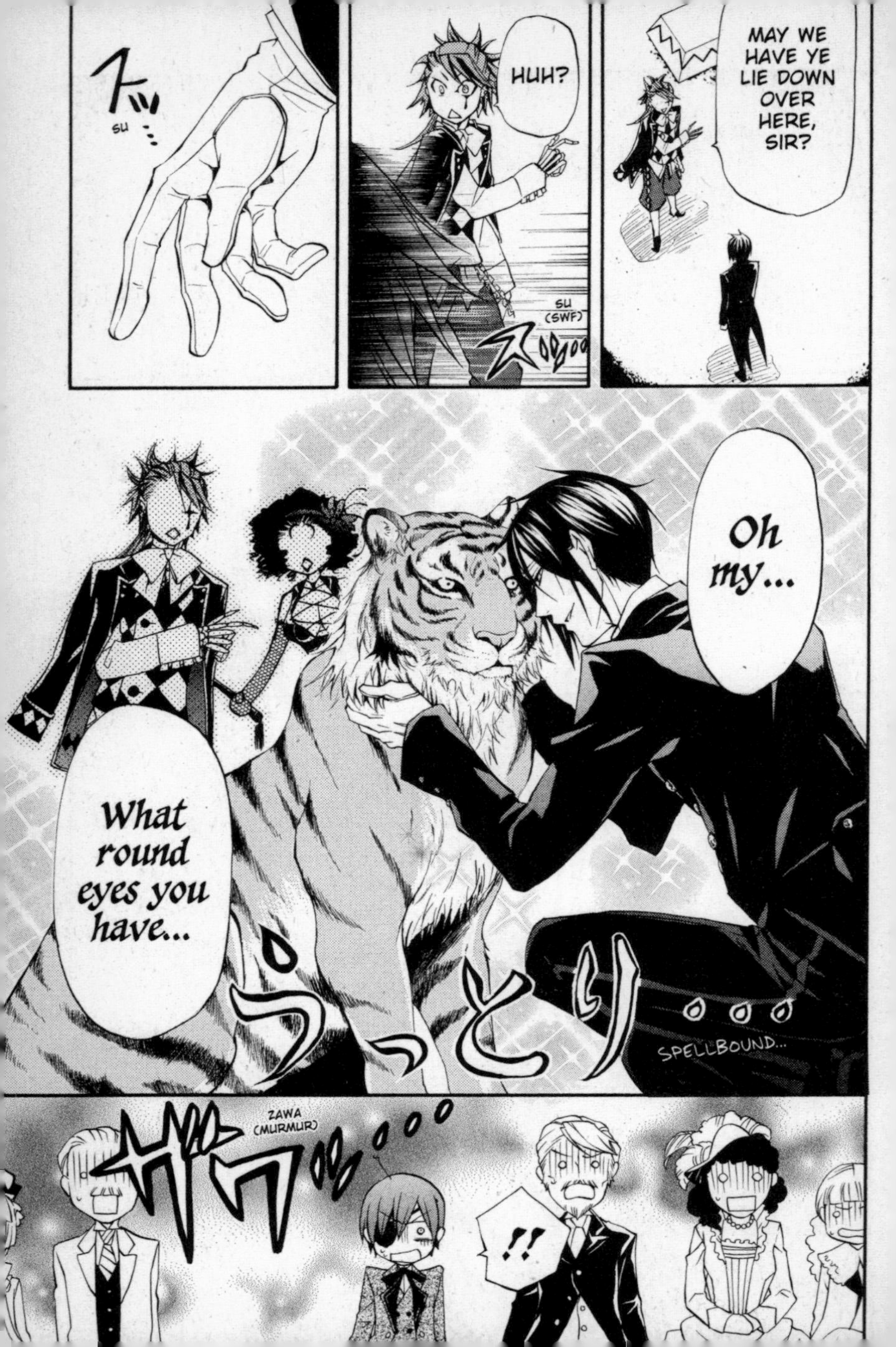
MAY WE HAVE YE LIE DOWN OVER HERE, SIR?
HUH?
SU (SWF)
SU
Oh my...
What round eyes you have...
SPELLBOUND...
ZAWA (MURMUR)
!!

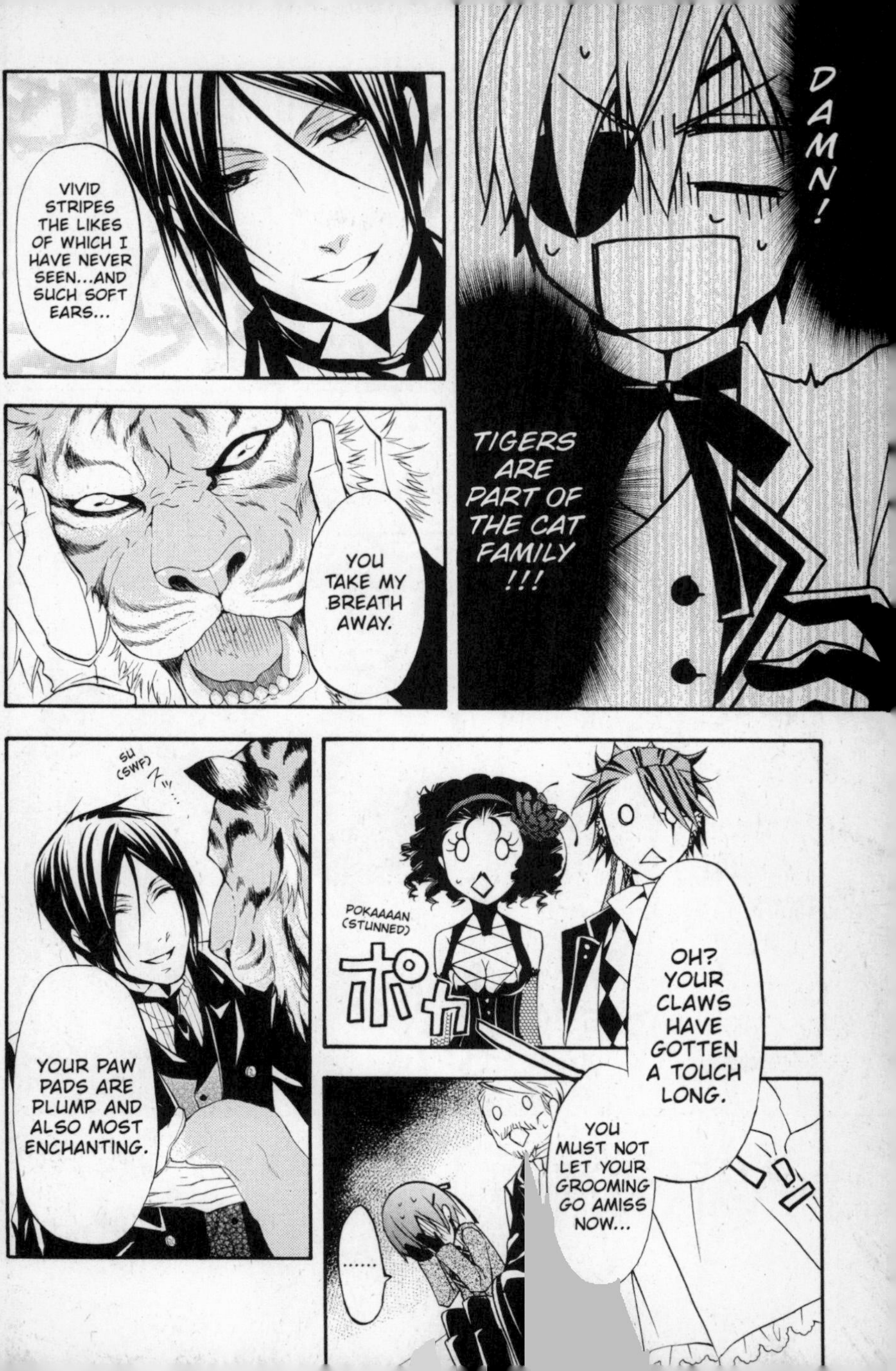
DAMN!
TIGERS ARE PART OF THE CAT FAMILY !!!
VIVID STRIPES THE LIKES OF WHICH I HAVE NEVER SEEN...AND SUCH SOFT EARS...
YOU TAKE MY BREATH AWAY.
OH? YOUR CLAWS HAVE GOTTEN A TOUCH LONG.
POKAAAAN (STUNNED)
YOU MUST NOT LET YOUR GROOMING GO AMISS NOW...
......
SU (SWF)
YOUR PAW PADS ARE PLUMP AND ALSO MOST ENCHANTING.

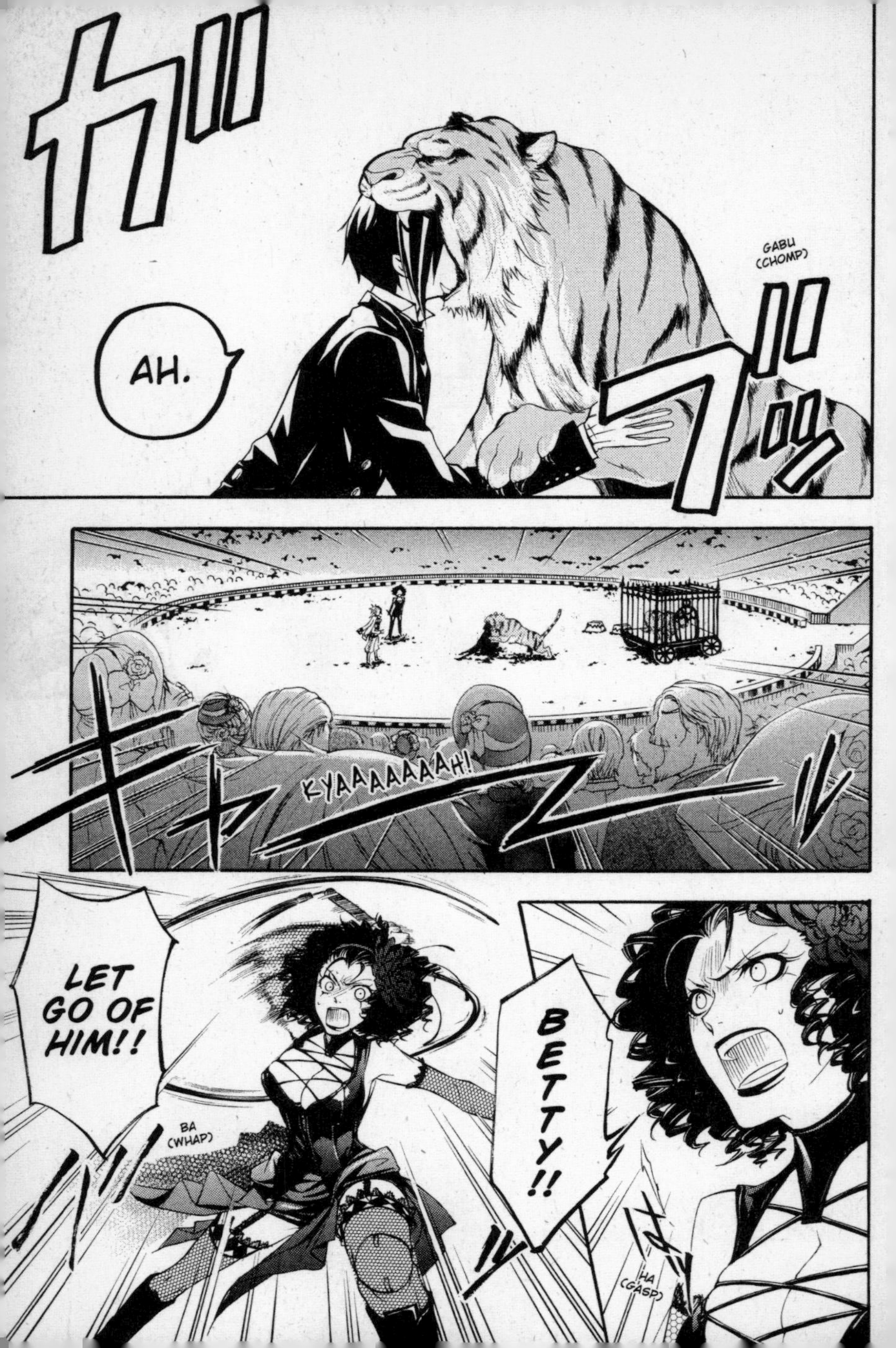
GABU
(CHOMP)
AH.
KYAAAAAAAH!
BETTY!!
HA
(GASP)
LET GO OF HIM!!
BA
(WHAP)

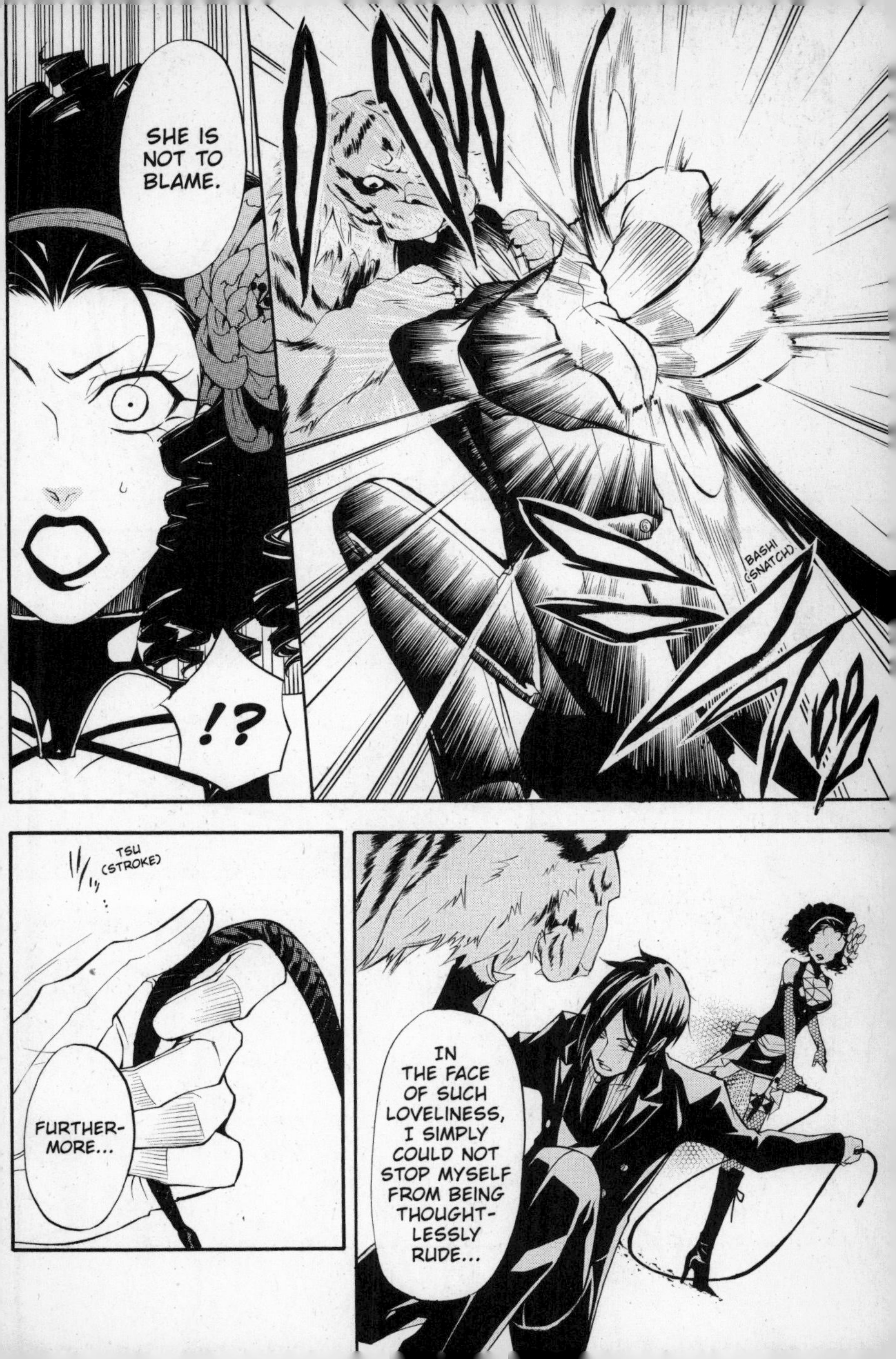
BASHI (SNATCH)
SHE IS NOT TO BLAME.
!?
IN THE FACE OF SUCH LOVELINESS, I SIMPLY COULD NOT STOP MYSELF FROM BEING THOUGHT-LESSLY RUDE...
TSU (STROKE)
FURTHER-MORE...

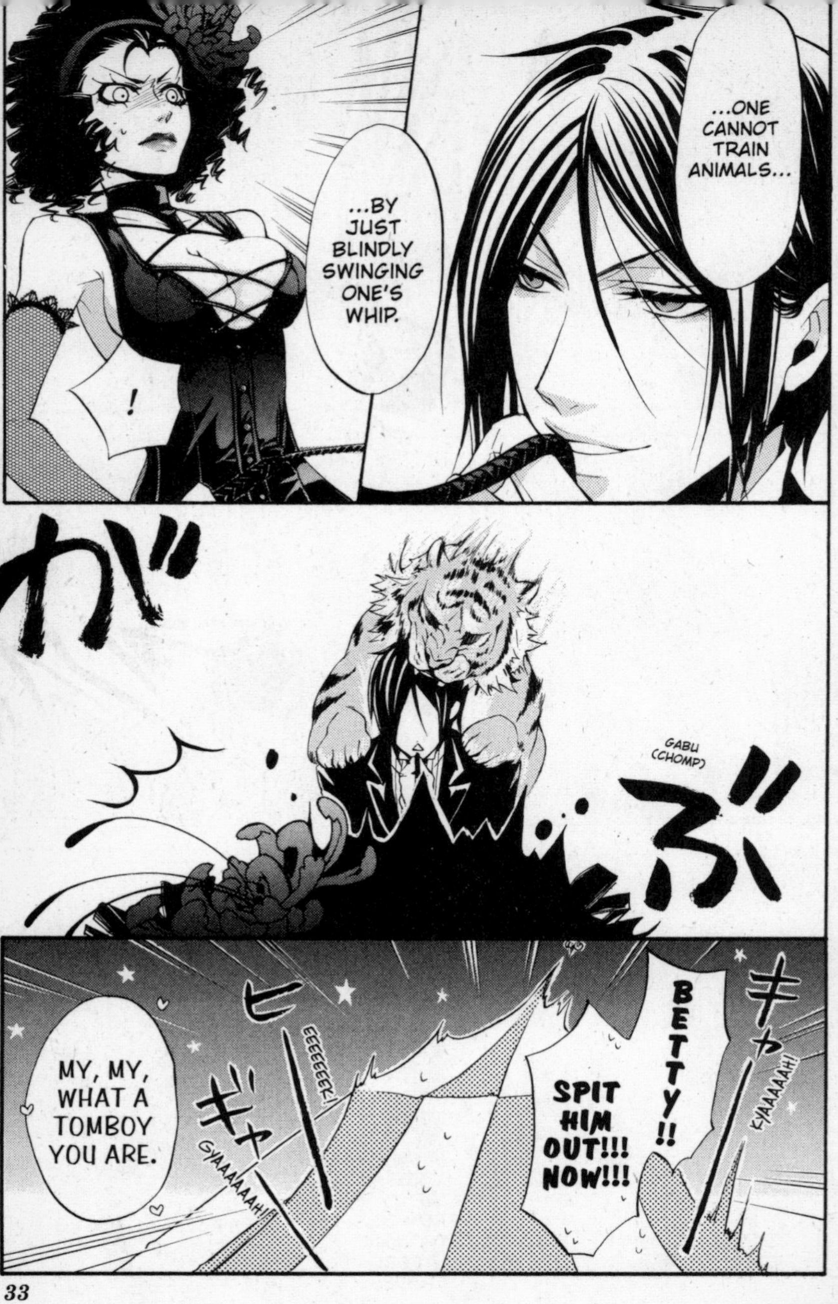

...ONE CANNOT TRAIN ANIMALS...
...BY JUST BLINDLY SWINGING ONE'S WHIP.
!
がぶ
GABU (CHOMP)
キャー
KYAAAAAH!
BETTY!!
SPIT HIM OUT!!! NOW!!!
ヒー
EEEEEEE!
ギャー
GYAAAAAAH!!
MY, MY, WHAT A TOMBOY YOU ARE.

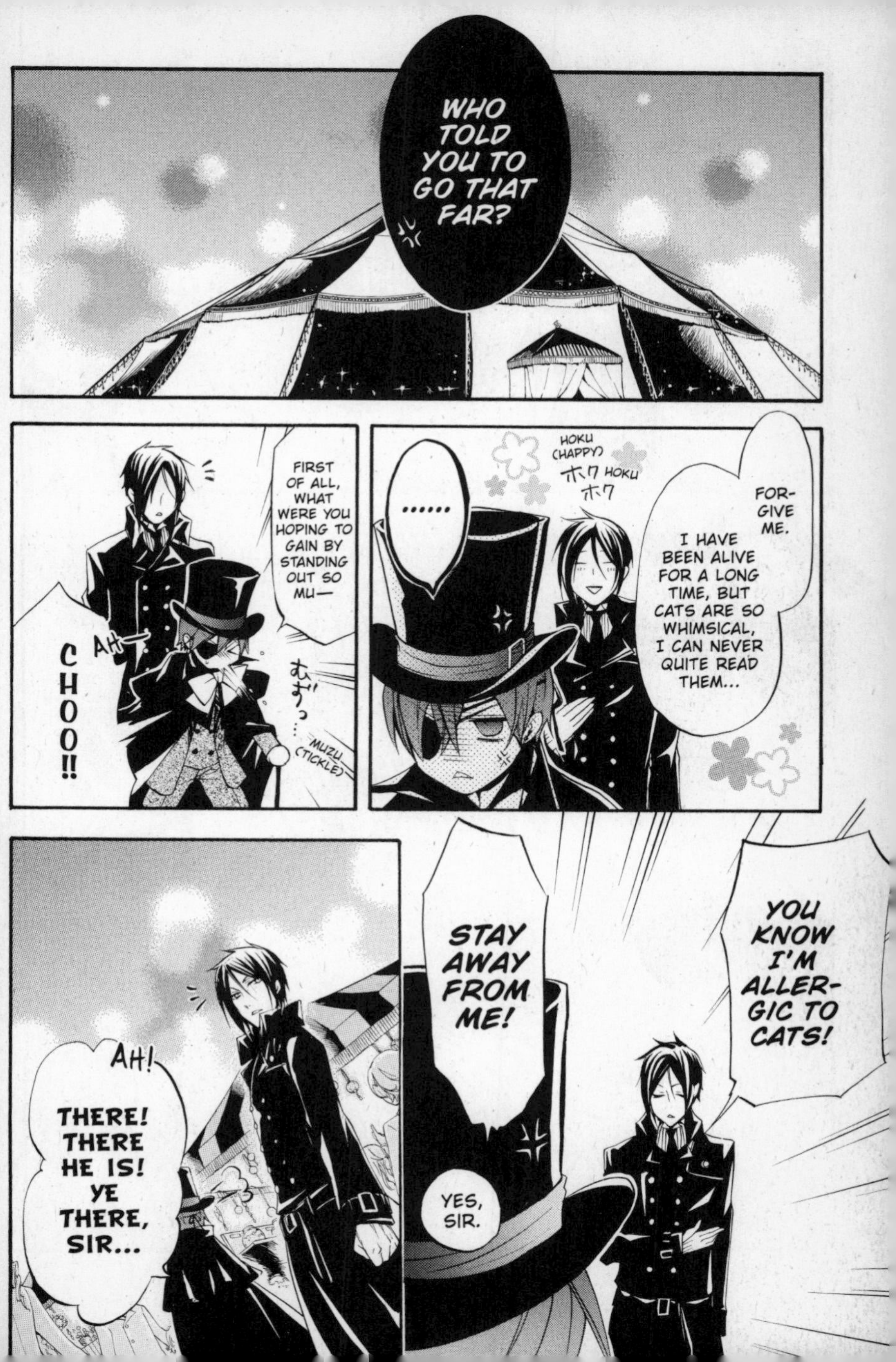
WHO TOLD YOU TO GO THAT FAR?
FOR-GIVE ME.
I HAVE BEEN ALIVE FOR A LONG TIME, BUT CATS ARE SO WHIMSICAL, I CAN NEVER QUITE READ THEM...
HOKU (HAPPY) ホク HOKU ホク
......
FIRST OF ALL, WHAT WERE YOU HOPING TO GAIN BY STANDING OUT SO MU—
むずっ…
MUZU (TICKLE)
AH CHOO!!
YOU KNOW I'M ALLER-GIC TO CATS!
STAY AWAY FROM ME!
YES, SIR.
AH!
THERE! THERE HE IS! YE THERE, SIR...

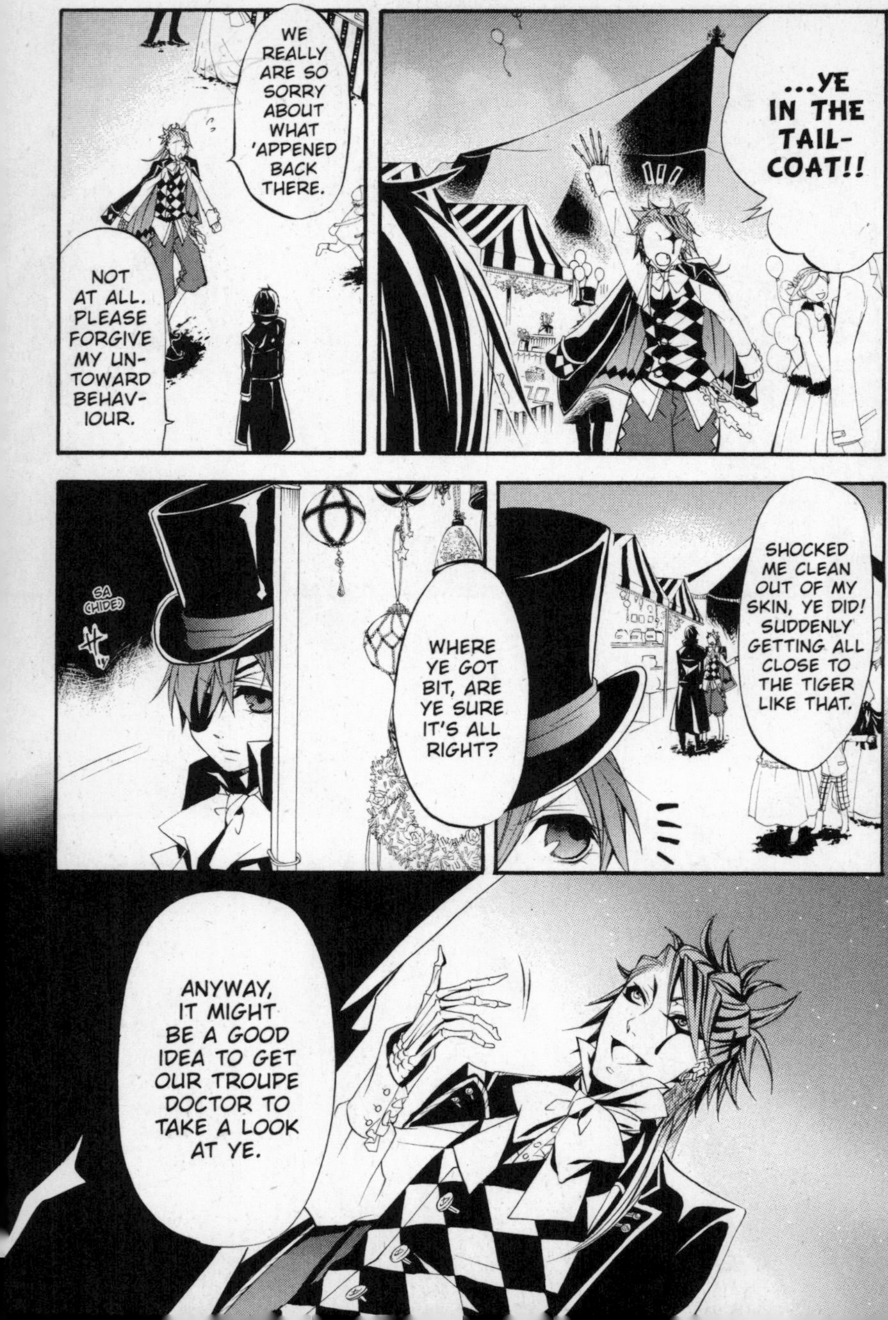
...YE IN THE TAIL-COAT!!
WE REALLY ARE SO SORRY ABOUT WHAT 'APPENED BACK THERE.
NOT AT ALL. PLEASE FORGIVE MY UNTOWARD BEHAVIOUR.
SHOCKED ME CLEAN OUT OF MY SKIN, YE DID! SUDDENLY GETTING ALL CLOSE TO THE TIGER LIKE THAT.
WHERE YE GOT BIT, ARE YE SURE IT'S ALL RIGHT?
SA (HIDE)
ANYWAY, IT MIGHT BE A GOOD IDEA TO GET OUR TROUPE DOCTOR TO TAKE A LOOK AT YE.

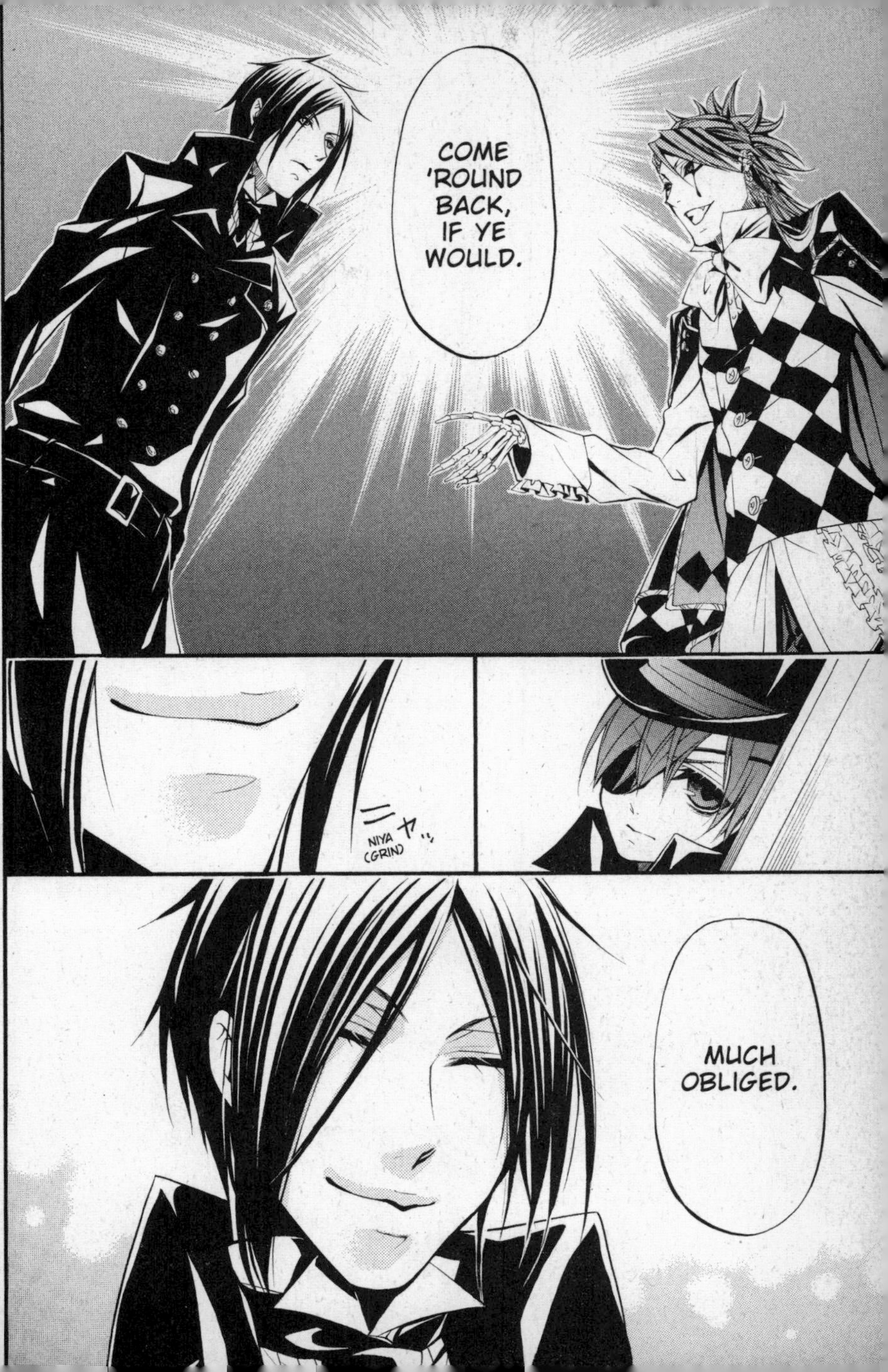
COME 'ROUND BACK, IF YE WOULD.
ニヤッ
NIYA (GRIN)
MUCH OBLIGED.

Black Butler

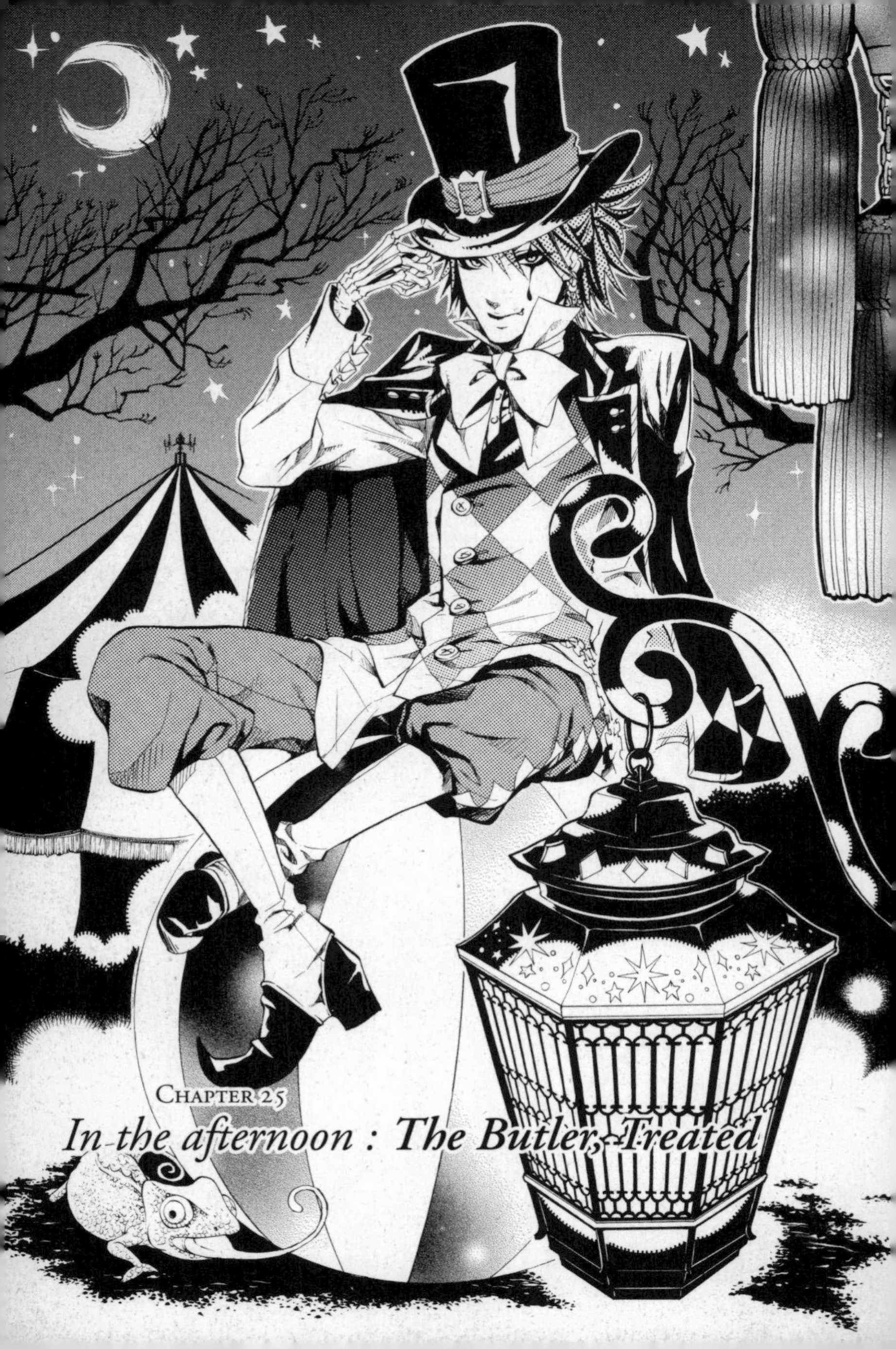
CHAPTER 25
In the afternoon : The Butler, Treated

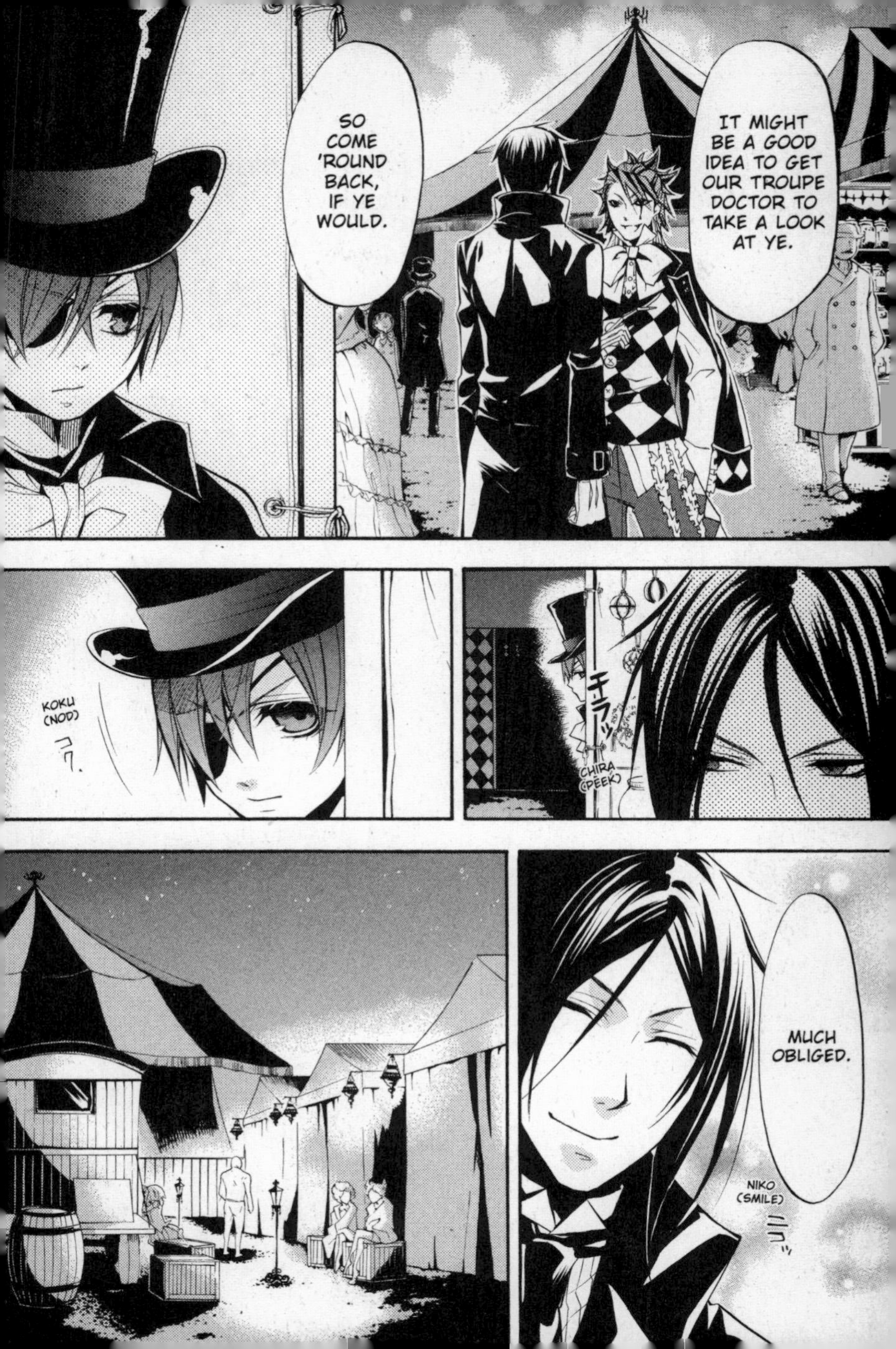
IT MIGHT BE A GOOD IDEA TO GET OUR TROUPE DOCTOR TO TAKE A LOOK AT YE.
SO COME 'ROUND BACK, IF YE WOULD.
チラッ
CHIRA (PEEK)
コク.
KOKU (NOD)
MUCH OBLIGED.
ニコッ
NIKO (SMILE)

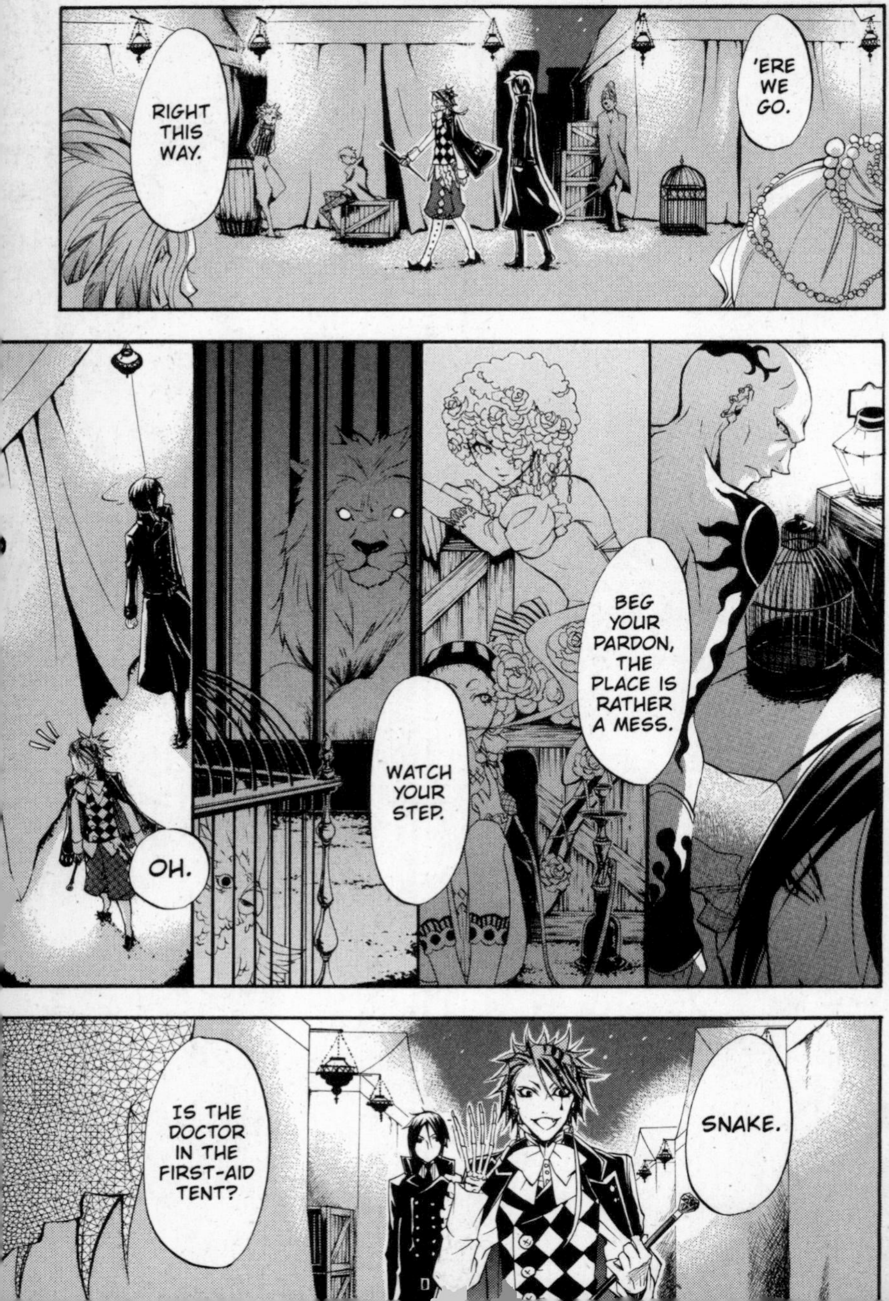
'ERE WE GO.
RIGHT THIS WAY.
BEG YOUR PARDON, THE PLACE IS RATHER A MESS.
WATCH YOUR STEP.
OH.
SNAKE.
IS THE DOCTOR IN THE FIRST-AID TENT?

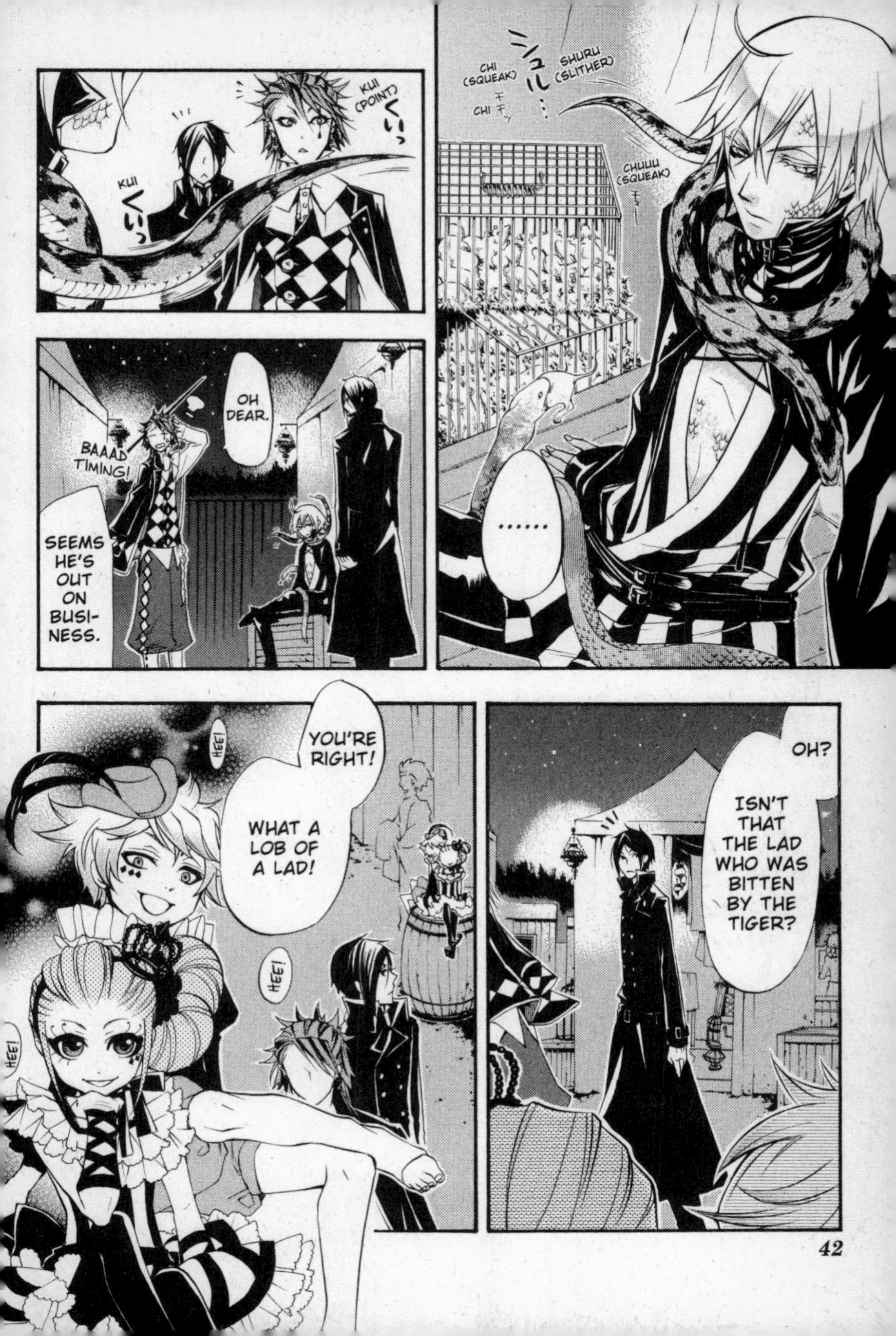
SHURU (SLITHER)
シュル…
CHI (SQUEAK)
CHI
チチッ
CHUUU (SQUEAK)
チュー
......
KUI (POINT)
くいっ
KUI
くいっ
OH DEAR.
BAAAD TIMING!
SEEMS HE'S OUT ON BUSINESS.
OH?
ISN'T THAT THE LAD WHO WAS BITTEN BY THE TIGER?
YOU'RE RIGHT!
WHAT A LOB OF A LAD!
HEE!
HEE!
HEE!

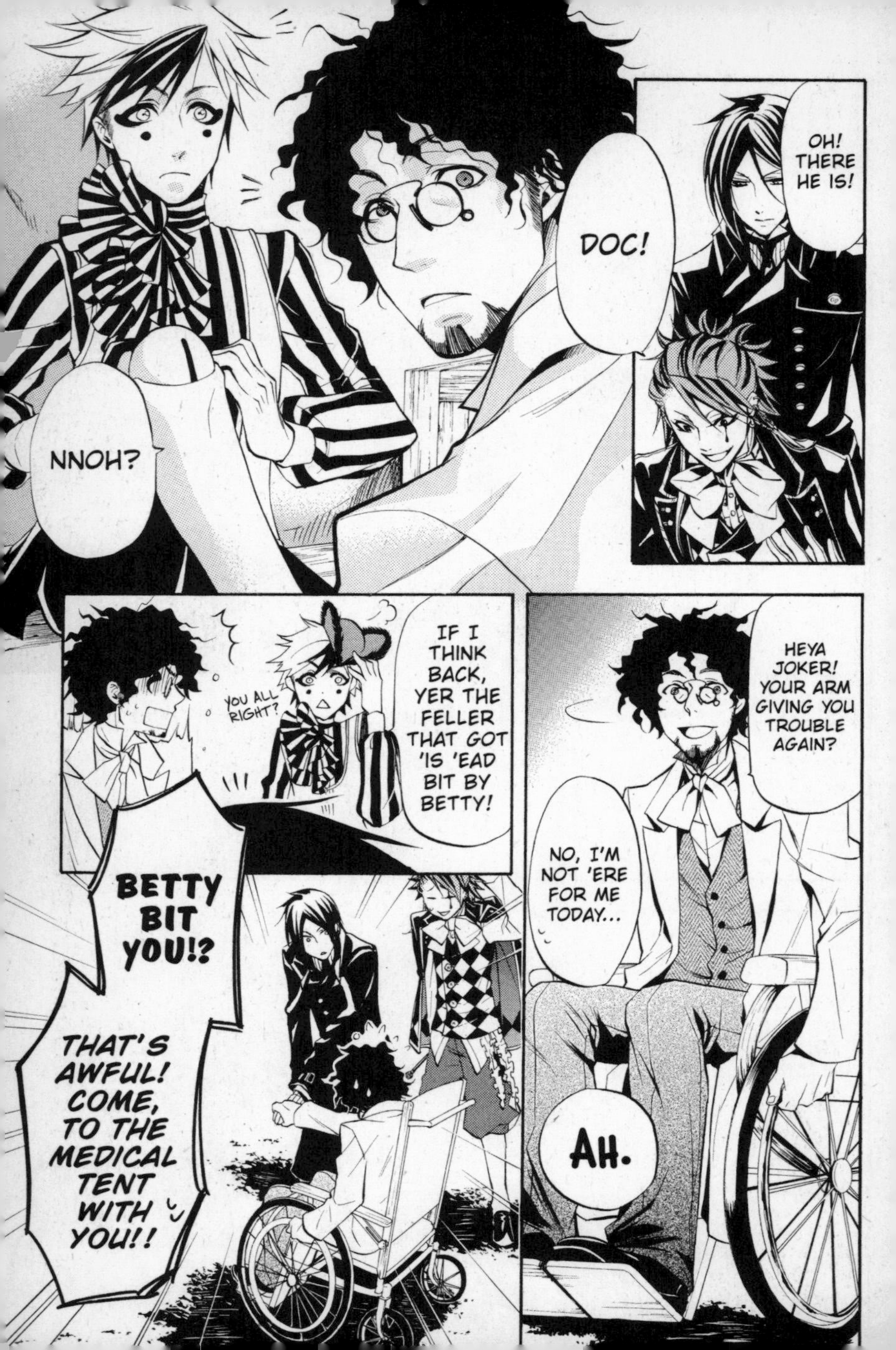
OH! THERE HE IS!
DOC!
NNOH?
HEYA JOKER! YOUR ARM GIVING YOU TROUBLE AGAIN?
NO, I'M NOT 'ERE FOR ME TODAY...
AH.
IF I THINK BACK, YER THE FELLER THAT GOT 'IS 'EAD BIT BY BETTY!
YOU ALL RIGHT?
BETTY BIT YOU!?
THAT'S AWFUL! COME, TO THE MEDICAL TENT WITH YOU!!

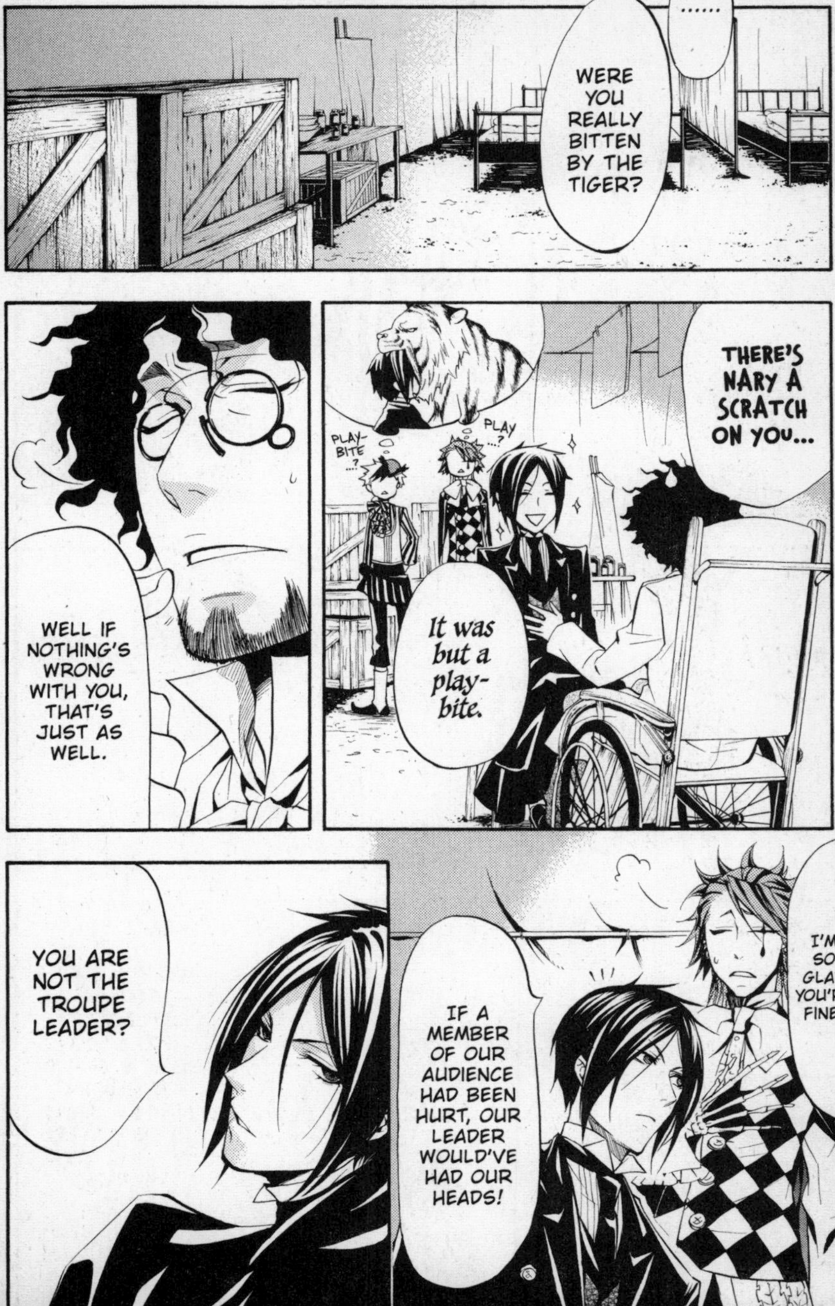
......
WERE YOU REALLY BITTEN BY THE TIGER?
THERE'S NARY A SCRATCH ON YOU...
PLAY ...?
PLAY-BITE ...?
It was but a play-bite.
WELL IF NOTHING'S WRONG WITH YOU, THAT'S JUST AS WELL.
I'M SO GLAD YOU'RE FINE.
IF A MEMBER OF OUR AUDIENCE HAD BEEN HURT, OUR LEADER WOULD'VE HAD OUR HEADS!
YOU ARE NOT THE TROUPE LEADER?

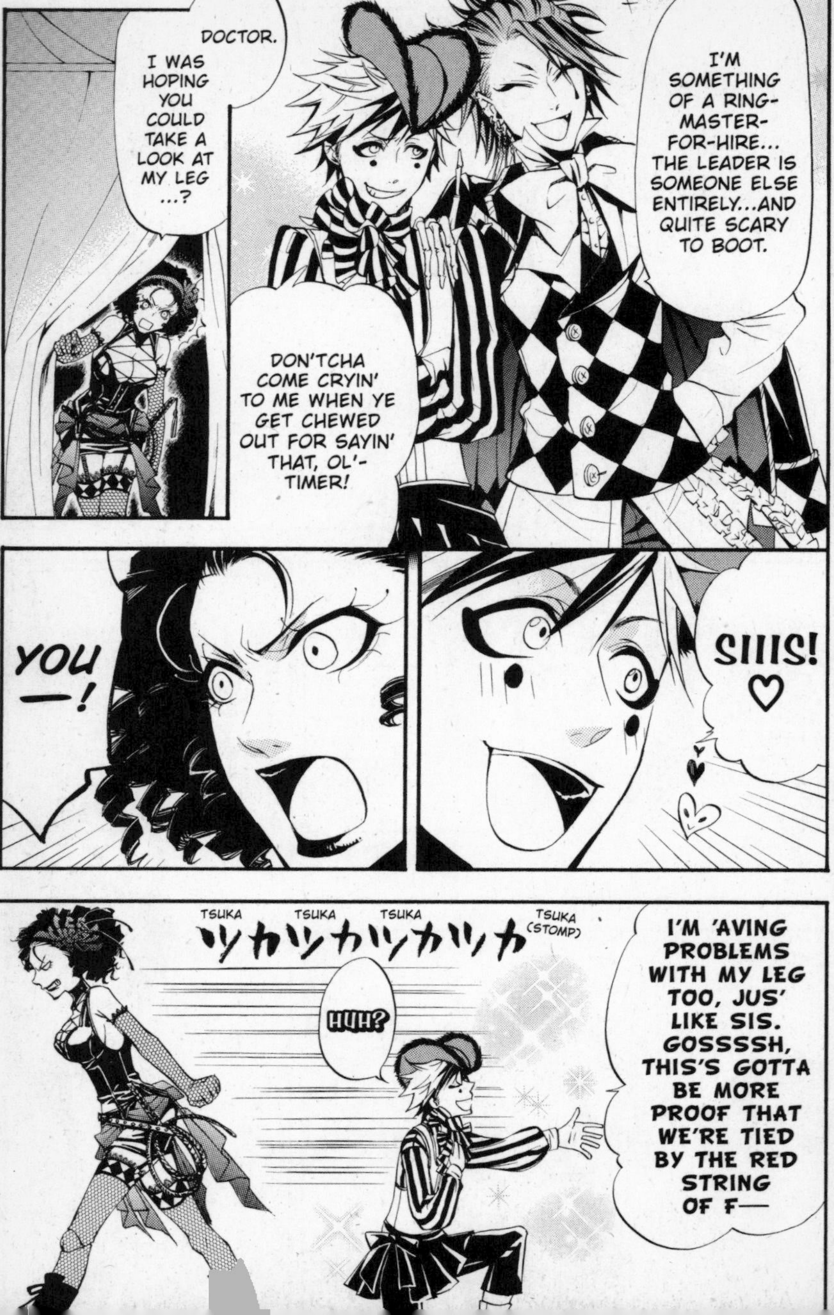
I'M SOMETHING OF A RING-MASTER-FOR-HIRE... THE LEADER IS SOMEONE ELSE ENTIRELY...AND QUITE SCARY TO BOOT.
DON'TCHA COME CRYIN' TO ME WHEN YE GET CHEWED OUT FOR SAYIN' THAT, OL'-TIMER!
DOCTOR. I WAS HOPING YOU COULD TAKE A LOOK AT MY LEG ...?
SIIIS! ♥
YOU—!
I'M 'AVING PROBLEMS WITH MY LEG TOO, JUS' LIKE SIS. GOSSSSH, THIS'S GOTTA BE MORE PROOF THAT WE'RE TIED BY THE RED STRING OF F—
ツカツカツカツカ
TSUKA TSUKA TSUKA TSUKA (STOMP)
HUH?

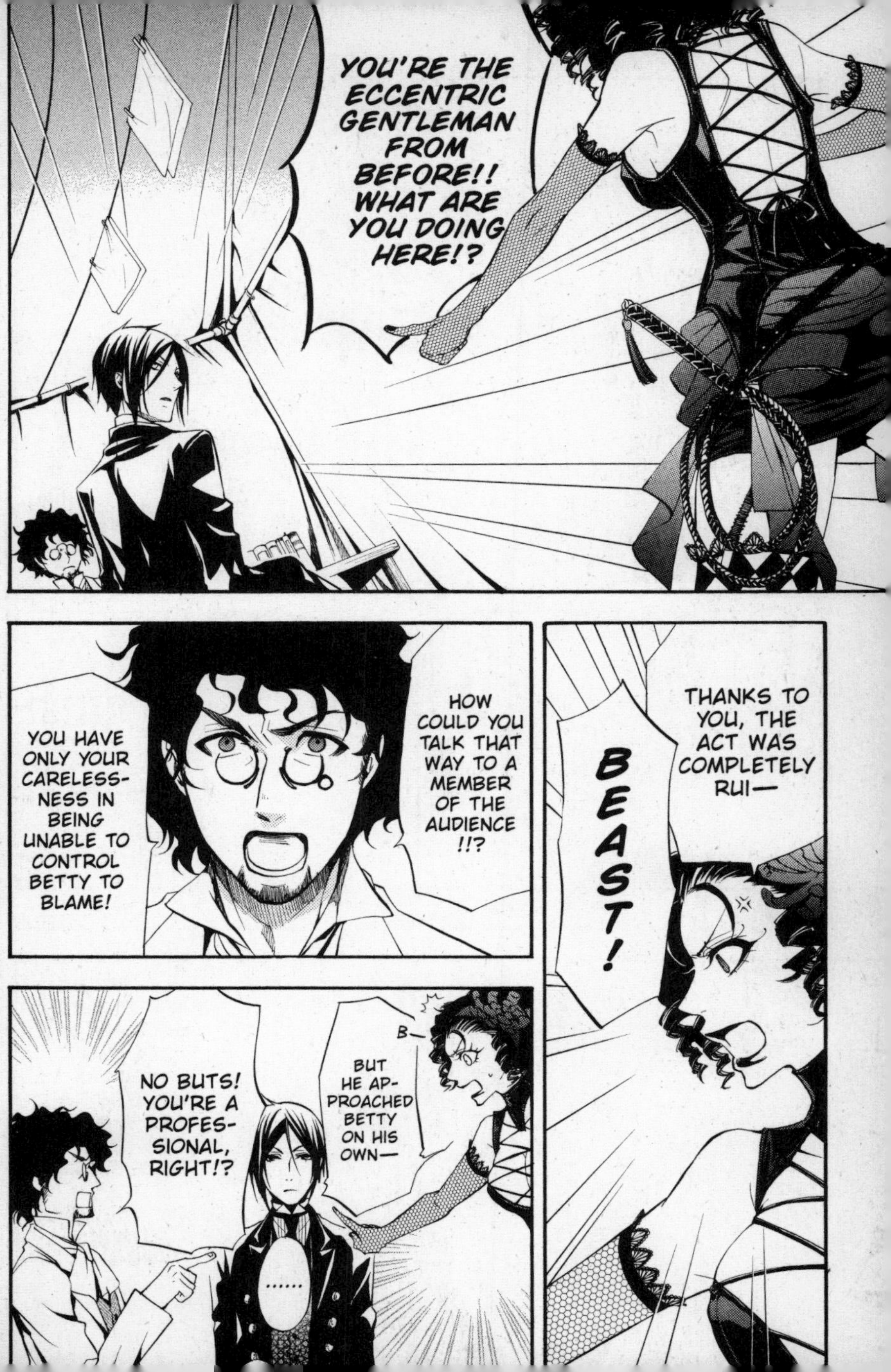
YOU'RE THE ECCENTRIC GENTLEMAN FROM BEFORE!! WHAT ARE YOU DOING HERE!?
THANKS TO YOU, THE ACT WAS COMPLETELY RUI—
BEAST!
HOW COULD YOU TALK THAT WAY TO A MEMBER OF THE AUDIENCE!!?
YOU HAVE ONLY YOUR CARELESS-NESS IN BEING UNABLE TO CONTROL BETTY TO BLAME!
B—
BUT HE AP-PROACHED BETTY ON HIS OWN—
NO BUTS! YOU'RE A PROFES-SIONAL, RIGHT!?
......

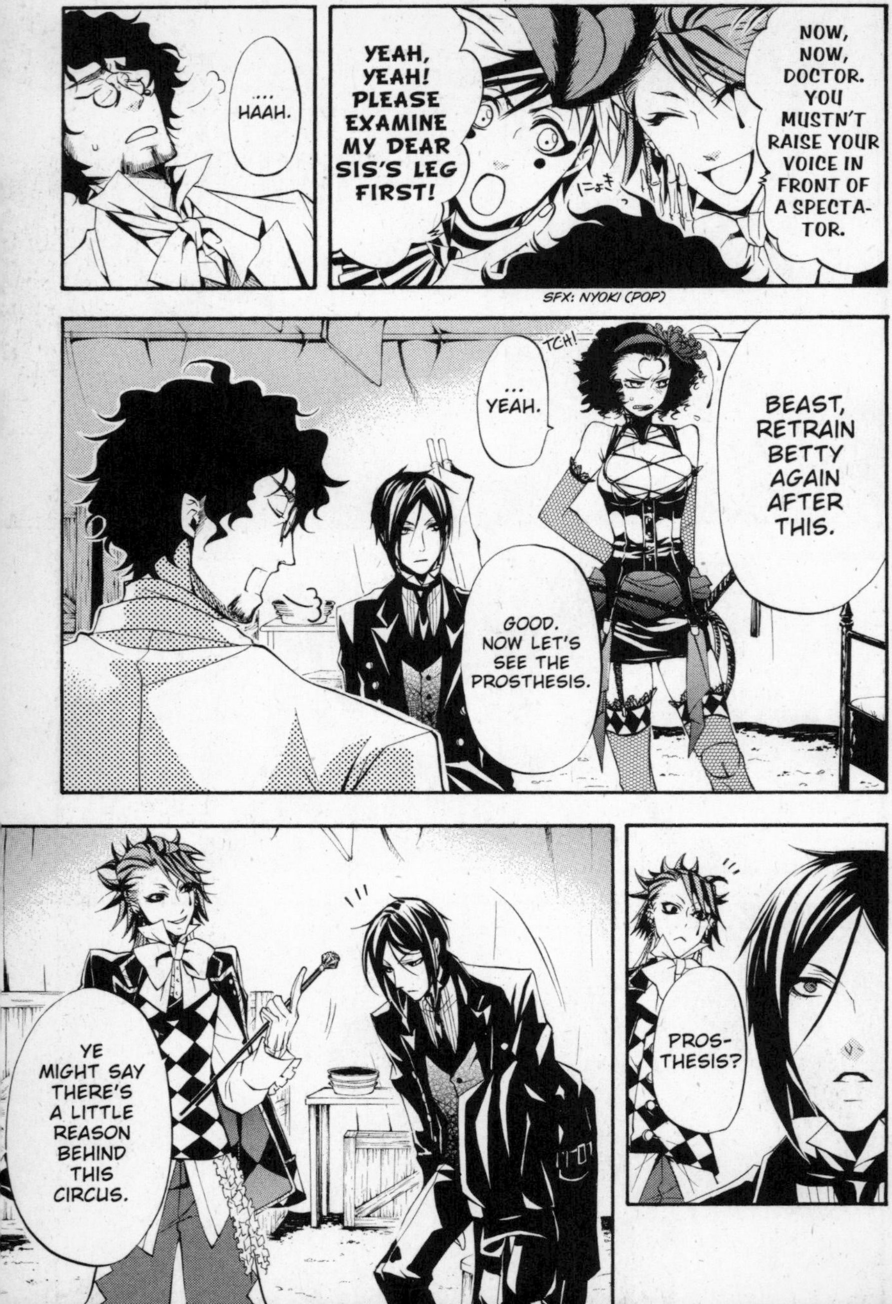
NOW, NOW, DOCTOR. YOU MUSTN'T RAISE YOUR VOICE IN FRONT OF A SPECTA-TOR.
にょきっ
YEAH, YEAH! PLEASE EXAMINE MY DEAR SIS'S LEG FIRST!
....HAAH.
SFX: NYOKI (POP)
BEAST, RETRAIN BETTY AGAIN AFTER THIS.
TCH!
...YEAH.
GOOD. NOW LET'S SEE THE PROSTHESIS.
PROS-THESIS?
YE MIGHT SAY THERE'S A LITTLE REASON BEHIND THIS CIRCUS.

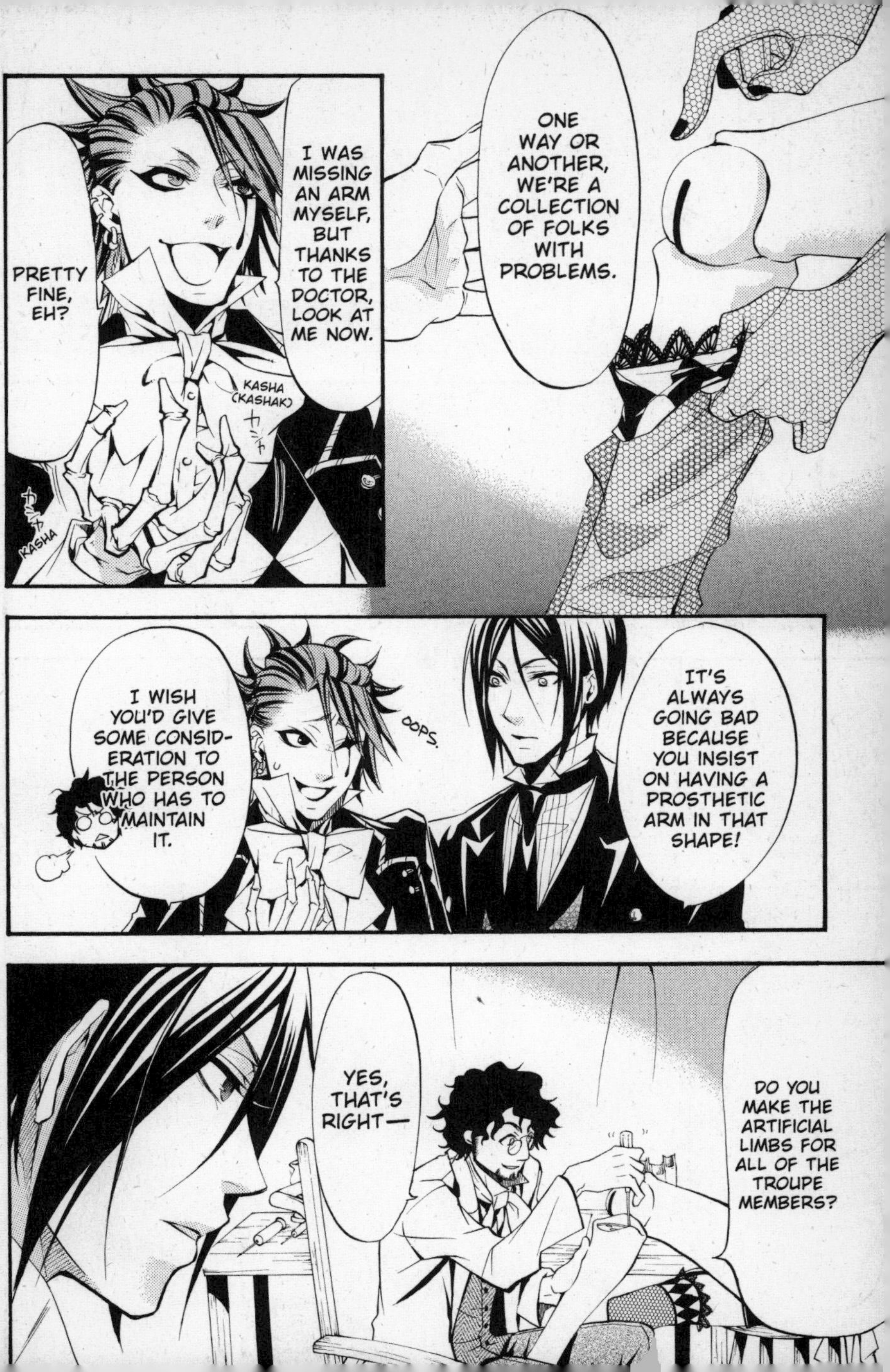
ONE WAY OR ANOTHER, WE'RE A COLLECTION OF FOLKS WITH PROBLEMS.
I WAS MISSING AN ARM MYSELF, BUT THANKS TO THE DOCTOR, LOOK AT ME NOW.
PRETTY FINE, EH?
KASHA (KASHAK)
KASHA
IT'S ALWAYS GOING BAD BECAUSE YOU INSIST ON HAVING A PROSTHETIC ARM IN THAT SHAPE!
OOPS.
I WISH YOU'D GIVE SOME CONSID-ERATION TO THE PERSON WHO HAS TO MAINTAIN IT.
DO YOU MAKE THE ARTIFICIAL LIMBS FOR ALL OF THE TROUPE MEMBERS?
YES, THAT'S RIGHT—

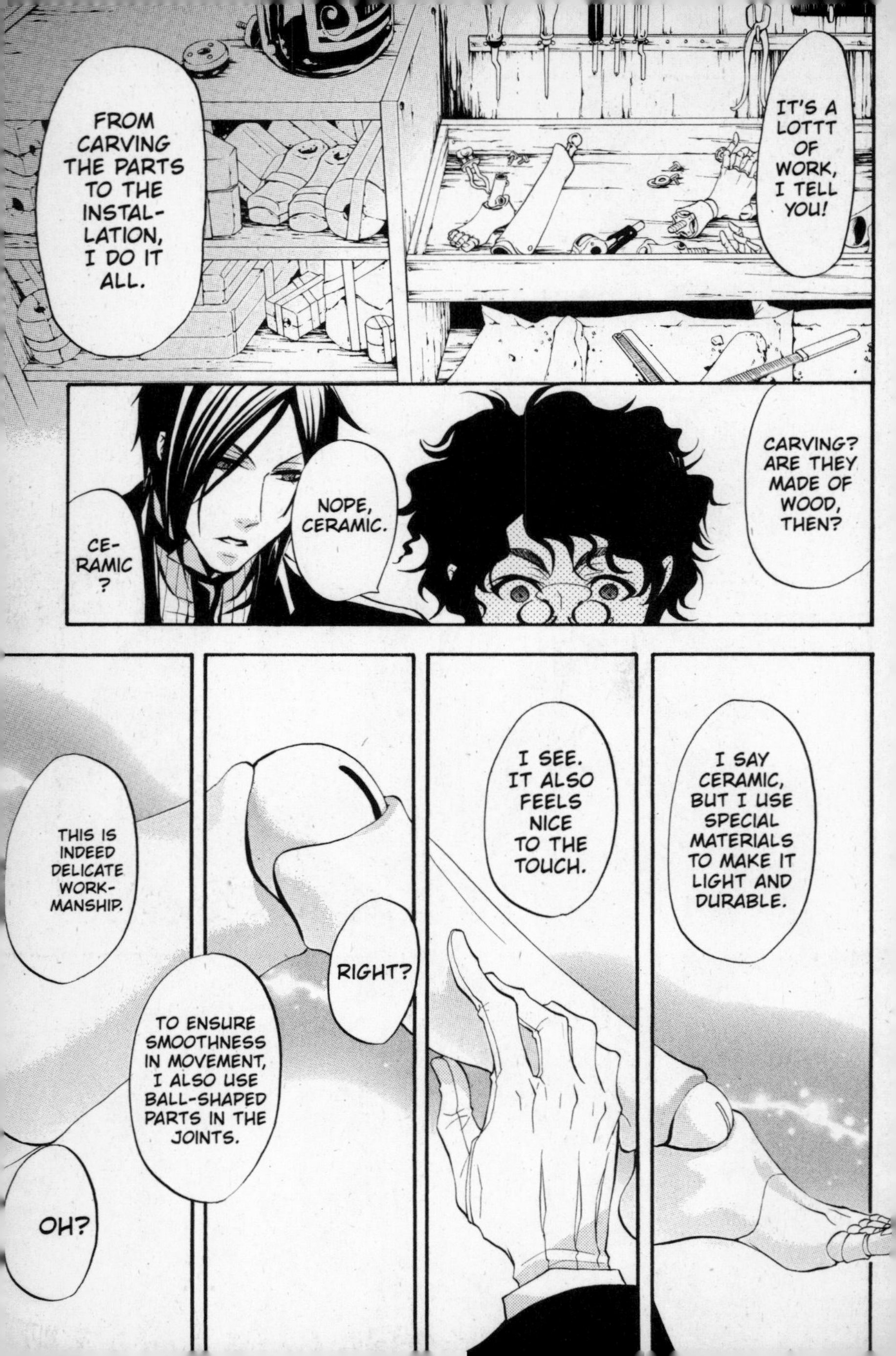
IT'S A LOTTT OF WORK, I TELL YOU!
FROM CARVING THE PARTS TO THE INSTAL-LATION, I DO IT ALL.
CARVING? ARE THEY MADE OF WOOD, THEN?
NOPE, CERAMIC.
CE-RAMIC?
I SAY CERAMIC, BUT I USE SPECIAL MATERIALS TO MAKE IT LIGHT AND DURABLE.
I SEE. IT ALSO FEELS NICE TO THE TOUCH.
RIGHT?
TO ENSURE SMOOTHNESS IN MOVEMENT, I ALSO USE BALL-SHAPED PARTS IN THE JOINTS.
THIS IS INDEED DELICATE WORK-MANSHIP.
OH?

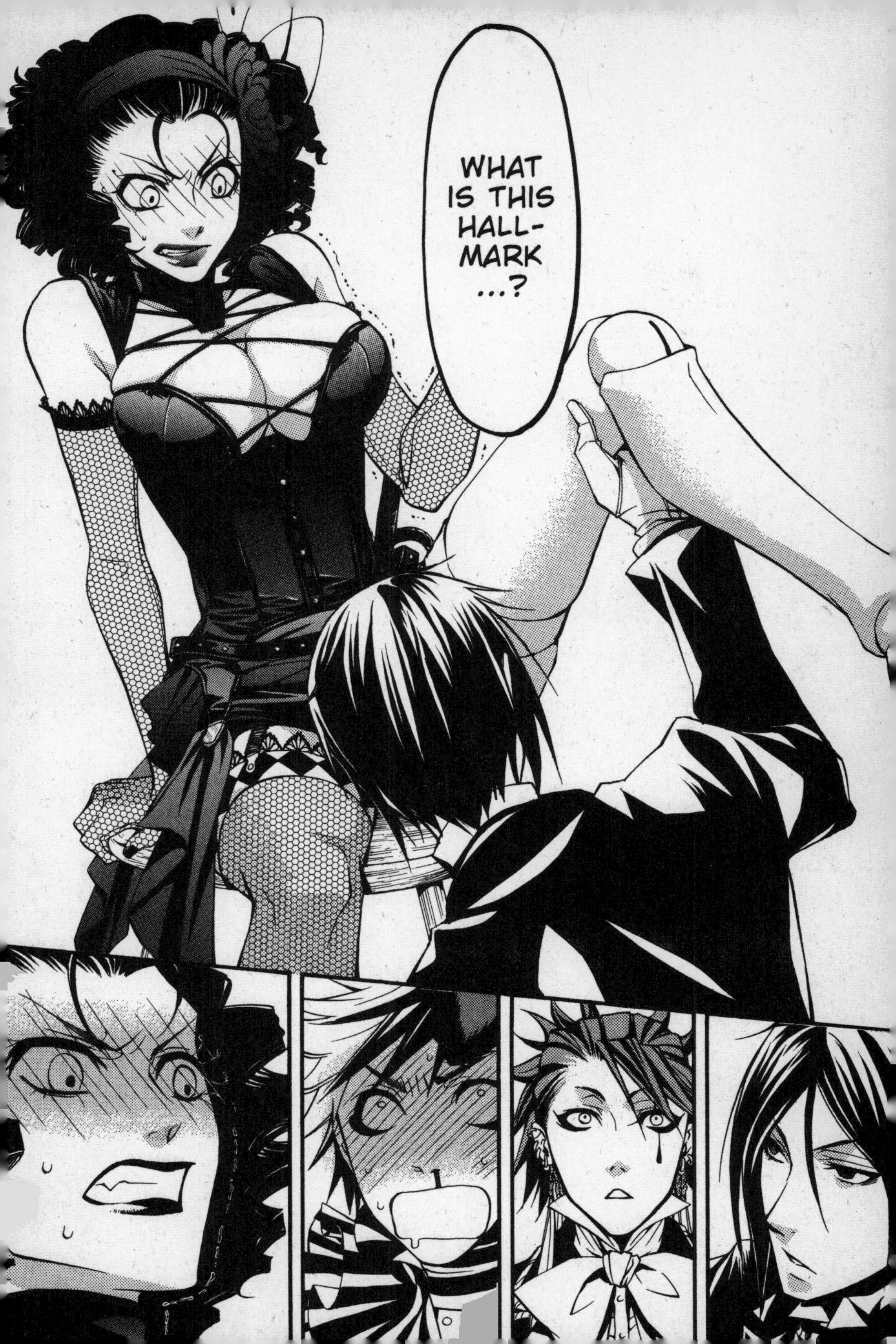
WHAT IS THIS HALL-MARK ...?

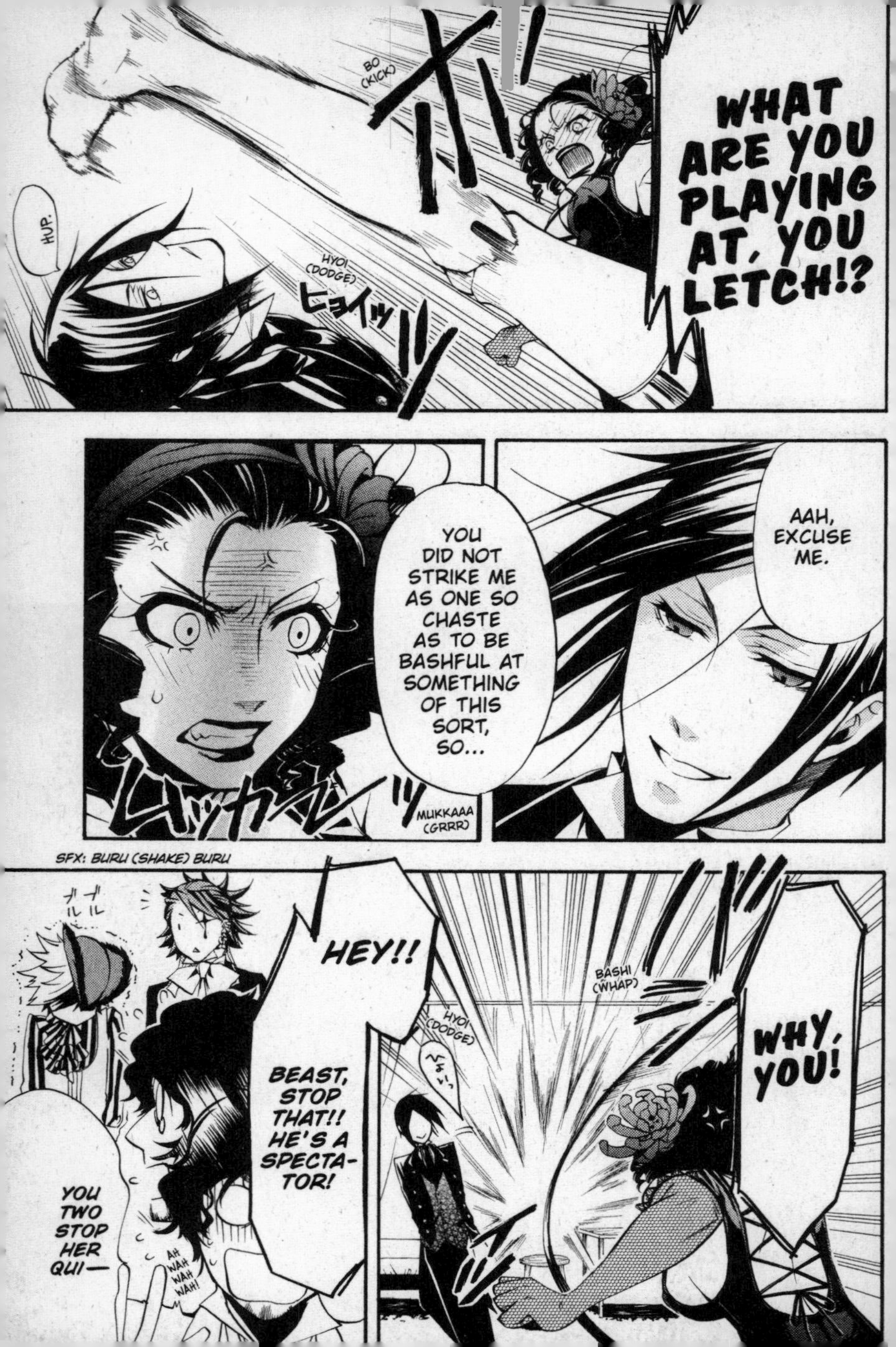
WHAT ARE YOU PLAYING AT, YOU LETCH!?
BO (KICK)
HUP.
HYOI (DODGE)
ヒョイッ
AAH, EXCUSE ME.
YOU DID NOT STRIKE ME AS ONE SO CHASTE AS TO BE BASHFUL AT SOMETHING OF THIS SORT, SO...
MUKKAAA (GRRR)
SFX: BURU (SHAKE) BURU
WHY, YOU!
BASHI (WHAP)
HYOI (DODGE)
HEY!!
BEAST, STOP THAT!! HE'S A SPECTATOR!
YOU TWO STOP HER QUI—
AH WAH WAH WAH!

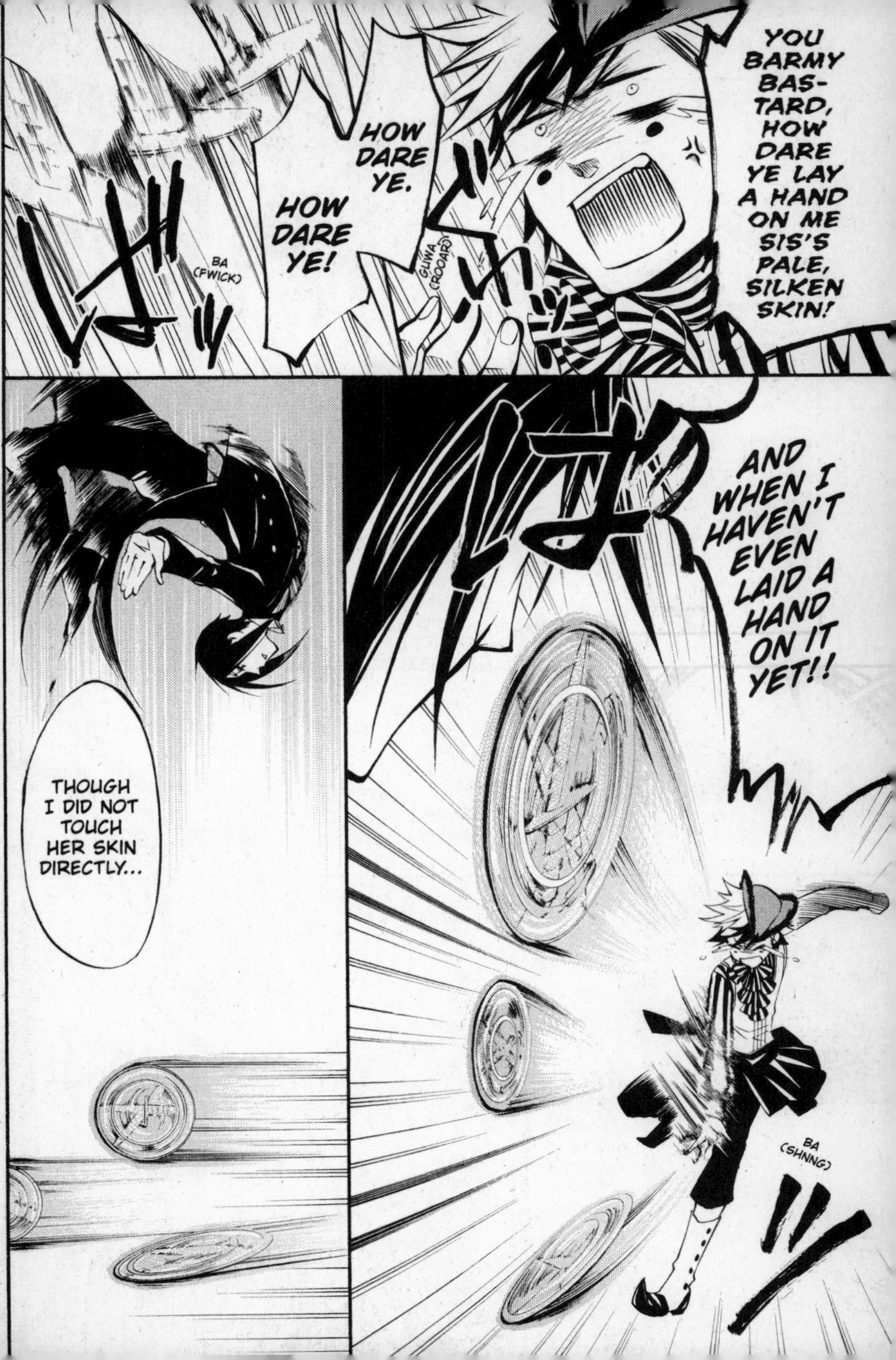
YOU BARMY BASTARD, HOW DARE YE LAY A HAND ON ME SIS'S PALE, SILKEN SKIN!
GUWA (ROOAR)
HOW DARE YE.
HOW DARE YE!
BA (FWICK)
AND WHEN I HAVEN'T EVEN LAID A HAND ON IT YET!!
BA (SHNNG)
THOUGH I DID NOT TOUCH HER SKIN DIRECTLY...

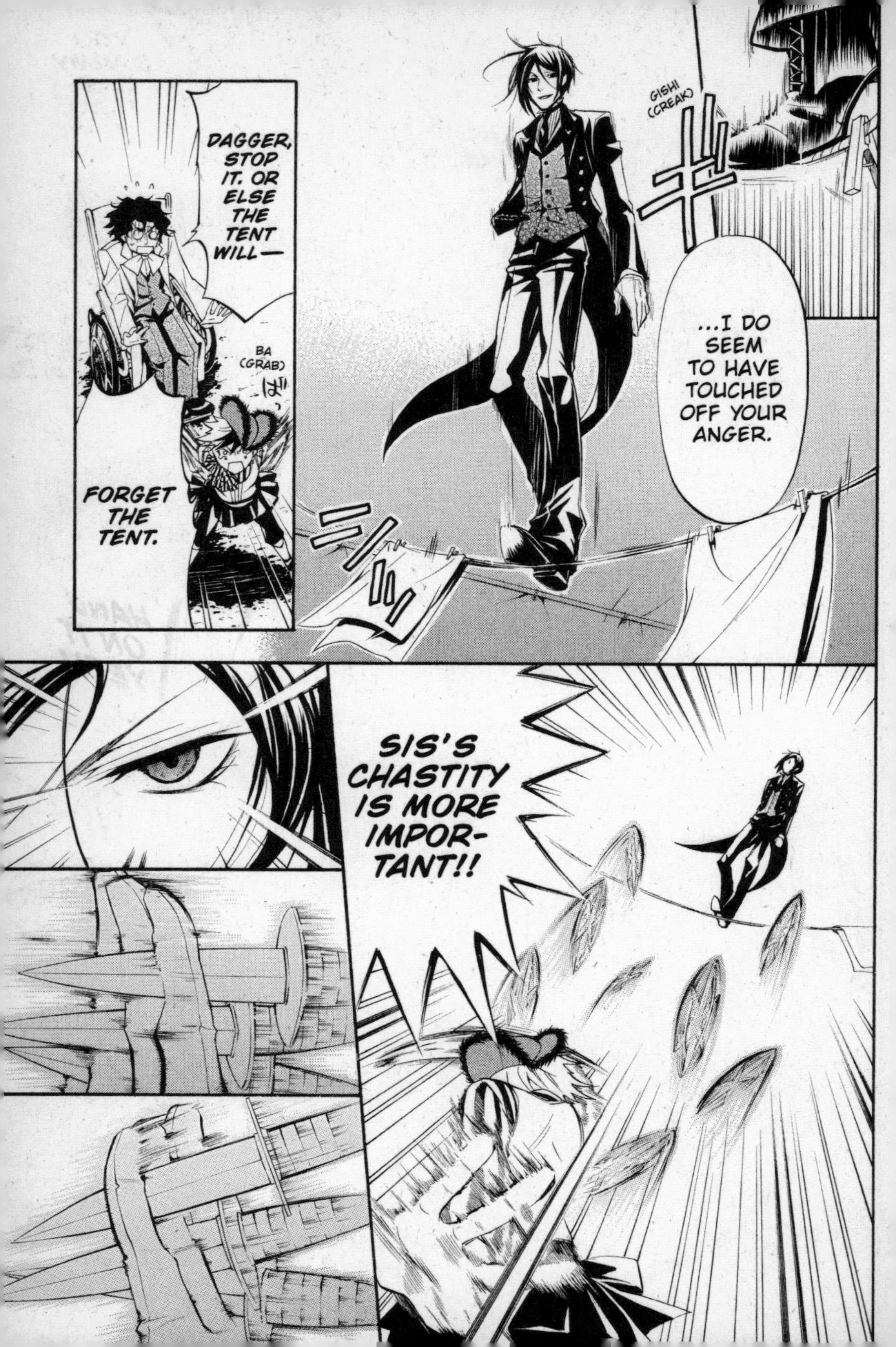
GISHI (CREAK)
...I DO SEEM TO HAVE TOUCHED OFF YOUR ANGER.
DAGGER, STOP IT. OR ELSE THE TENT WILL—
BA (GRAB)
ばっ
FORGET THE TENT.
SIS'S CHASTITY IS MORE IMPOR-TANT!!

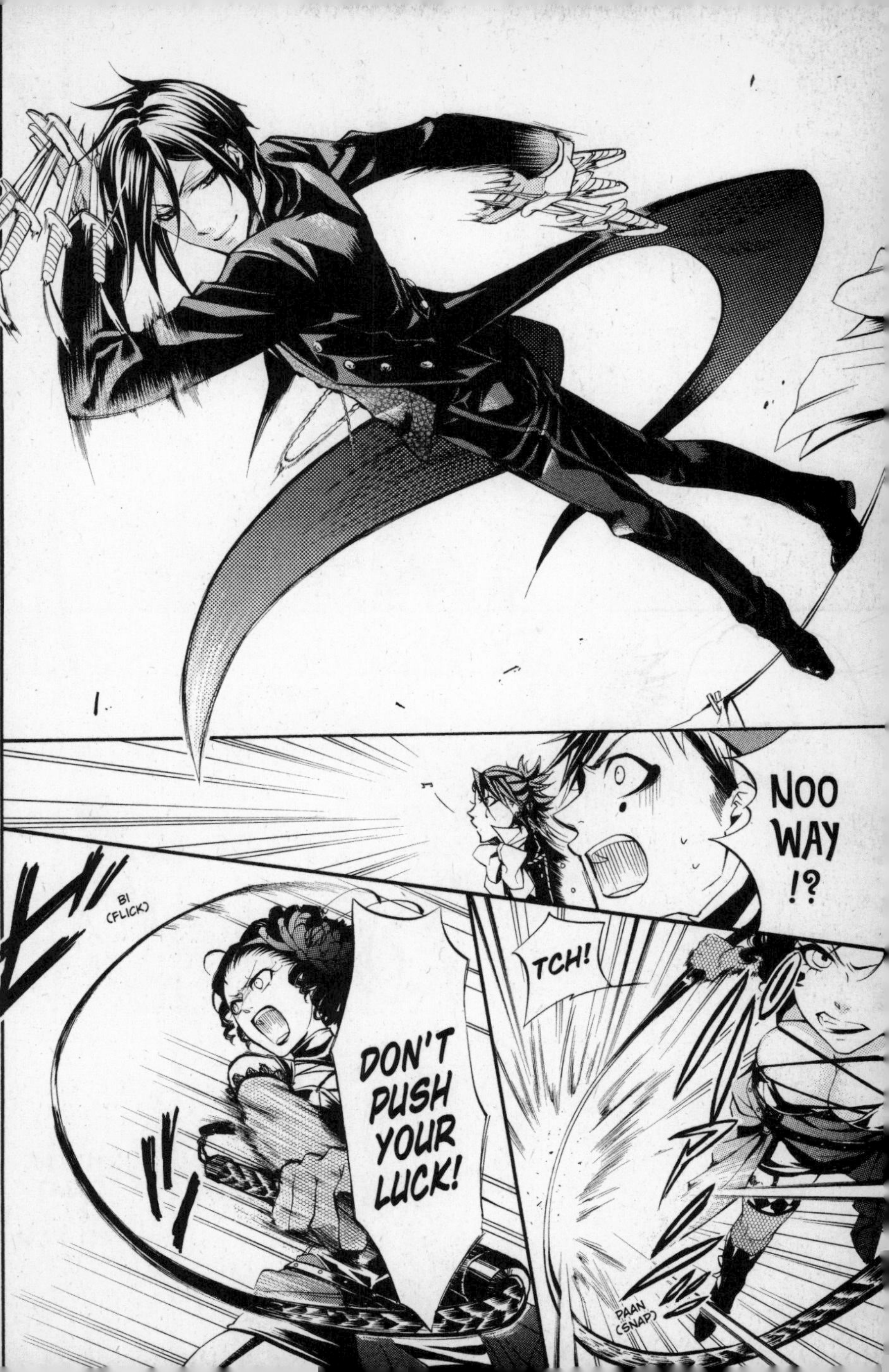
NOO WAY !?
TCH!
PAAN (SNAP)
DON'T PUSH YOUR LUCK!
BI (FLICK)

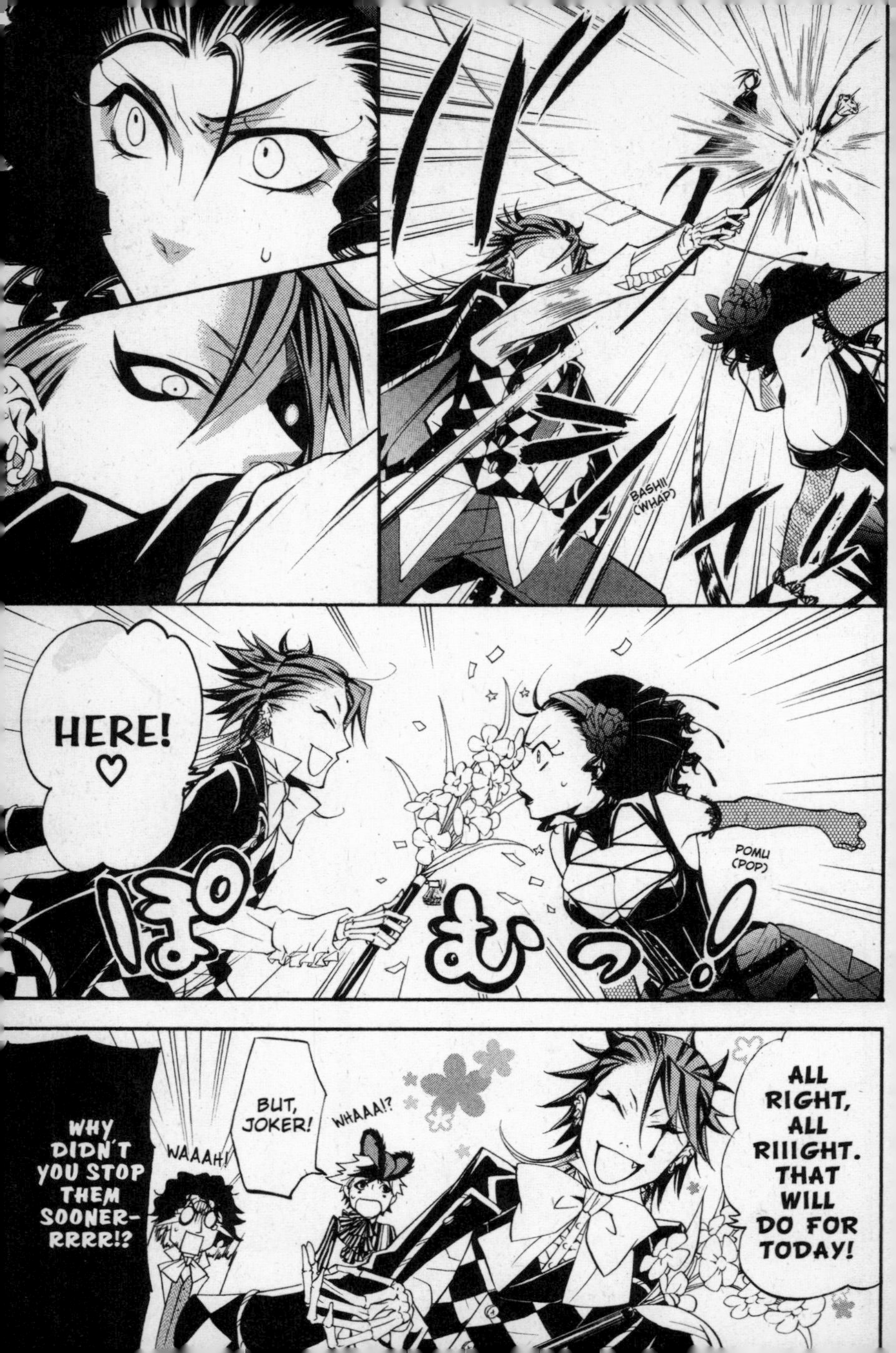
BASHII (WHAP)
HERE! ♡
ぽむっ!
POMU (POP)
ALL RIGHT, ALL RIIIGHT. THAT WILL DO FOR TODAY!
WHAAA!?
BUT, JOKER!
WAAAH!
WHY DIDN'T YOU STOP THEM SOONER-RRRR!?

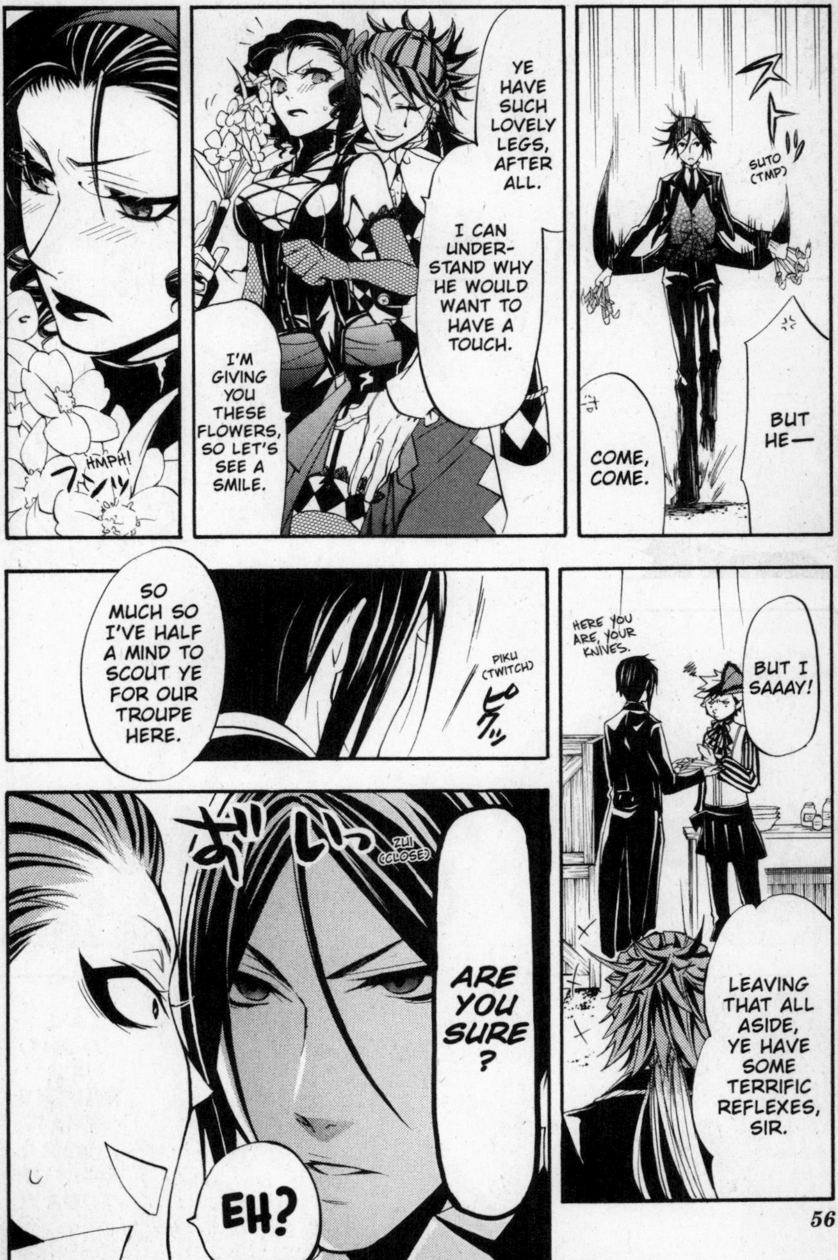
SUTO (TMP)
BUT HE—
COME, COME.
YE HAVE SUCH LOVELY LEGS, AFTER ALL.
I CAN UNDER-STAND WHY HE WOULD WANT TO HAVE A TOUCH.
I'M GIVING YOU THESE FLOWERS, SO LET'S SEE A SMILE.
HMPH!
HERE YOU ARE, YOUR KNIVES.
BUT I SAAAY!
LEAVING THAT ALL ASIDE, YE HAVE SOME TERRIFIC REFLEXES, SIR.
SO MUCH SO I'VE HALF A MIND TO SCOUT YE FOR OUR TROUPE HERE.
PIKU (TWITCH)
ZUI (CLOSE)
ARE YOU SURE?
EH?

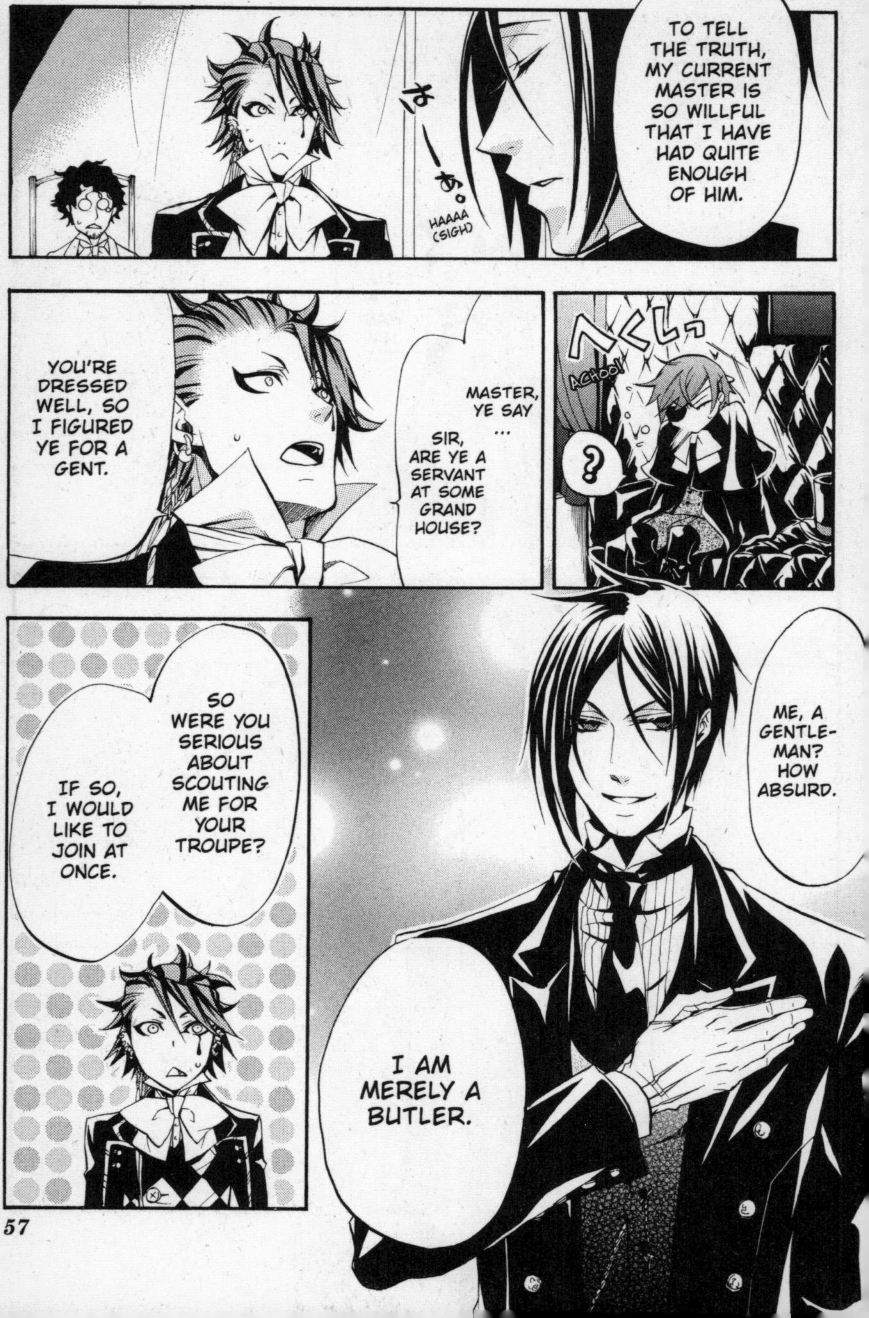
TO TELL THE TRUTH, MY CURRENT MASTER IS SO WILLFUL THAT I HAVE HAD QUITE ENOUGH OF HIM.
はーあ。
HAAAA (SIGH)
へくしっ
ACHOO!
?
MASTER, YE SAY ...
SIR, ARE YE A SERVANT AT SOME GRAND HOUSE?
YOU'RE DRESSED WELL, SO I FIGURED YE FOR A GENT.
ME, A GENTLE-MAN? HOW ABSURD.
I AM MERELY A BUTLER.
SO WERE YOU SERIOUS ABOUT SCOUTING ME FOR YOUR TROUPE?
IF SO, I WOULD LIKE TO JOIN AT ONCE.

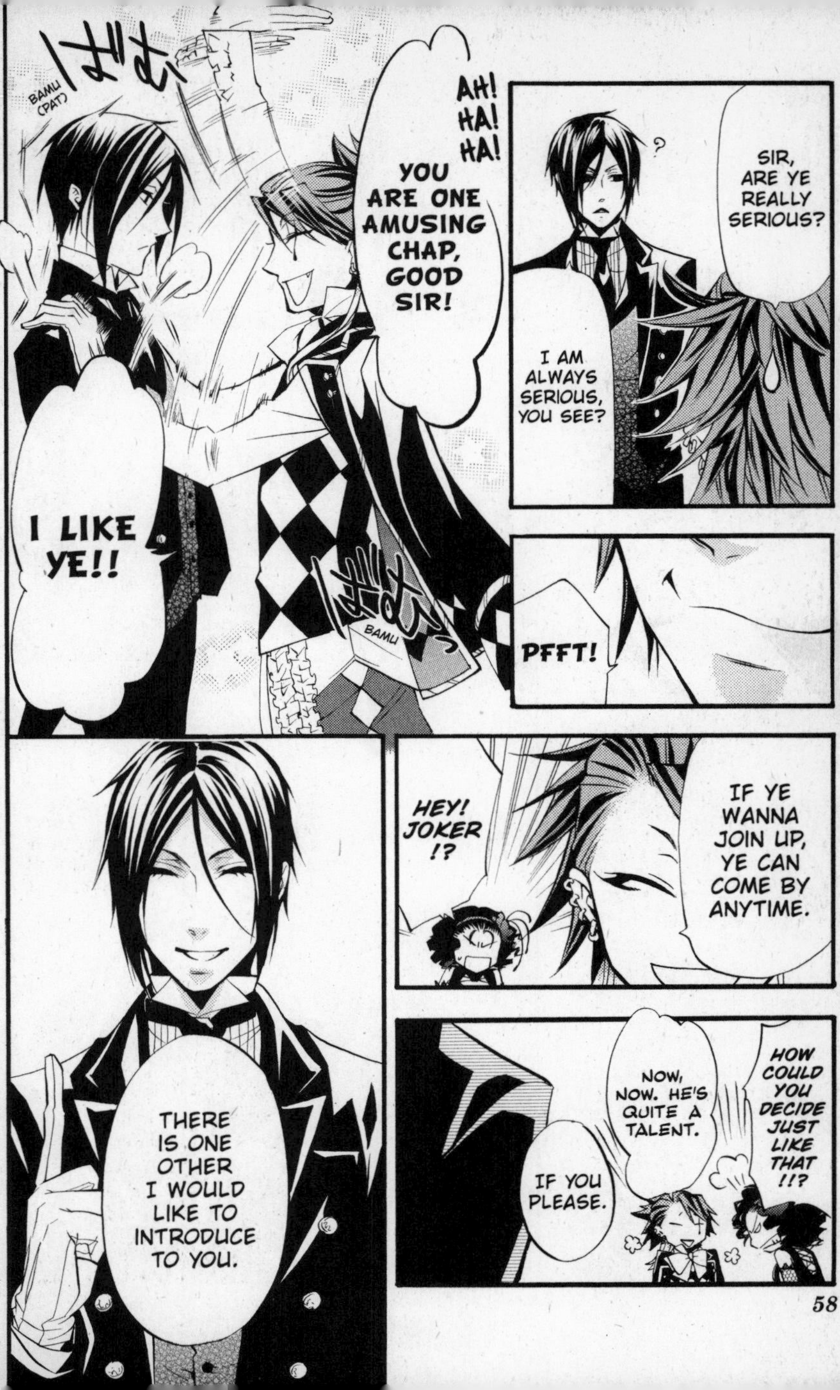
SIR, ARE YE REALLY SERIOUS?
I AM ALWAYS SERIOUS, YOU SEE?
PFFT!
AH! HA! HA!
YOU ARE ONE AMUSING CHAP, GOOD SIR!
ばむ!
BAMU (PAT)
I LIKE YE!!
ばむ
BAMU
IF YE WANNA JOIN UP, YE CAN COME BY ANYTIME.
HEY! JOKER !?
HOW COULD YOU DECIDE JUST LIKE THAT !!?
NOW, NOW. HE'S QUITE A TALENT.
IF YOU PLEASE.
THERE IS ONE OTHER I WOULD LIKE TO INTRODUCE TO YOU.

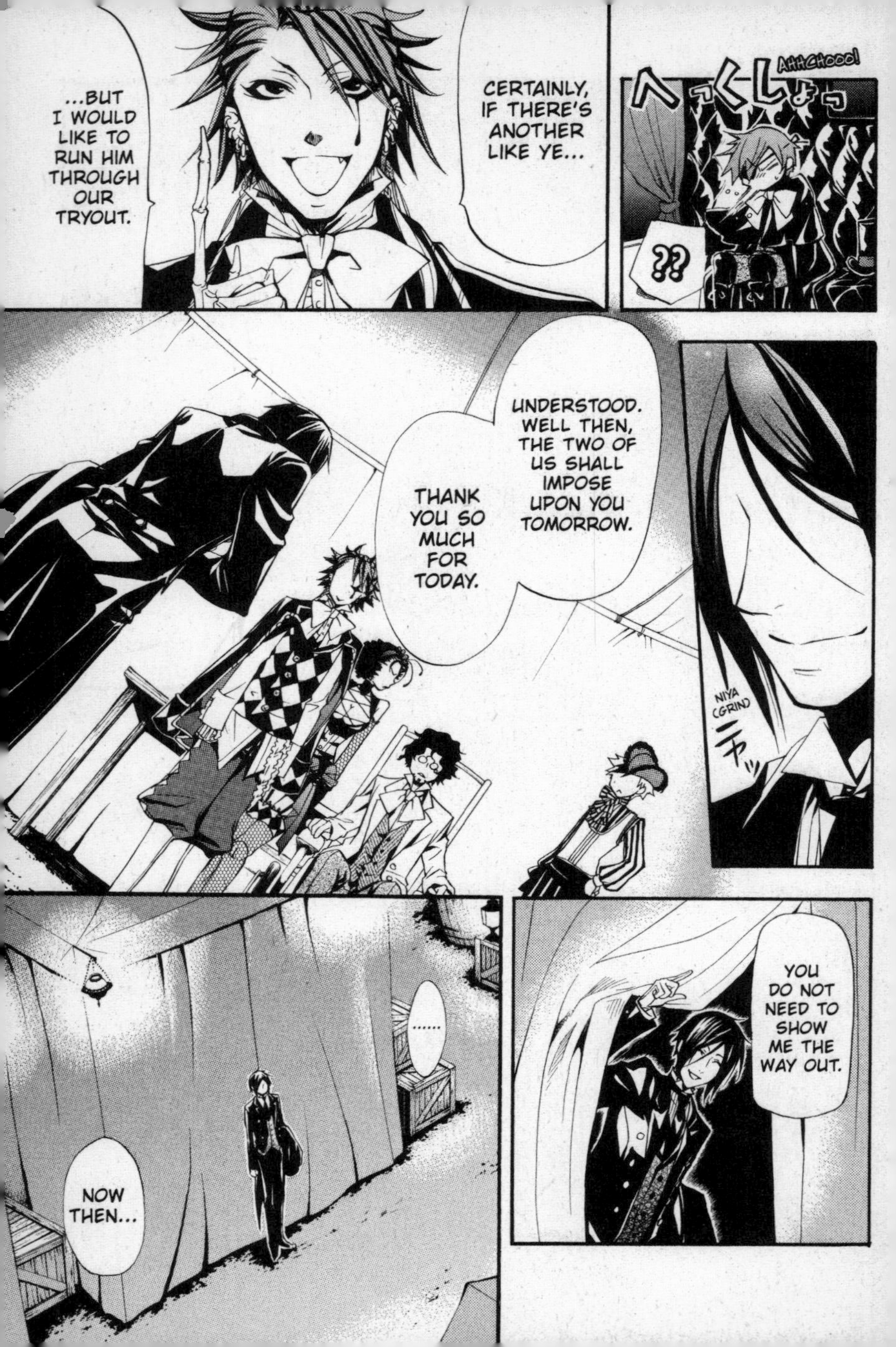
へっくしょっ
AHHCHOOO!
??
CERTAINLY, IF THERE'S ANOTHER LIKE YE...
...BUT I WOULD LIKE TO RUN HIM THROUGH OUR TRYOUT.
ニヤッ
NIYA (GRIN)
UNDERSTOOD. WELL THEN, THE TWO OF US SHALL IMPOSE UPON YOU TOMORROW.
THANK YOU SO MUCH FOR TODAY.
YOU DO NOT NEED TO SHOW ME THE WAY OUT.
......
NOW THEN...

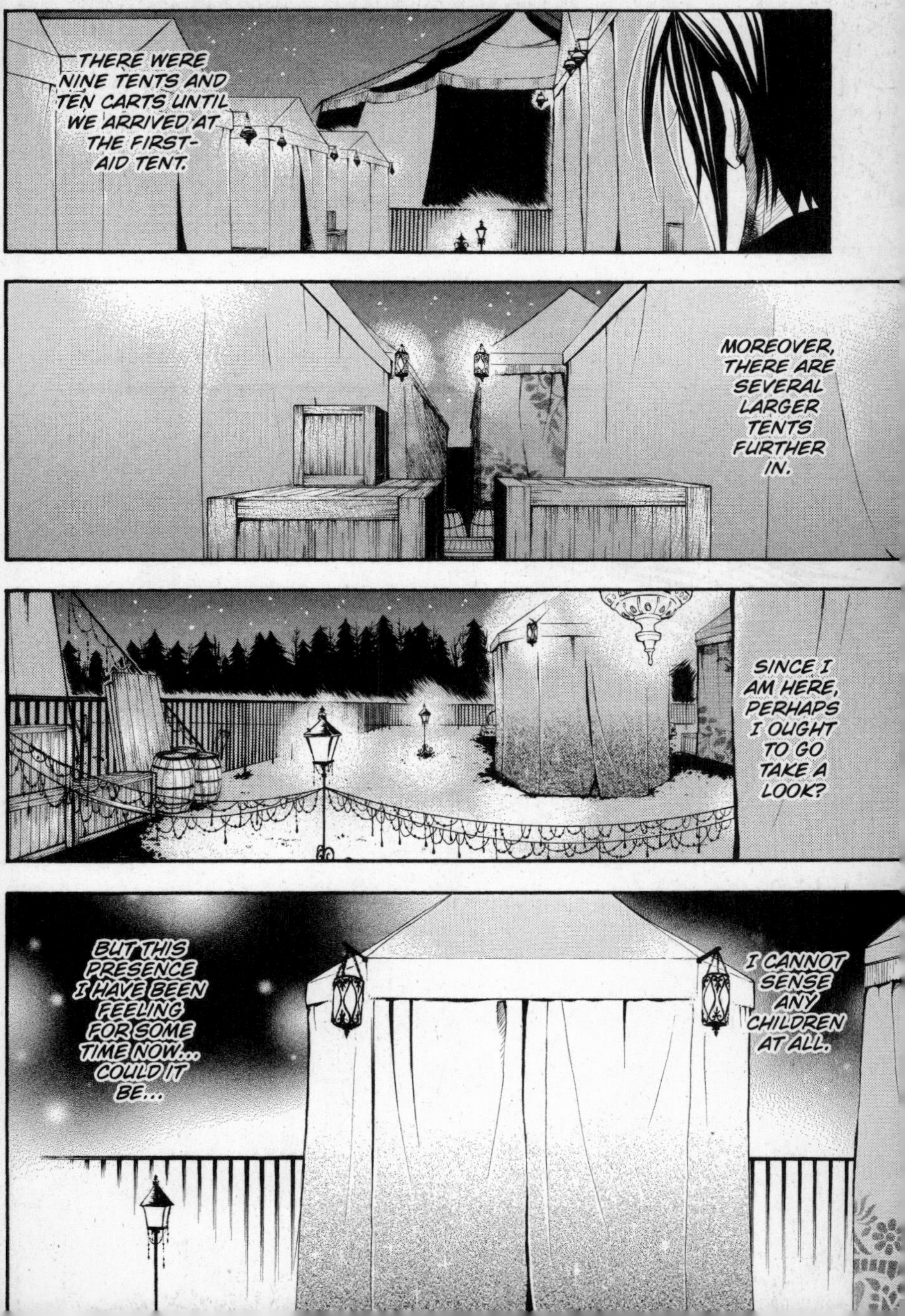
THERE WERE NINE TENTS AND TEN CARTS UNTIL WE ARRIVED AT THE FIRST-AID TENT.
MOREOVER, THERE ARE SEVERAL LARGER TENTS FURTHER IN.
SINCE I AM HERE, PERHAPS I OUGHT TO GO TAKE A LOOK?
I CANNOT SENSE ANY CHILDREN AT ALL.
BUT THIS PRESENCE I HAVE BEEN FEELING FOR SOME TIME NOW... COULD IT BE...

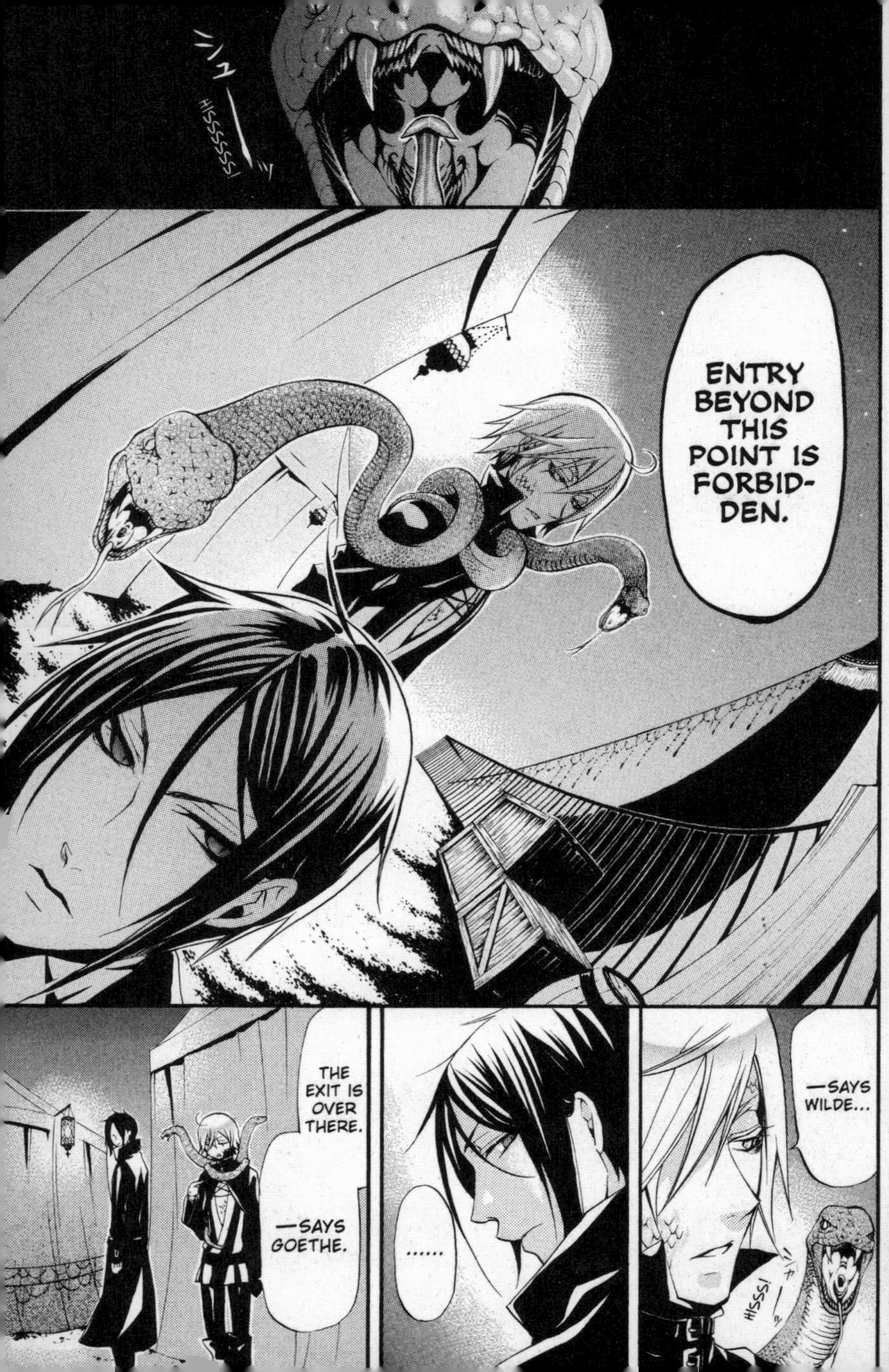
HISSSSS!
ENTRY BEYOND THIS POINT IS FORBIDDEN.
—SAYS WILDE...
HISSS!
......
THE EXIT IS OVER THERE.
—SAYS GOETHE.

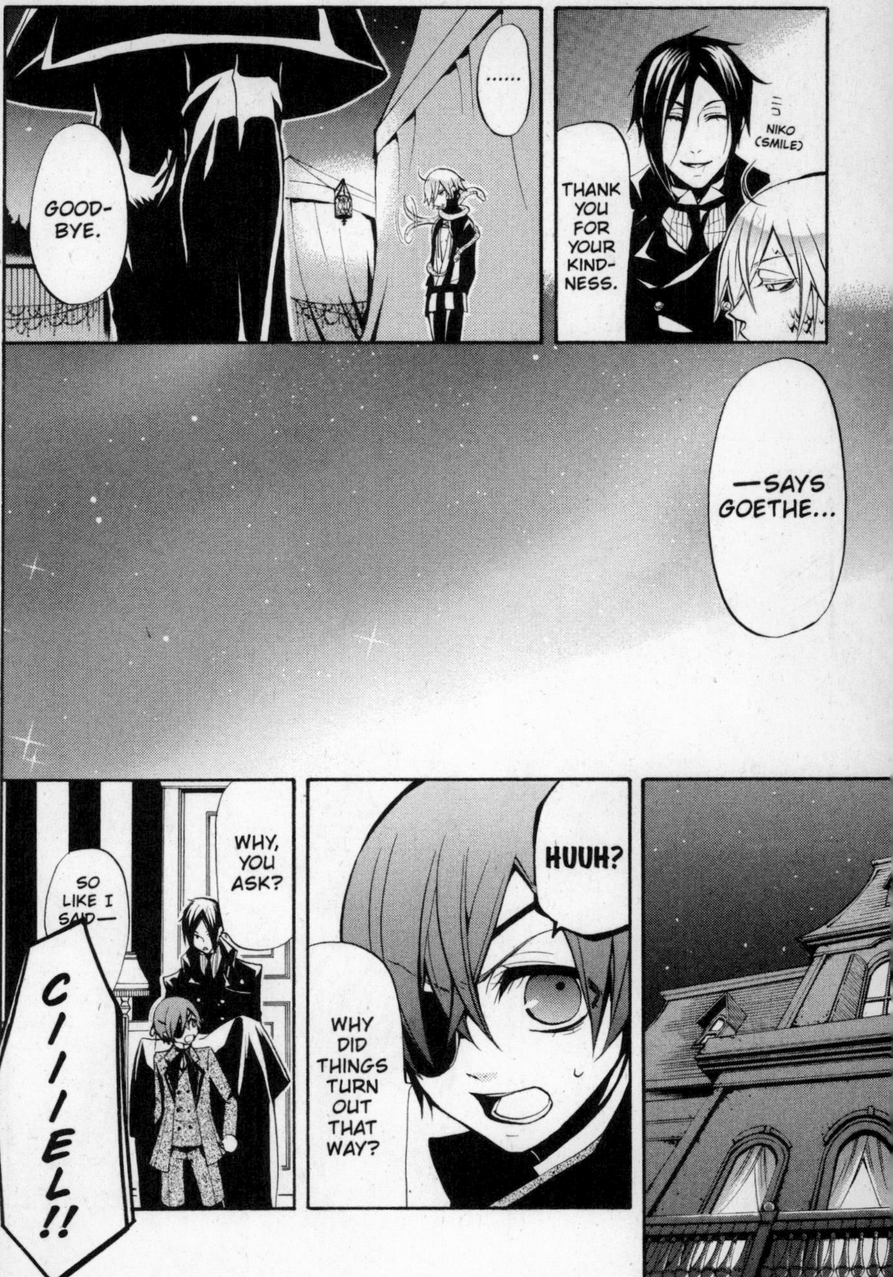

ニコ
NIKO (SMILE)
THANK YOU FOR YOUR KINDNESS.
......
GOOD-BYE.
—SAYS GOETHE...
HUUH?
WHY DID THINGS TURN OUT THAT WAY?
WHY, YOU ASK?
SO LIKE I SAID—
CIIIEL!!

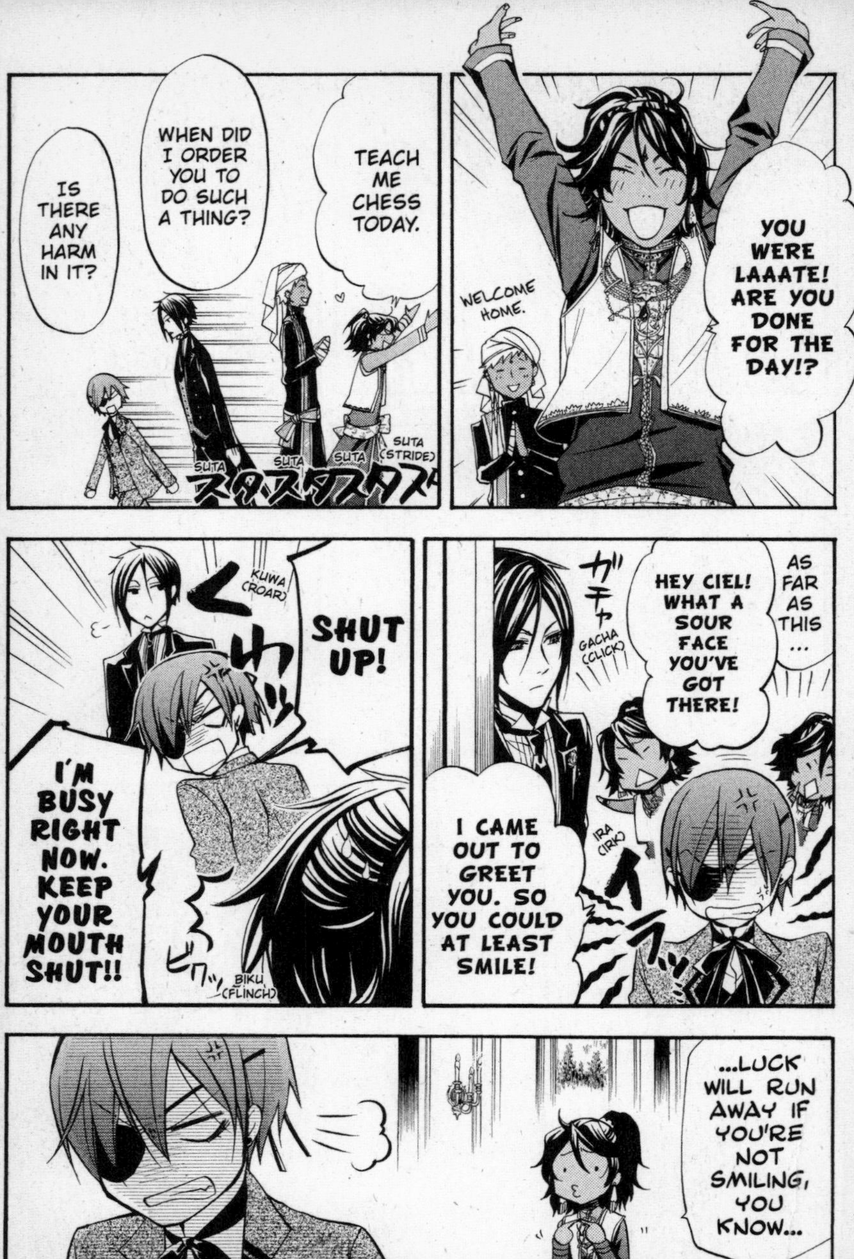
YOU WERE LAAATE! ARE YOU DONE FOR THE DAY!?
WELCOME HOME.
TEACH ME CHESS TODAY.
WHEN DID I ORDER YOU TO DO SUCH A THING?
IS THERE ANY HARM IN IT?
SUTA (STRIDE)
SUTA
SUTA
SUTA
AS FAR AS THIS...
HEY CIEL! WHAT A SOUR FACE YOU'VE GOT THERE!
ガチャ
GACHA (CLICK)
I CAME OUT TO GREET YOU. SO YOU COULD AT LEAST SMILE!
IRA (IRK)
SHUT UP!
KUWA (ROAR)
I'M BUSY RIGHT NOW. KEEP YOUR MOUTH SHUT!!
BIKU (FLINCH)
...LUCK WILL RUN AWAY IF YOU'RE NOT SMILING, YOU KNOW...

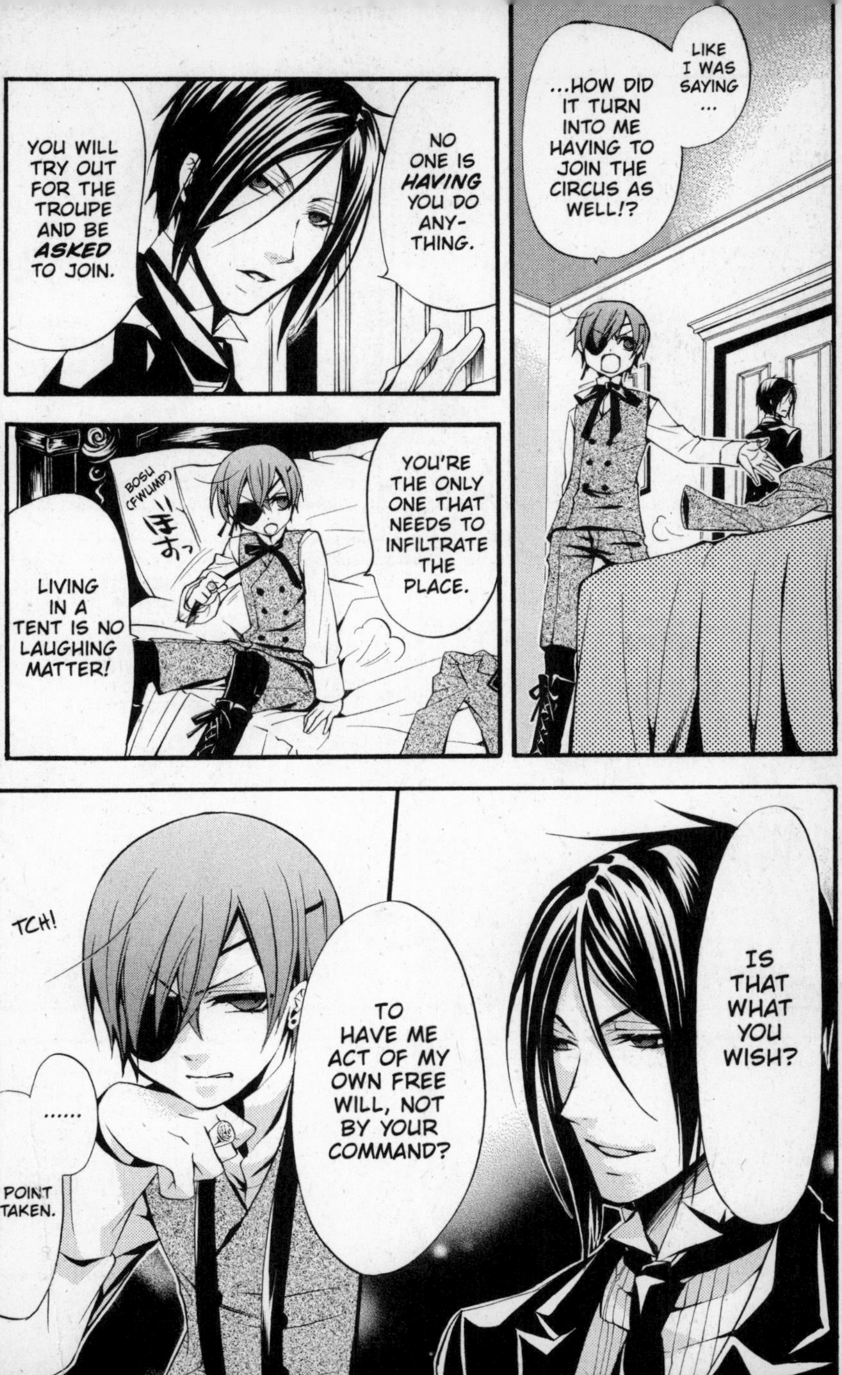
LIKE I WAS SAYING ...
...HOW DID IT TURN INTO ME HAVING TO JOIN THE CIRCUS AS WELL!?
NO ONE IS HAVING YOU DO ANY-THING.
YOU WILL TRY OUT FOR THE TROUPE AND BE ASKED TO JOIN.
YOU'RE THE ONLY ONE THAT NEEDS TO INFILTRATE THE PLACE.
ぼすっ
BOSU (FWUMP)
LIVING IN A TENT IS NO LAUGHING MATTER!
IS THAT WHAT YOU WISH?
TO HAVE ME ACT OF MY OWN FREE WILL, NOT BY YOUR COMMAND?
TCH!
......
POINT TAKEN.

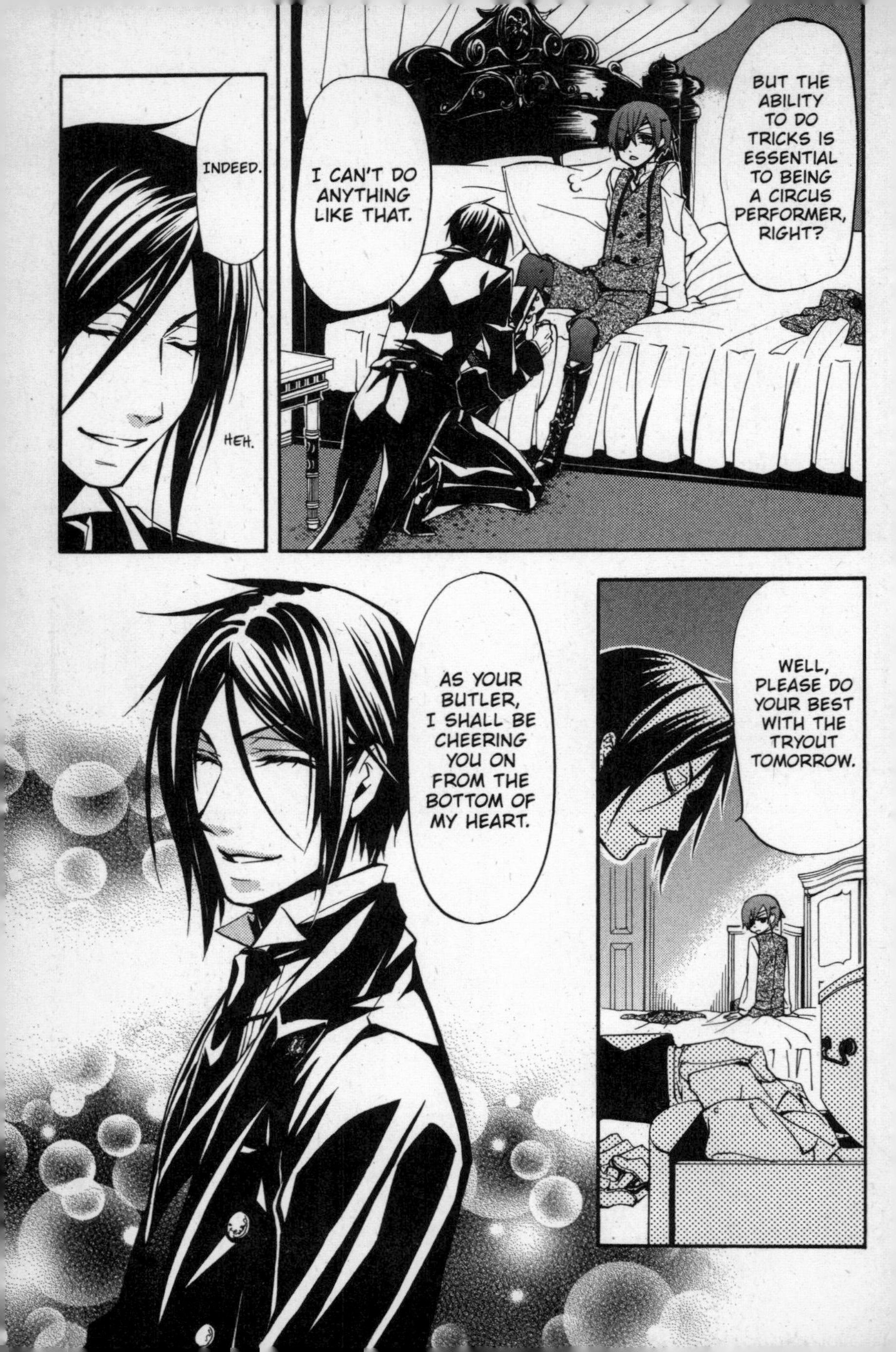
BUT THE ABILITY TO DO TRICKS IS ESSENTIAL TO BEING A CIRCUS PERFORMER, RIGHT?
I CAN'T DO ANYTHING LIKE THAT.
INDEED.
HEH.
WELL, PLEASE DO YOUR BEST WITH THE TRYOUT TOMORROW.
AS YOUR BUTLER, I SHALL BE CHEERING YOU ON FROM THE BOTTOM OF MY HEART.

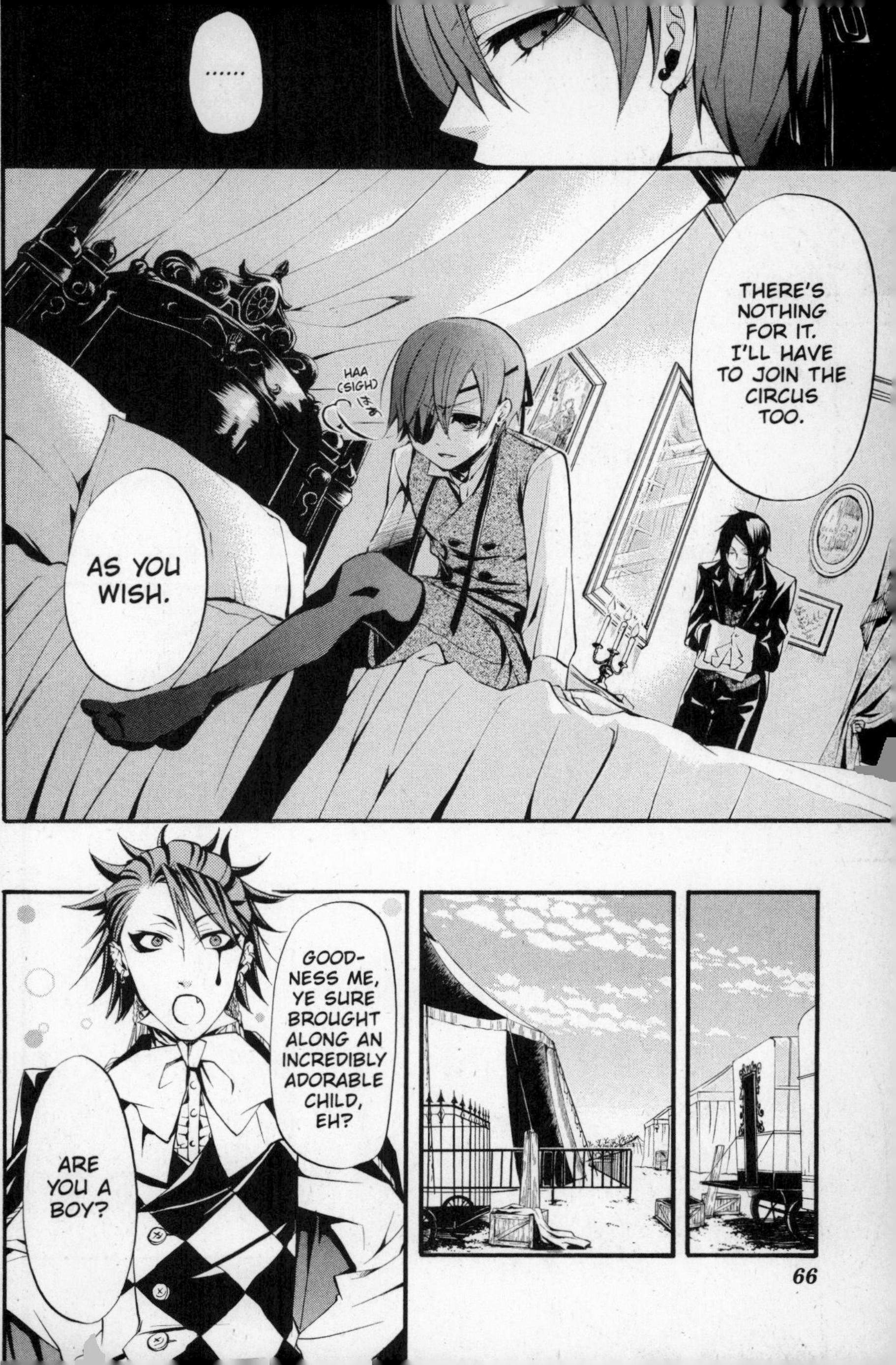

......
THERE'S NOTHING FOR IT. I'LL HAVE TO JOIN THE CIRCUS TOO.
HAA (SIGH)
AS YOU WISH.
GOOD-NESS ME, YE SURE BROUGHT ALONG AN INCREDIBLY ADORABLE CHILD, EH?
ARE YOU A BOY?

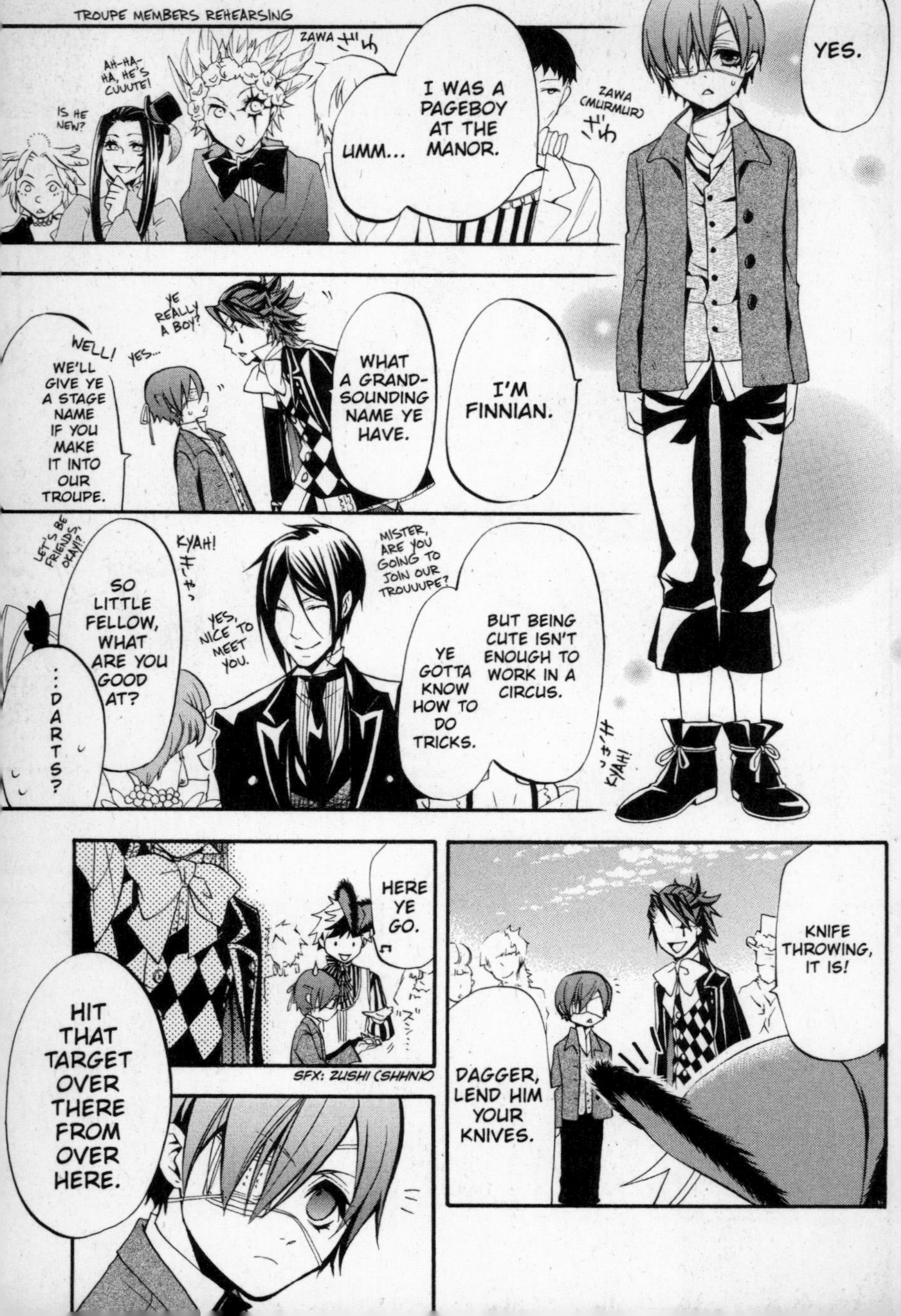
YES.
TROUPE MEMBERS REHEARSING
UMM... I WAS A PAGEBOY AT THE MANOR.
ZAWA
ZAWA (MURMUR)
AH-HA-HA, HE'S CUUUTE!
IS HE NEW?
I'M FINNIAN.
WHAT A GRAND-SOUNDING NAME YE HAVE.
YE REALLY A BOY?
YES...
WELL! WE'LL GIVE YE A STAGE NAME IF YOU MAKE IT INTO OUR TROUPE.
BUT BEING CUTE ISN'T ENOUGH TO WORK IN A CIRCUS. YE GOTTA KNOW HOW TO DO TRICKS.
KYAH!
MISTER, ARE YOU GOING TO JOIN OUR TROUUUPE?
YES, NICE TO MEET YOU.
KYAH!
LET'S BE FRIENDS, OKAY!?
SO LITTLE FELLOW, WHAT ARE YOU GOOD AT?
...DARTS?
KNIFE THROWING, IT IS!
DAGGER, LEND HIM YOUR KNIVES.
HERE YE GO.
SFX: ZUSHI (SHHNK)
HIT THAT TARGET OVER THERE FROM OVER HERE.

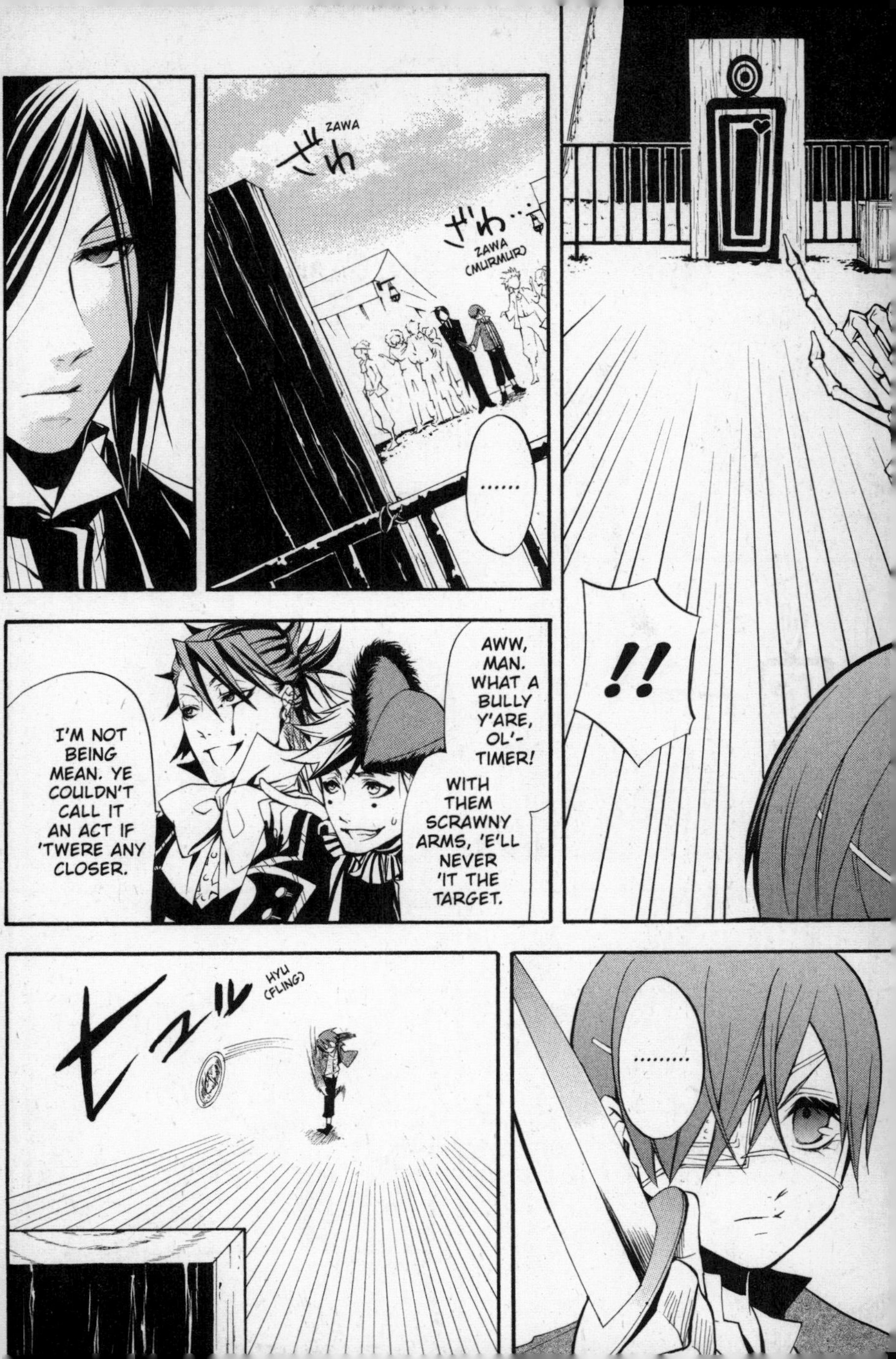
!!
ZAWA
ざわ
ざわ…
ZAWA (MURMUR)
......
AWW, MAN. WHAT A BULLY Y'ARE, OL'-TIMER!
WITH THEM SCRAWNY ARMS, 'E'LL NEVER 'IT THE TARGET.
I'M NOT BEING MEAN. YE COULDN'T CALL IT AN ACT IF 'TWERE ANY CLOSER.
....
ヒュル
HYU (FLING)

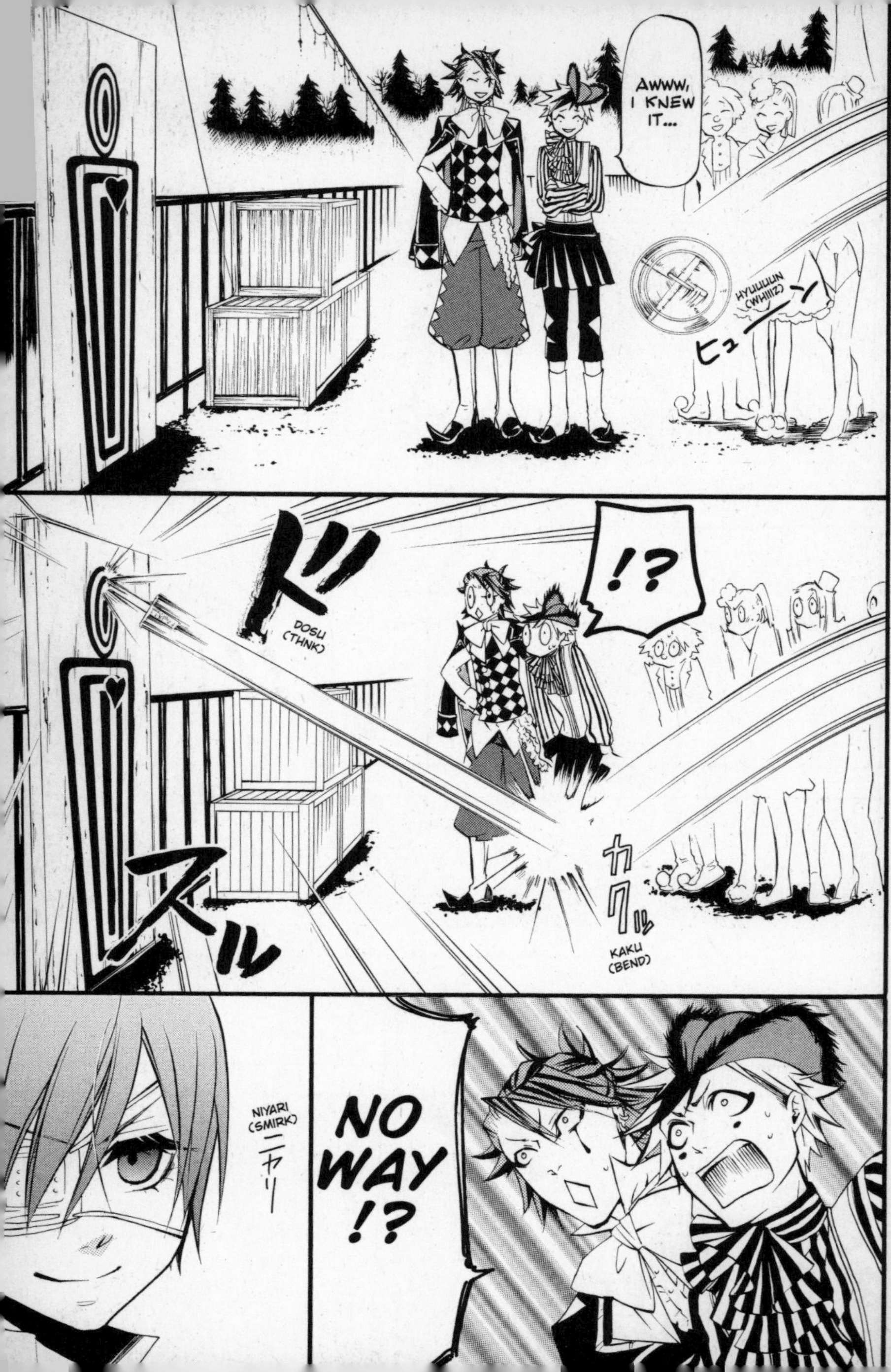
AWWW, I KNEW IT...
HYUUUUN (WHIIIZ)
ヒューン
!?
DOSU (THNK)
カクッ
KAKU (BEND)
スル
NO WAY!?
NIYARI (SMIRK)
ニヤリ

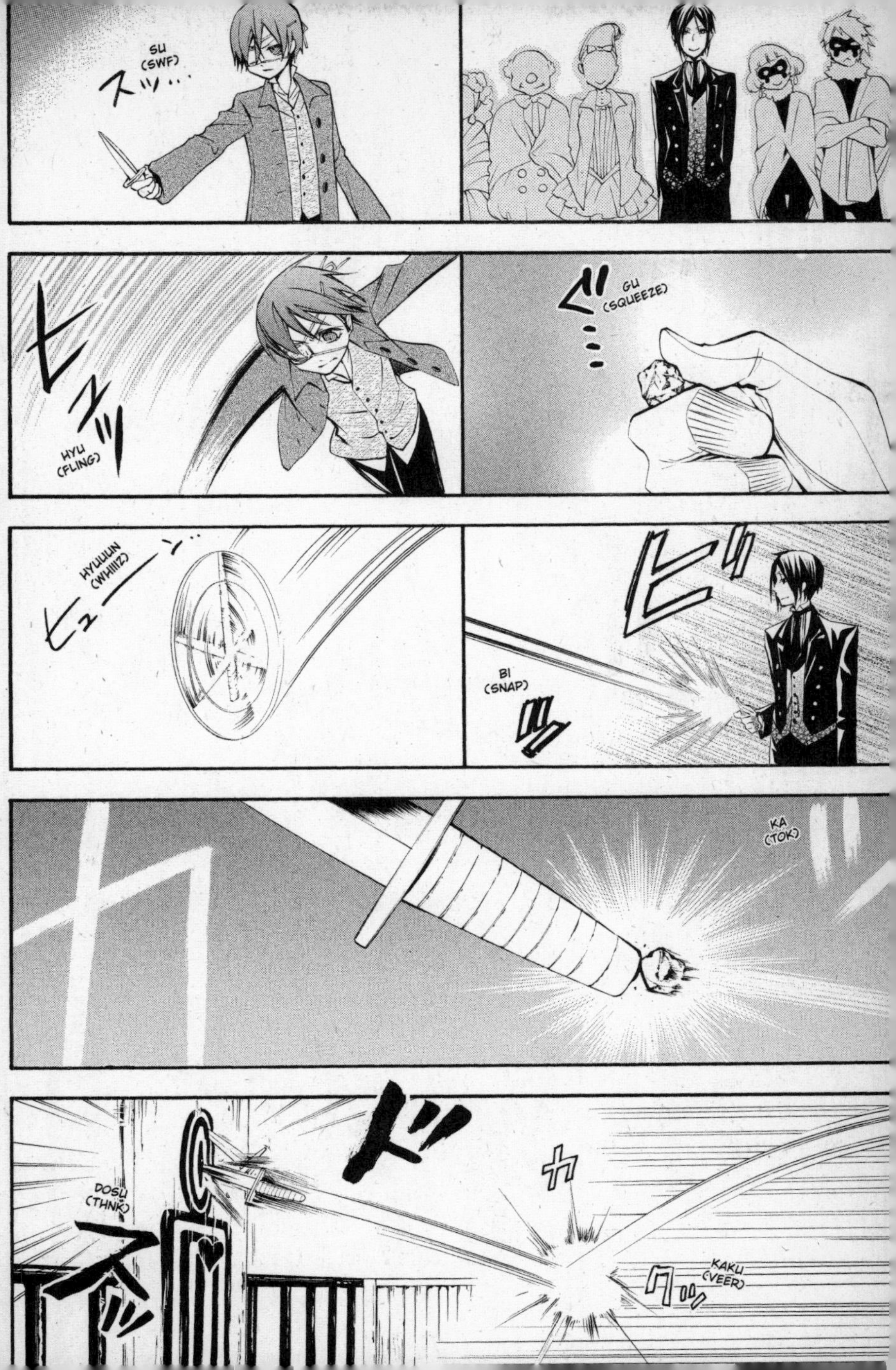

スッ…
SU (SWF)
ぐ…
GU (SQUEEZE)
ヒュッ
HYU (FLING)
ビッ
BI (SNAP)
ヒューン…
HYUUUN (WHIIIZ)
KA (TOK)
クッ
KAKU (VEER)
カ
ド
ズッ
DOSU (THNK)

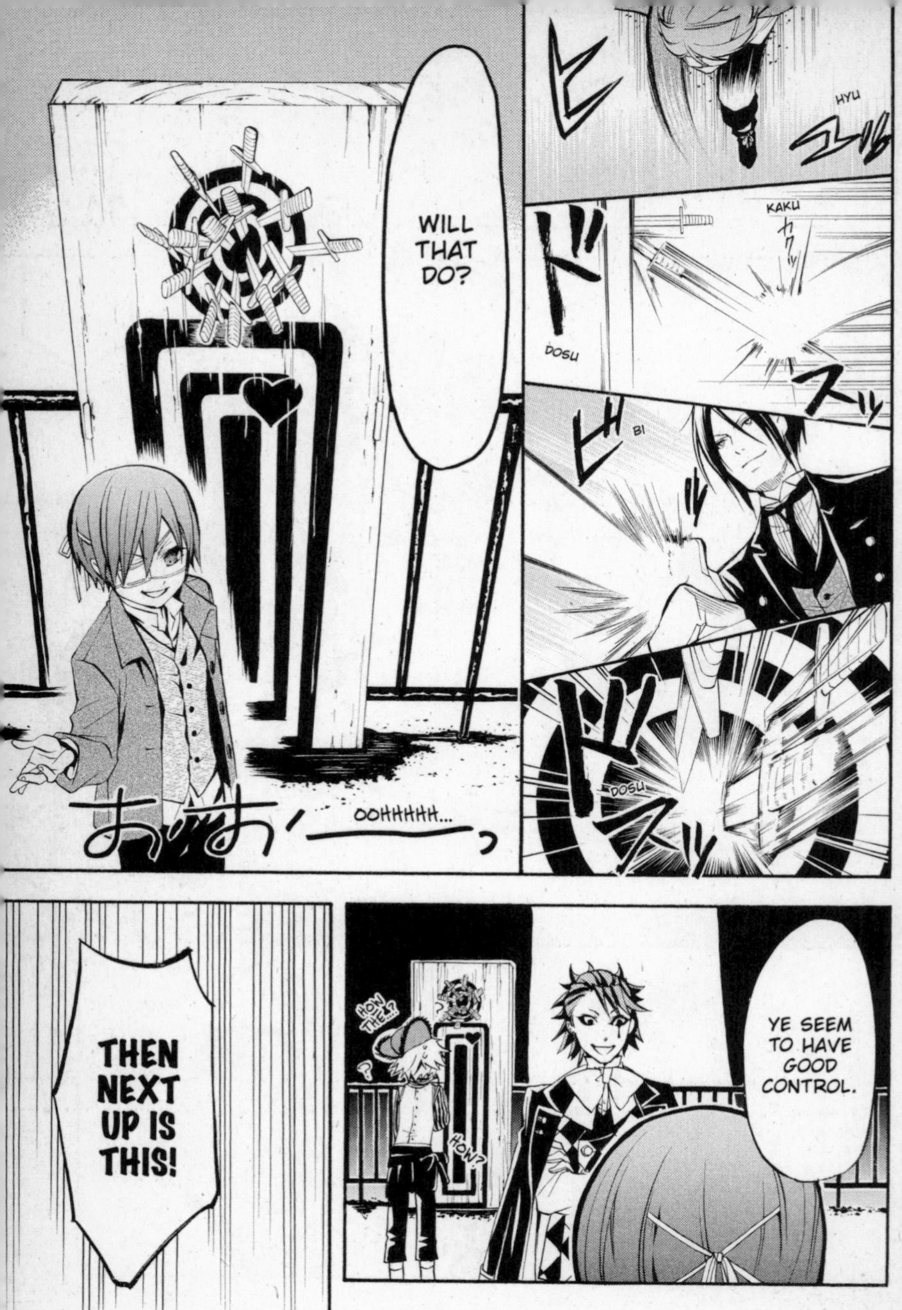
HYU
KAKU
DOSU
BI
DOSU
WILL THAT DO?
OOHHHHH...
YE SEEM TO HAVE GOOD CONTROL.
HOW THE...?
HOW?
THEN NEXT UP IS THIS!

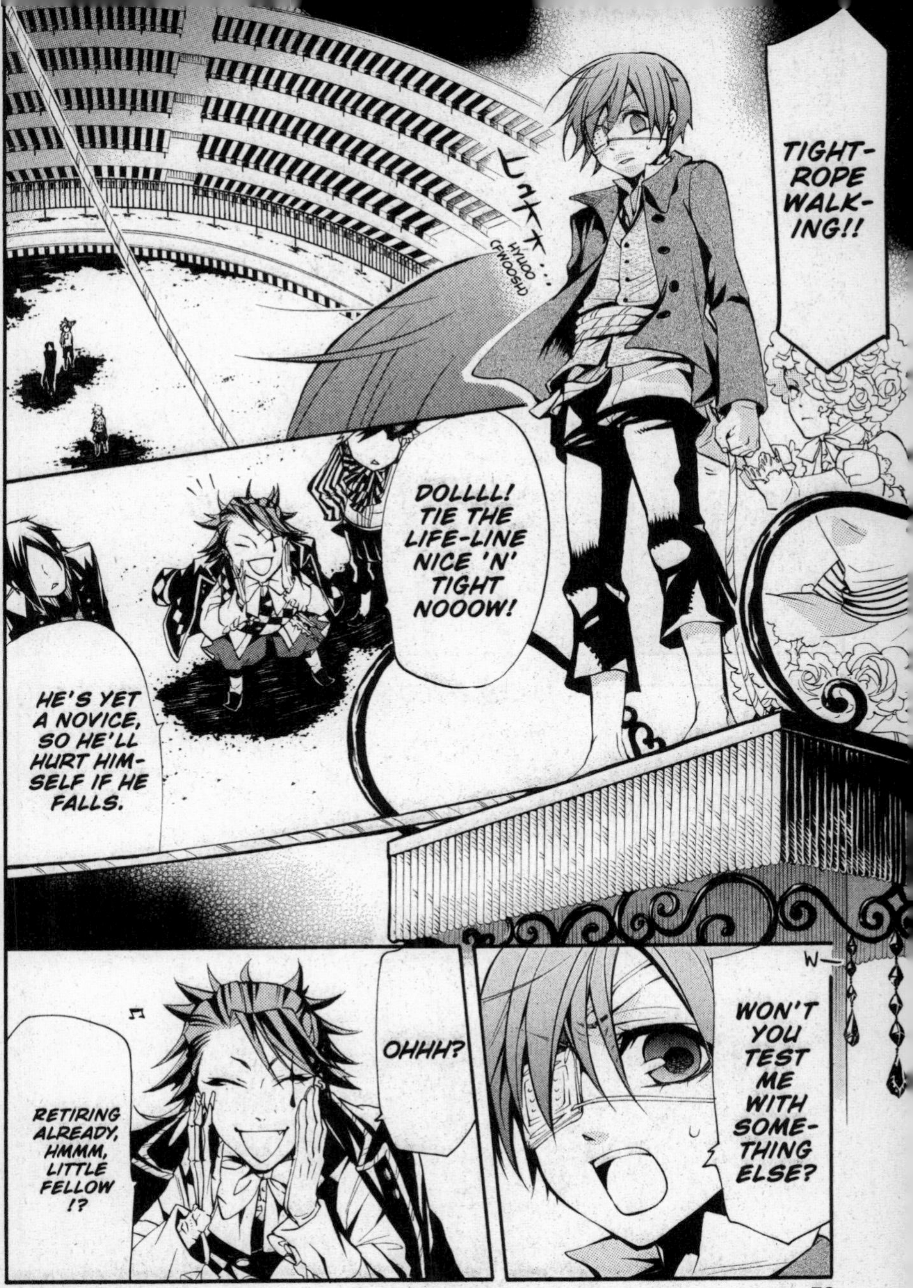
TIGHT-ROPE WALKING!!
HYUOO CFWOOSH
DOLLLL! TIE THE LIFE-LINE NICE 'N' TIGHT NOOOW!
HE'S YET A NOVICE, SO HE'LL HURT HIMSELF IF HE FALLS.
W—
WON'T YOU TEST ME WITH SOME-THING ELSE?
OHHH?
RETIRING ALREADY, HMMM, LITTLE FELLOW!?

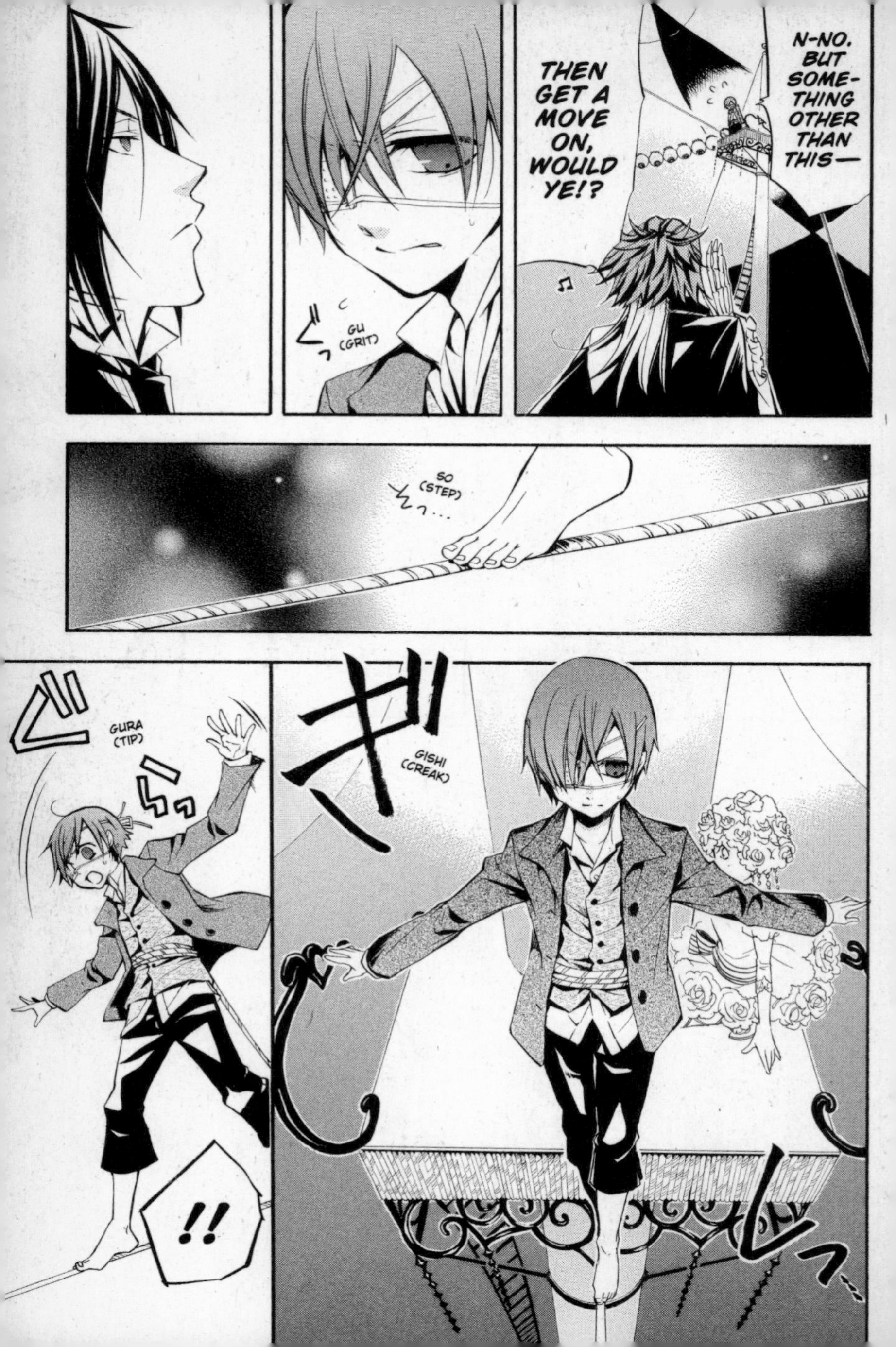
N-NO. BUT SOMETHING OTHER THAN THIS—
THEN GET A MOVE ON, WOULD YE!?
GU (GRIT)
SO (STEP)
GISHI (CREAK)
GURA (TIP)
!!

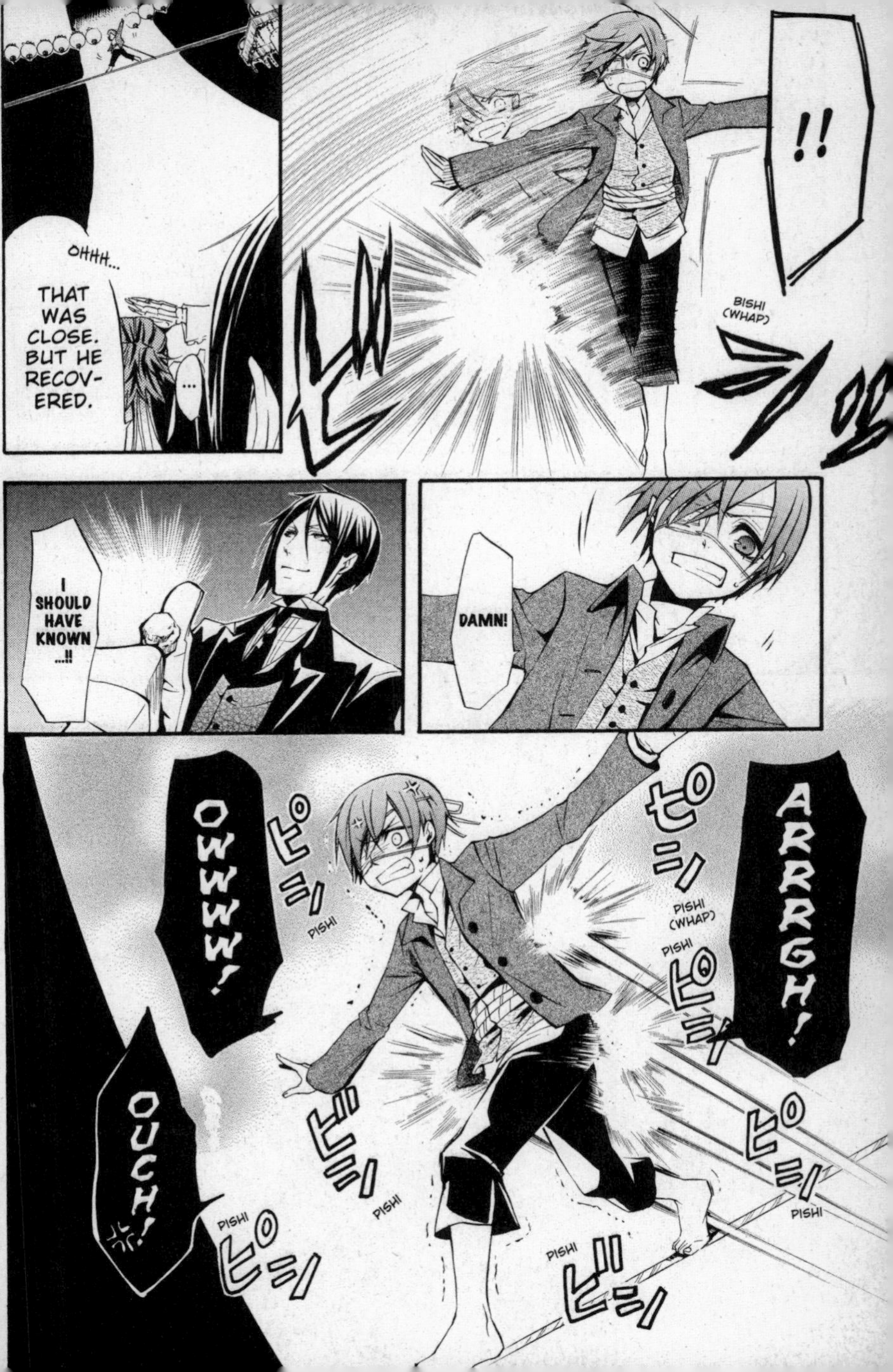

!!
BISHI (WHAP)
OHHH...
THAT WAS CLOSE. BUT HE RECOVERED.
...
DAMN!
I SHOULD HAVE KNOWN ...!!
ARRRGH!
PISHI (WHAP)
PISHI
OWWWW!
PISHI
PISHI
PISHI
OUCH!
PISHI
PISHI

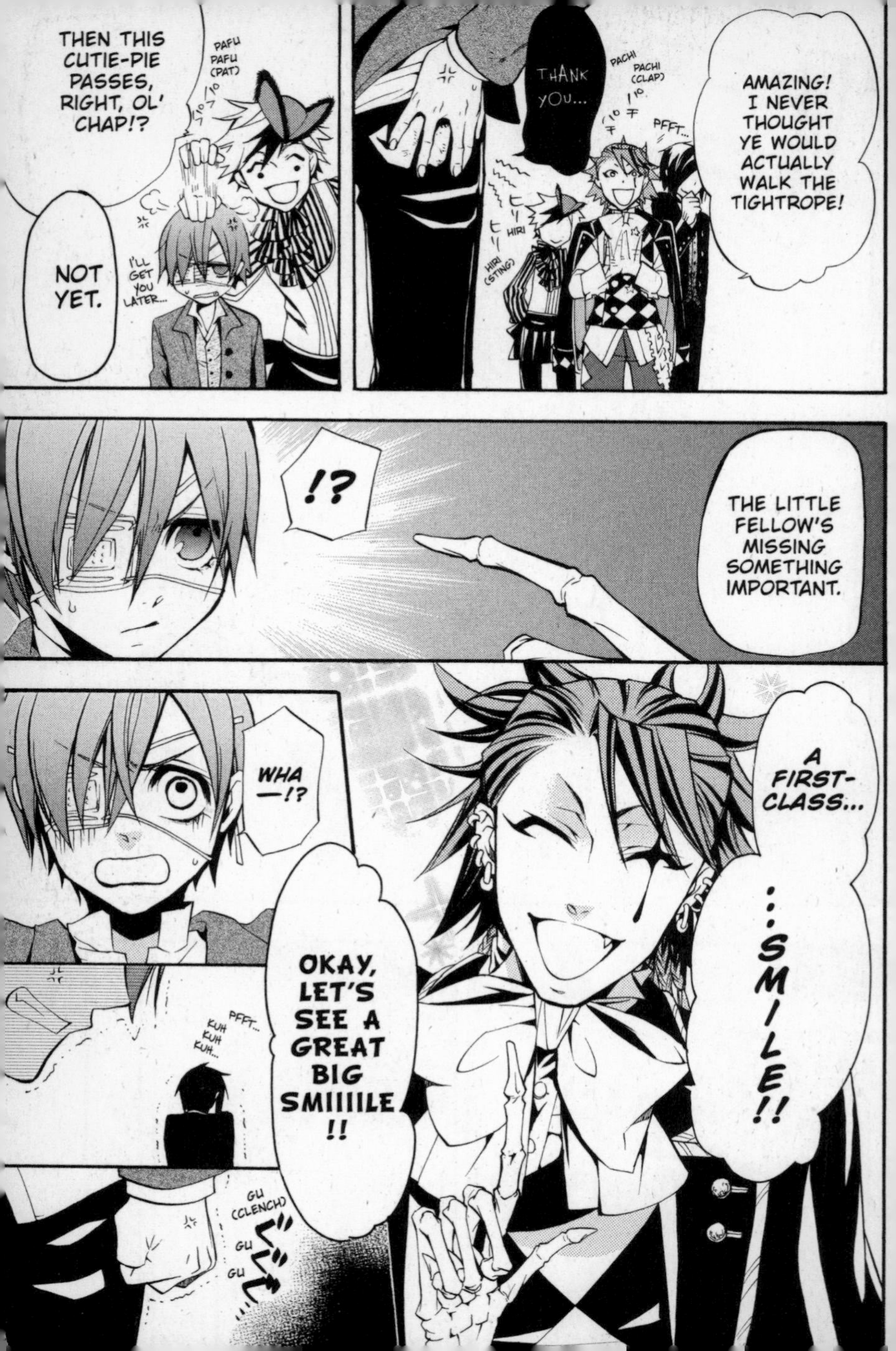
AMAZING! I NEVER THOUGHT YE WOULD ACTUALLY WALK THE TIGHTROPE!
PFFT...
PACHI PACHI (CLAP)
THANK YOU...
HIRI HIRI HIRI (STING)
THEN THIS CUTIE-PIE PASSES, RIGHT, OL' CHAP!?
PAFU PAFU (PAT)
NOT YET.
I'LL GET YOU LATER...
THE LITTLE FELLOW'S MISSING SOMETHING IMPORTANT.
!?
A FIRST-CLASS...
...SMILE!!
OKAY, LET'S SEE A GREAT BIG SMIIIIILE!!
WHA—!?
PFFT... KUH KUH KUH...
GU (CLENCH) GU GU

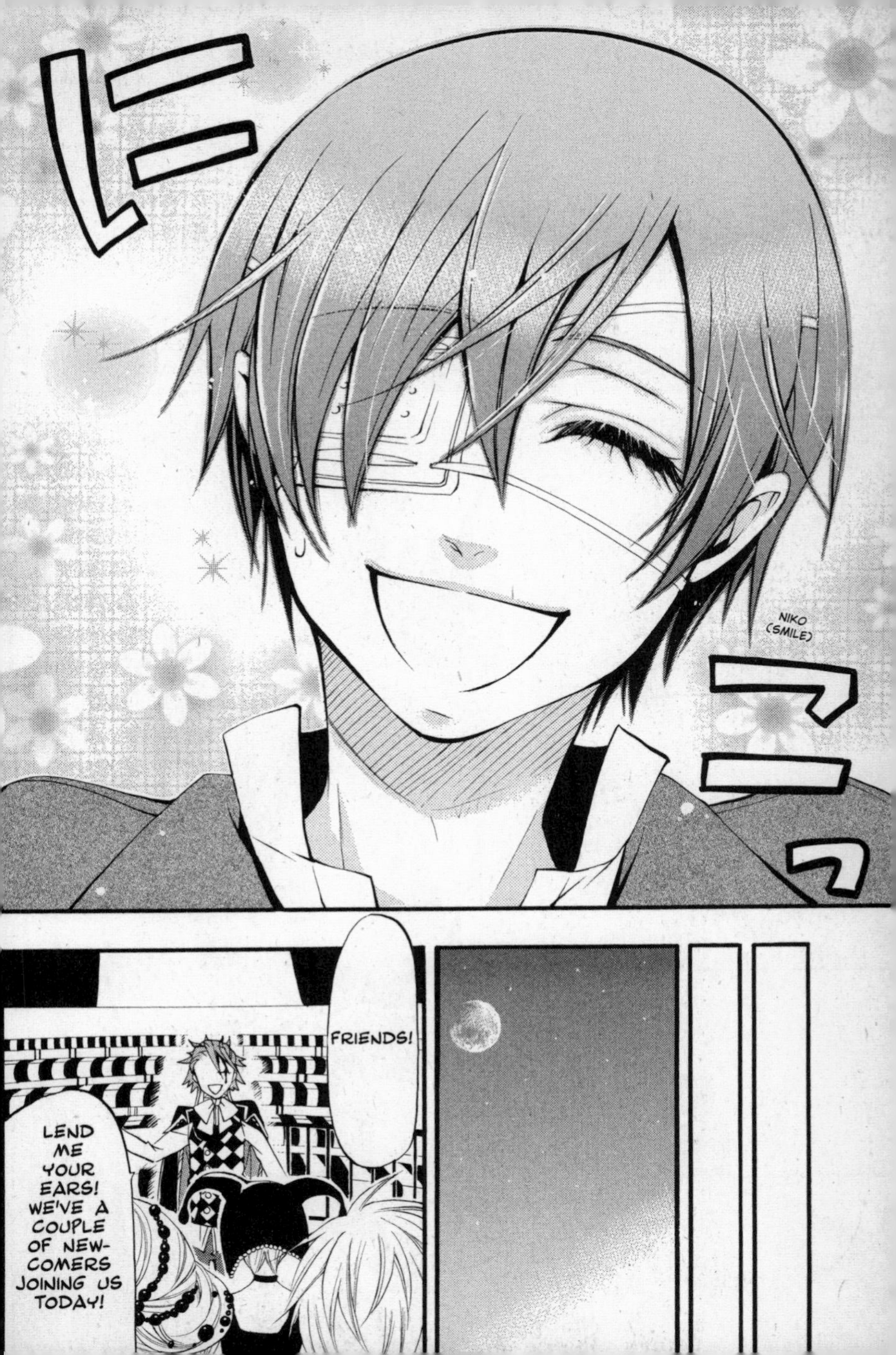
NIKO (SMILE)
FRIENDS!
LEND ME YOUR EARS! WE'VE A COUPLE OF NEW-COMERS JOINING US TODAY!

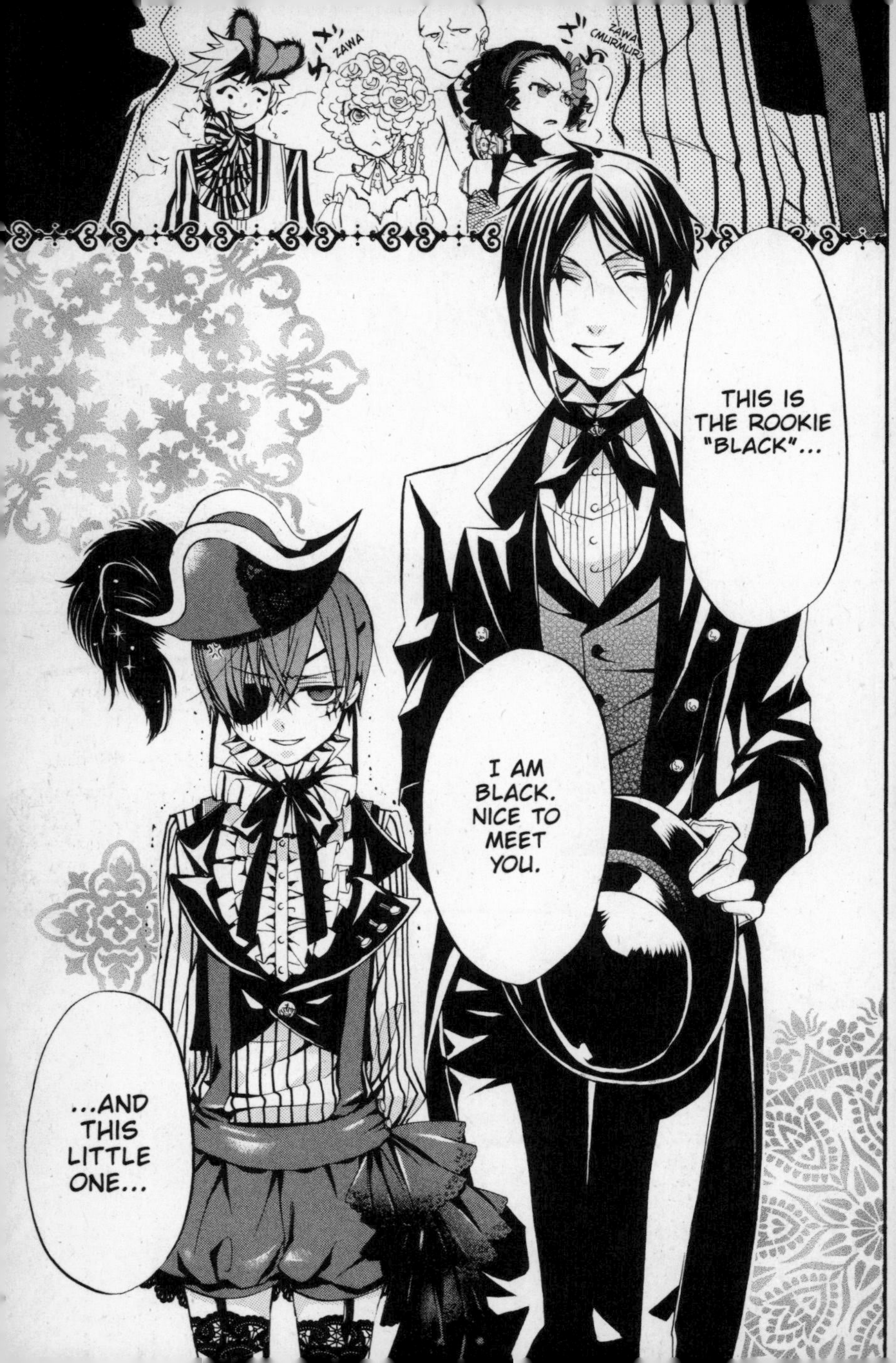
ざわ
ZAWA (MURMUR)
ざわ
ZAWA
THIS IS THE ROOKIE "BLACK"...
I AM BLACK. NICE TO MEET YOU.
...AND THIS LITTLE ONE...

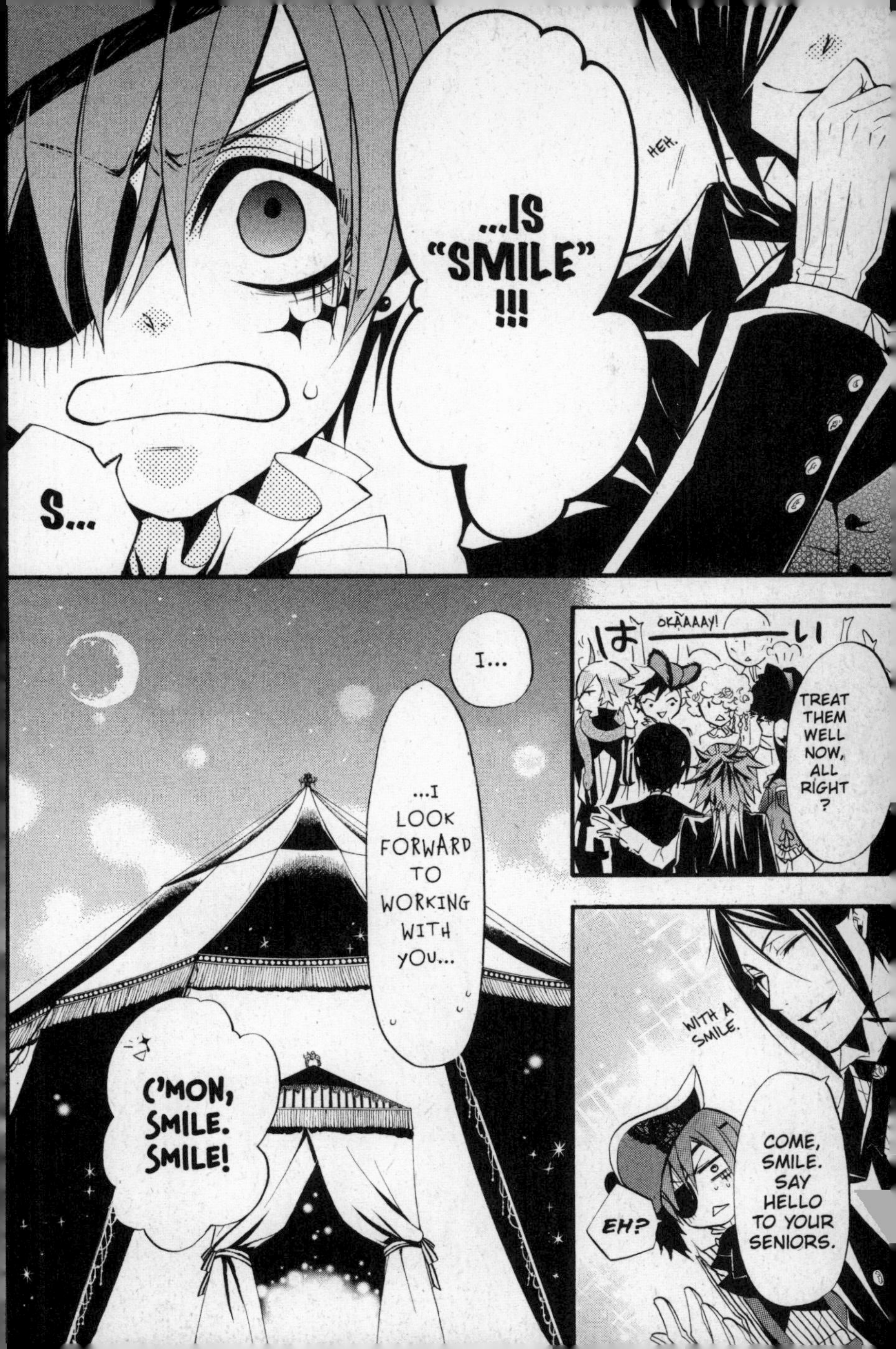

HEH.
...IS "SMILE" !!!
S...
TREAT THEM WELL NOW, ALL RIGHT?
はーい
OKAAAAY!
COME, SMILE. SAY HELLO TO YOUR SENIORS.
EH?
WITH A SMILE.
I...
...I LOOK FORWARD TO WORKING WITH YOU...
C'MON, SMILE. SMILE!

Black Butler

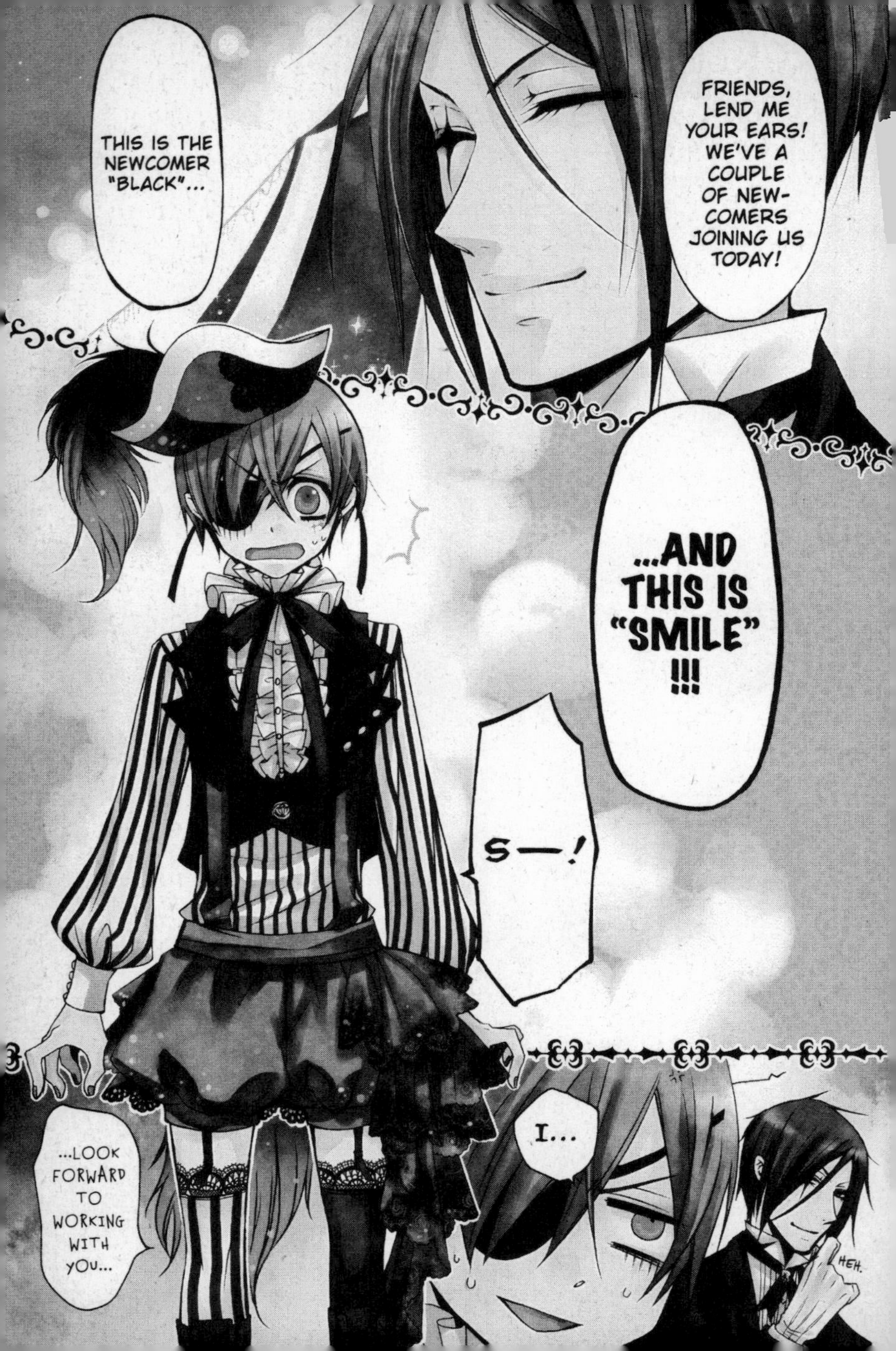
FRIENDS, LEND ME YOUR EARS! WE'VE A COUPLE OF NEW-COMERS JOINING US TODAY!
THIS IS THE NEWCOMER "BLACK"...
...AND THIS IS "SMILE"!!!
S—!
I...
HEH.
...LOOK FORWARD TO WORKING WITH YOU...

Chapter 26
At night : The Butler, A Colleague

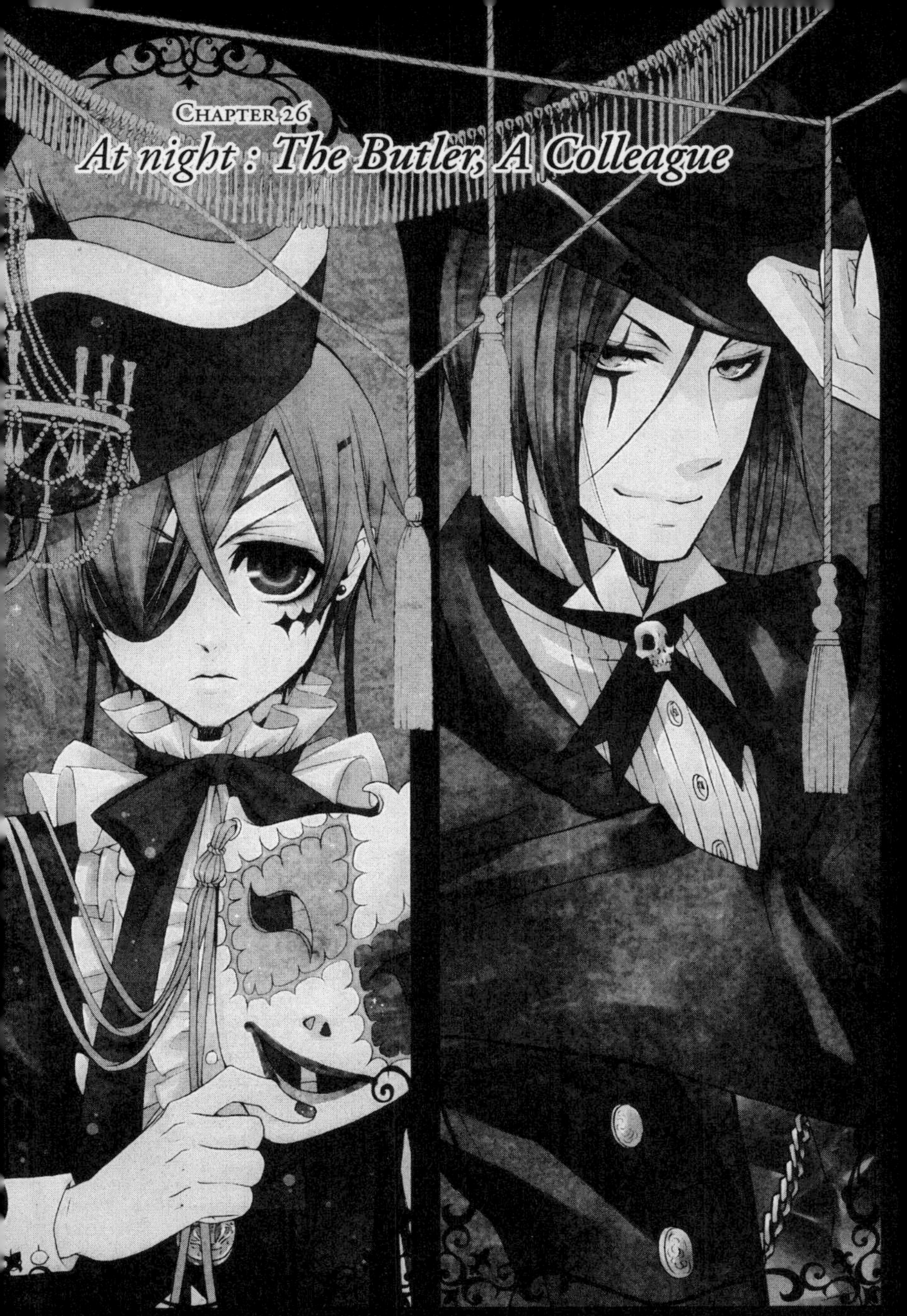

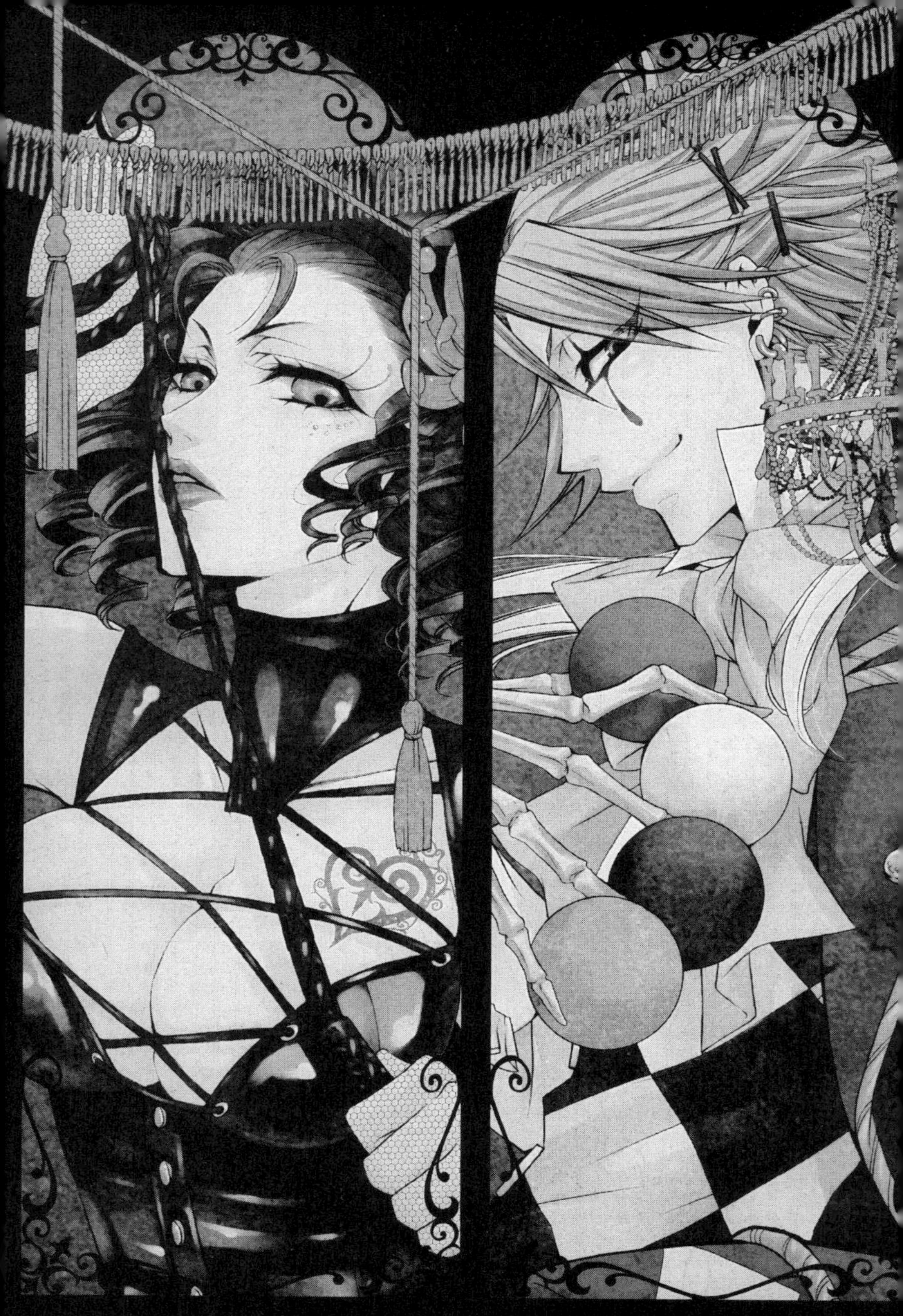

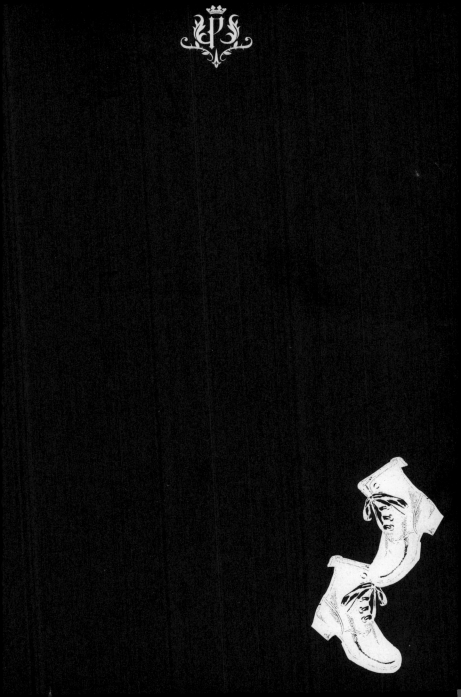

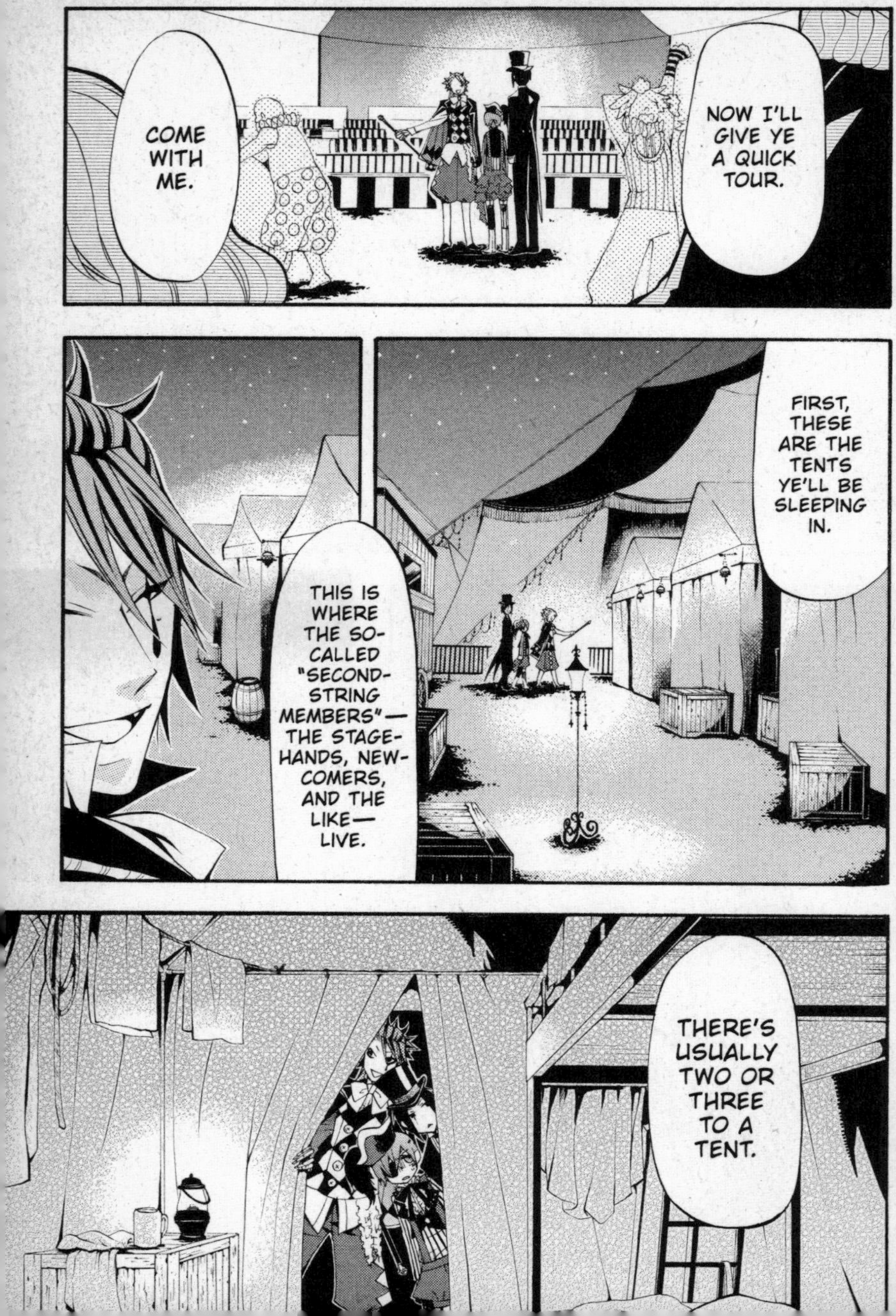
NOW I'LL GIVE YE A QUICK TOUR.
COME WITH ME.
FIRST, THESE ARE THE TENTS YE'LL BE SLEEPING IN.
THIS IS WHERE THE SO-CALLED "SECOND-STRING MEMBERS"—THE STAGE-HANDS, NEW-COMERS, AND THE LIKE—LIVE.
THERE'S USUALLY TWO OR THREE TO A TENT.

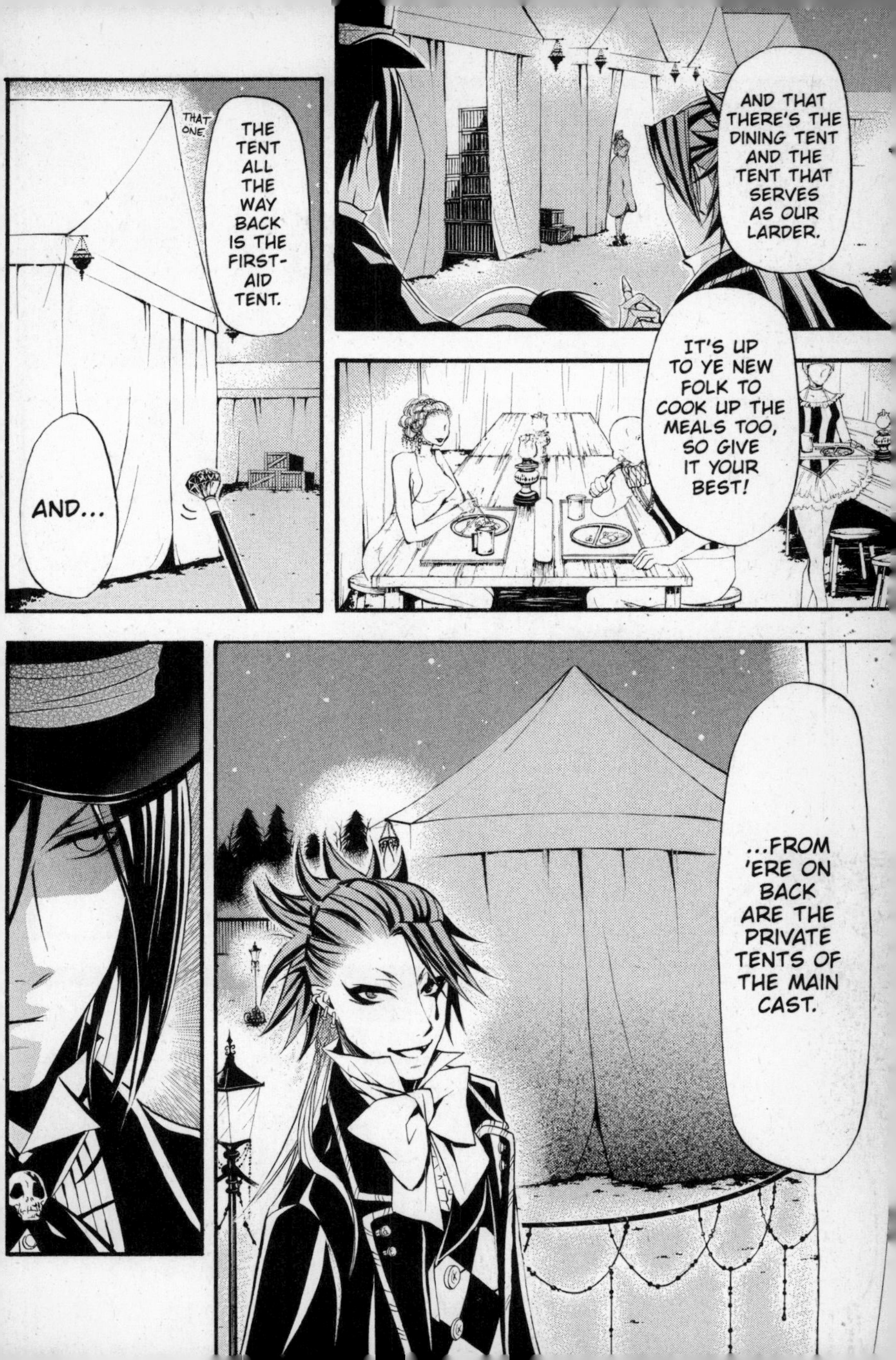
AND THAT THERE'S THE DINING TENT AND THE TENT THAT SERVES AS OUR LARDER.
IT'S UP TO YE NEW FOLK TO COOK UP THE MEALS TOO, SO GIVE IT YOUR BEST!
THAT ONE.
THE TENT ALL THE WAY BACK IS THE FIRST-AID TENT.
AND...
...FROM 'ERE ON BACK ARE THE PRIVATE TENTS OF THE MAIN CAST.

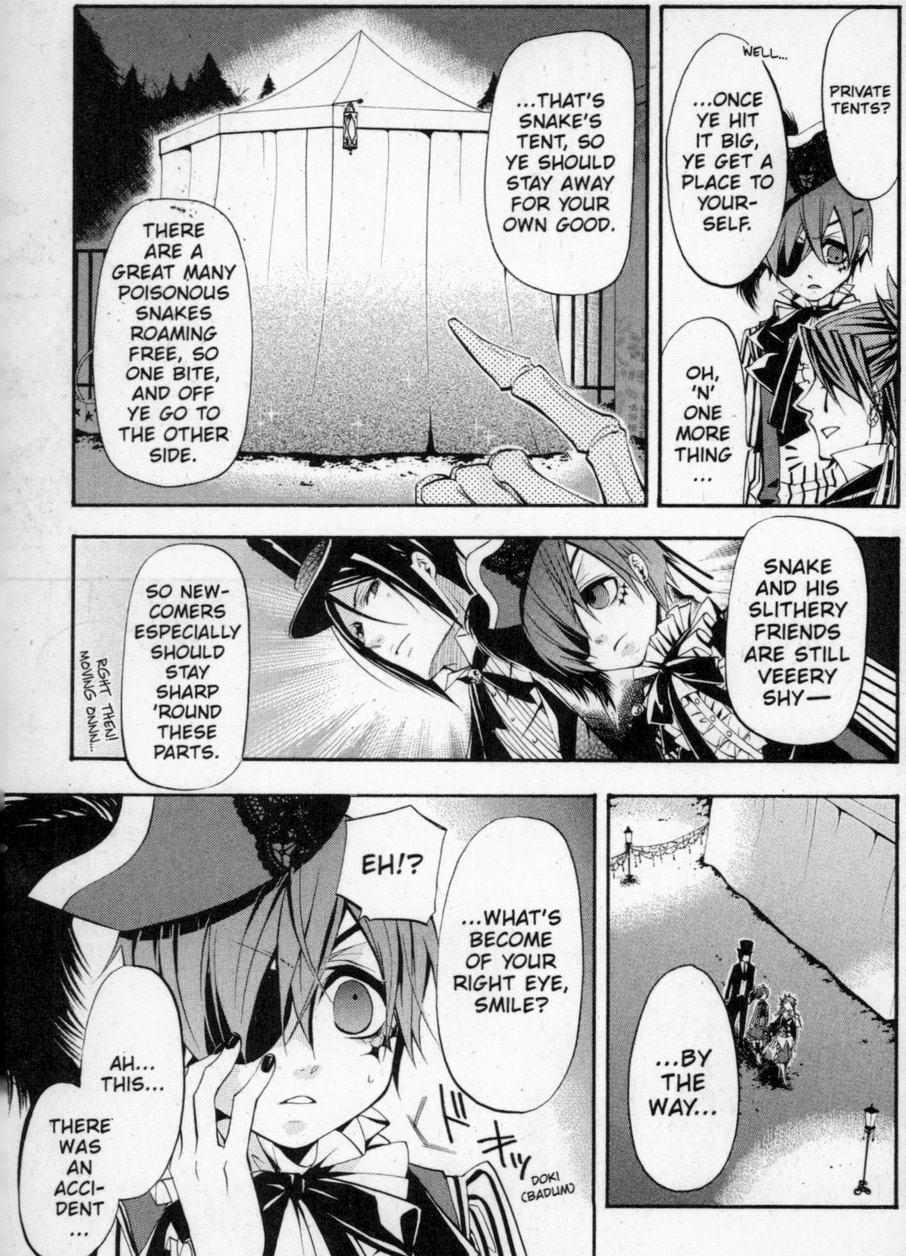
PRIVATE TENTS?
WELL...
...ONCE YE HIT IT BIG, YE GET A PLACE TO YOURSELF.
OH, 'N' ONE MORE THING ...
...THAT'S SNAKE'S TENT, SO YE SHOULD STAY AWAY FOR YOUR OWN GOOD.
THERE ARE A GREAT MANY POISONOUS SNAKES ROAMING FREE, SO ONE BITE, AND OFF YE GO TO THE OTHER SIDE.
SNAKE AND HIS SLITHERY FRIENDS ARE STILL VEEERY SHY—
SO NEWCOMERS ESPECIALLY SHOULD STAY SHARP 'ROUND THESE PARTS.
RIGHT THEN! MOVING ONN...
...BY THE WAY...
...WHAT'S BECOME OF YOUR RIGHT EYE, SMILE?
EH!?
DOKI (BADUM)
AH... THIS...
THERE WAS AN ACCIDENT ...

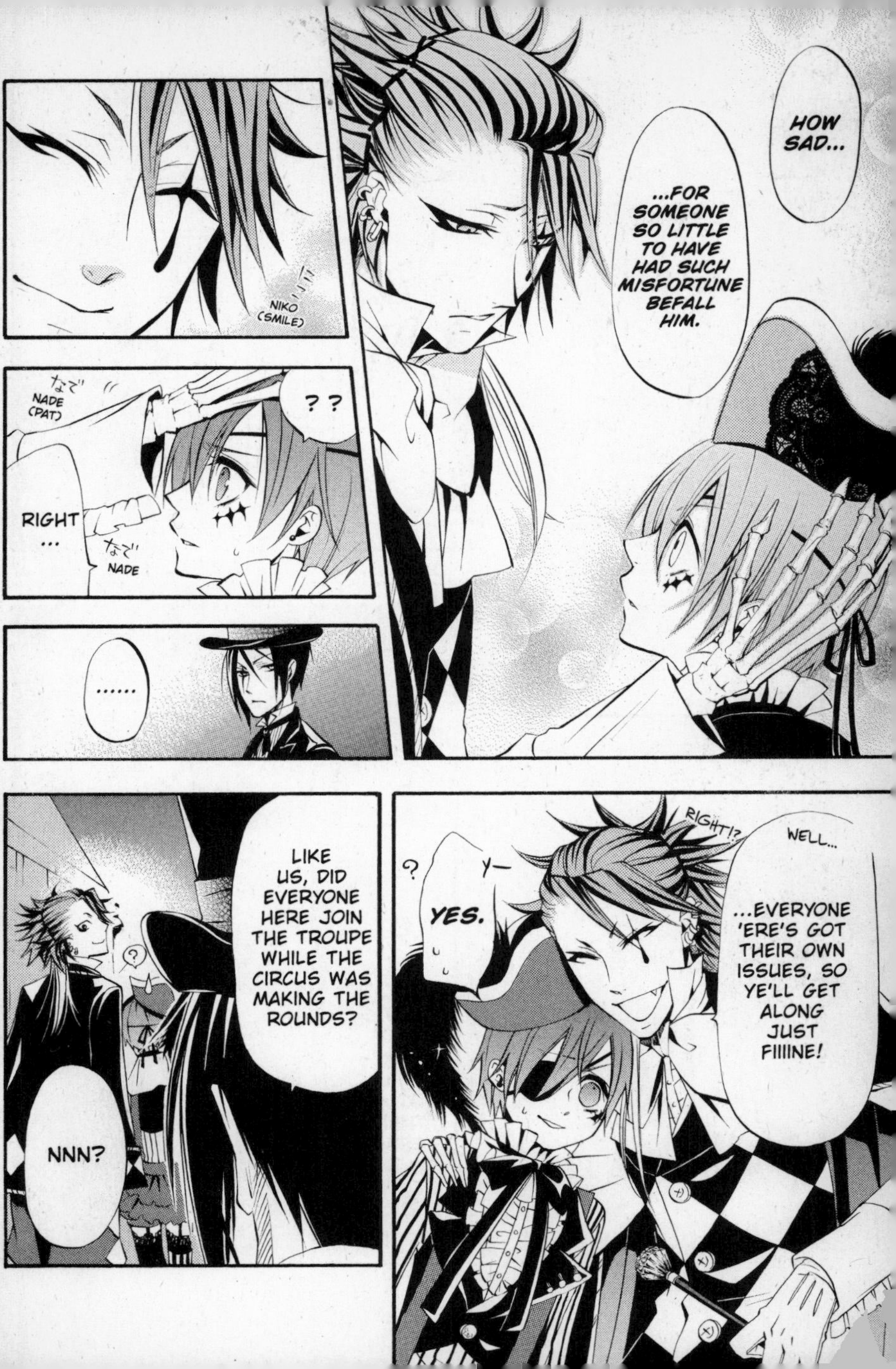
HOW SAD...
...FOR SOMEONE SO LITTLE TO HAVE HAD SUCH MISFORTUNE BEFALL HIM.
NIKO (SMILE)
なで NADE (PAT)
? ?
RIGHT ...
なで NADE
......
WELL...
...EVERYONE 'ERE'S GOT THEIR OWN ISSUES, SO YE'LL GET ALONG JUST FIIIINE!
RIGHT!?
Y—
YES.
?
LIKE US, DID EVERYONE HERE JOIN THE TROUPE WHILE THE CIRCUS WAS MAKING THE ROUNDS?
?
NNN?

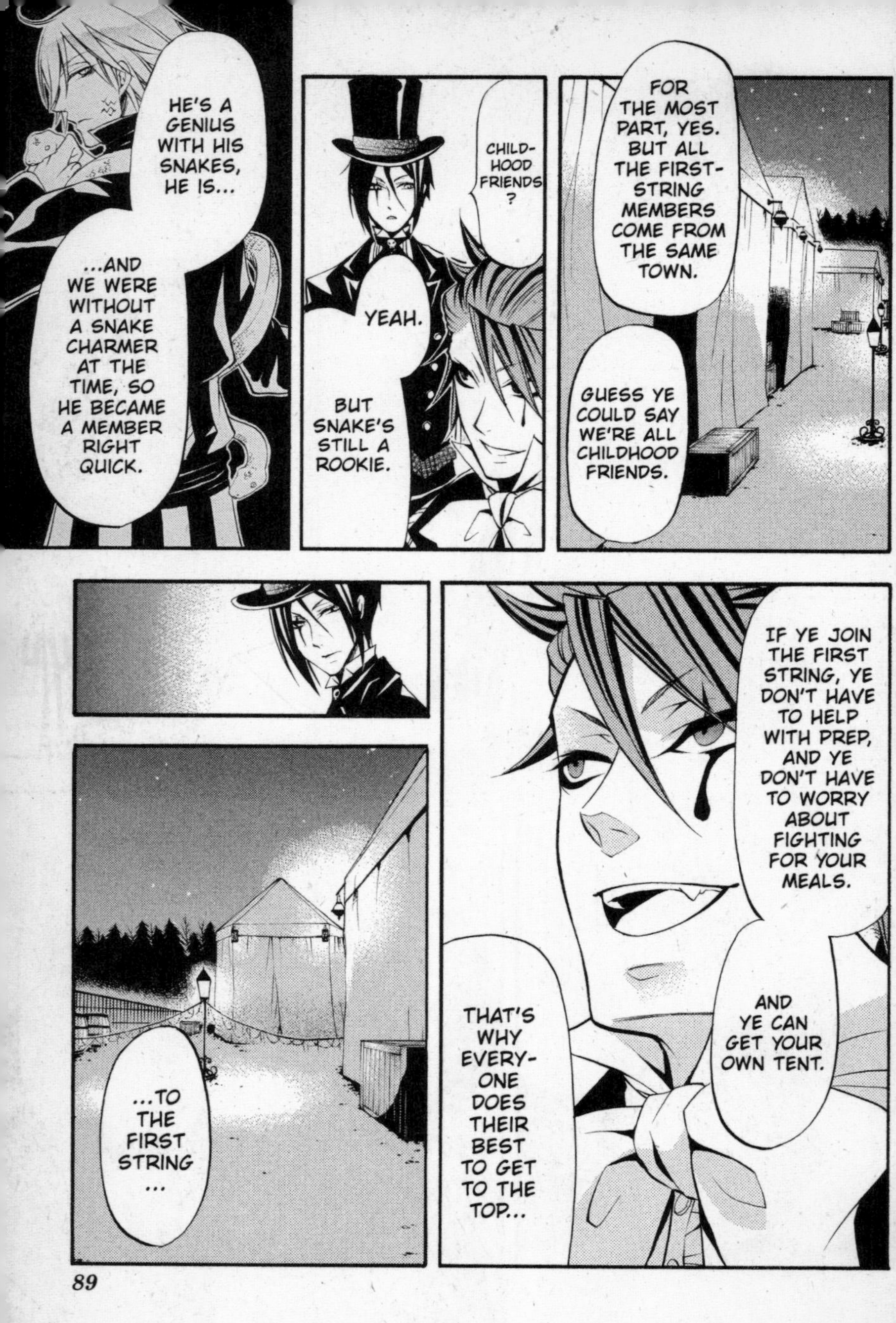
FOR THE MOST PART, YES. BUT ALL THE FIRST-STRING MEMBERS COME FROM THE SAME TOWN.
GUESS YE COULD SAY WE'RE ALL CHILDHOOD FRIENDS.
CHILD-HOOD FRIENDS?
YEAH.
BUT SNAKE'S STILL A ROOKIE.
HE'S A GENIUS WITH HIS SNAKES, HE IS...
...AND WE WERE WITHOUT A SNAKE CHARMER AT THE TIME, SO HE BECAME A MEMBER RIGHT QUICK.
IF YE JOIN THE FIRST STRING, YE DON'T HAVE TO HELP WITH PREP, AND YE DON'T HAVE TO WORRY ABOUT FIGHTING FOR YOUR MEALS.
AND YE CAN GET YOUR OWN TENT.
THAT'S WHY EVERY-ONE DOES THEIR BEST TO GET TO THE TOP...
...TO THE FIRST STRING...

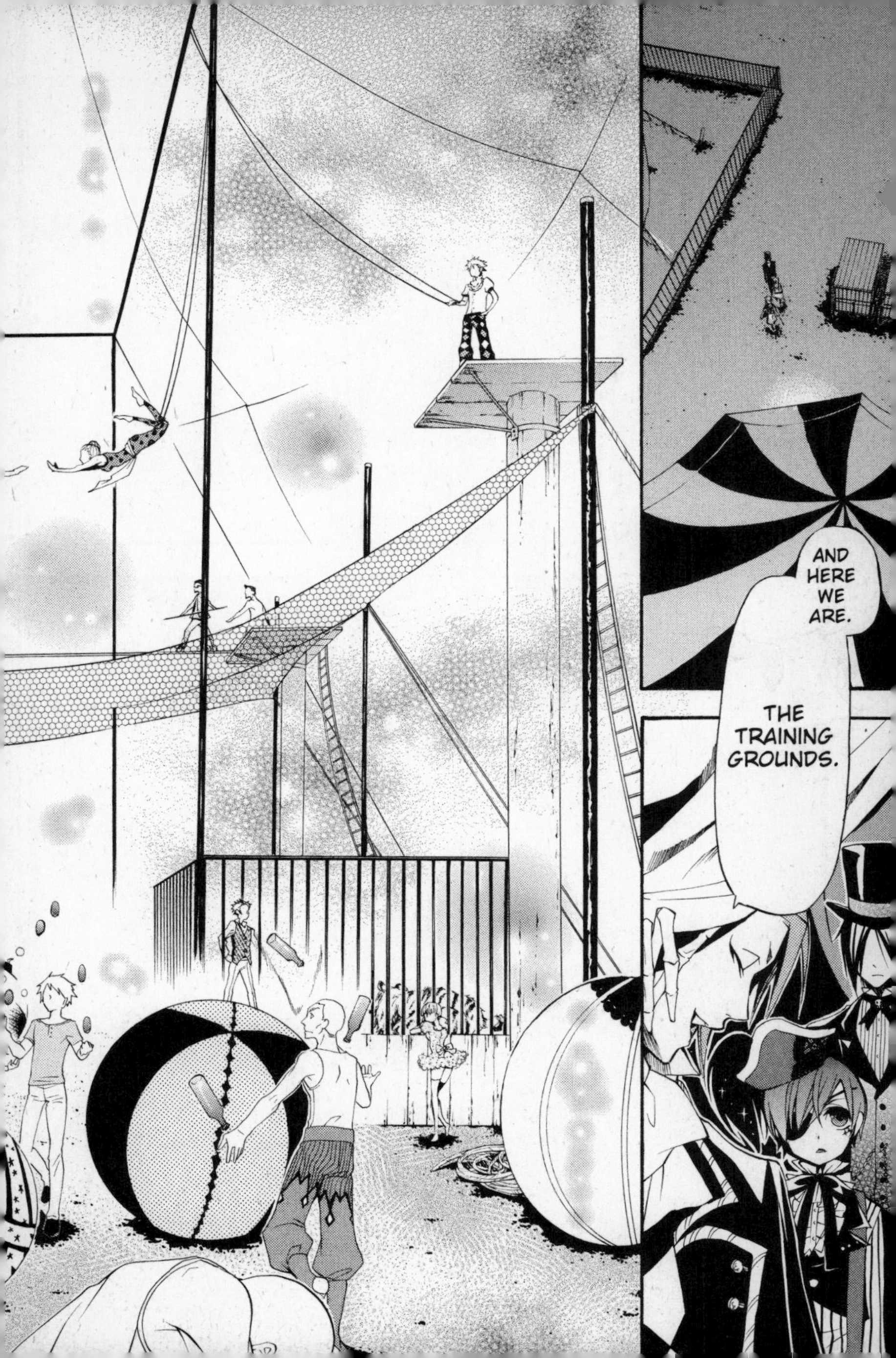
AND HERE WE ARE.
THE TRAINING GROUNDS.

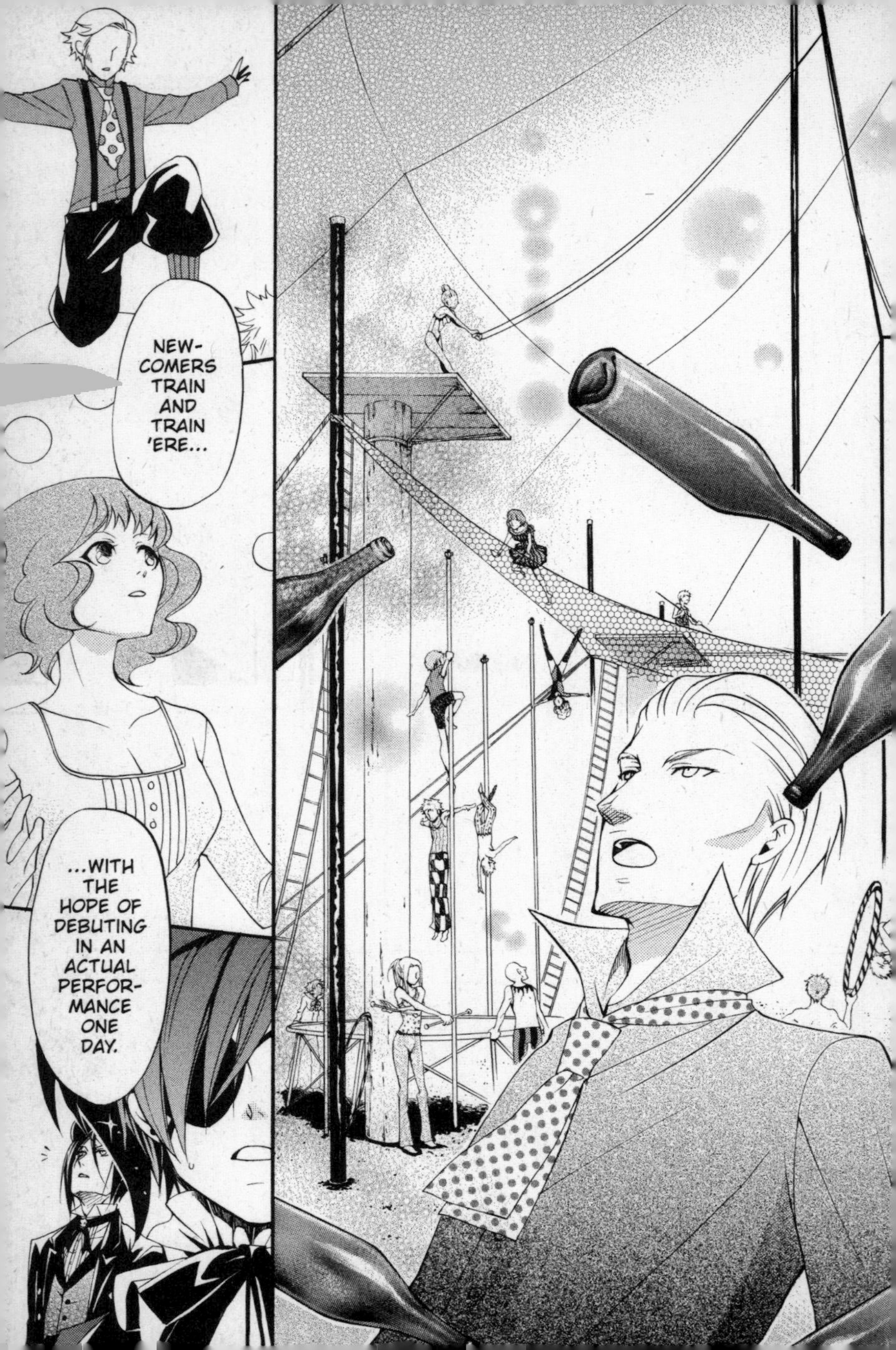
NEW-COMERS TRAIN AND TRAIN 'ERE...
...WITH THE HOPE OF DEBUTING IN AN ACTUAL PERFORMANCE ONE DAY.

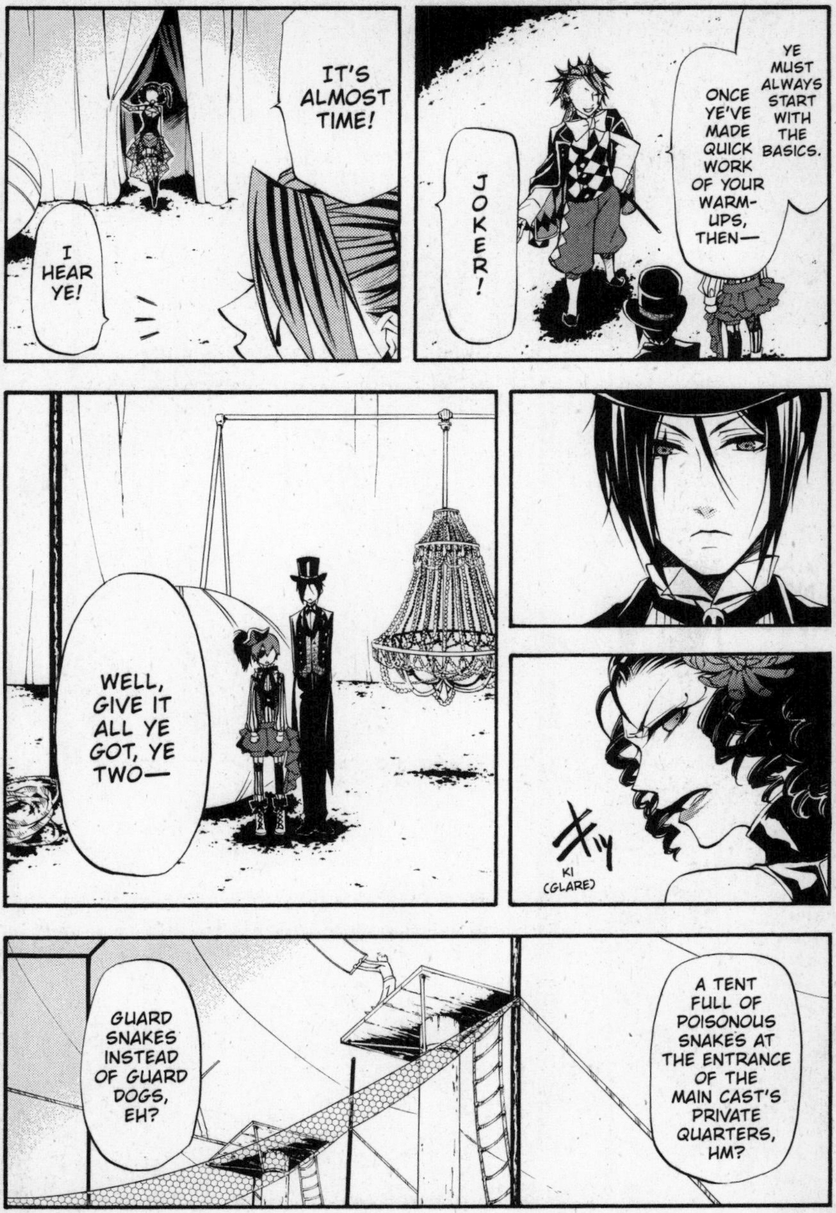
YE MUST ALWAYS START WITH THE BASICS.
ONCE YE'VE MADE QUICK WORK OF YOUR WARM-UPS, THEN—
JOKER!
IT'S ALMOST TIME!
I HEAR YE!
KI (GLARE)
WELL, GIVE IT ALL YE GOT, YE TWO—
A TENT FULL OF POISONOUS SNAKES AT THE ENTRANCE OF THE MAIN CAST'S PRIVATE QUARTERS, HM?
GUARD SNAKES INSTEAD OF GUARD DOGS, EH?

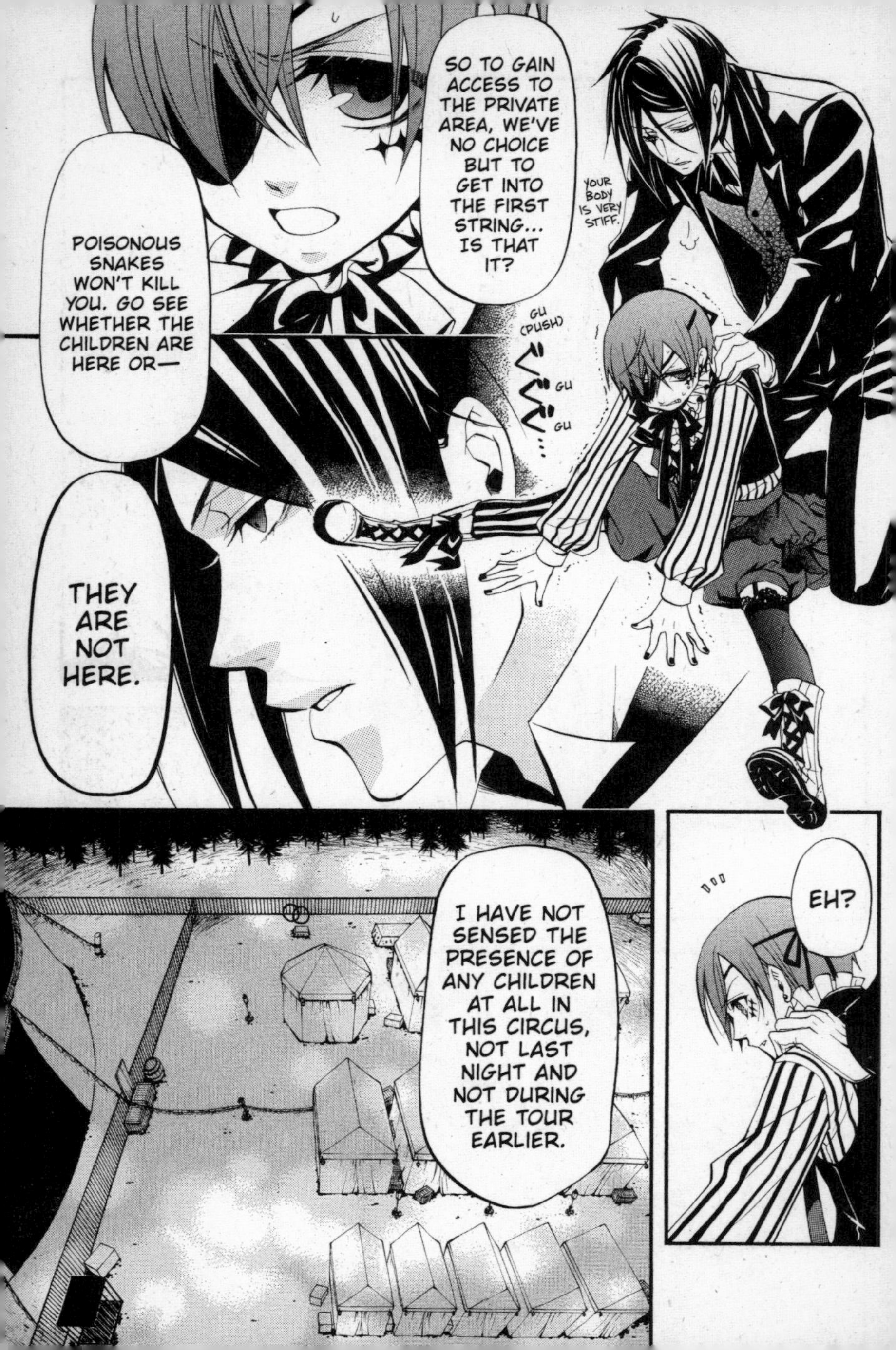

YOUR BODY IS VERY STIFF.
GU (PUSH)
GU
GU
SO TO GAIN ACCESS TO THE PRIVATE AREA, WE'VE NO CHOICE BUT TO GET INTO THE FIRST STRING... IS THAT IT?
POISONOUS SNAKES WON'T KILL YOU. GO SEE WHETHER THE CHILDREN ARE HERE OR—
THEY ARE NOT HERE.
EH?
I HAVE NOT SENSED THE PRESENCE OF ANY CHILDREN AT ALL IN THIS CIRCUS, NOT LAST NIGHT AND NOT DURING THE TOUR EARLIER.

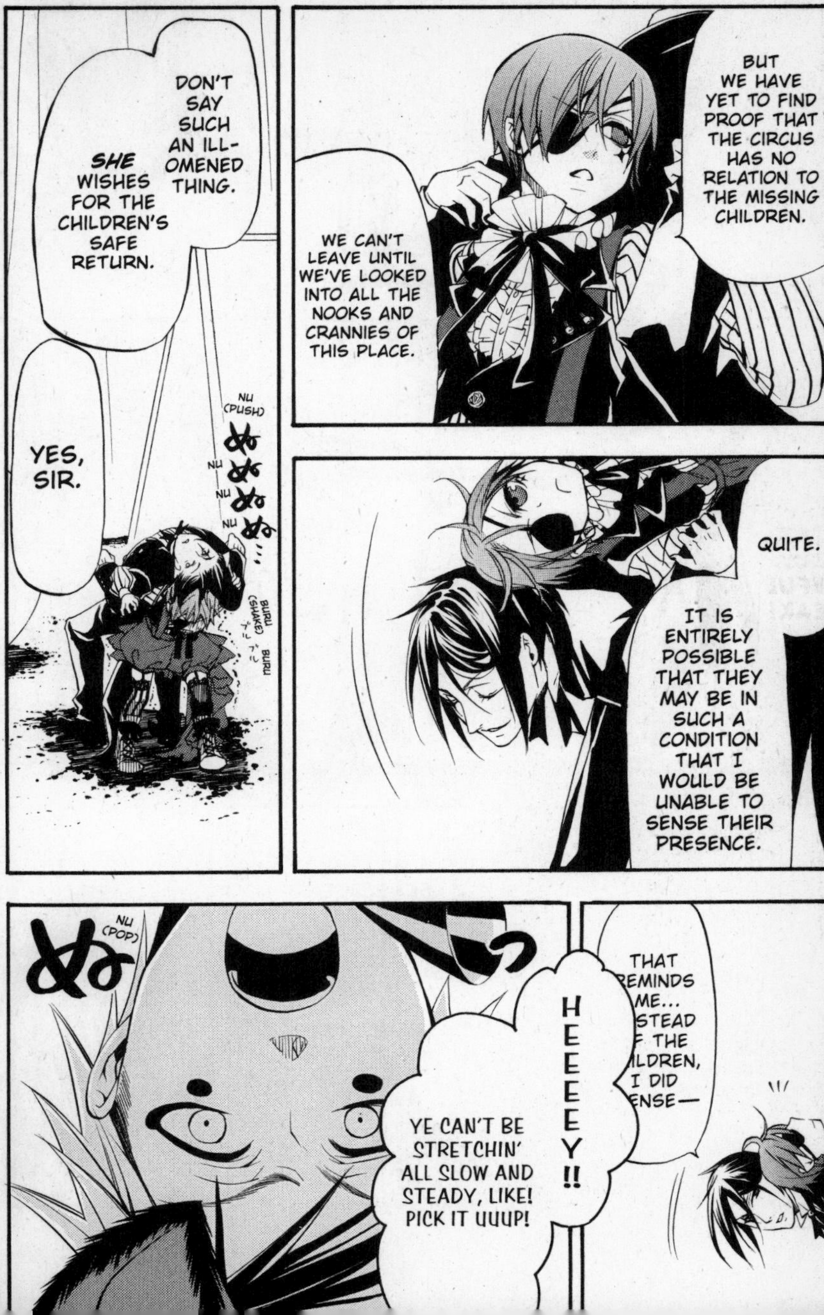
BUT WE HAVE YET TO FIND PROOF THAT THE CIRCUS HAS NO RELATION TO THE MISSING CHILDREN.
WE CAN'T LEAVE UNTIL WE'VE LOOKED INTO ALL THE NOOKS AND CRANNIES OF THIS PLACE.
QUITE.
IT IS ENTIRELY POSSIBLE THAT THEY MAY BE IN SUCH A CONDITION THAT I WOULD BE UNABLE TO SENSE THEIR PRESENCE.
DON'T SAY SUCH AN ILL-OMENED THING.
SHE WISHES FOR THE CHILDREN'S SAFE RETURN.
YES, SIR.
NU (PUSH)
ぬ
NU
ぬ
NU
ぬ
NU
ぬ…
BURU (SHAKE) ブル
BURU ブル
THAT EMINDS ME... STEAD F THE ILDREN, I DID ENSE—
NU (POP)
ぬっ
HEEEEEY!!
YE CAN'T BE STRETCHIN' ALL SLOW AND STEADY, LIKE! PICK IT UUUP!

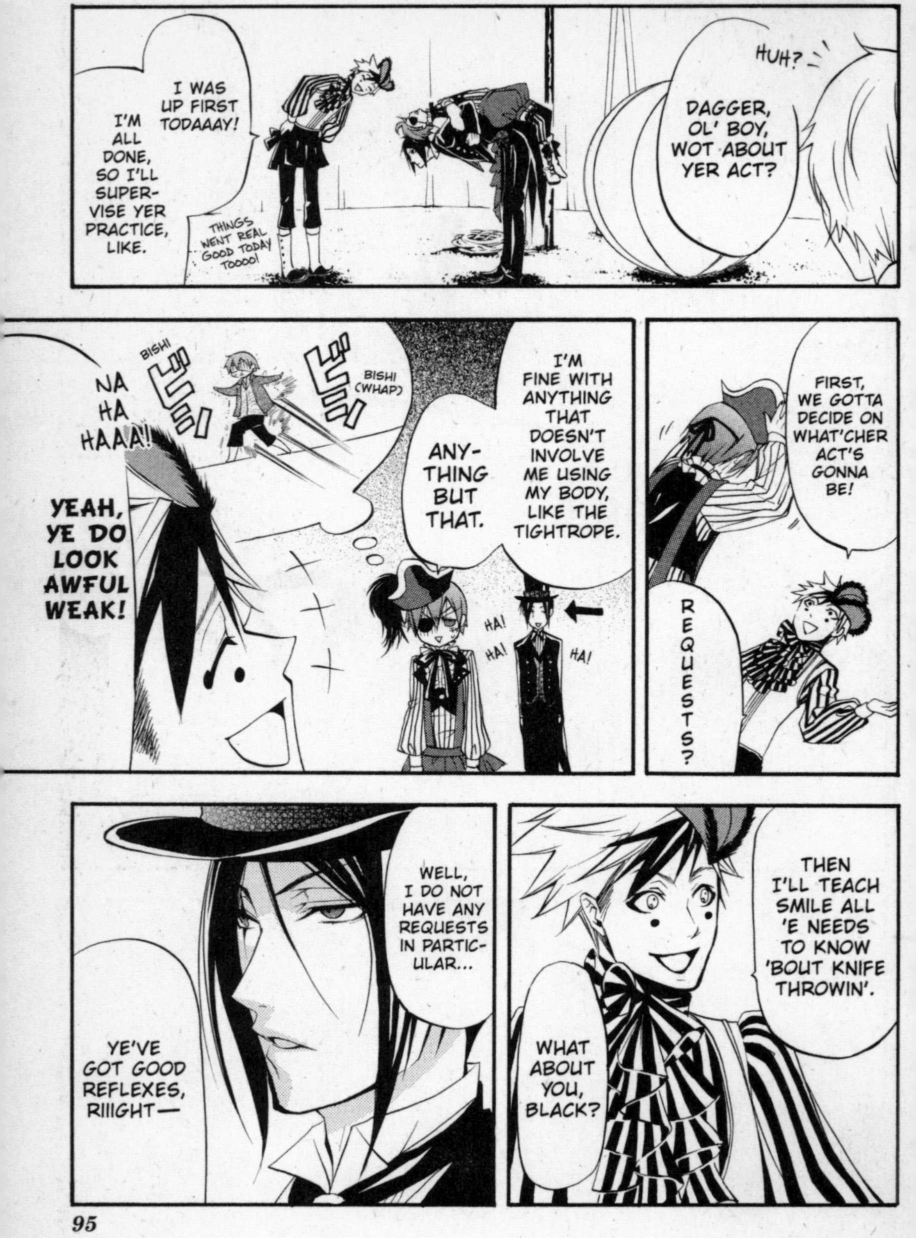
HUH?
DAGGER, OL' BOY, WOT ABOUT YER ACT?
I WAS UP FIRST TODAAAY!
I'M ALL DONE, SO I'LL SUPER-VISE YER PRACTICE, LIKE.
THINGS WENT REAL GOOD TODAY TOOOO!
FIRST, WE GOTTA DECIDE ON WHAT'CHER ACT'S GONNA BE!
REQUESTS?
I'M FINE WITH ANYTHING THAT DOESN'T INVOLVE ME USING MY BODY, LIKE THE TIGHTROPE.
ANY-THING BUT THAT.
HA! HA! HA!
BISHI (WHAP)
BISHI
NA HA HAAAA!
YEAH, YE DO LOOK AWFUL WEAK!
THEN I'LL TEACH SMILE ALL 'E NEEDS TO KNOW 'BOUT KNIFE THROWIN'.
WHAT ABOUT YOU, BLACK?
WELL, I DO NOT HAVE ANY REQUESTS IN PARTIC-ULAR...
YE'VE GOT GOOD REFLEXES, RIIIGHT—

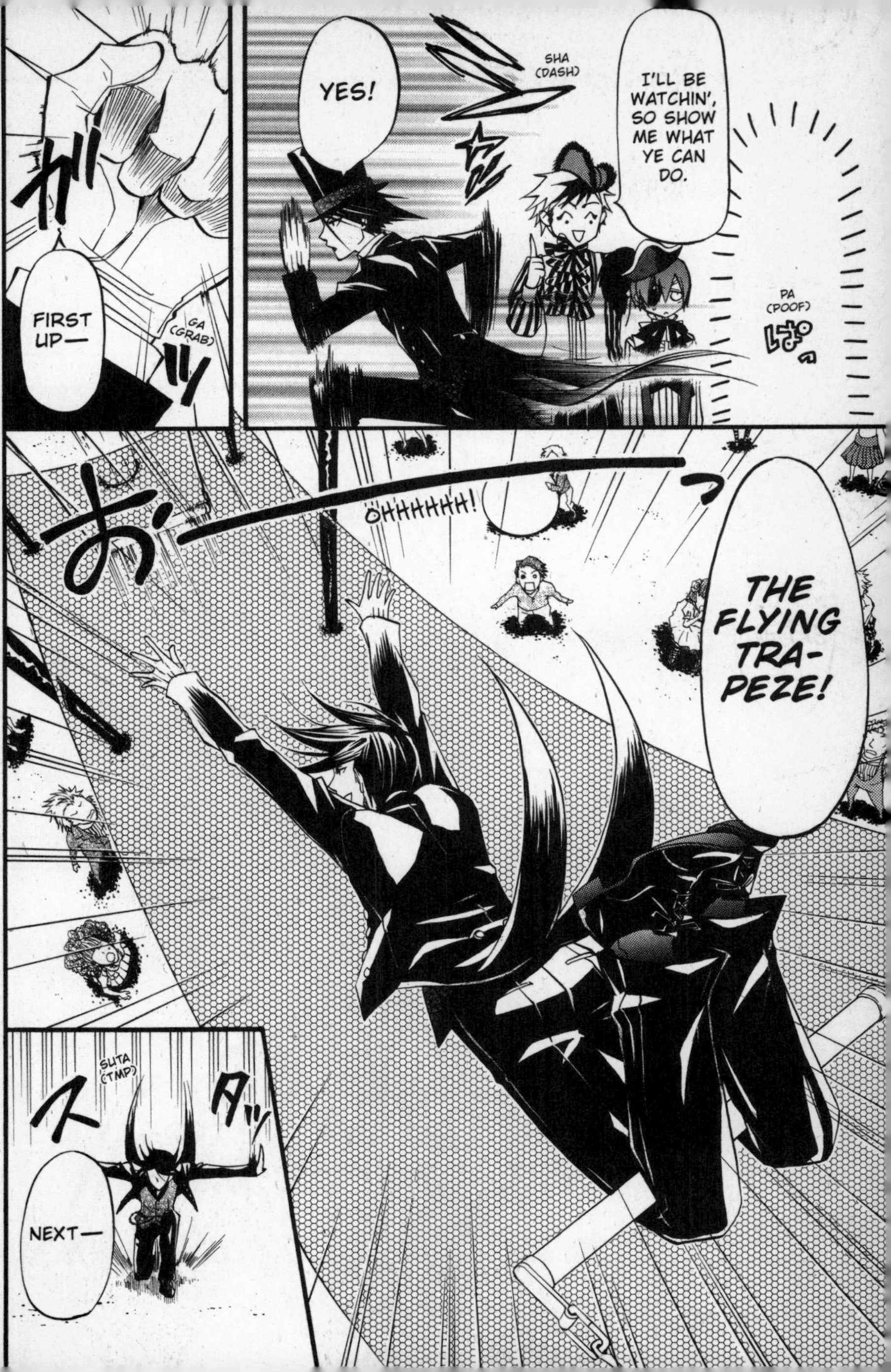
I'LL BE WATCHIN', SO SHOW ME WHAT YE CAN DO.
PA (POOF)
SHA (DASH)
YES!
FIRST UP—
GA (GRAB)
THE FLYING TRA-PEZE!
OHHHHHHH!
SUTA (TMP)
NEXT—

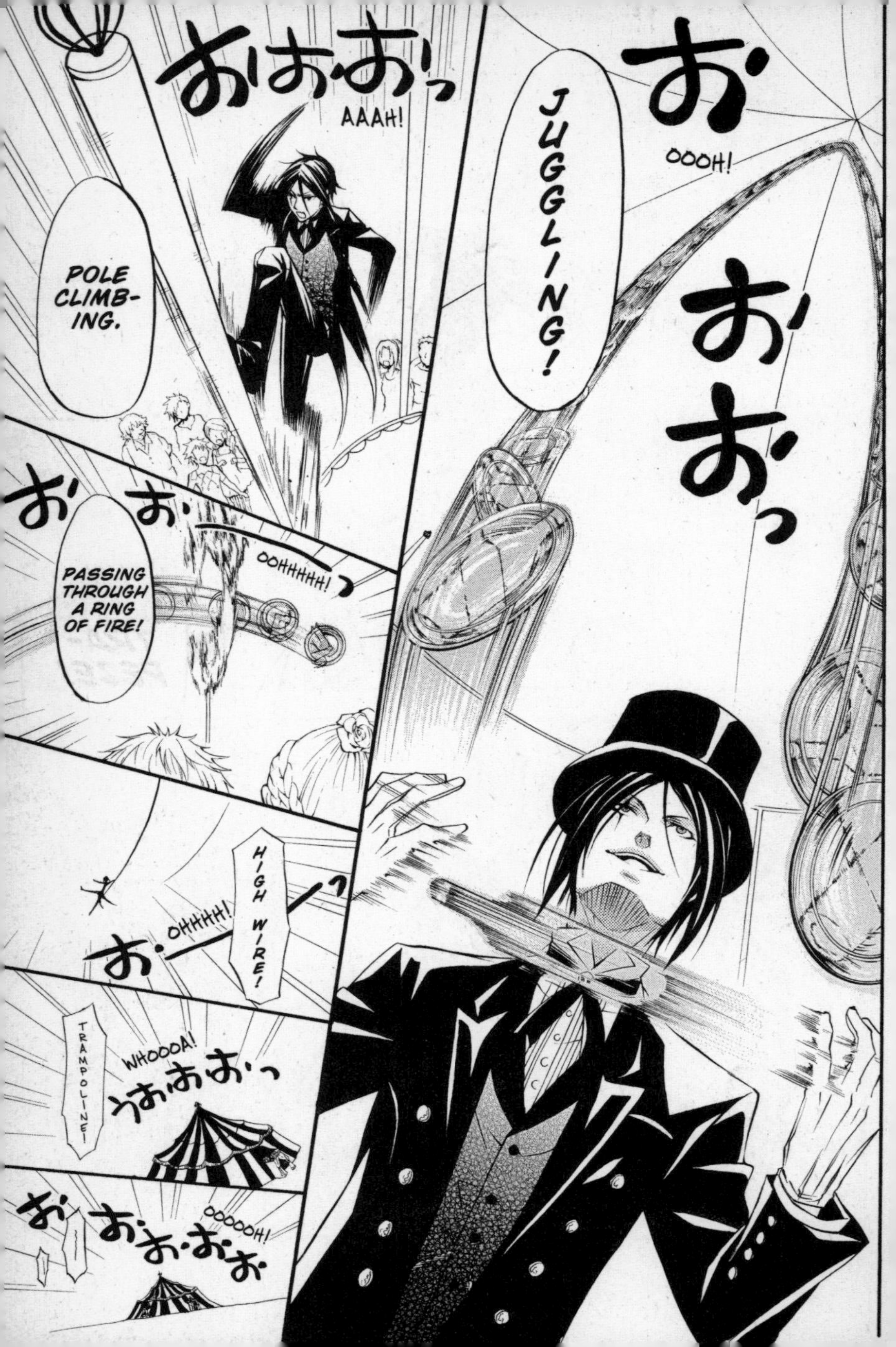

おおおっ
JUGGLING!
OOOH!
おおっ
おおおっ
AAAH!
POLE CLIMBING.
おお
OOHHHHH!
PASSING THROUGH A RING OF FIRE!
HIGH WIRE!
おー
OHHHHH!
TRAMPOLINE!
WHOOOA!
うおおおっ
おーおお・おお
OOOOOH!

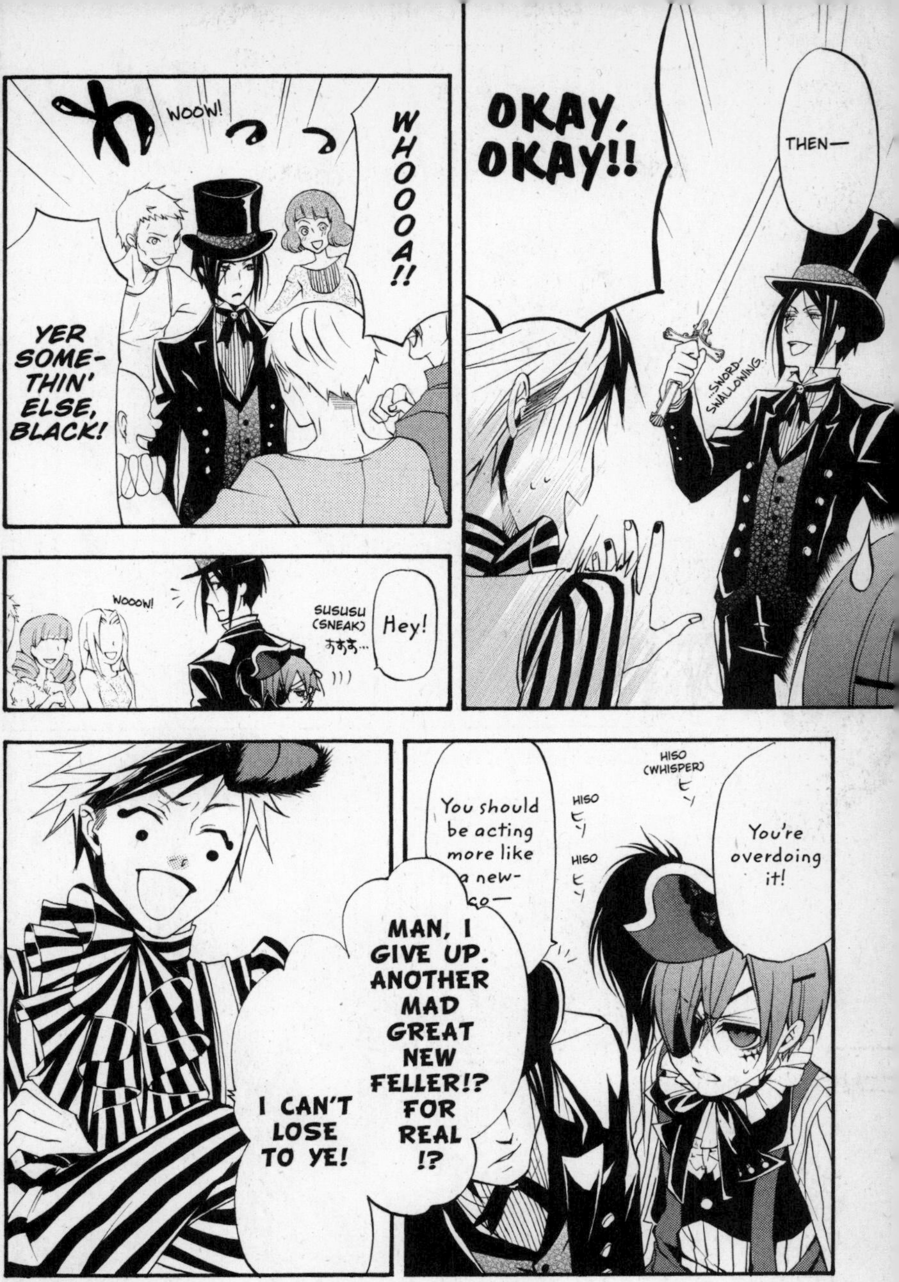
THEN—
OKAY, OKAY!!
...SWORD-SWALLOWING.
わっっ
WOOW!
WHOOOOA!!
YER SOME-THIN' ELSE, BLACK!
Hey!
SUSUSU (SNEAK)
すすす…
WOOOW!
You're overdoing it!
HISO (WHISPER)
ヒソ
HISO
ヒソ
HISO
ヒソ
You should be acting more like a new-co—
MAN, I GIVE UP. ANOTHER MAD GREAT NEW FELLER!? FOR REAL!?
I CAN'T LOSE TO YE!

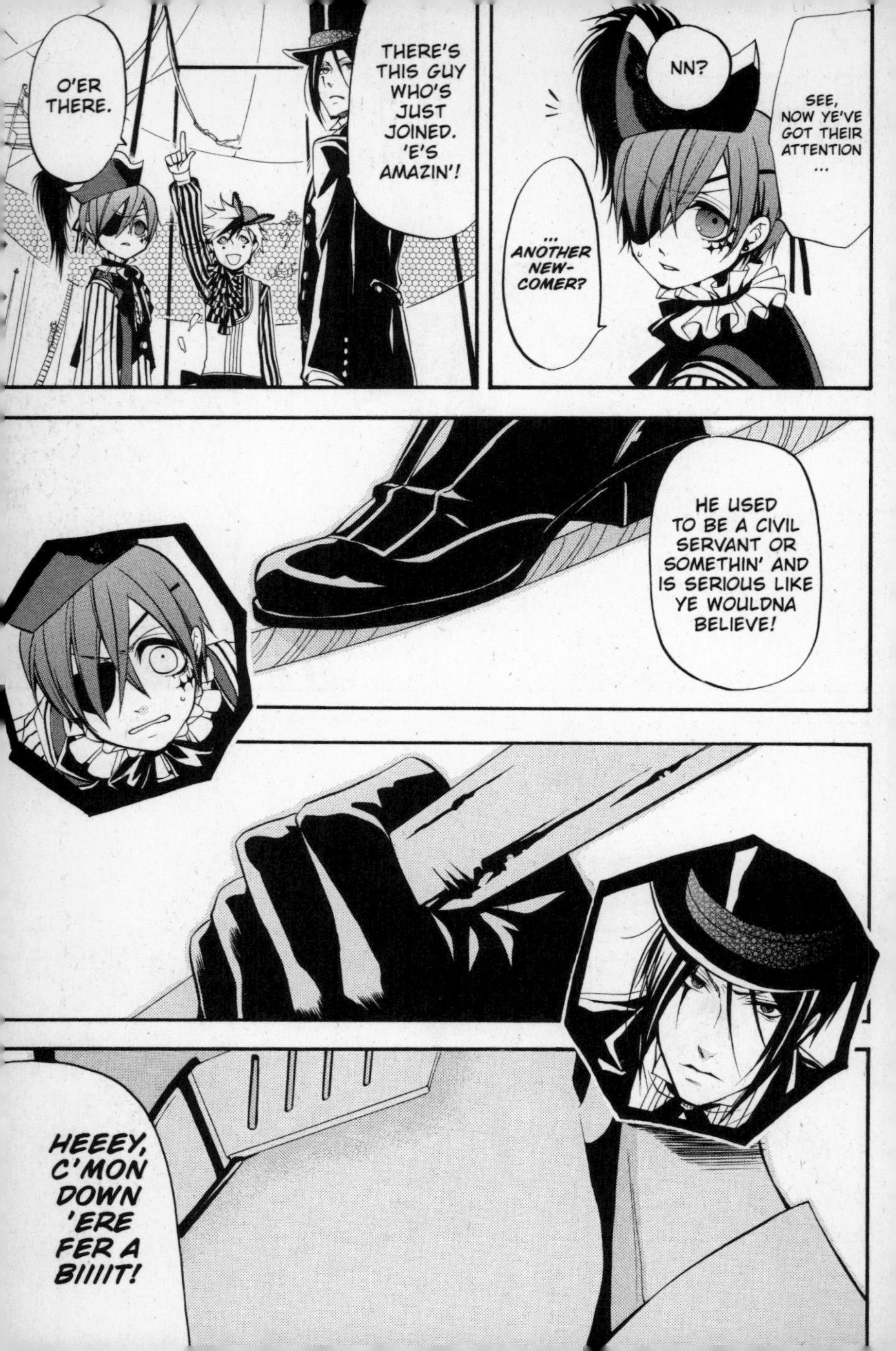
NN?
SEE, NOW YE'VE GOT THEIR ATTENTION ...
... ANOTHER NEW-COMER?
THERE'S THIS GUY WHO'S JUST JOINED. 'E'S AMAZIN'!
O'ER THERE.
HE USED TO BE A CIVIL SERVANT OR SOMETHIN' AND IS SERIOUS LIKE YE WOULDNA BELIEVE!
HEEEY, C'MON DOWN 'ERE FER A BIIIIT!

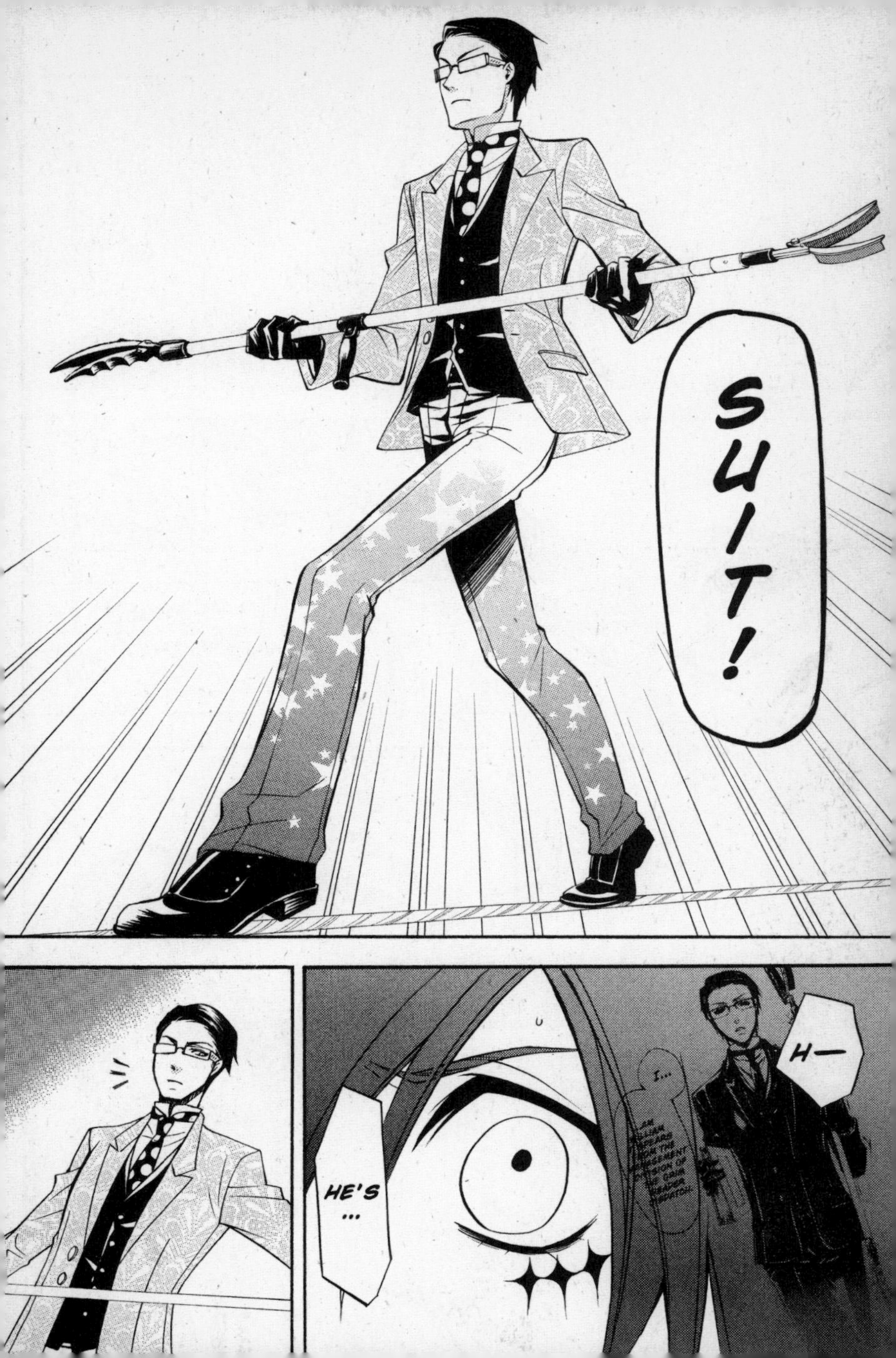
SUIT!
H—
I...
HE'S ...

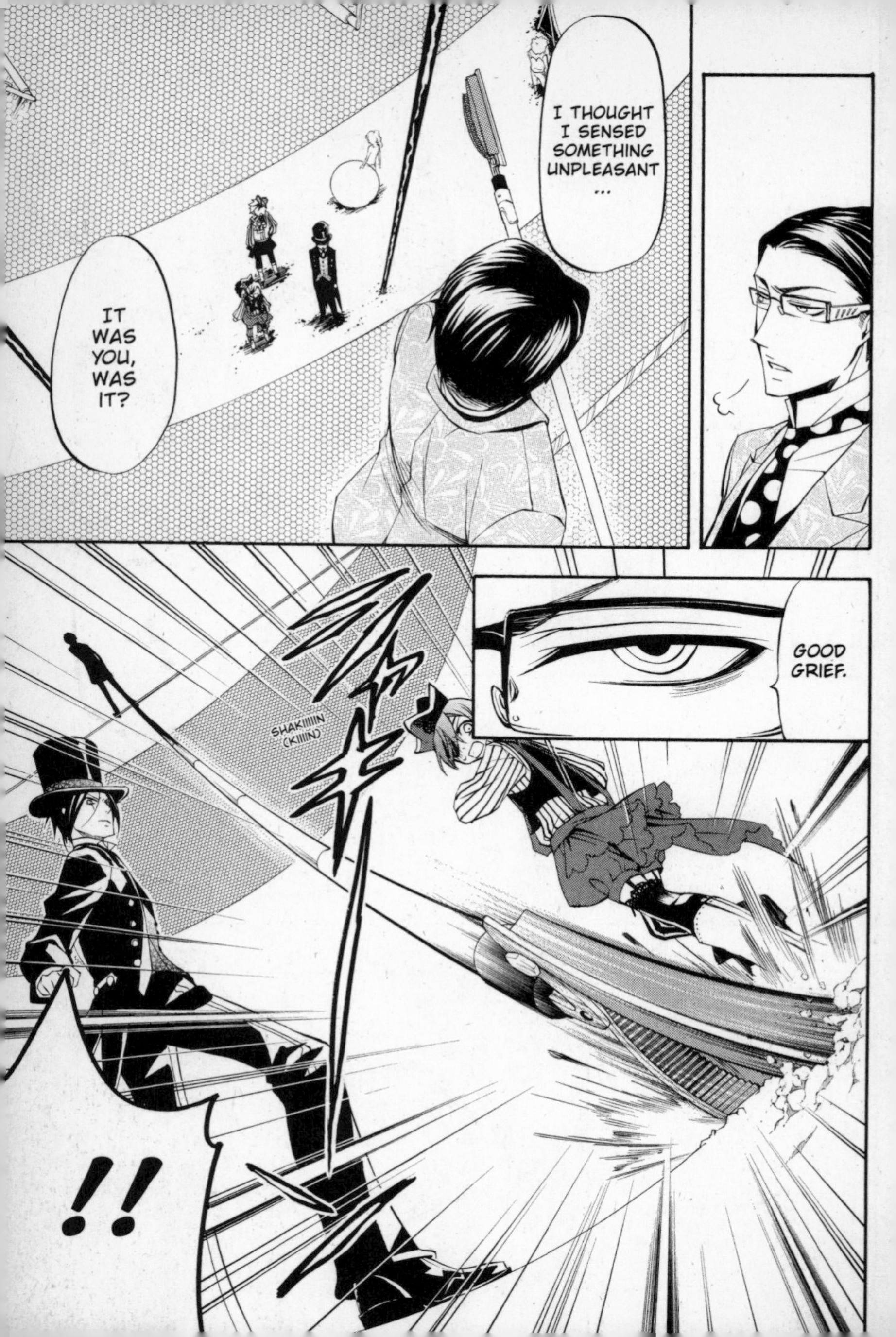
I THOUGHT I SENSED SOMETHING UNPLEASANT ...
IT WAS YOU, WAS IT?
GOOD GRIEF.
SHAKIIIIIIN (KIIIIN)
!!

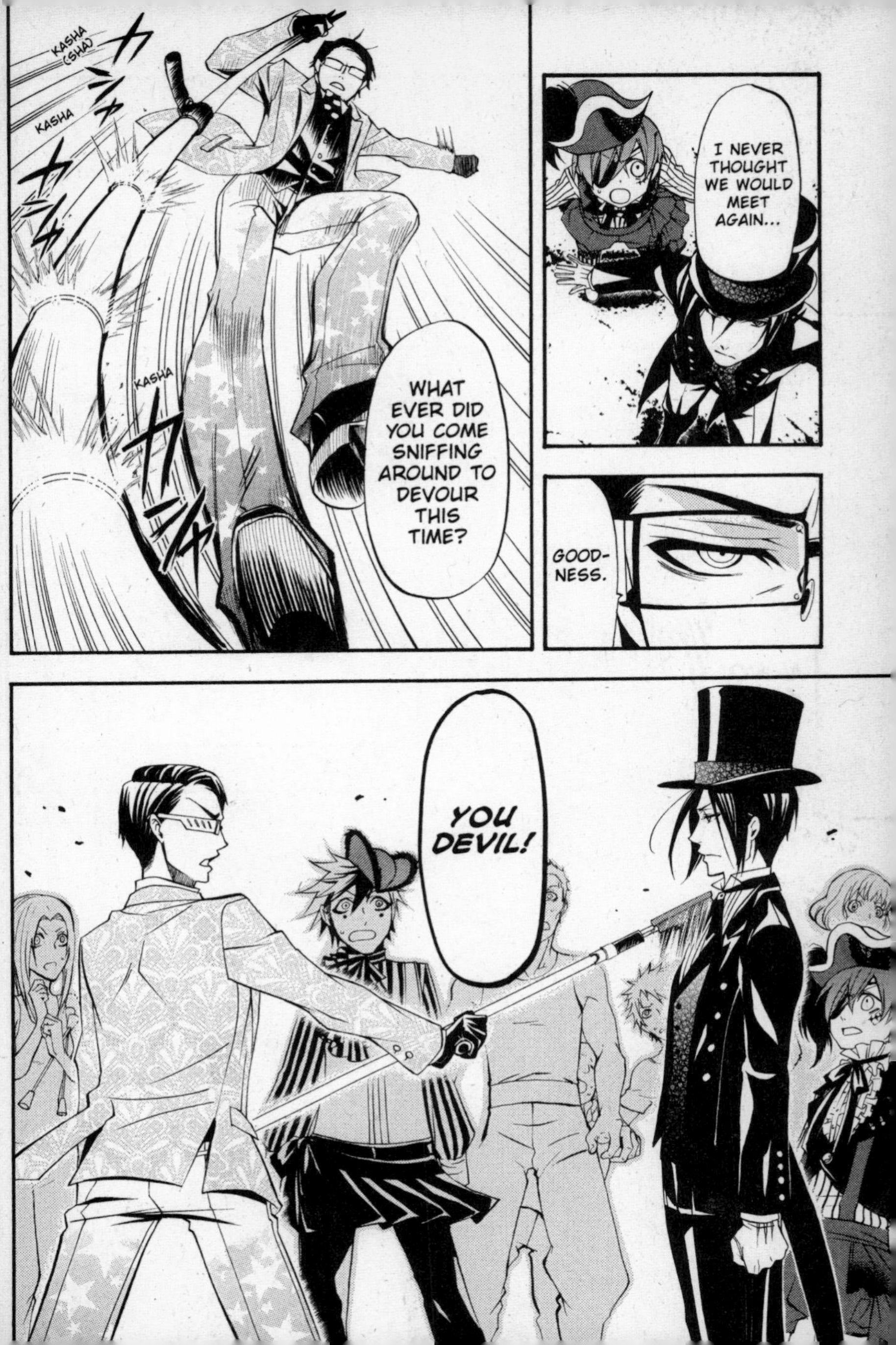
I NEVER THOUGHT WE WOULD MEET AGAIN...
GOOD-NESS.
KASHA (SHA)
KASHA
KASHA
WHAT EVER DID YOU COME SNIFFING AROUND TO DEVOUR THIS TIME?
YOU DEVIL!

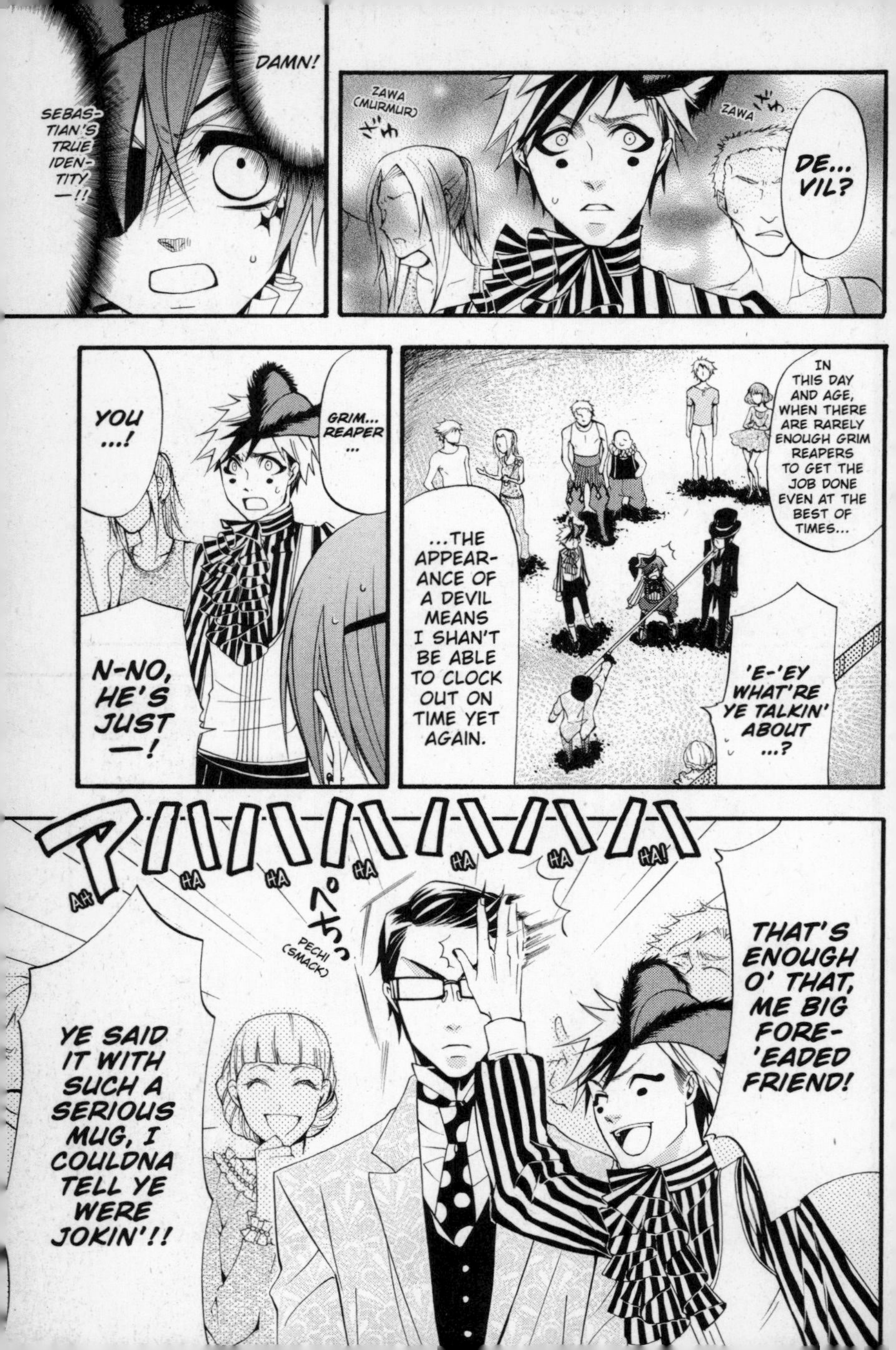
ZAWA (MURMUR)
ZAWA
DE... VIL?
DAMN!
SEBAS-TIAN'S TRUE IDEN-TITY —!!
IN THIS DAY AND AGE, WHEN THERE ARE RARELY ENOUGH GRIM REAPERS TO GET THE JOB DONE EVEN AT THE BEST OF TIMES...
...THE APPEAR-ANCE OF A DEVIL MEANS I SHAN'T BE ABLE TO CLOCK OUT ON TIME YET AGAIN.
'E-'EY WHAT'RE YE TALKIN' ABOUT ...?
GRIM... REAPER ...
YOU ...!
N-NO, HE'S JUST —!
AH HA HA HA HA HA HA!
THAT'S ENOUGH O' THAT, ME BIG FORE-'EADED FRIEND!
PECHI (SMACK)
YE SAID IT WITH SUCH A SERIOUS MUG, I COULDNA TELL YE WERE JOKIN'!!

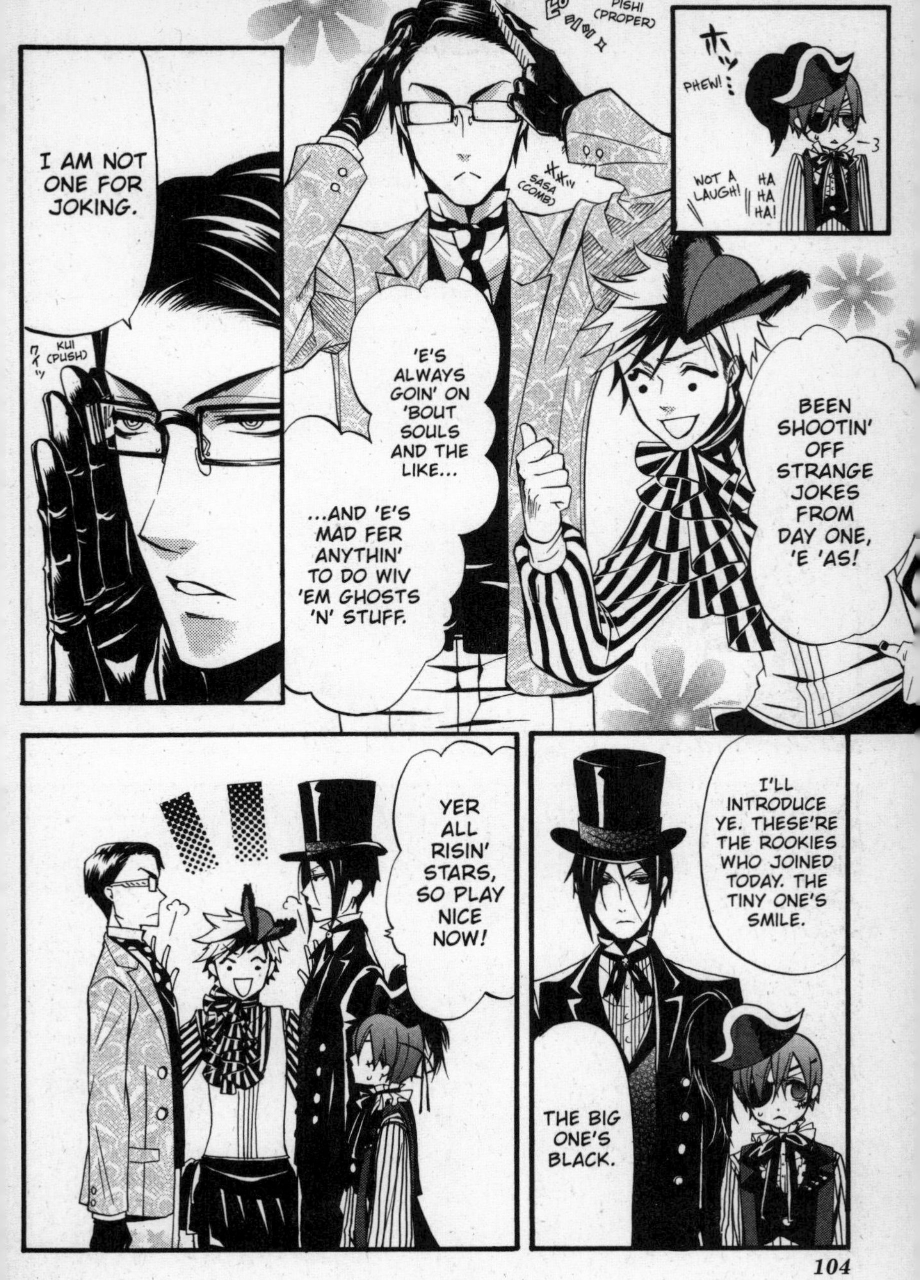
PHEW!
NOT A LAUGH!
HA HA HA!
BEEN SHOOTIN' OFF STRANGE JOKES FROM DAY ONE, 'E 'AS!
PISHI (PROPER)
SASA (COMB)
'E'S ALWAYS GOIN' ON 'BOUT SOULS AND THE LIKE...
...AND 'E'S MAD FER ANYTHIN' TO DO WIV 'EM GHOSTS 'N' STUFF.
KUI (PUSH)
I AM NOT ONE FOR JOKING.
I'LL INTRODUCE YE. THESE'RE THE ROOKIES WHO JOINED TODAY. THE TINY ONE'S SMILE.
THE BIG ONE'S BLACK.
YER ALL RISIN' STARS, SO PLAY NICE NOW!

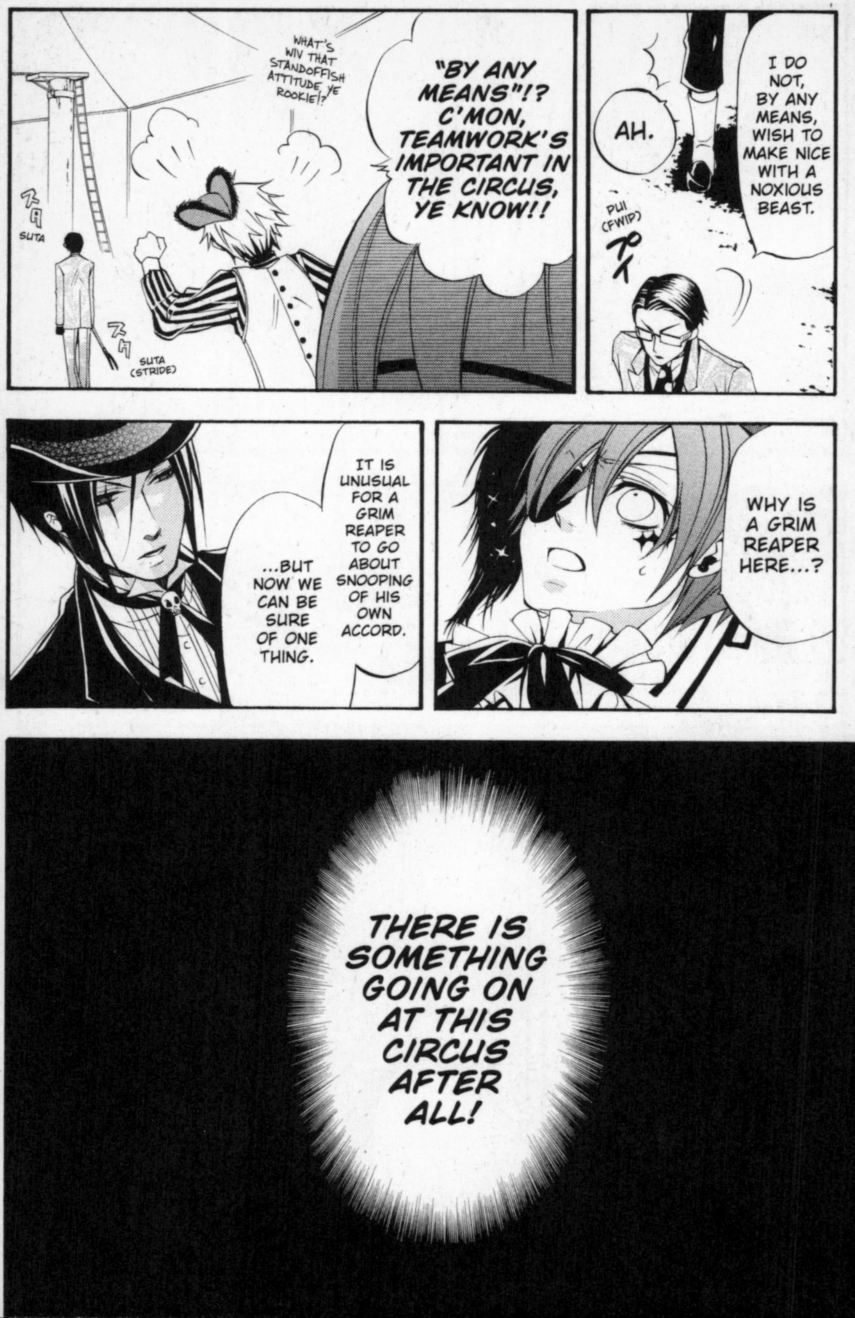

I DO NOT, BY ANY MEANS, WISH TO MAKE NICE WITH A NOXIOUS BEAST.
AH.
PUI (FWIP)
"BY ANY MEANS"!? C'MON, TEAMWORK'S IMPORTANT IN THE CIRCUS, YE KNOW!!
WHAT'S WIV THAT STANDOFFISH ATTITUDE, YE ROOKIE!?
SUTA
SUTA (STRIDE)
WHY IS A GRIM REAPER HERE...?
IT IS UNUSUAL FOR A GRIM REAPER TO GO ABOUT SNOOPING OF HIS OWN ACCORD.
...BUT NOW WE CAN BE SURE OF ONE THING.
THERE IS SOMETHING GOING ON AT THIS CIRCUS AFTER ALL!

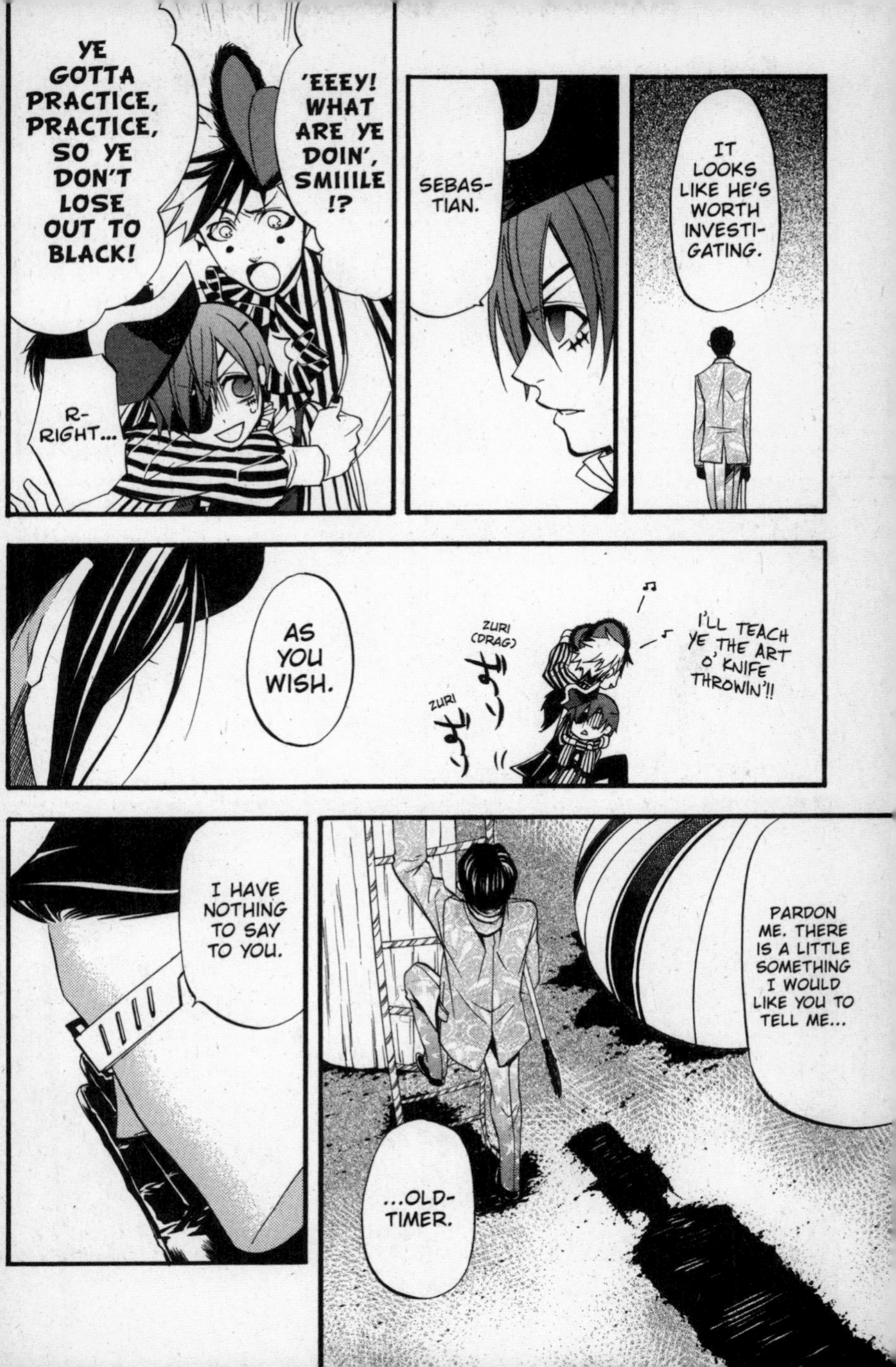
IT LOOKS LIKE HE'S WORTH INVESTIGATING.
SEBASTIAN.
'EEEY! WHAT ARE YE DOIN', SMIIILE!?
YE GOTTA PRACTICE, PRACTICE, SO YE DON'T LOSE OUT TO BLACK!
R-RIGHT...
I'LL TEACH YE THE ART O' KNIFE THROWIN'!!
ZURI (DRAG)
ZURI
AS YOU WISH.
PARDON ME. THERE IS A LITTLE SOMETHING I WOULD LIKE YOU TO TELL ME...
...OLD-TIMER.
I HAVE NOTHING TO SAY TO YOU.

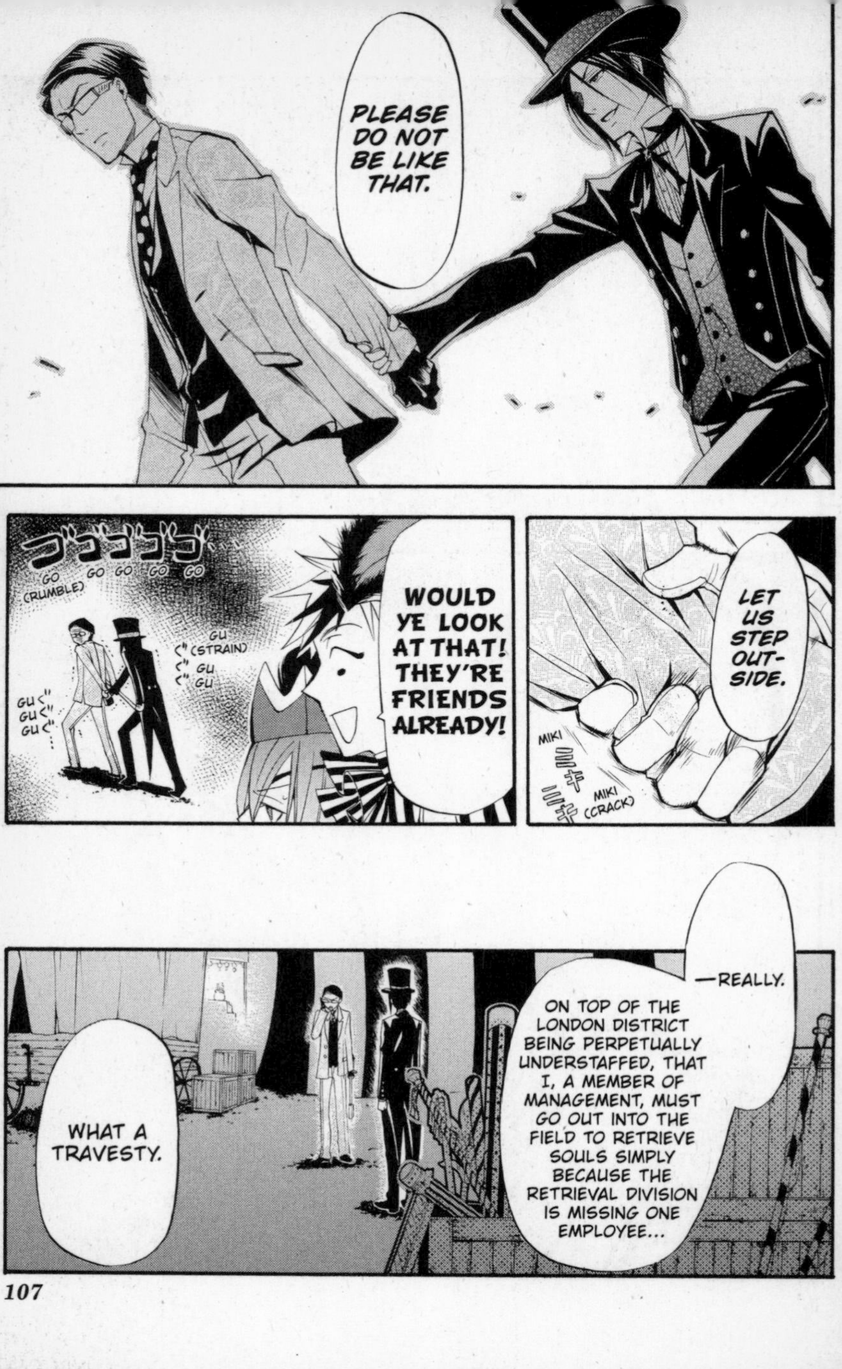

PLEASE DO NOT BE LIKE THAT.
LET US STEP OUT-SIDE.
MIKI MIKI (CRACK)
WOULD YE LOOK AT THAT! THEY'RE FRIENDS ALREADY!
GO GO GO GO GO (RUMBLE)
GU GU GU (STRAIN)
GU GU GU
—REALLY.
ON TOP OF THE LONDON DISTRICT BEING PERPETUALLY UNDERSTAFFED, THAT I, A MEMBER OF MANAGEMENT, MUST GO OUT INTO THE FIELD TO RETRIEVE SOULS SIMPLY BECAUSE THE RETRIEVAL DIVISION IS MISSING ONE EMPLOYEE...
WHAT A TRAVESTY.

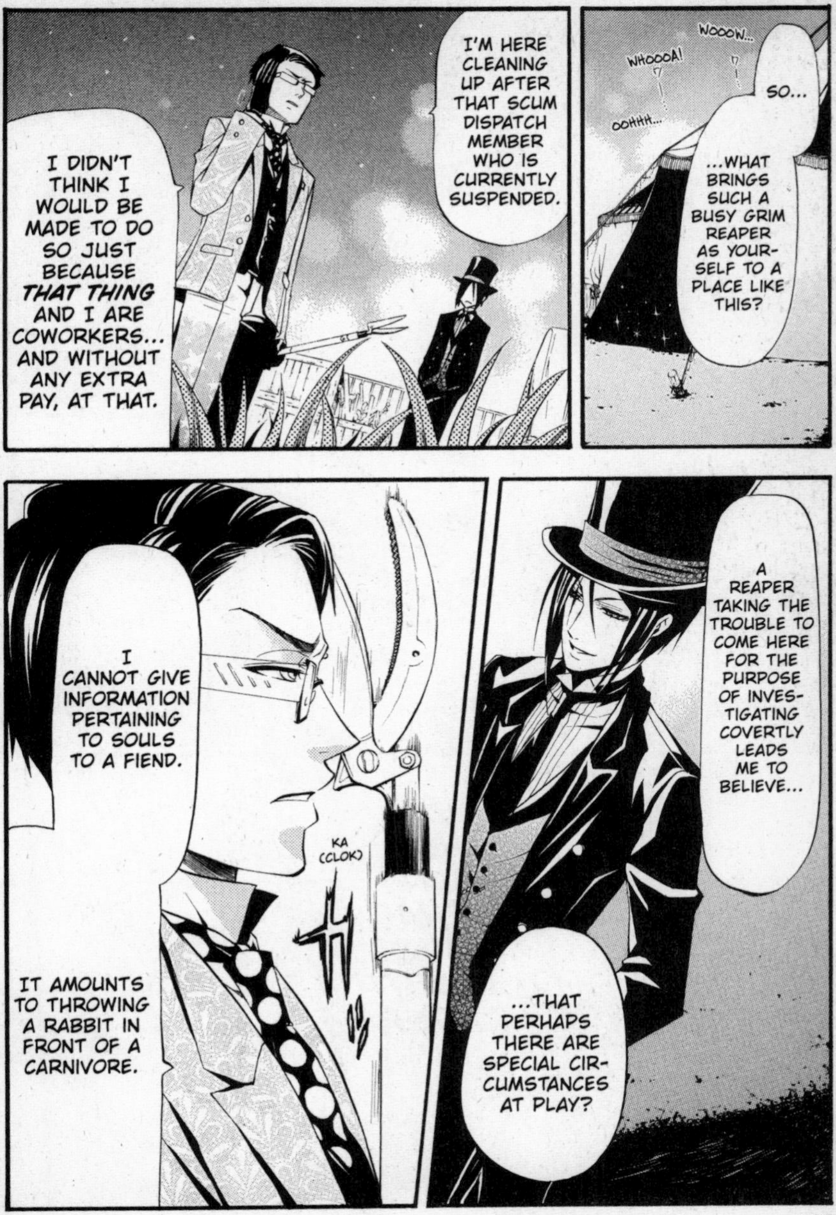
WOOOW...
WHOOOA!
OOHHH...
SO...
...WHAT BRINGS SUCH A BUSY GRIM REAPER AS YOUR-SELF TO A PLACE LIKE THIS?
I'M HERE CLEANING UP AFTER THAT SCUM DISPATCH MEMBER WHO IS CURRENTLY SUSPENDED.
I DIDN'T THINK I WOULD BE MADE TO DO SO JUST BECAUSE *THAT THING* AND I ARE COWORKERS... AND WITHOUT ANY EXTRA PAY, AT THAT.
A REAPER TAKING THE TROUBLE TO COME HERE FOR THE PURPOSE OF INVES-TIGATING COVERTLY LEADS ME TO BELIEVE...
...THAT PERHAPS THERE ARE SPECIAL CIR-CUMSTANCES AT PLAY?
I CANNOT GIVE INFORMATION PERTAINING TO SOULS TO A FIEND.
KA (CLOK)
IT AMOUNTS TO THROWING A RABBIT IN FRONT OF A CARNIVORE.

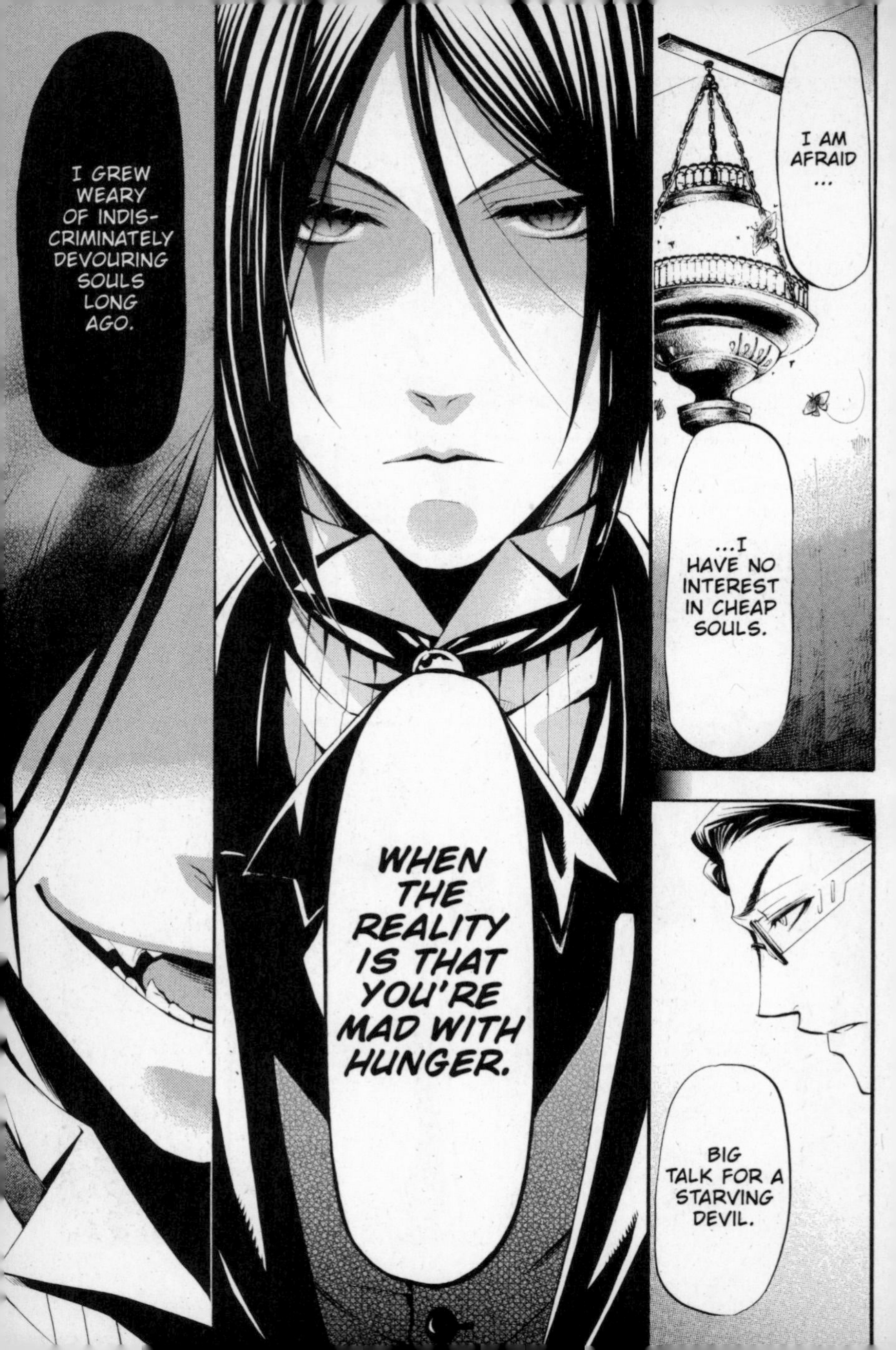
I AM AFRAID ...
...I HAVE NO INTEREST IN CHEAP SOULS.
BIG TALK FOR A STARVING DEVIL.
WHEN THE REALITY IS THAT YOU'RE MAD WITH HUNGER.
I GREW WEARY OF INDIS-CRIMINATELY DEVOURING SOULS LONG AGO.

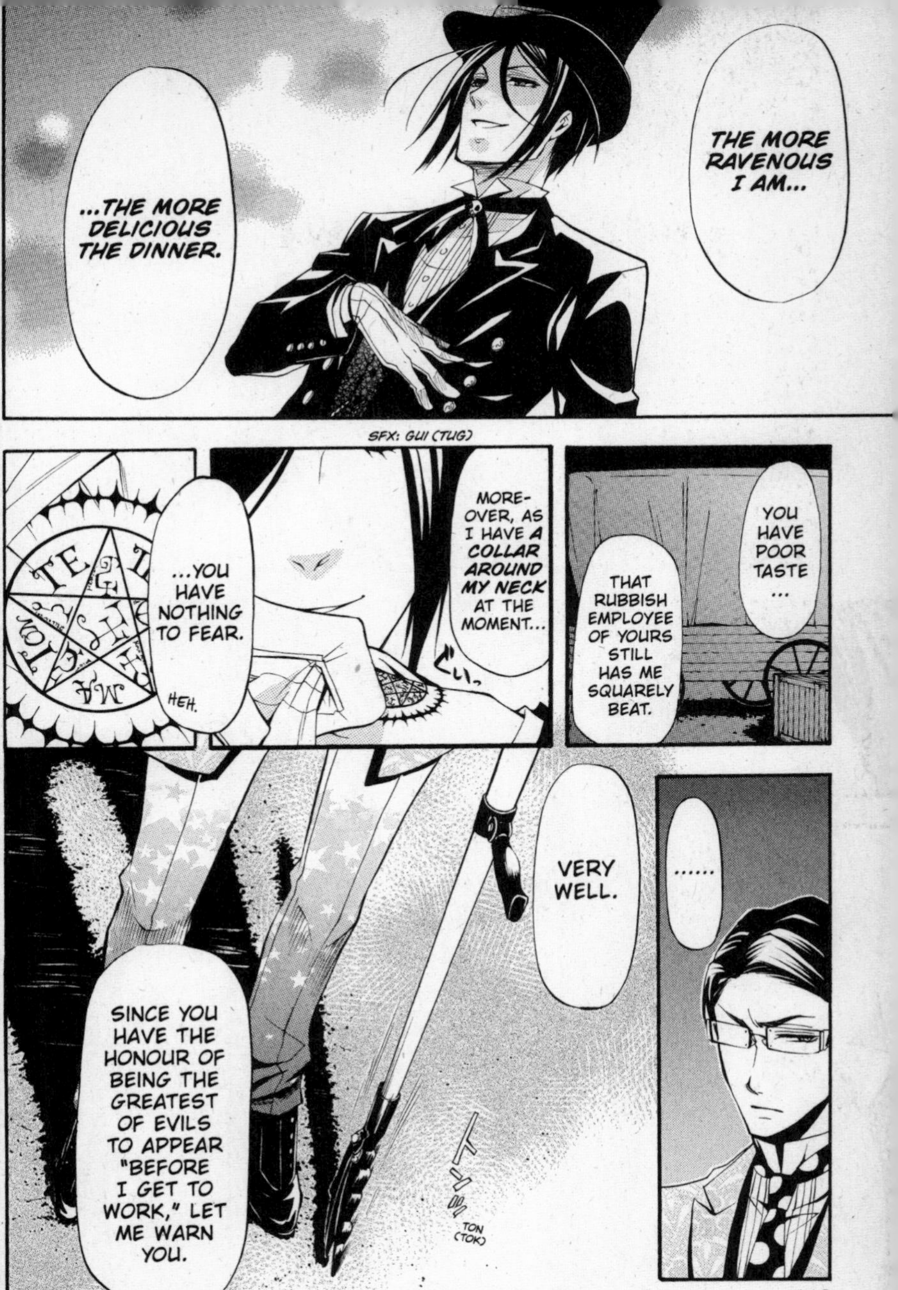
THE MORE RAVENOUS I AM...
...THE MORE DELICIOUS THE DINNER.
SFX: GUI (TUG)
YOU HAVE POOR TASTE...
THAT RUBBISH EMPLOYEE OF YOURS STILL HAS ME SQUARELY BEAT.
MORE-OVER, AS I HAVE A COLLAR AROUND MY NECK AT THE MOMENT...
...YOU HAVE NOTHING TO FEAR.
HEH.
......
VERY WELL.
SINCE YOU HAVE THE HONOUR OF BEING THE GREATEST OF EVILS TO APPEAR "BEFORE I GET TO WORK," LET ME WARN YOU.
TON (TOK)

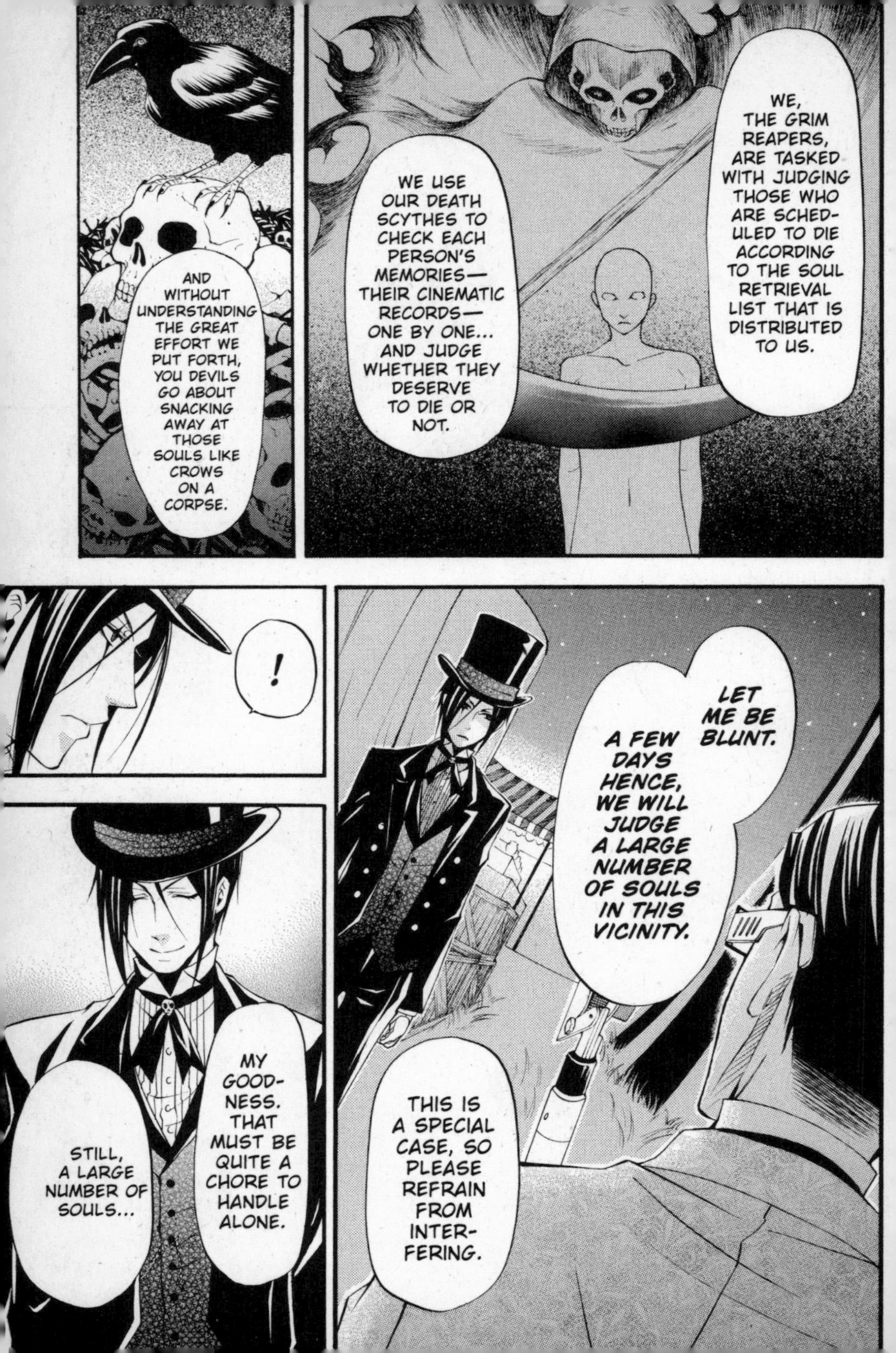
WE, THE GRIM REAPERS, ARE TASKED WITH JUDGING THOSE WHO ARE SCHED-ULED TO DIE ACCORDING TO THE SOUL RETRIEVAL LIST THAT IS DISTRIBUTED TO US.
WE USE OUR DEATH SCYTHES TO CHECK EACH PERSON'S MEMORIES—THEIR CINEMATIC RECORDS—ONE BY ONE... AND JUDGE WHETHER THEY DESERVE TO DIE OR NOT.
AND WITHOUT UNDERSTANDING THE GREAT EFFORT WE PUT FORTH, YOU DEVILS GO ABOUT SNACKING AWAY AT THOSE SOULS LIKE CROWS ON A CORPSE.
LET ME BE BLUNT.
A FEW DAYS HENCE, WE WILL JUDGE A LARGE NUMBER OF SOULS IN THIS VICINITY.
THIS IS A SPECIAL CASE, SO PLEASE REFRAIN FROM INTER-FERING.
!
MY GOOD-NESS. THAT MUST BE QUITE A CHORE TO HANDLE ALONE.
STILL, A LARGE NUMBER OF SOULS...

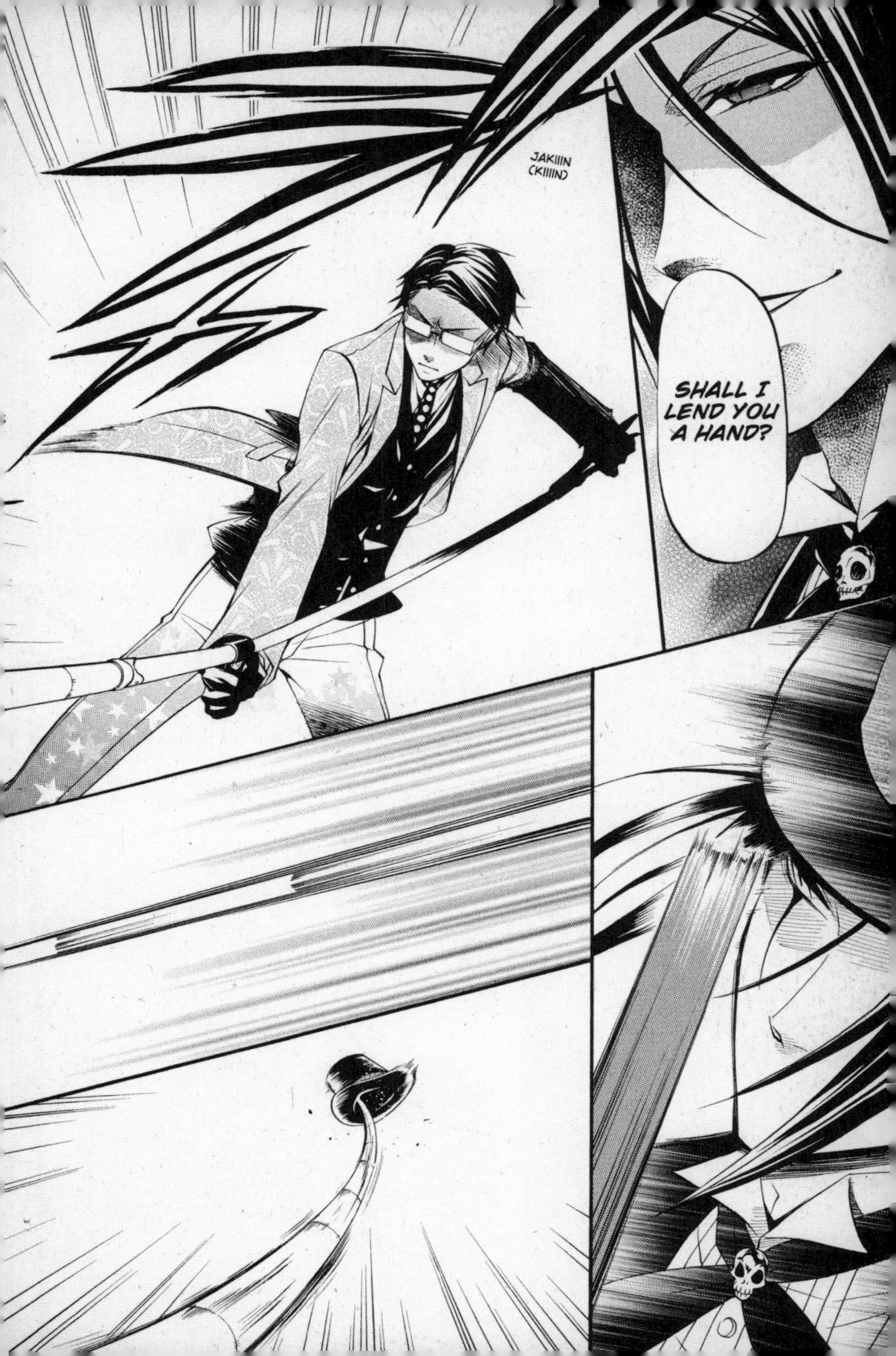
SHALL I LEND YOU A HAND?
JAKIIIN (KIIIN)

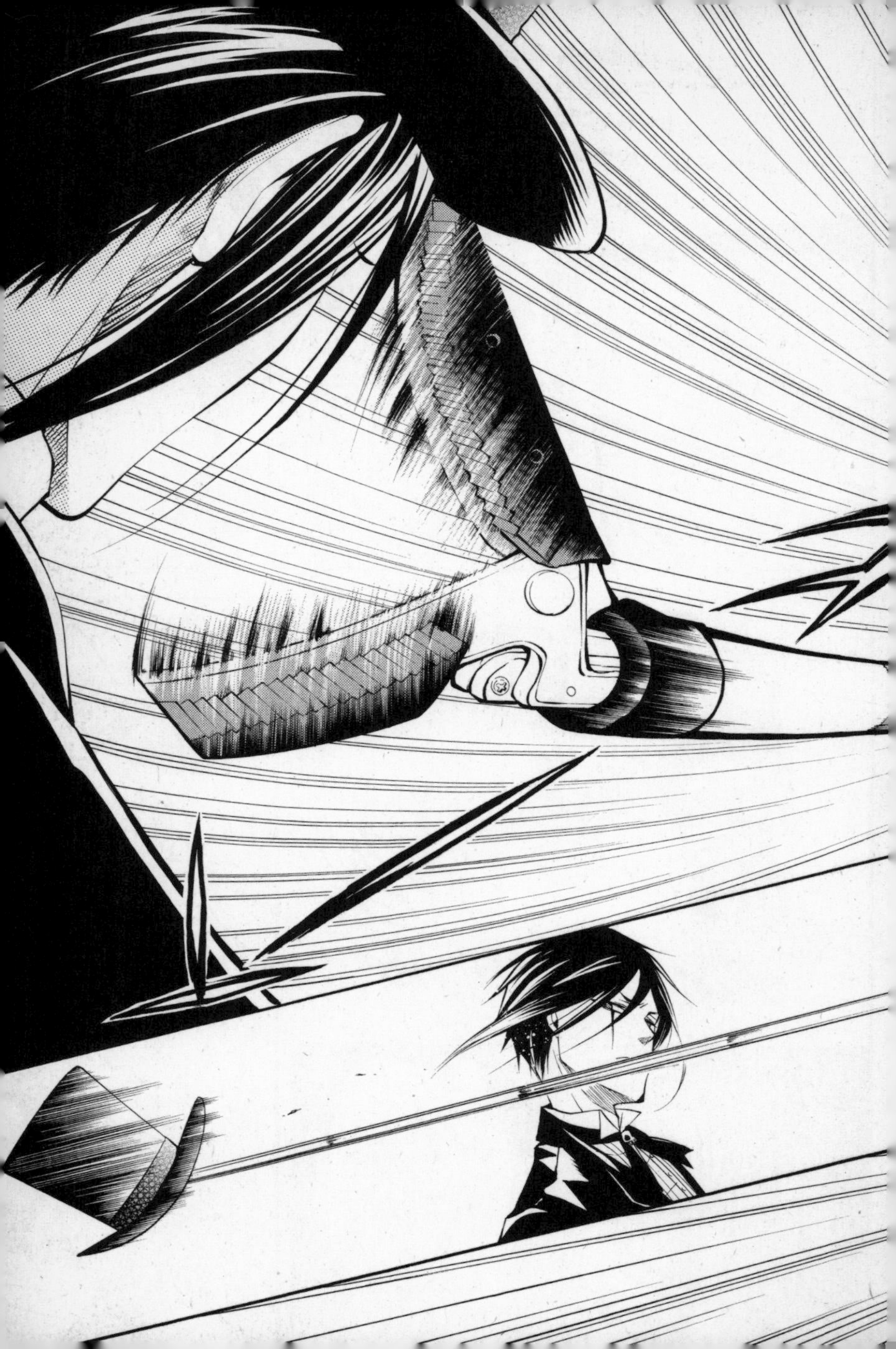

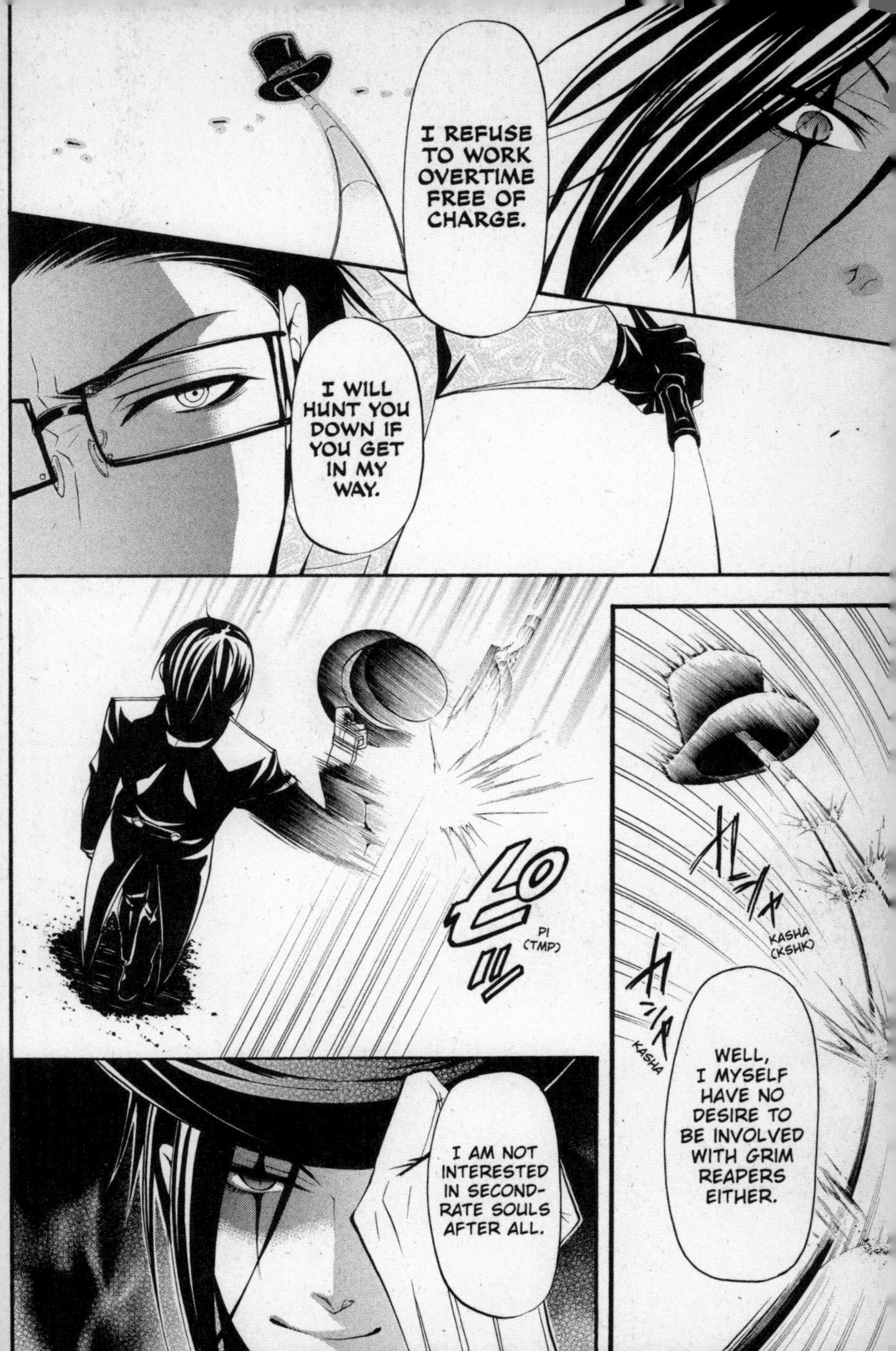
I REFUSE TO WORK OVERTIME FREE OF CHARGE.
I WILL HUNT YOU DOWN IF YOU GET IN MY WAY.
KASHA (KSHK)
KASHA
WELL, I MYSELF HAVE NO DESIRE TO BE INVOLVED WITH GRIM REAPERS EITHER.
PI (TMP)
I AM NOT INTERESTED IN SECOND-RATE SOULS AFTER ALL.

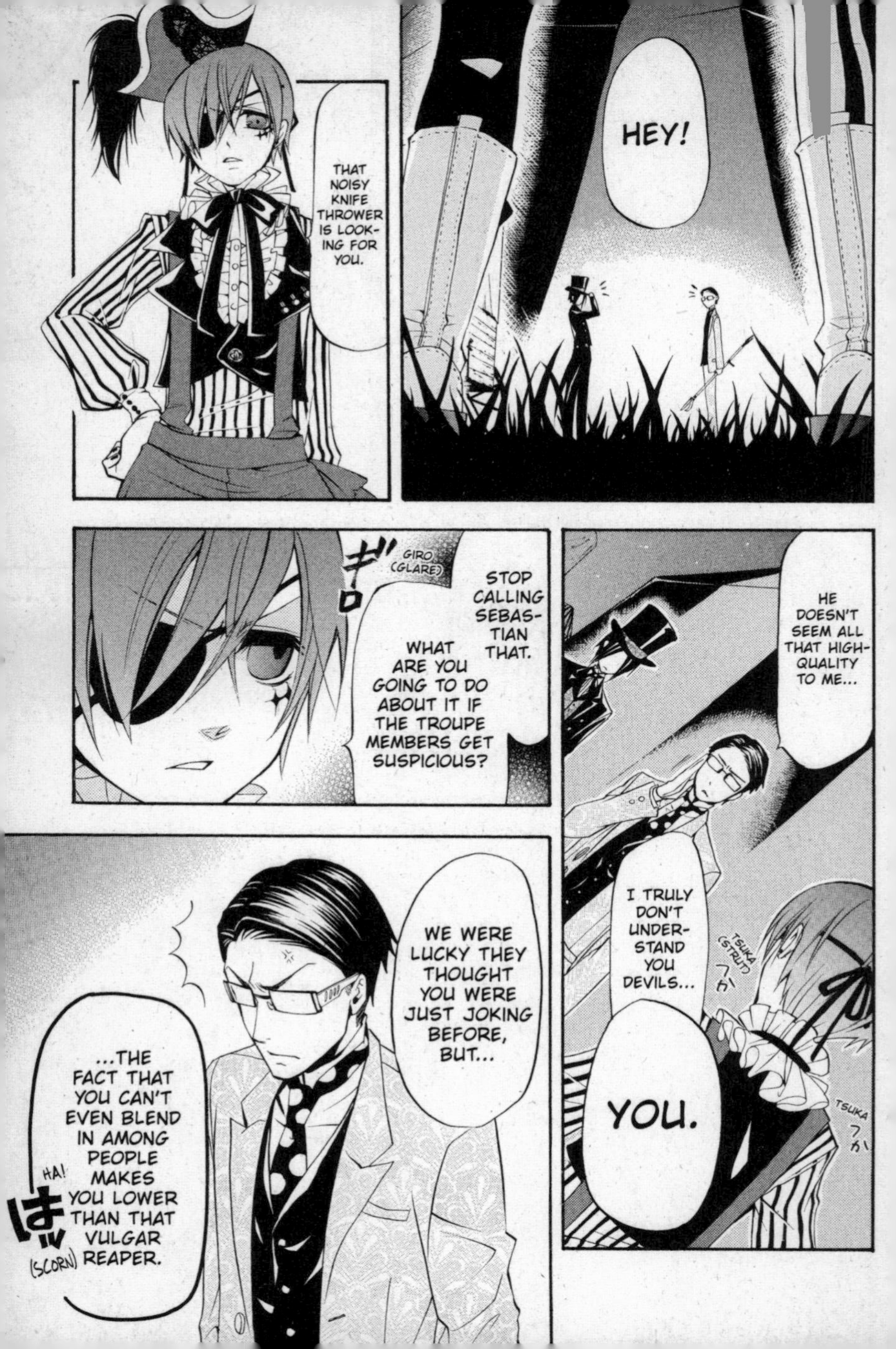

HEY!
THAT NOISY KNIFE THROWER IS LOOKING FOR YOU.
HE DOESN'T SEEM ALL THAT HIGH-QUALITY TO ME...
I TRULY DON'T UNDERSTAND YOU DEVILS...
TSUKA (STRUT)
YOU.
TSUKA
GIRO (GLARE)
STOP CALLING SEBASTIAN THAT.
WHAT ARE YOU GOING TO DO ABOUT IT IF THE TROUPE MEMBERS GET SUSPICIOUS?
WE WERE LUCKY THEY THOUGHT YOU WERE JUST JOKING BEFORE, BUT...
...THE FACT THAT YOU CAN'T EVEN BLEND IN AMONG PEOPLE MAKES YOU LOWER THAN THAT VULGAR REAPER.
HA! (SCORN)

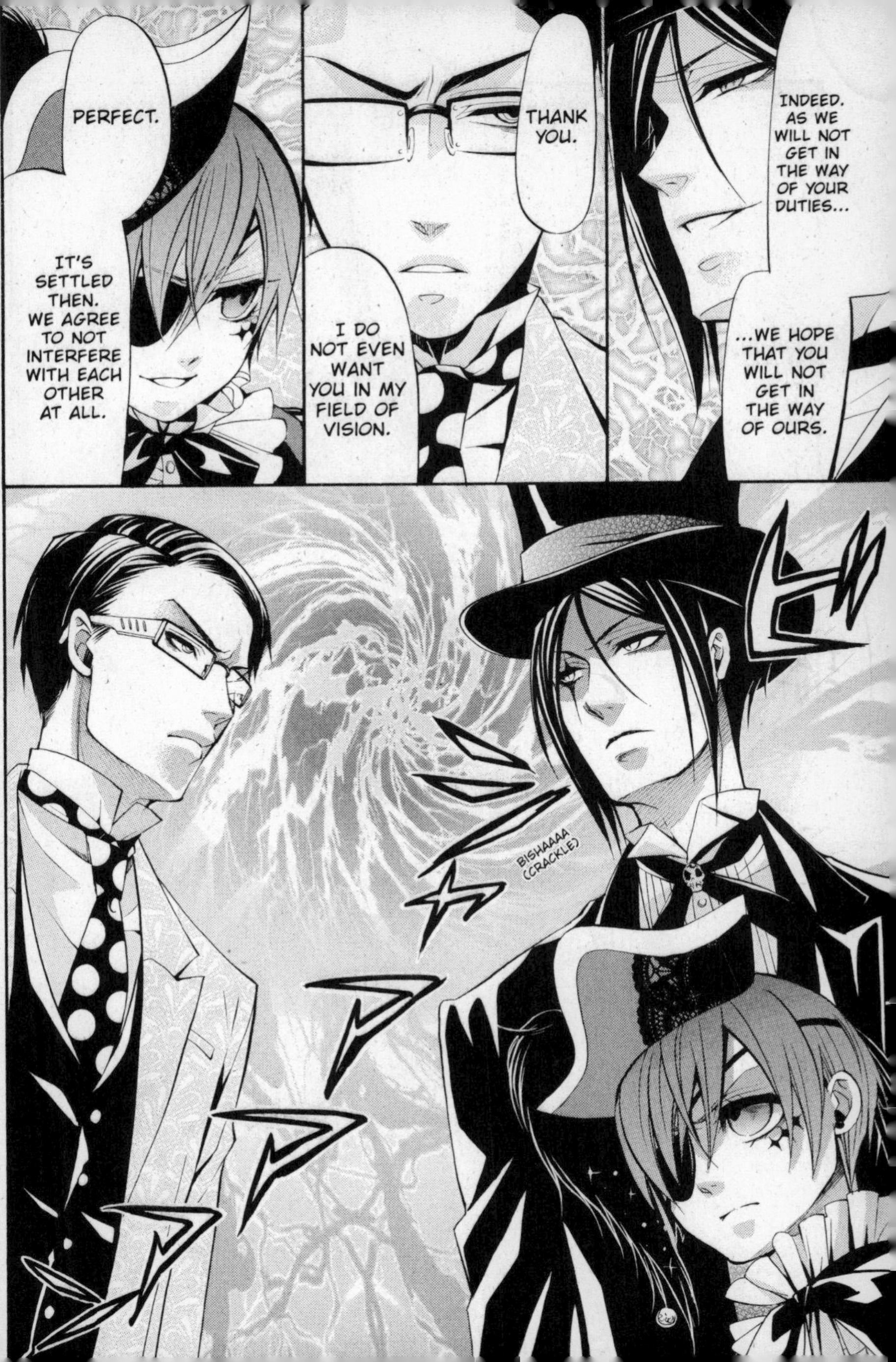
INDEED. AS WE WILL NOT GET IN THE WAY OF YOUR DUTIES...
...WE HOPE THAT YOU WILL NOT GET IN THE WAY OF OURS.
THANK YOU.
I DO NOT EVEN WANT YOU IN MY FIELD OF VISION.
PERFECT.
IT'S SETTLED THEN. WE AGREE TO NOT INTERFERE WITH EACH OTHER AT ALL.
BISHAAAA (CRACKLE)

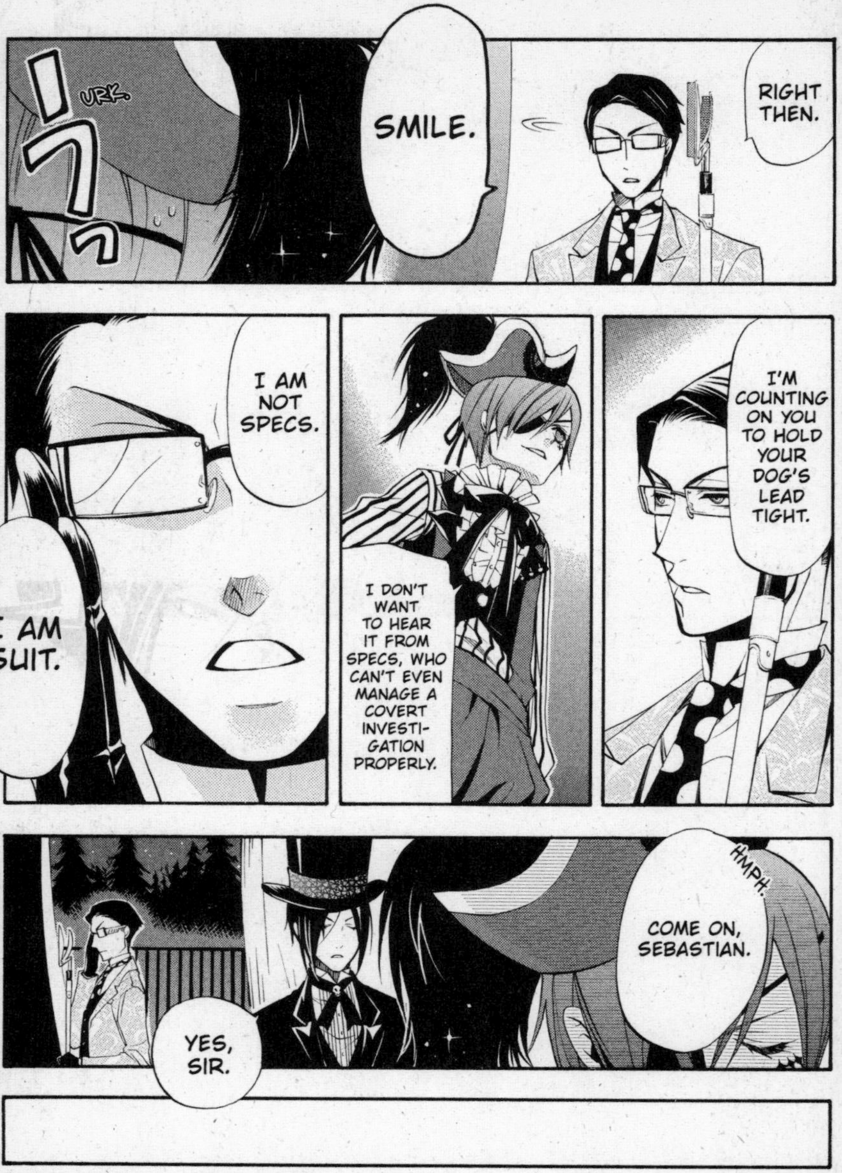
RIGHT THEN.
SMILE.
URK.
I'M COUNTING ON YOU TO HOLD YOUR DOG'S LEAD TIGHT.
I DON'T WANT TO HEAR IT FROM SPECS, WHO CAN'T EVEN MANAGE A COVERT INVESTI-GATION PROPERLY.
I AM NOT SPECS.
I AM SUIT.
HMPH.
COME ON, SEBASTIAN.
YES, SIR.

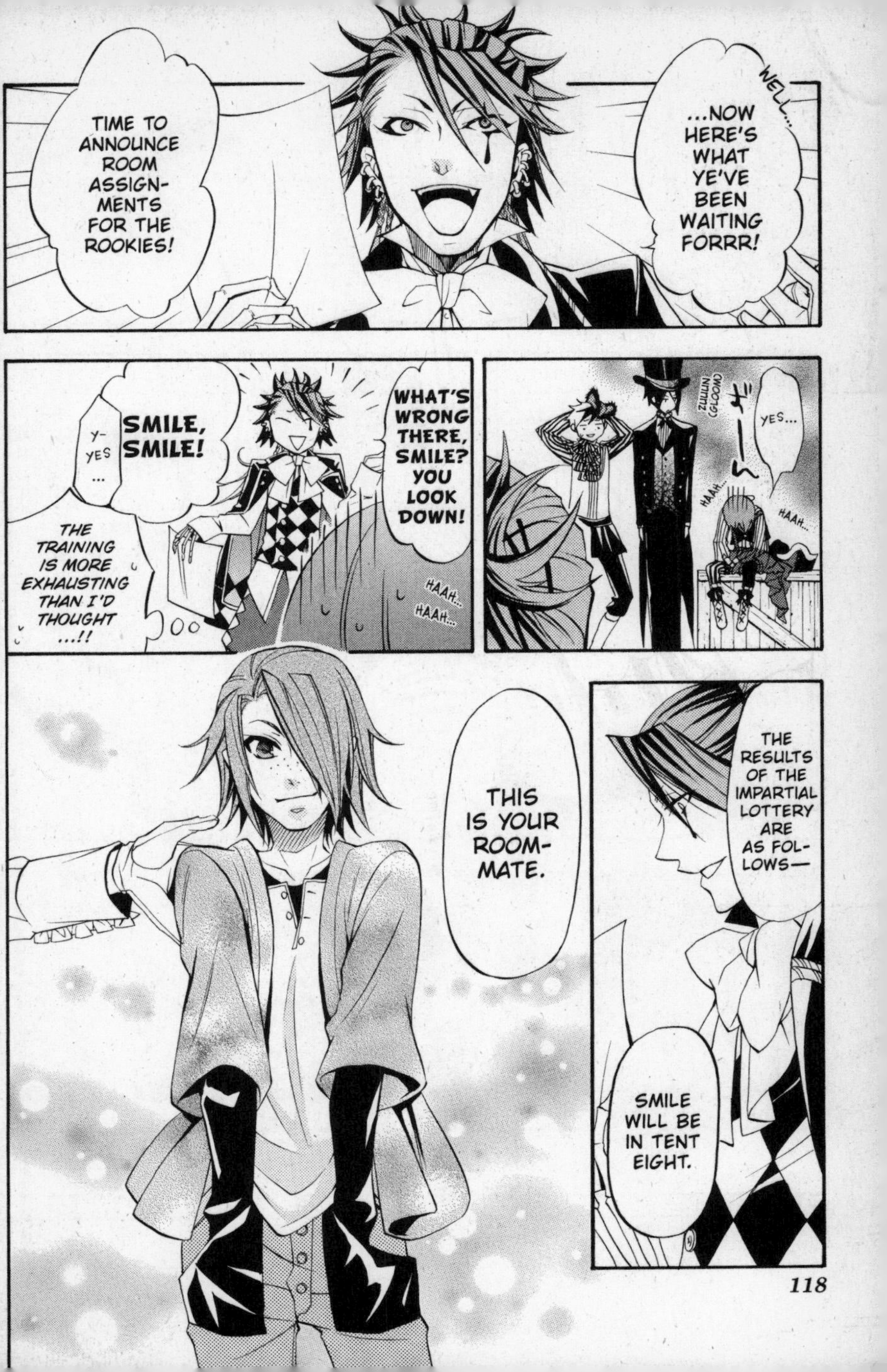
WELL...
...NOW HERE'S WHAT YE'VE BEEN WAITING FORRR!
TIME TO ANNOUNCE ROOM ASSIGN-MENTS FOR THE ROOKIES!
ZUUUN (GLOOM)
YES...
HAAH... HAAH...
WHAT'S WRONG THERE, SMILE? YOU LOOK DOWN!
SMILE, SMILE!
Y-YES...
THE TRAINING IS MORE EXHAUSTING THAN I'D THOUGHT ...!!
HAAH... HAAH...
THE RESULTS OF THE IMPARTIAL LOTTERY ARE AS FOL-LOWS—
SMILE WILL BE IN TENT EIGHT.
THIS IS YOUR ROOM-MATE.

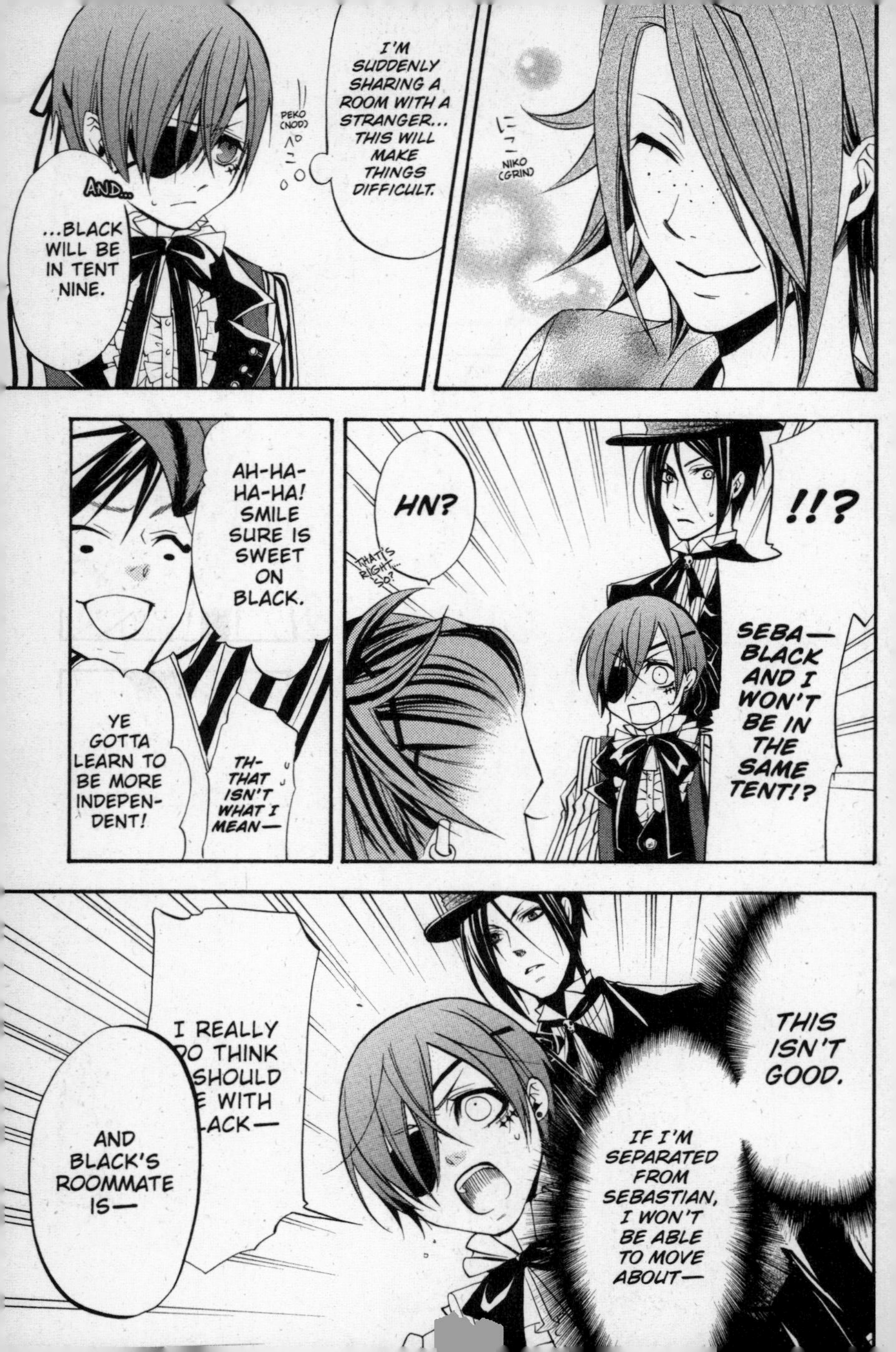
NIKO (GRIN)
I'M SUDDENLY SHARING A ROOM WITH A STRANGER... THIS WILL MAKE THINGS DIFFICULT.
PEKO (NOD)
AND...
...BLACK WILL BE IN TENT NINE.
!!?
SEBA— BLACK AND I WON'T BE IN THE SAME TENT!?
HN?
THAT'S RIGHT... SO?
AH-HA-HA-HA! SMILE SURE IS SWEET ON BLACK.
TH-THAT ISN'T WHAT I MEAN—
YE GOTTA LEARN TO BE MORE INDEPENDENT!
THIS ISN'T GOOD.
IF I'M SEPARATED FROM SEBASTIAN, I WON'T BE ABLE TO MOVE ABOUT—
I REALLY DO THINK SHOULD E WITH LACK—
AND BLACK'S ROOMMATE IS—

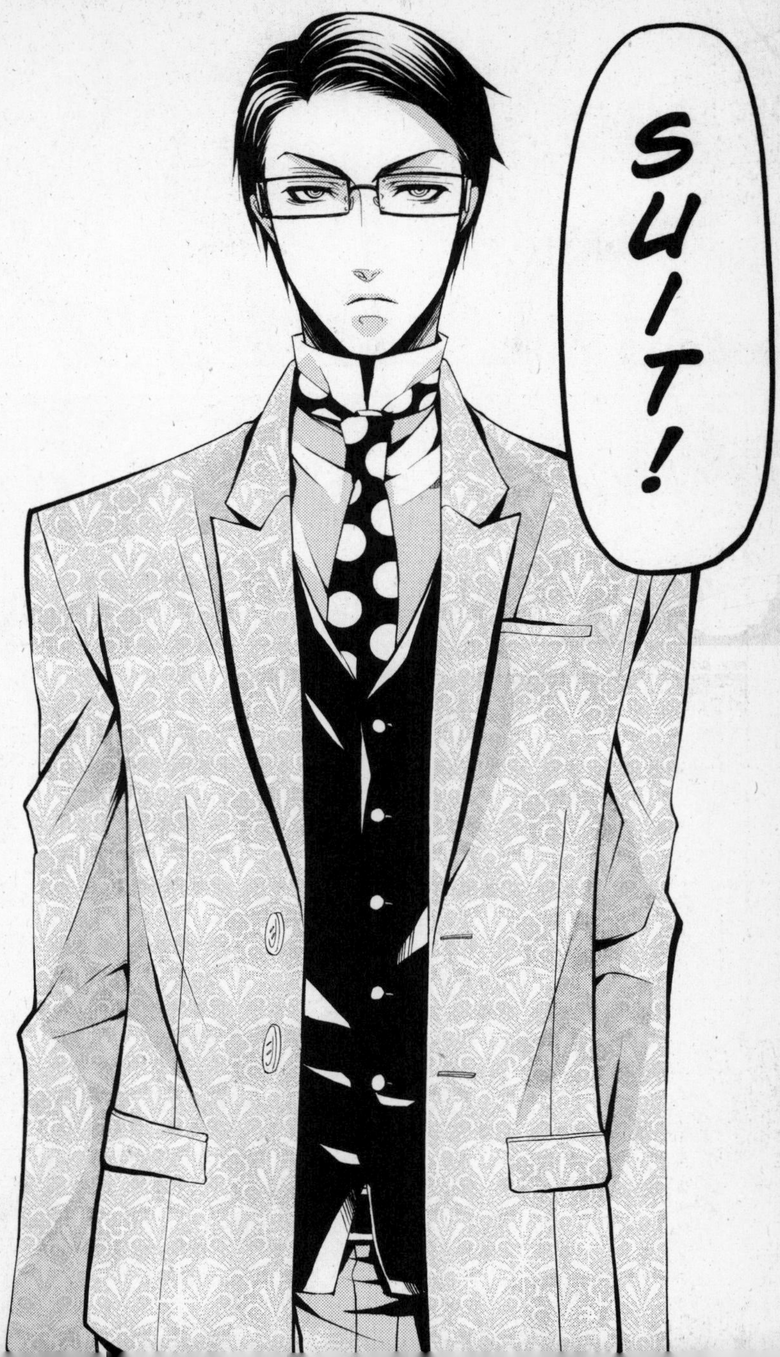
SUIT!

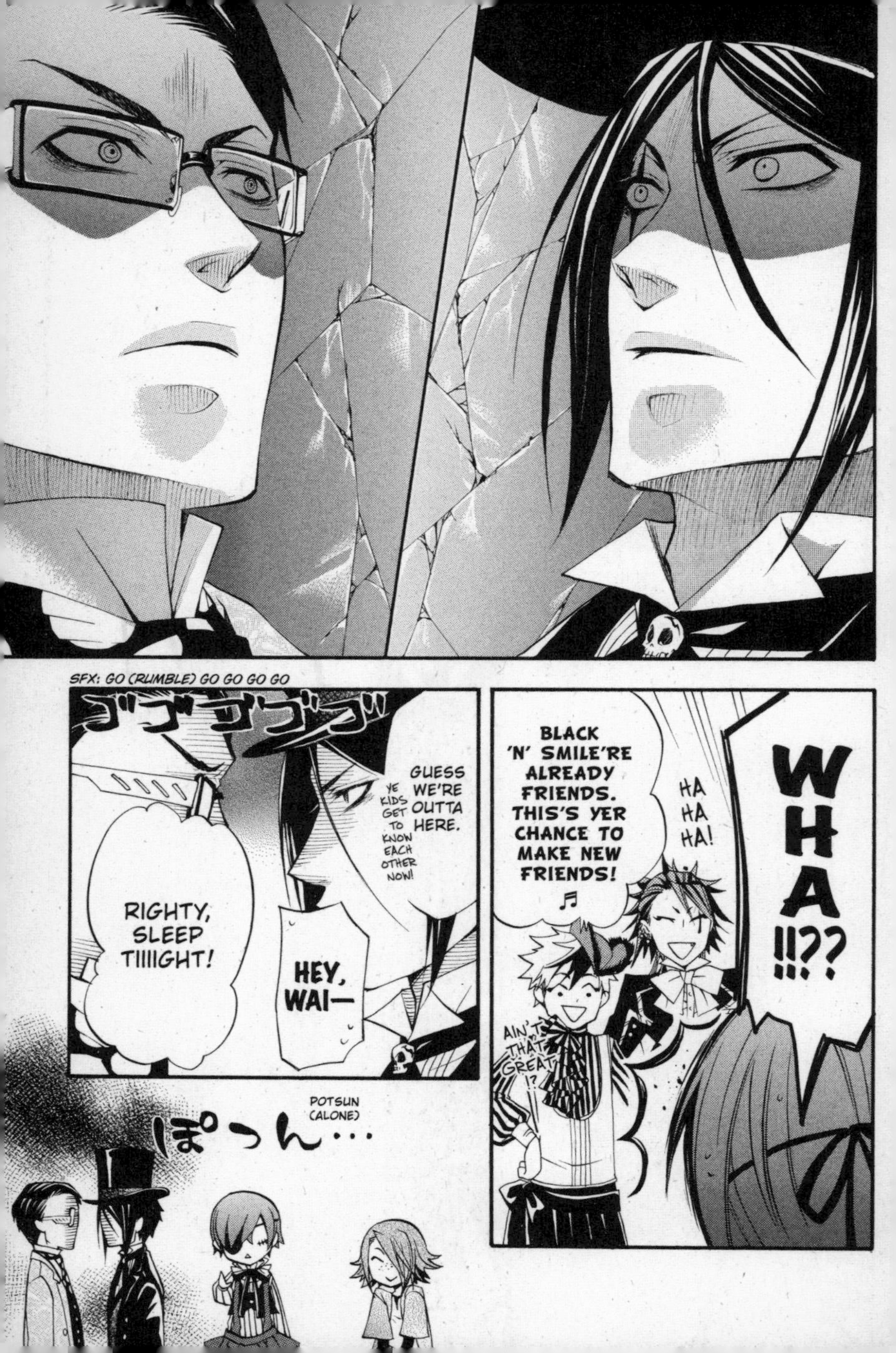
WHA!!??
HA HA HA!
BLACK 'N' SMILE'RE ALREADY FRIENDS. THIS'S YER CHANCE TO MAKE NEW FRIENDS! ♬
AIN'T THAT GREAT!?
SFX: GO (RUMBLE) GO GO GO GO
ゴゴゴゴゴ
GUESS WE'RE OUTTA HERE.
YE KIDS GET TO KNOW EACH OTHER NOW!
HEY, WAI—
RIGHTY, SLEEP TIIIIGHT!
POTSUN (ALONE)
ぽつん…

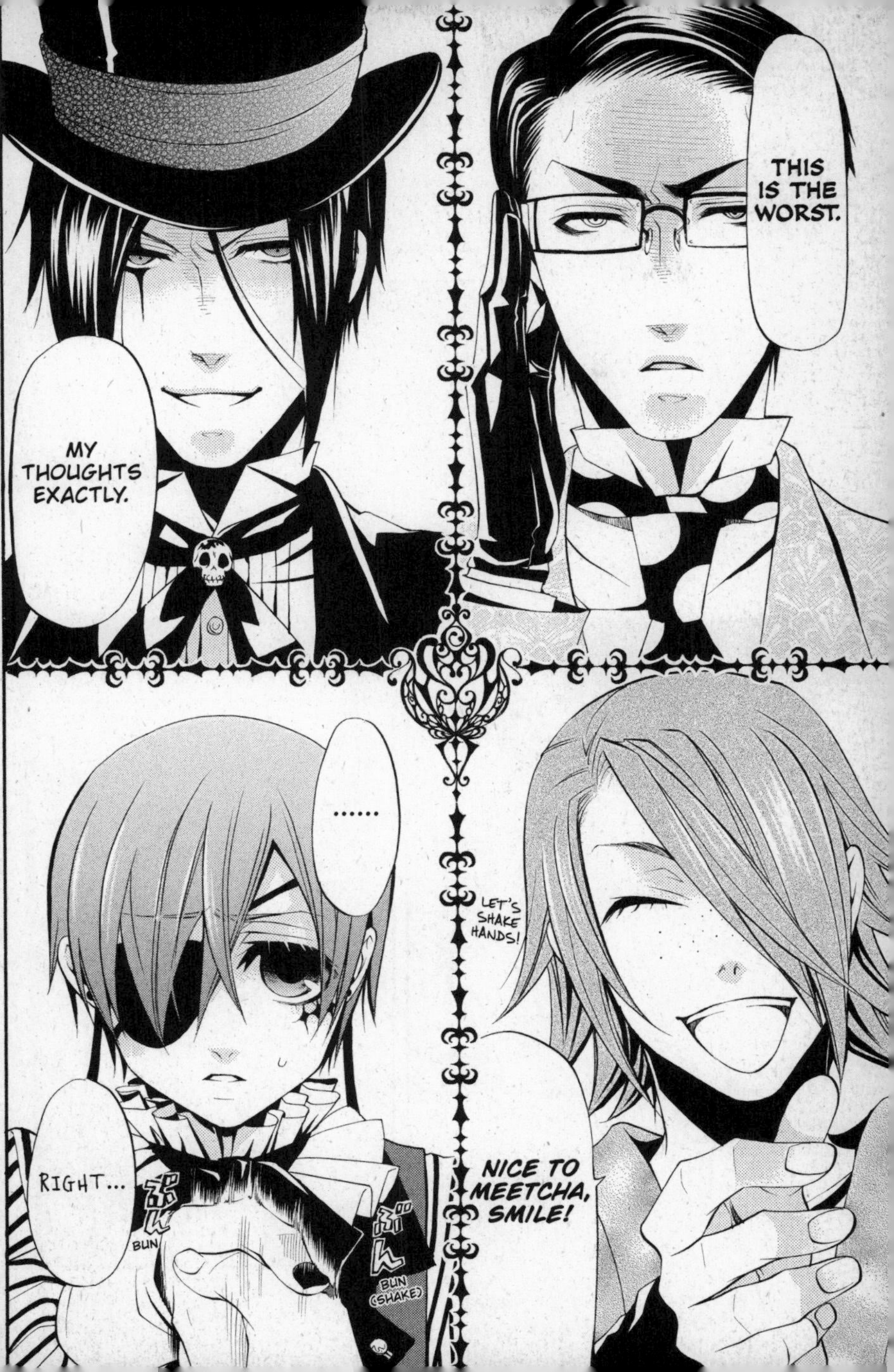
THIS IS THE WORST.
MY THOUGHTS EXACTLY.
LET'S SHAKE HANDS!
NICE TO MEETCHA, SMILE!
......
RIGHT...
BUN (SHAKE)
BUN

Black Butler

Chapter 27

At midnight : The Butler, Performs

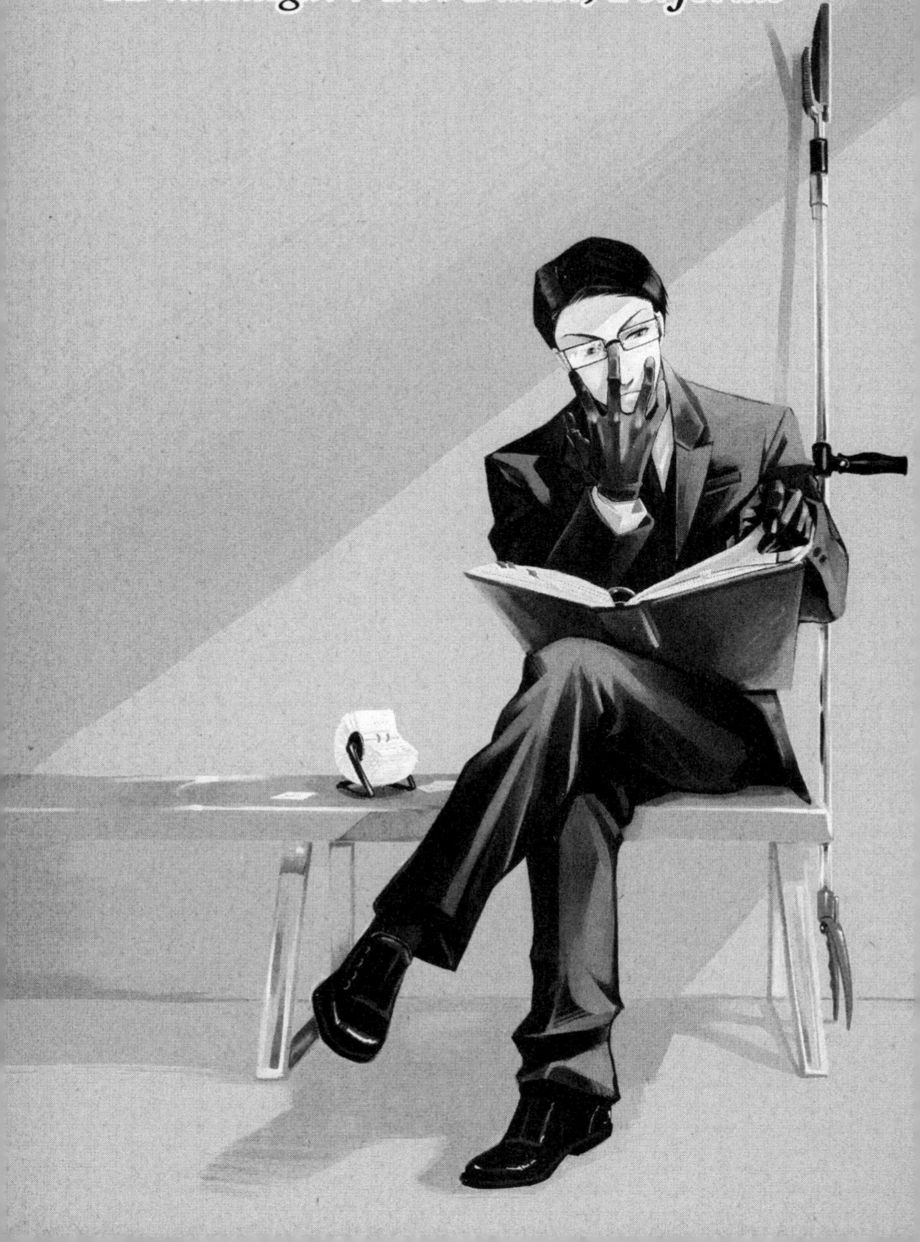

Black Butler

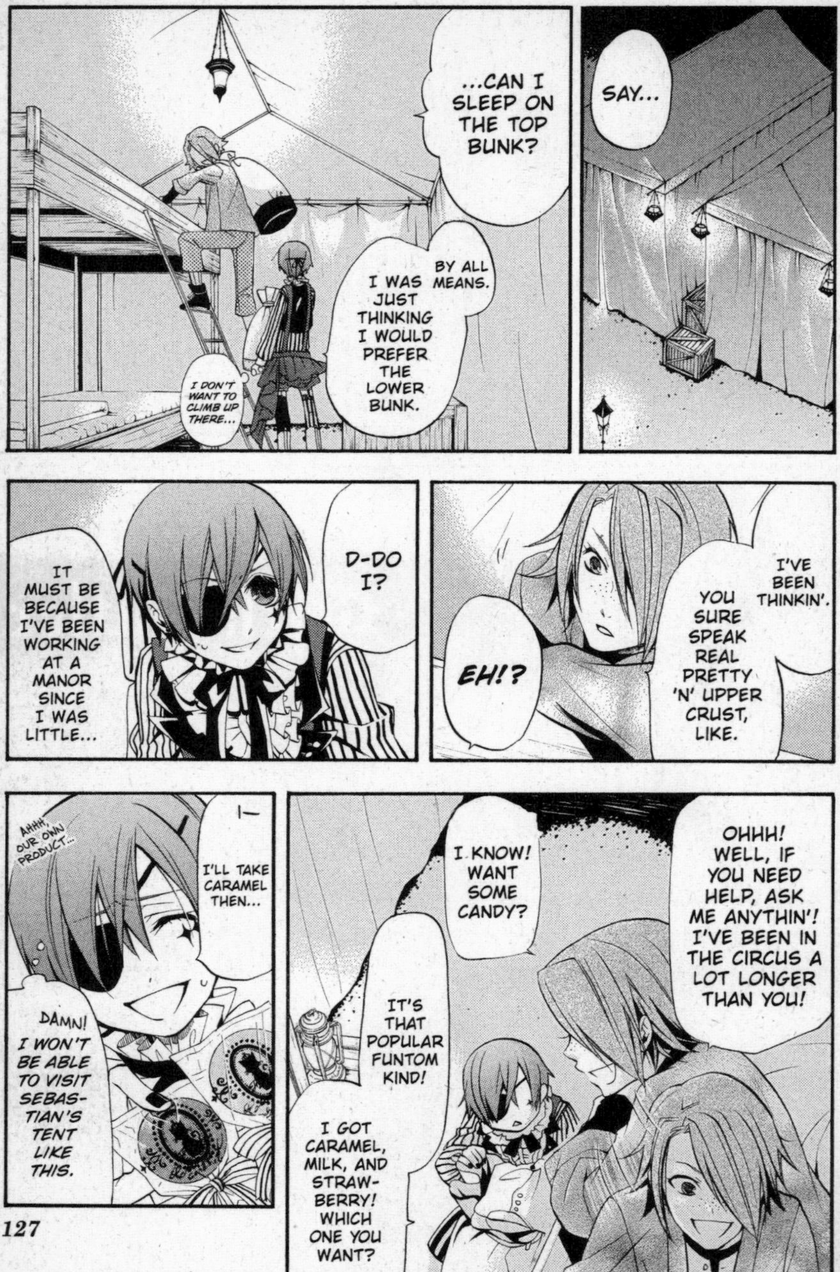
SAY...
...CAN I SLEEP ON THE TOP BUNK?
BY ALL MEANS. I WAS JUST THINKING I WOULD PREFER THE LOWER BUNK.
I DON'T WANT TO CLIMB UP THERE...
I'VE BEEN THINKIN'.
YOU SURE SPEAK REAL PRETTY 'N' UPPER CRUST, LIKE.
EH!?
D-DO I?
IT MUST BE BECAUSE I'VE BEEN WORKING AT A MANOR SINCE I WAS LITTLE...
OHHH! WELL, IF YOU NEED HELP, ASK ME ANYTHIN'! I'VE BEEN IN THE CIRCUS A LOT LONGER THAN YOU!
I KNOW! WANT SOME CANDY?
IT'S THAT POPULAR FUNTOM KIND!
I GOT CARAMEL, MILK, AND STRAW-BERRY! WHICH ONE YOU WANT?
I—
I'LL TAKE CARAMEL THEN...
AHHH, OUR OWN PRODUCT...
DAMN! I WON'T BE ABLE TO VISIT SEBAS-TIAN'S TENT LIKE THIS.

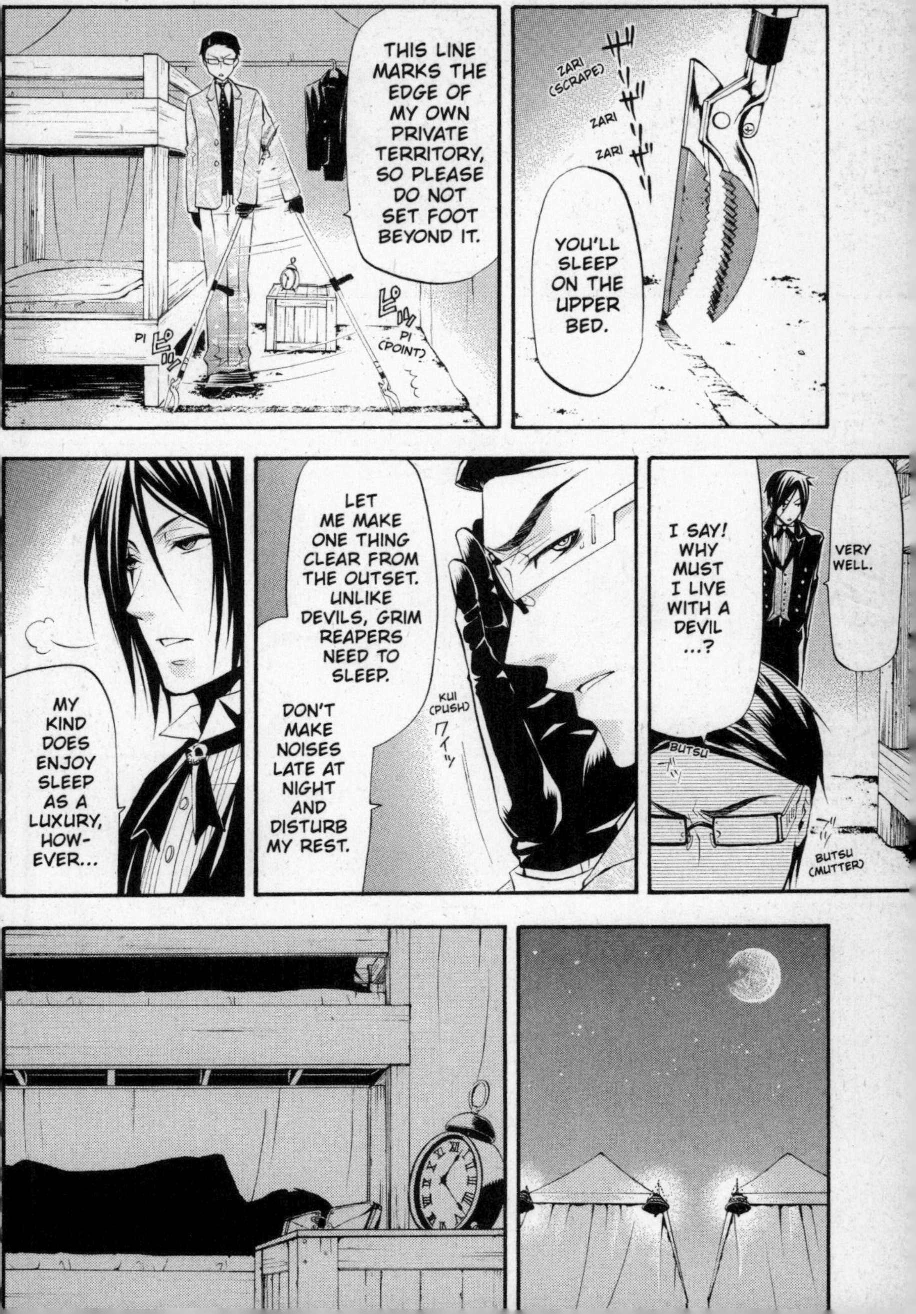
ZARI (SCRAPE)
ZARI
ZARI
YOU'LL SLEEP ON THE UPPER BED.
THIS LINE MARKS THE EDGE OF MY OWN PRIVATE TERRITORY, SO PLEASE DO NOT SET FOOT BEYOND IT.
PI (POINT)
PI
VERY WELL.
I SAY! WHY MUST I LIVE WITH A DEVIL ...?
BUTSU
BUTSU (MUTTER)
LET ME MAKE ONE THING CLEAR FROM THE OUTSET. UNLIKE DEVILS, GRIM REAPERS NEED TO SLEEP.
KUI (PUSH)
DON'T MAKE NOISES LATE AT NIGHT AND DISTURB MY REST.
MY KIND DOES ENJOY SLEEP AS A LUXURY, HOWEVER...

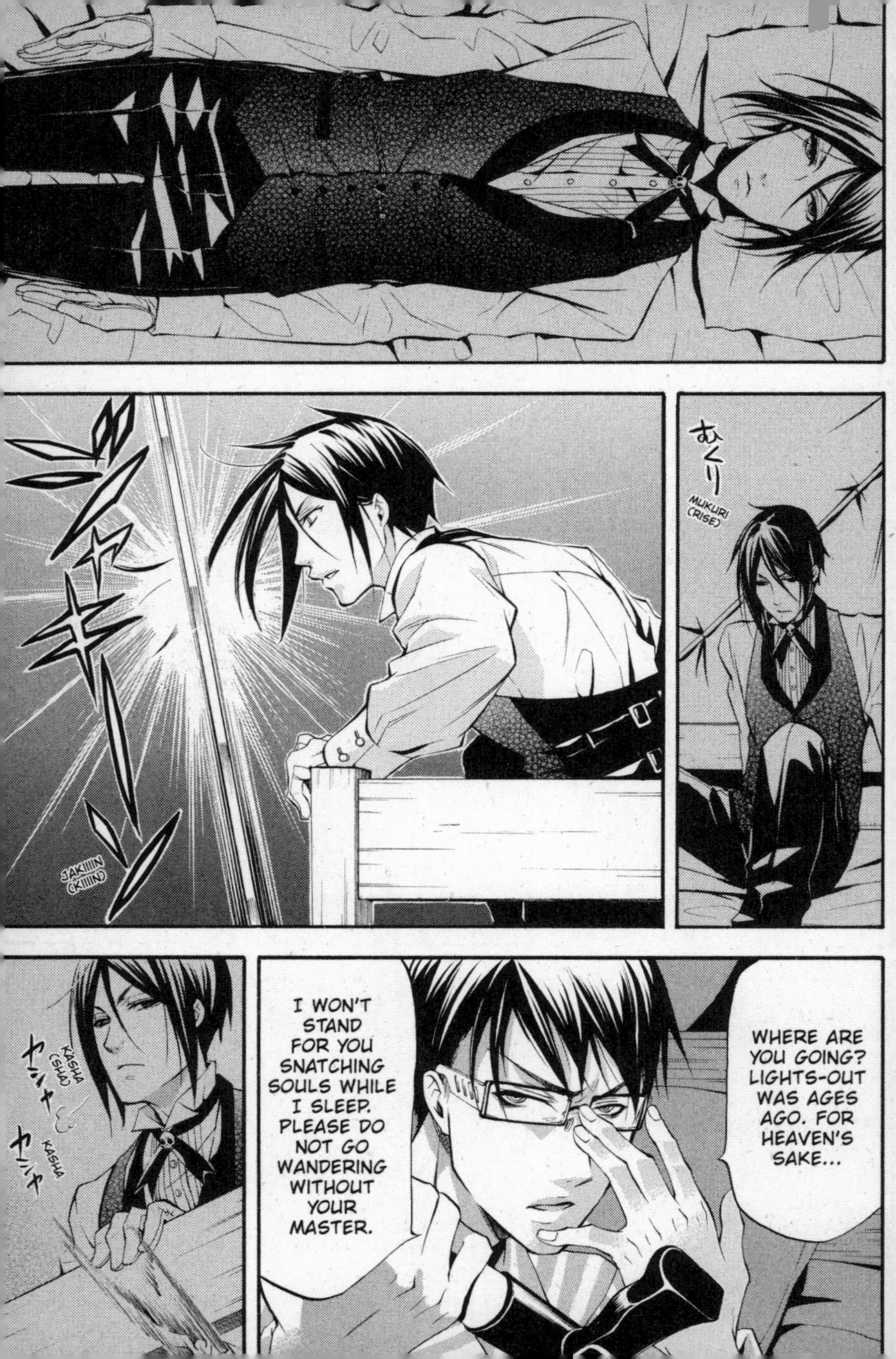

むくり
MUKURI (RISE)
JAKIIIN (KIIIN)
WHERE ARE YOU GOING? LIGHTS-OUT WAS AGES AGO. FOR HEAVEN'S SAKE...
I WON'T STAND FOR YOU SNATCHING SOULS WHILE I SLEEP. PLEASE DO NOT GO WANDERING WITHOUT YOUR MASTER.
KASHA (SHA)
KASHA

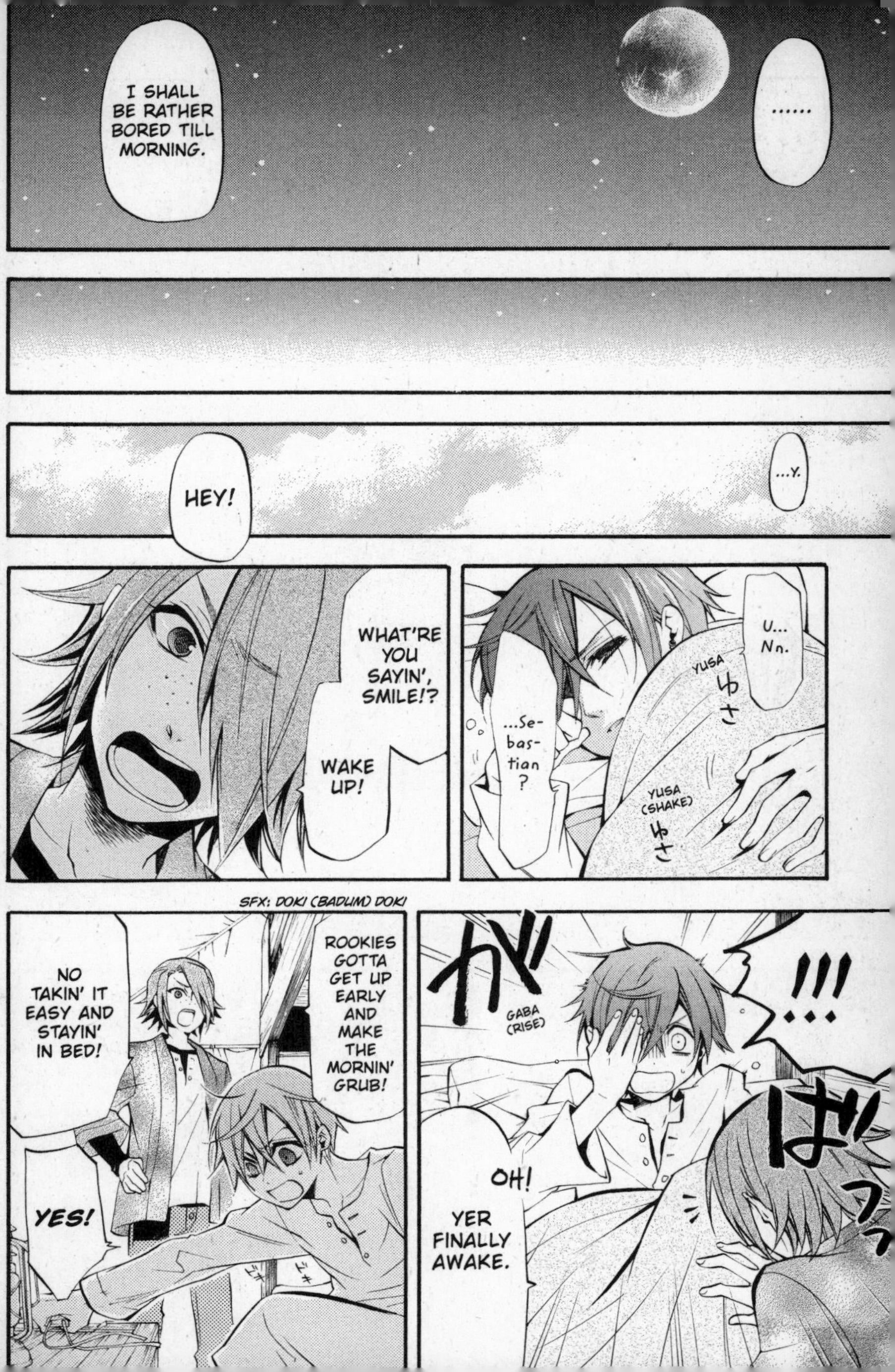
......
I SHALL BE RATHER BORED TILL MORNING.
...Y.
HEY!
U... Nn.
YUSA
ゆさ
...Se-bas-tian?
YUSA (SHAKE)
ゆさ
WHAT'RE YOU SAYIN', SMILE!?
WAKE UP!
SFX: DOKI (BADUM) DOKI
!!!
GABA (RISE)
OH!
YER FINALLY AWAKE.
ROOKIES GOTTA GET UP EARLY AND MAKE THE MORNIN' GRUB!
NO TAKIN' IT EASY AND STAYIN' IN BED!
YES!

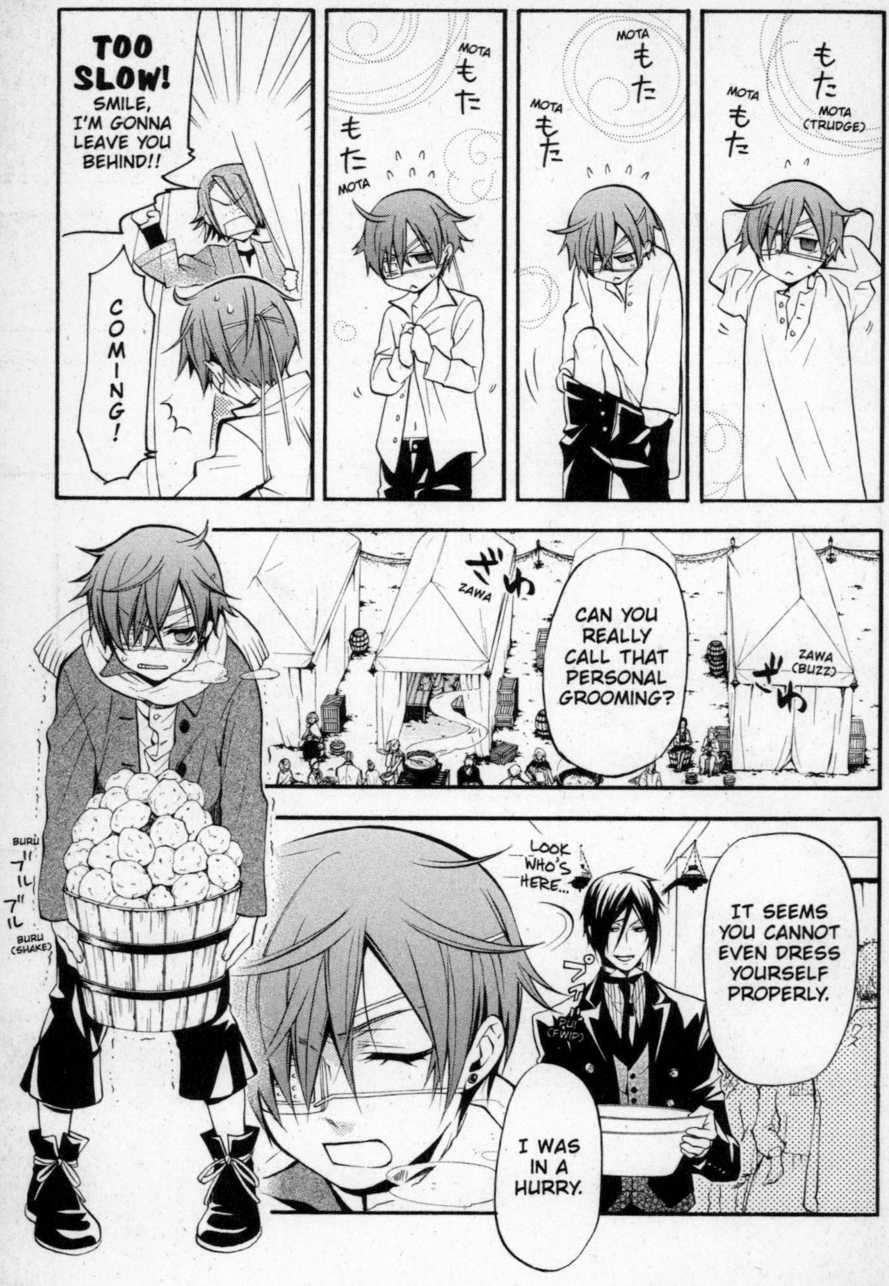

もた
MOTA (TRUDGE)
MOTA もた
MOTA もた
MOTA もた
MOTA もた
もた MOTA
TOO SLOW! SMILE, I'M GONNA LEAVE YOU BEHIND!!
COMING!
ざわ ZAWA
CAN YOU REALLY CALL THAT PERSONAL GROOMING?
ZAWA (BUZZ) ざわ
IT SEEMS YOU CANNOT EVEN DRESS YOURSELF PROPERLY.
LOOK WHO'S HERE...
PUI (FWIP)
I WAS IN A HURRY.
BURU ブル ブル BURU (SHAKE)

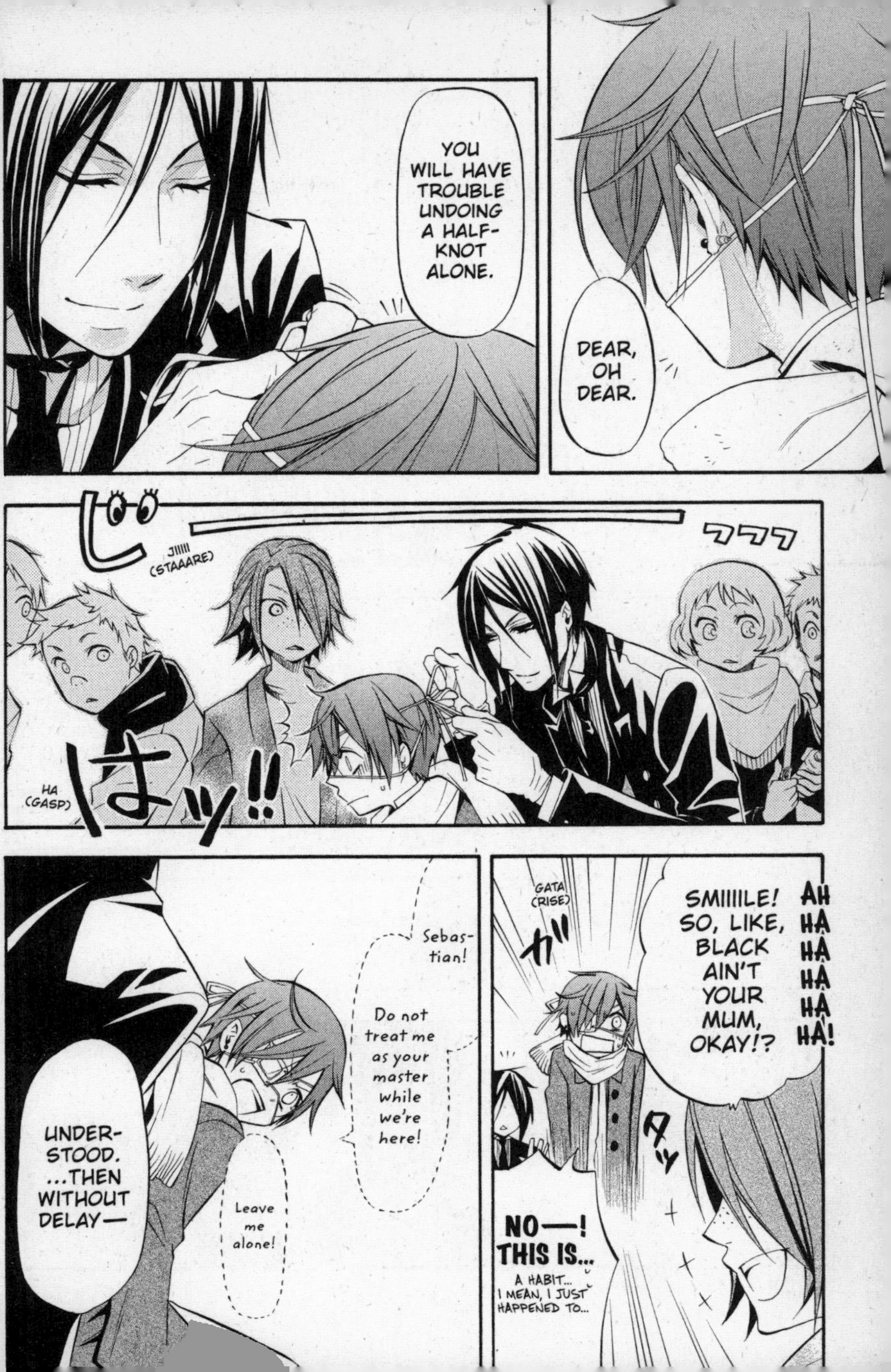

DEAR, OH DEAR.
YOU WILL HAVE TROUBLE UNDOING A HALF-KNOT ALONE.
フフフ
じー
JIIII (STAAARE)
はッ!!
HA (GASP)
AH HA HA HA HA HA!
SMIIIILE! SO, LIKE, BLACK AIN'T YOUR MUM, OKAY!?
ガ
GATA (RISE)
NO—! THIS IS...
A HABIT... I MEAN, I JUST HAPPENED TO...
Sebastian!
Do not treat me as your master while we're here!
Leave me alone!
UNDERSTOOD. ...THEN WITHOUT DELAY—

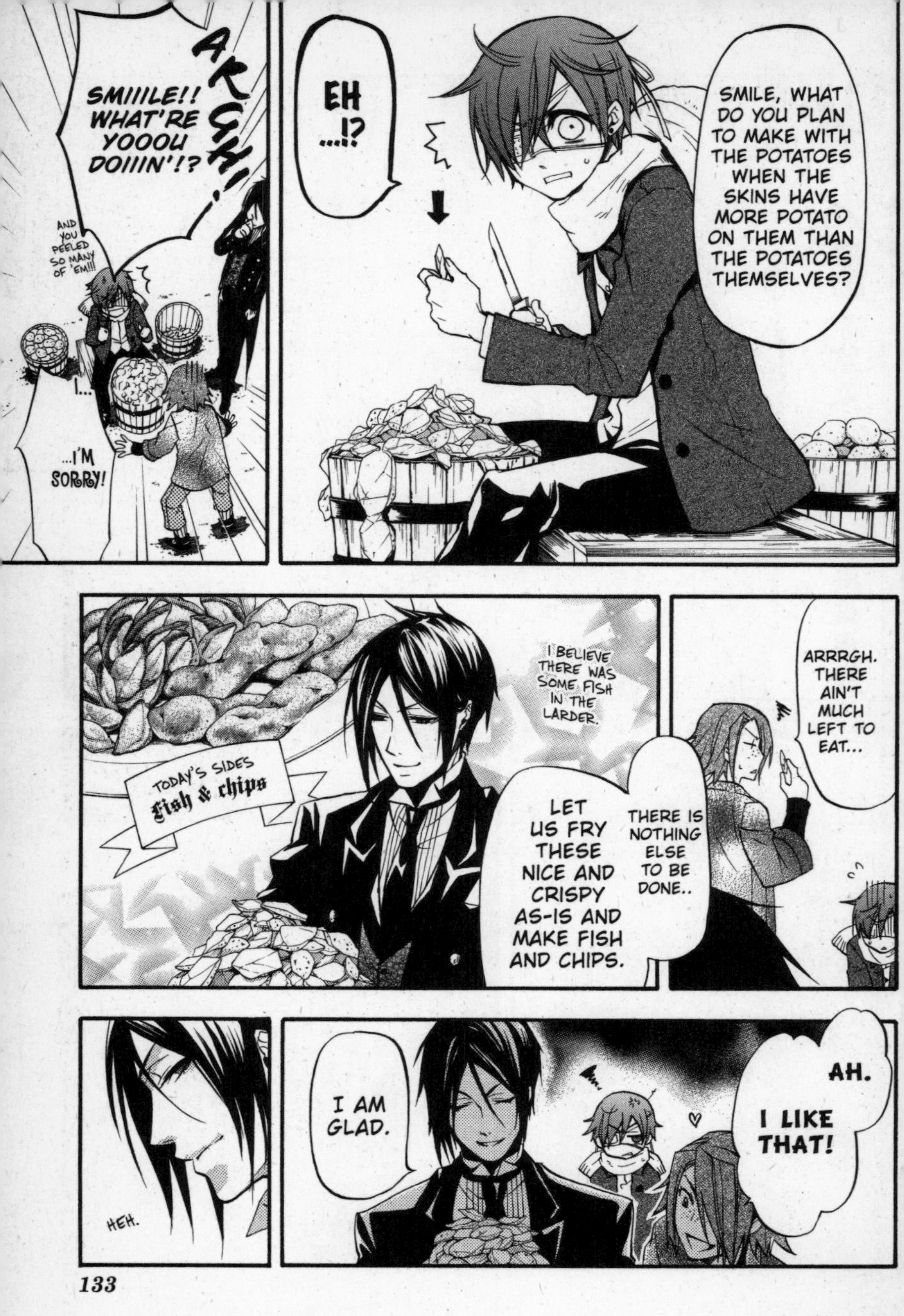
SMILE, WHAT DO YOU PLAN TO MAKE WITH THE POTATOES WHEN THE SKINS HAVE MORE POTATO ON THEM THAN THE POTATOES THEMSELVES?
EH ...!?
ARGH!
SMIIILE!! WHAT'RE YOOOU DOIIIN'!?
AND YOU PEELED SO MANY OF 'EM!!!
I...
...I'M SORRY!
ARRRGH. THERE AIN'T MUCH LEFT TO EAT...
I BELIEVE THERE WAS SOME FISH IN THE LARDER.
THERE IS NOTHING ELSE TO BE DONE..
LET US FRY THESE NICE AND CRISPY AS-IS AND MAKE FISH AND CHIPS.
TODAY'S SIDES
fish & chips
AH.
I LIKE THAT!
I AM GLAD.
HEH.

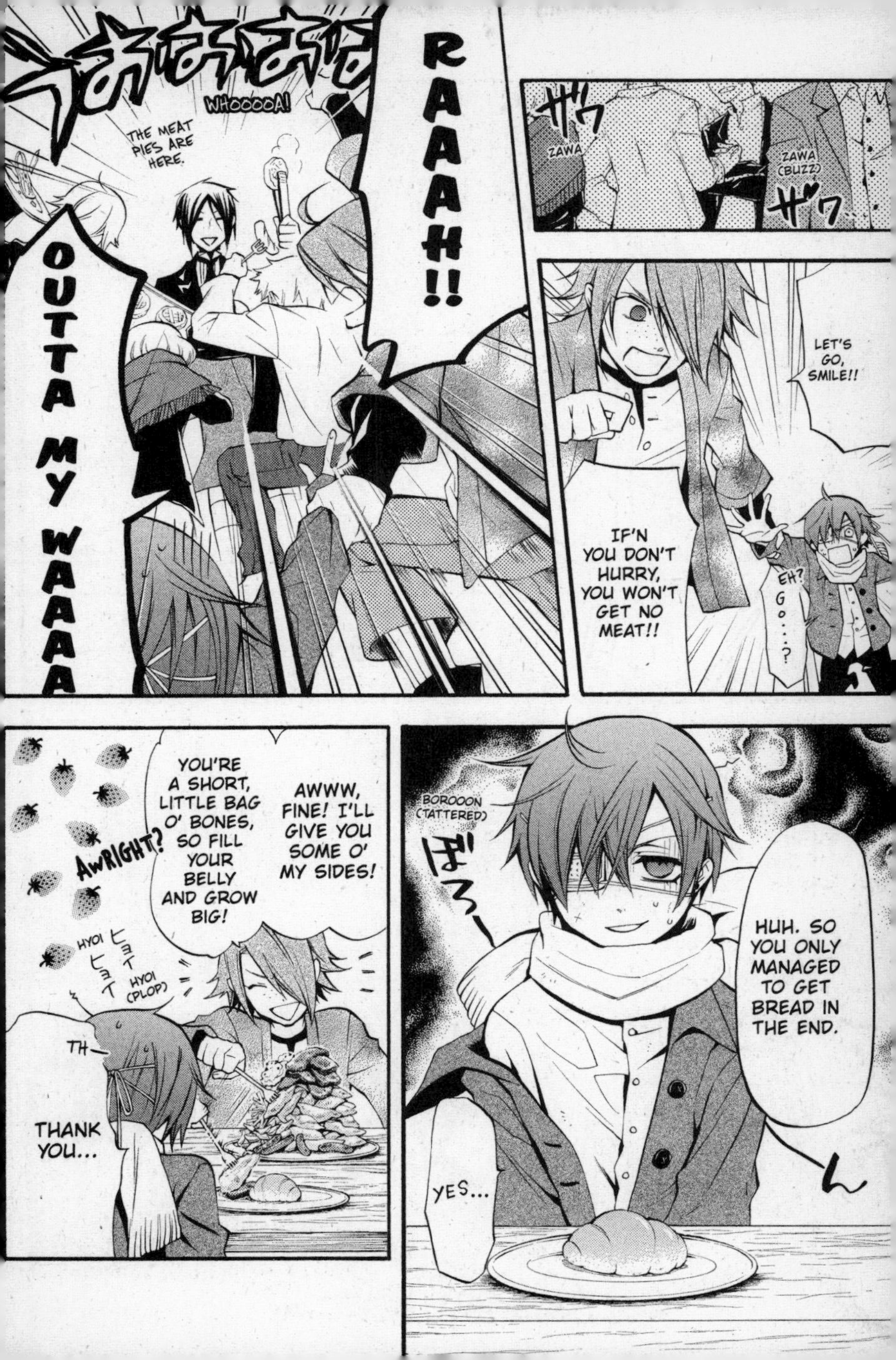
ザワ
ZAWA
ZAWA (BUZZ)
ザワ
LET'S GO, SMILE!!
IF'N YOU DON'T HURRY, YOU WON'T GET NO MEAT!!
EH? Go...?
WHOOOOA!
THE MEAT PIES ARE HERE.
RAAAAH!!
OUTTA MY WAAAAA
BOROOON (TATTERED)
ぼろ
HUH. SO YOU ONLY MANAGED TO GET BREAD IN THE END.
ん
YES...
YOU'RE A SHORT, LITTLE BAG O' BONES, SO FILL YOUR BELLY AND GROW BIG!
AWRIGHT?
AWWW, FINE! I'LL GIVE YOU SOME O' MY SIDES!
HYOI ヒョイ
ヒョイ HYOI (PLOP)
TH—
THANK YOU...

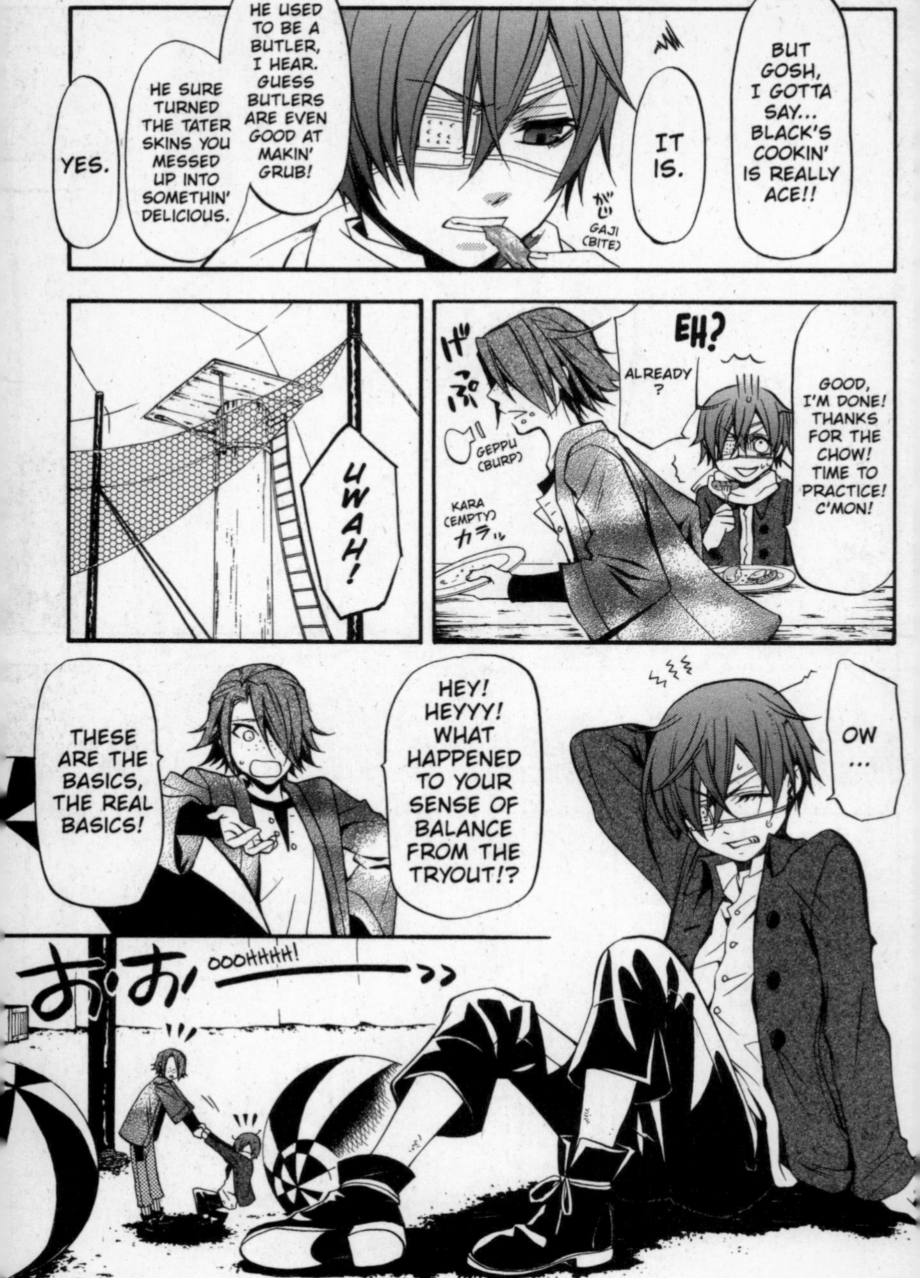

BUT GOSH, I GOTTA SAY... BLACK'S COOKIN' IS REALLY ACE!!
IT IS.
がじ
GAJI (BITE)
HE USED TO BE A BUTLER, I HEAR. GUESS BUTLERS ARE EVEN GOOD AT MAKIN' GRUB!
HE SURE TURNED THE TATER SKINS YOU MESSED UP INTO SOMETHIN' DELICIOUS.
YES.
GOOD, I'M DONE! THANKS FOR THE CHOW! TIME TO PRACTICE! C'MON!
EH?
ALREADY?
げぷ
GEPPU (BURP)
KARA (EMPTY) カラッ
UWAH!
OW...
HEY! HEYYY! WHAT HAPPENED TO YOUR SENSE OF BALANCE FROM THE TRYOUT!?
THESE ARE THE BASICS, THE REAL BASICS!
おお
OOOHHHH!

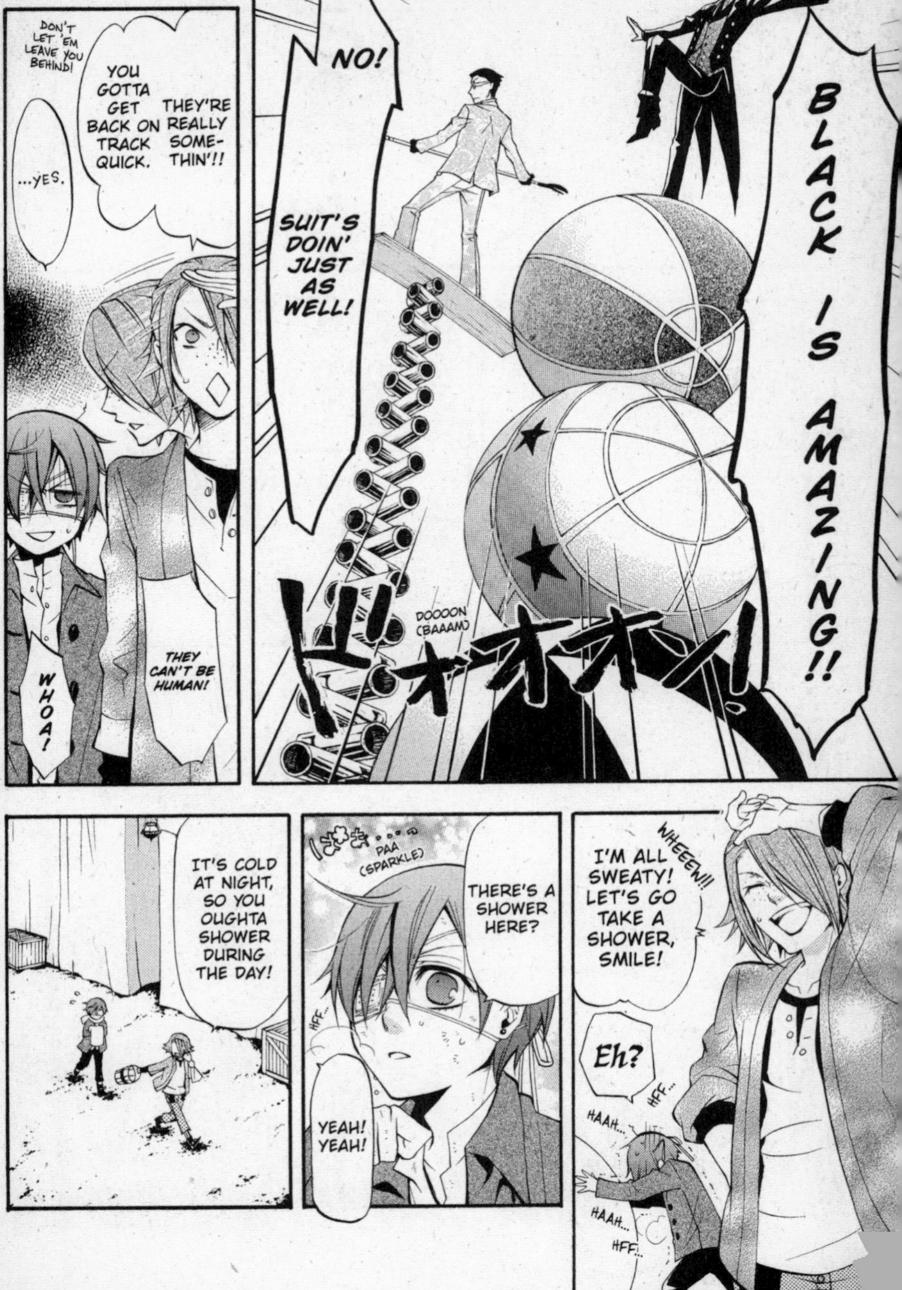
BLACK IS AMAZING!!
NO!
SUIT'S DOIN' JUST AS WELL!
DOOOON (BAAAM)
DON'T LET 'EM LEAVE YOU BEHIND!
THEY'RE REALLY SOME-THIN'!!
YOU GOTTA GET BACK ON TRACK QUICK.
...YES.
THEY CAN'T BE HUMAN!
WHOA!
WHEEEW!!
I'M ALL SWEATY! LET'S GO TAKE A SHOWER, SMILE!
Eh?
HFF...
HAAH...
HAAH...
HFF...
PAA (SPARKLE)
THERE'S A SHOWER HERE?
HFF...
YEAH! YEAH!
IT'S COLD AT NIGHT, SO YOU OUGHTA SHOWER DURING THE DAY!

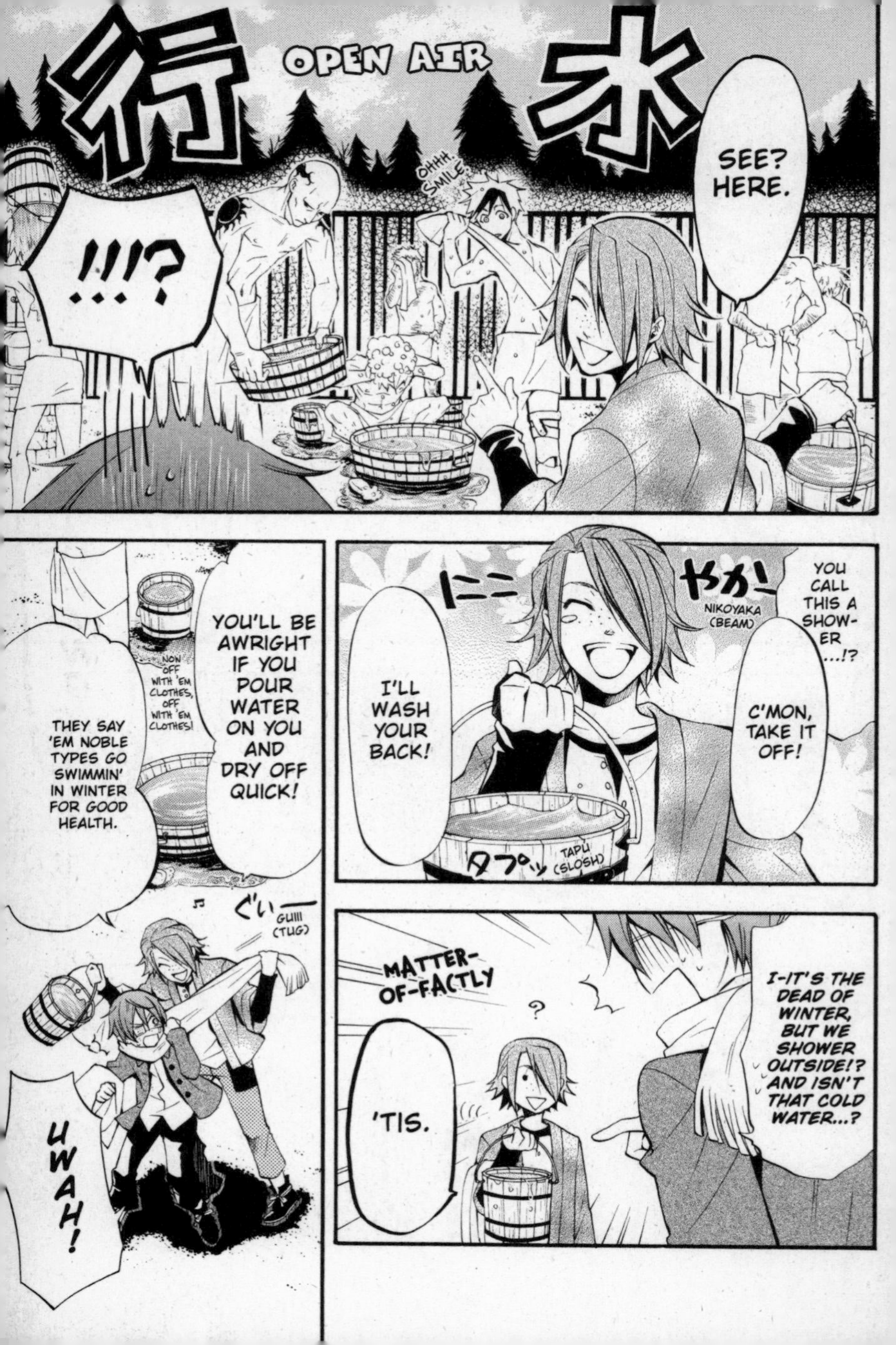
行 水
OPEN AIR
SEE? HERE.
OHHH, SMILE.
!!!?
にこー やかー
NIKOYAKA (BEAM)
YOU CALL THIS A SHOWER ...!?
C'MON, TAKE IT OFF!
I'LL WASH YOUR BACK!
タプッ
TAPU (SLOSH)
I-IT'S THE DEAD OF WINTER, BUT WE SHOWER OUTSIDE!? AND ISN'T THAT COLD WATER...?
MATTER-OF-FACTLY
?
'TIS.
YOU'LL BE AWRIGHT IF YOU POUR WATER ON YOU AND DRY OFF QUICK!
NOW OFF WITH 'EM CLOTHES, OFF WITH 'EM CLOTHES!
THEY SAY 'EM NOBLE TYPES GO SWIMMIN' IN WINTER FOR GOOD HEALTH.
ぐいー
GUIII (TUG)
UWAH!

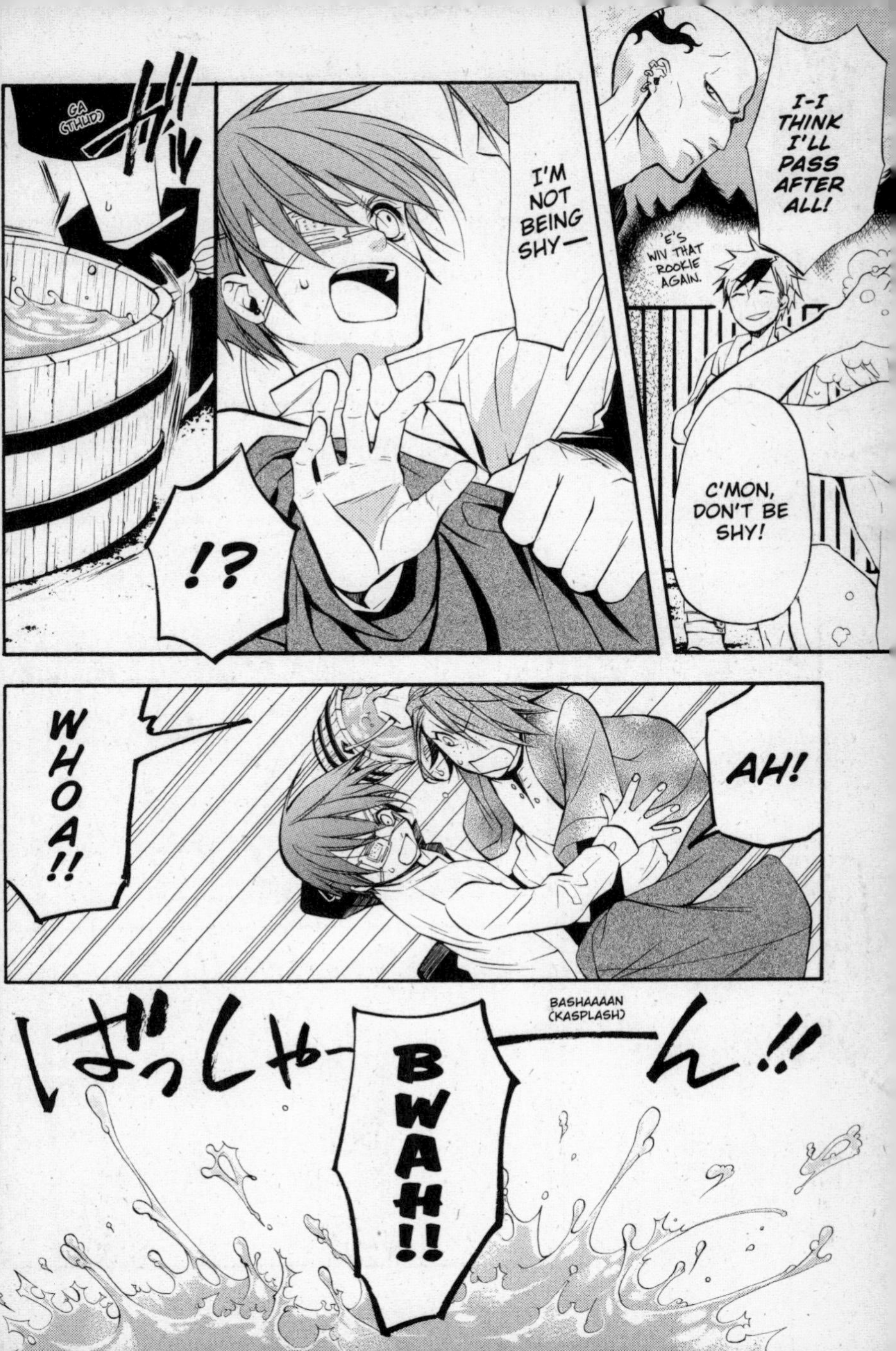
I-I THINK I'LL PASS AFTER ALL!
'E'S WIV THAT ROOKIE AGAIN.
C'MON, DON'T BE SHY!
I'M NOT BEING SHY—
!?
GA (THUD)
AH!
WHOA!!
BASHAAAAN (KASPLASH)
ばっしゃーーん!!
BWAH!!

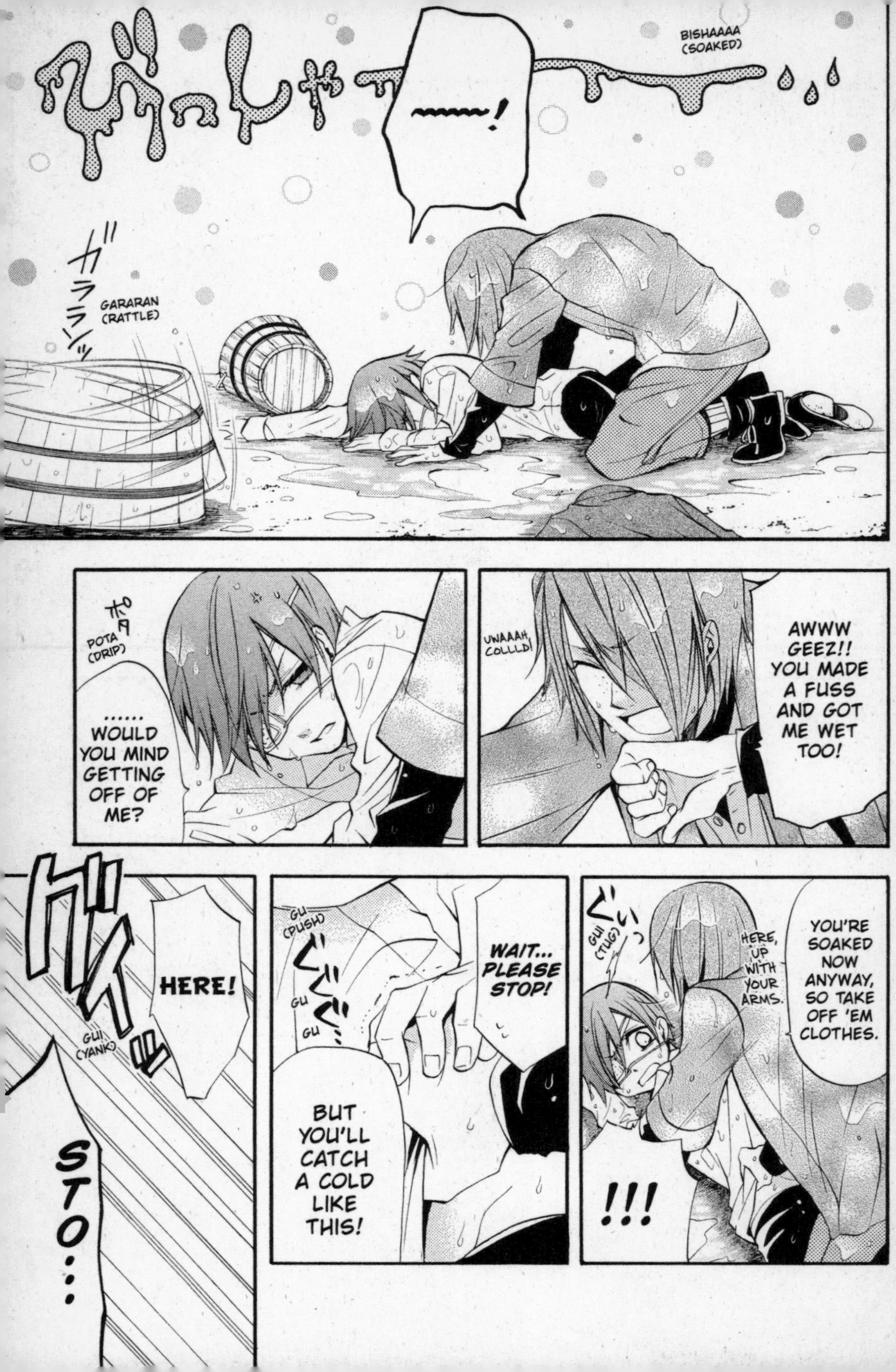
BISHAAAA (SOAKED)
——!
GARARAN (RATTLE)
AWWW GEEZ!! YOU MADE A FUSS AND GOT ME WET TOO!
UWAAAH, COLLLD!
POTA (DRIP)
......WOULD YOU MIND GETTING OFF OF ME?
YOU'RE SOAKED NOW ANYWAY, SO TAKE OFF 'EM CLOTHES.
HERE, UP WITH YOUR ARMS.
GUI (TUG)
!!!
WAIT... PLEASE STOP!
GU (PUSH)
GU
GU
BUT YOU'LL CATCH A COLD LIKE THIS!
HERE!
GUI (YANK)
STO...

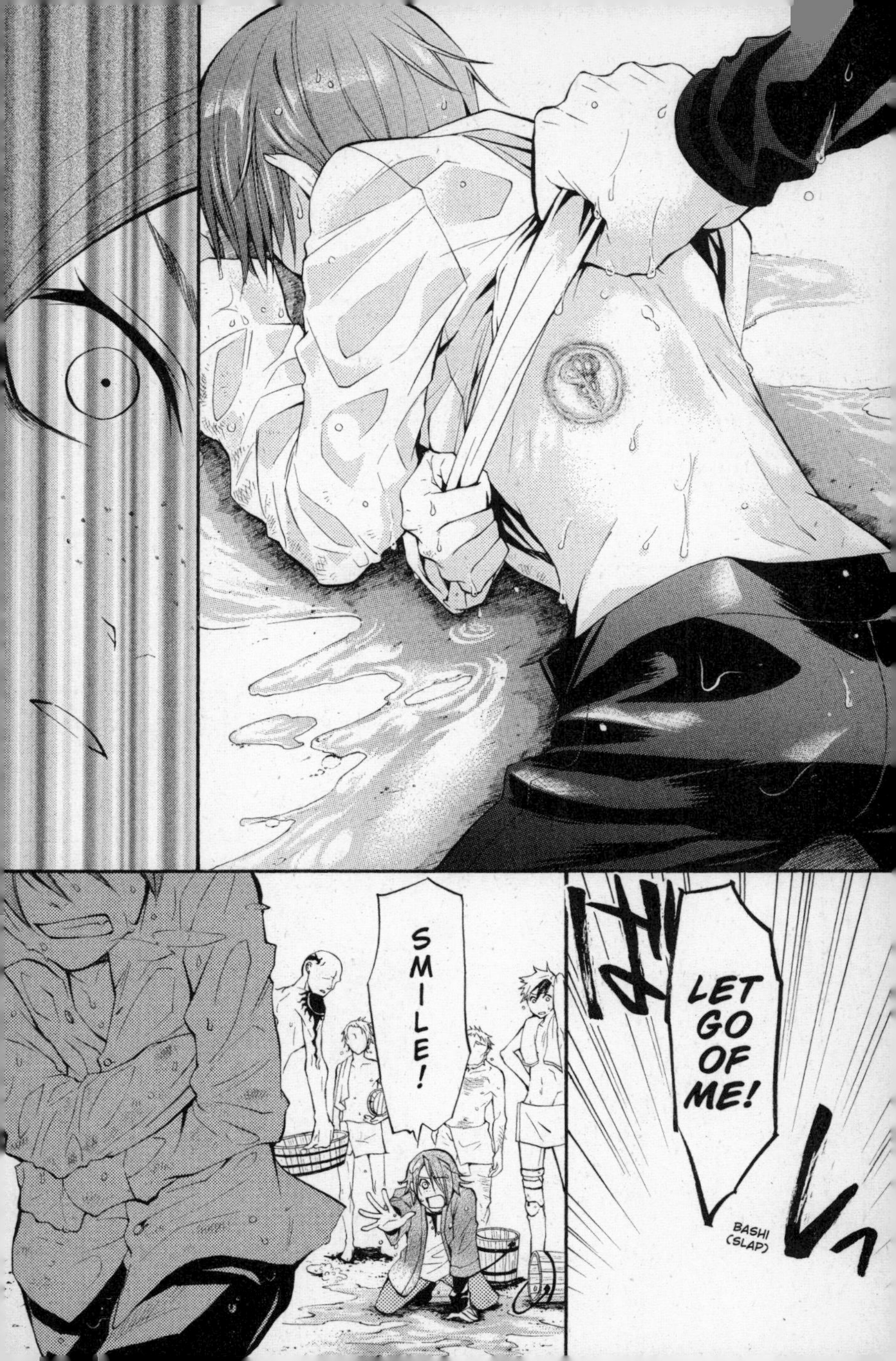
LET GO OF ME!
BASHI (SLAP)
SMILE!

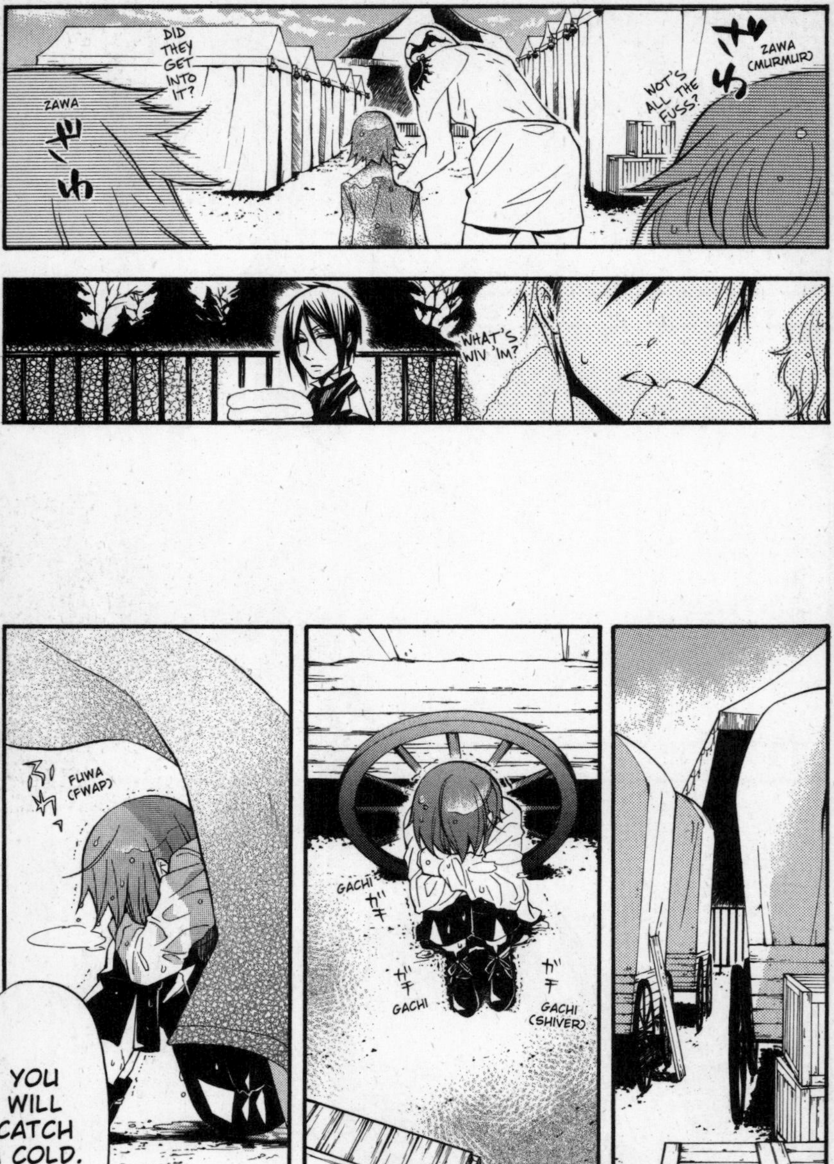
ざわ
ZAWA (MURMUR)
WOT'S ALL THE FUSS?
DID THEY GET INTO IT?
ZAWA
ざわ
WHAT'S WIV 'IM?
GACHI
ガチ
ガチ
GACHI (SHIVER)
ガチ
GACHI
ふわ
FUWA (FWAP)
YOU WILL CATCH A COLD.

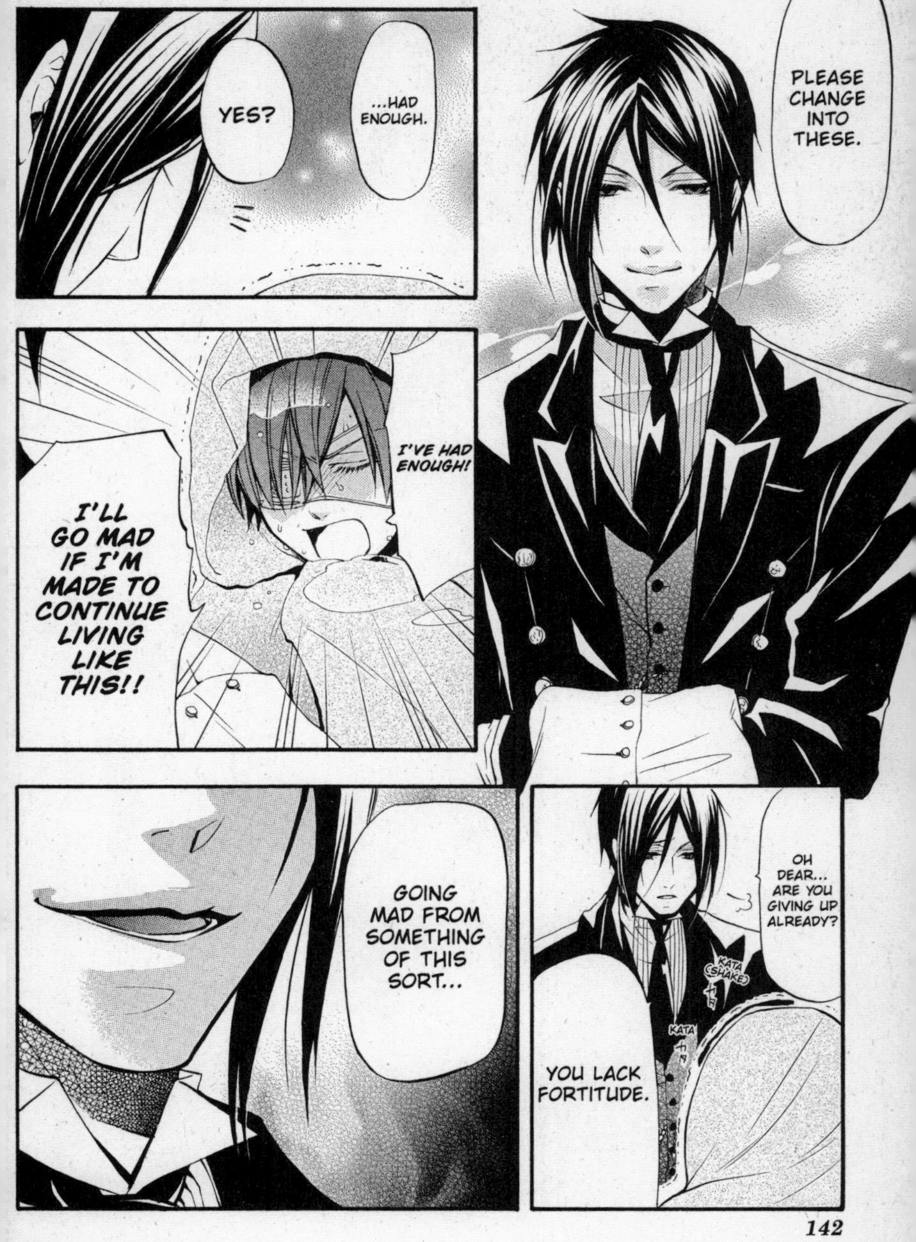
PLEASE CHANGE INTO THESE.
...HAD ENOUGH.
YES?
I'VE HAD ENOUGH!
I'LL GO MAD IF I'M MADE TO CONTINUE LIVING LIKE THIS!!
OH DEAR... ARE YOU GIVING UP ALREADY?
KATA (SHAKE)
KATA
YOU LACK FORTITUDE.
GOING MAD FROM SOMETHING OF THIS SORT...

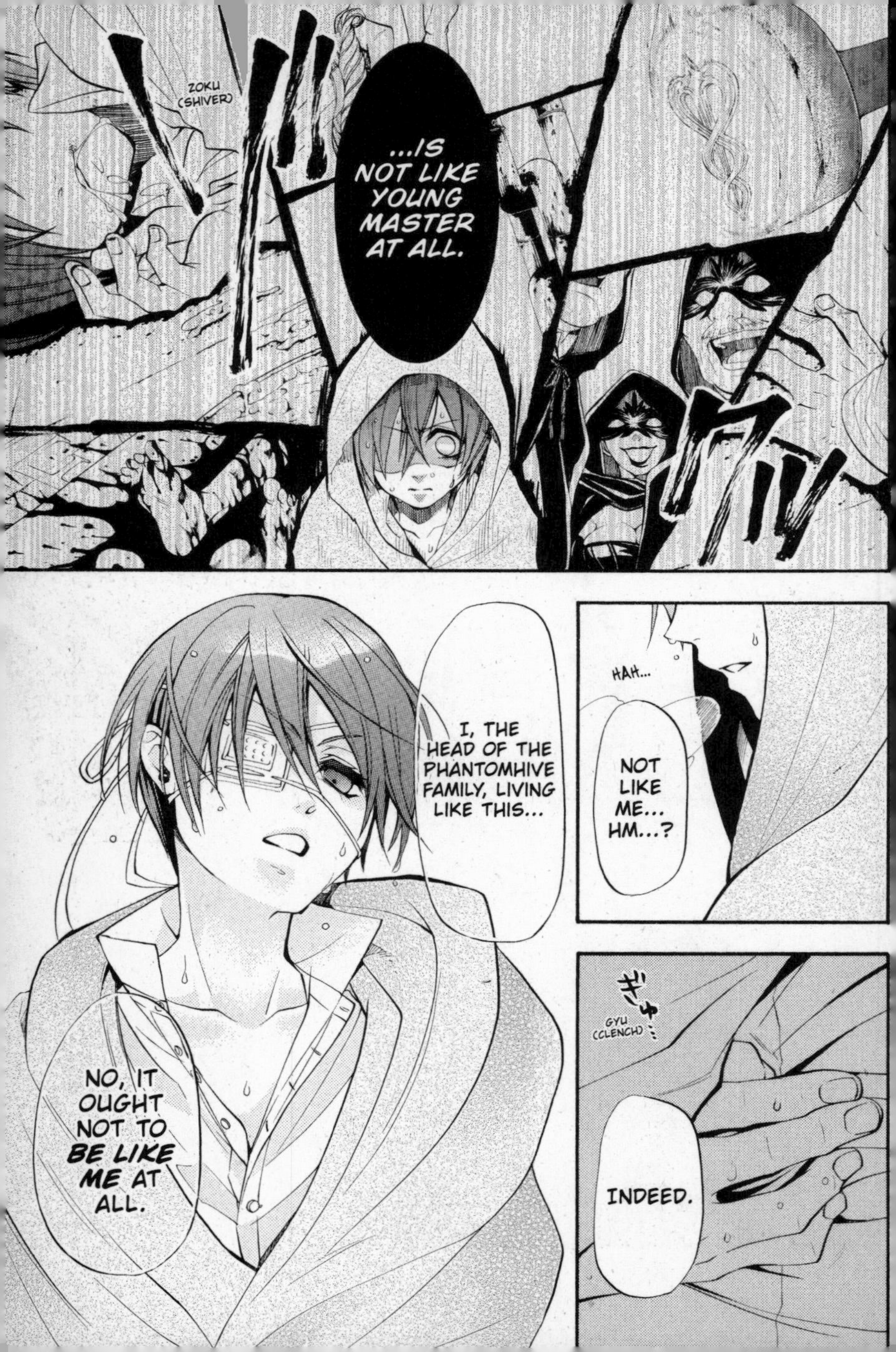
...IS NOT LIKE YOUNG MASTER AT ALL.
ZOKU (SHIVER)
HAH...
NOT LIKE ME... HM...?
GYU (CLENCH)
INDEED.
I, THE HEAD OF THE PHANTOMHIVE FAMILY, LIVING LIKE THIS...
NO, IT OUGHT NOT TO BE LIKE ME AT ALL.

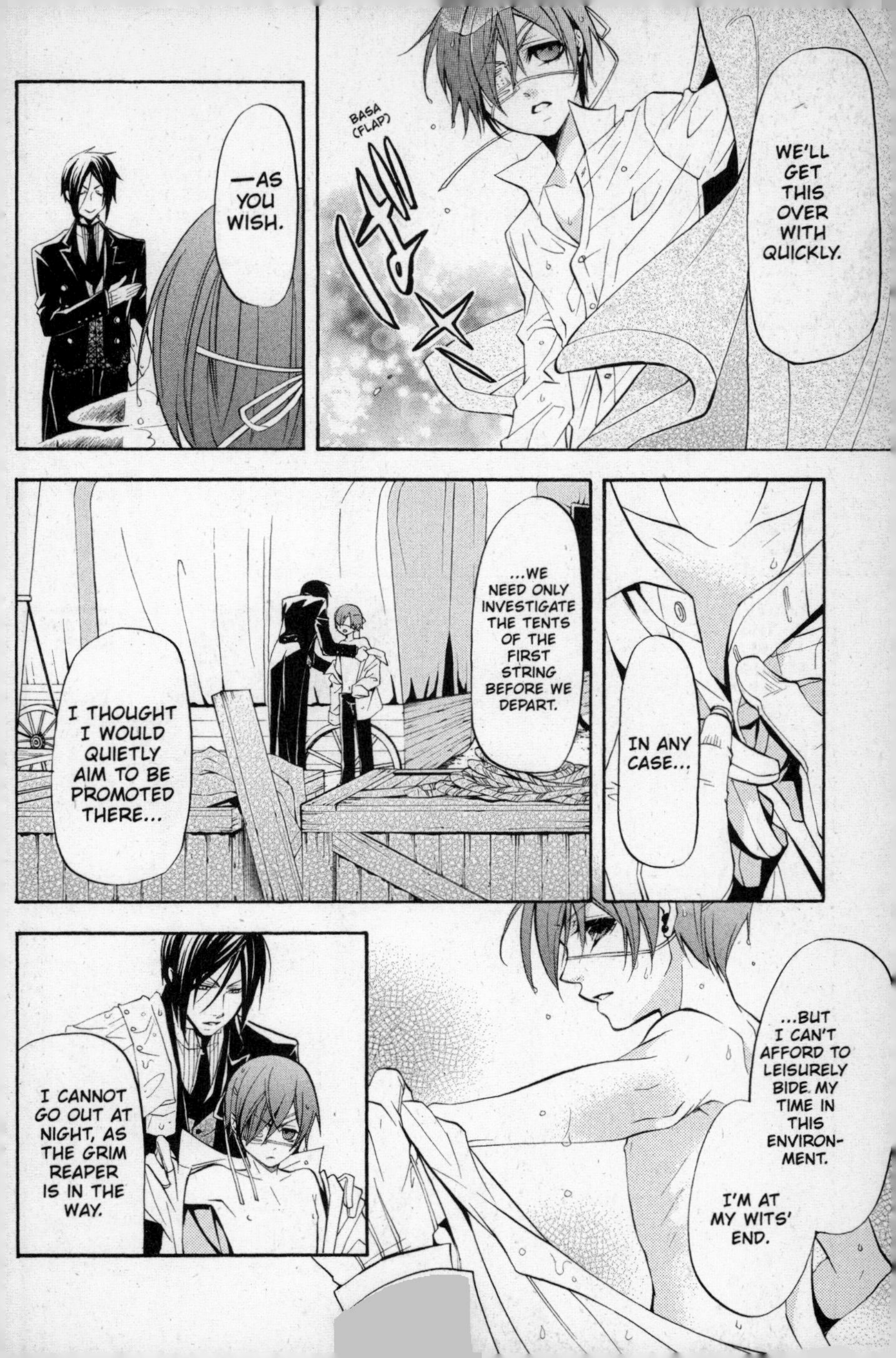
WE'LL GET THIS OVER WITH QUICKLY.
BASA (FLAP)
—AS YOU WISH.
IN ANY CASE...
...WE NEED ONLY INVESTIGATE THE TENTS OF THE FIRST STRING BEFORE WE DEPART.
I THOUGHT I WOULD QUIETLY AIM TO BE PROMOTED THERE...
...BUT I CAN'T AFFORD TO LEISURELY BIDE MY TIME IN THIS ENVIRON-MENT.
I'M AT MY WITS' END.
I CANNOT GO OUT AT NIGHT, AS THE GRIM REAPER IS IN THE WAY.

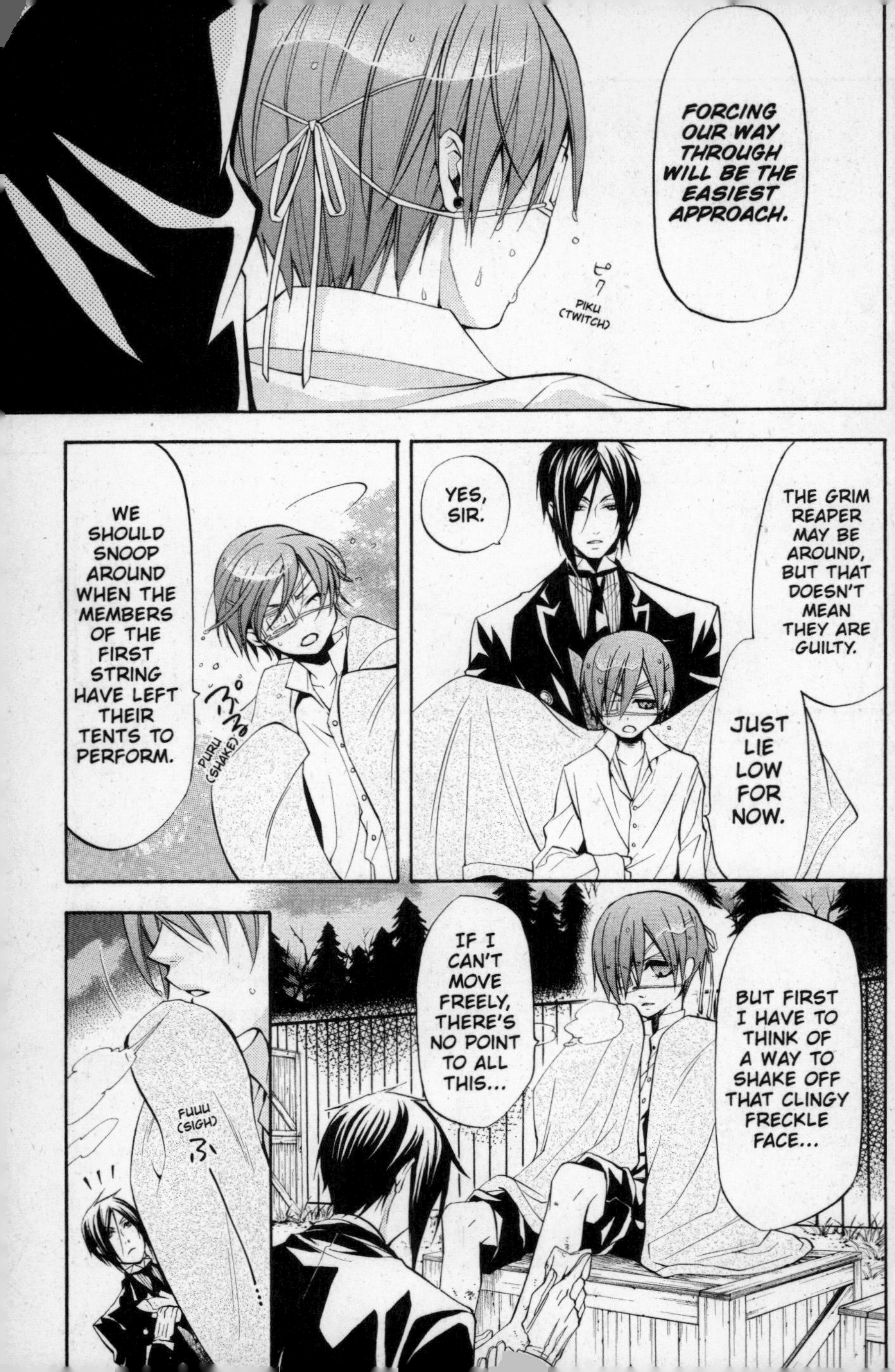
FORCING OUR WAY THROUGH WILL BE THE EASIEST APPROACH.
ピク
PIKU (TWITCH)
THE GRIM REAPER MAY BE AROUND, BUT THAT DOESN'T MEAN THEY ARE GUILTY.
JUST LIE LOW FOR NOW.
YES, SIR.
WE SHOULD SNOOP AROUND WHEN THE MEMBERS OF THE FIRST STRING HAVE LEFT THEIR TENTS TO PERFORM.
ぷる
PURU (SHAKE)
BUT FIRST I HAVE TO THINK OF A WAY TO SHAKE OFF THAT CLINGY FRECKLE FACE...
IF I CAN'T MOVE FREELY, THERE'S NO POINT TO ALL THIS...
FUUU (SIGH)
ふ

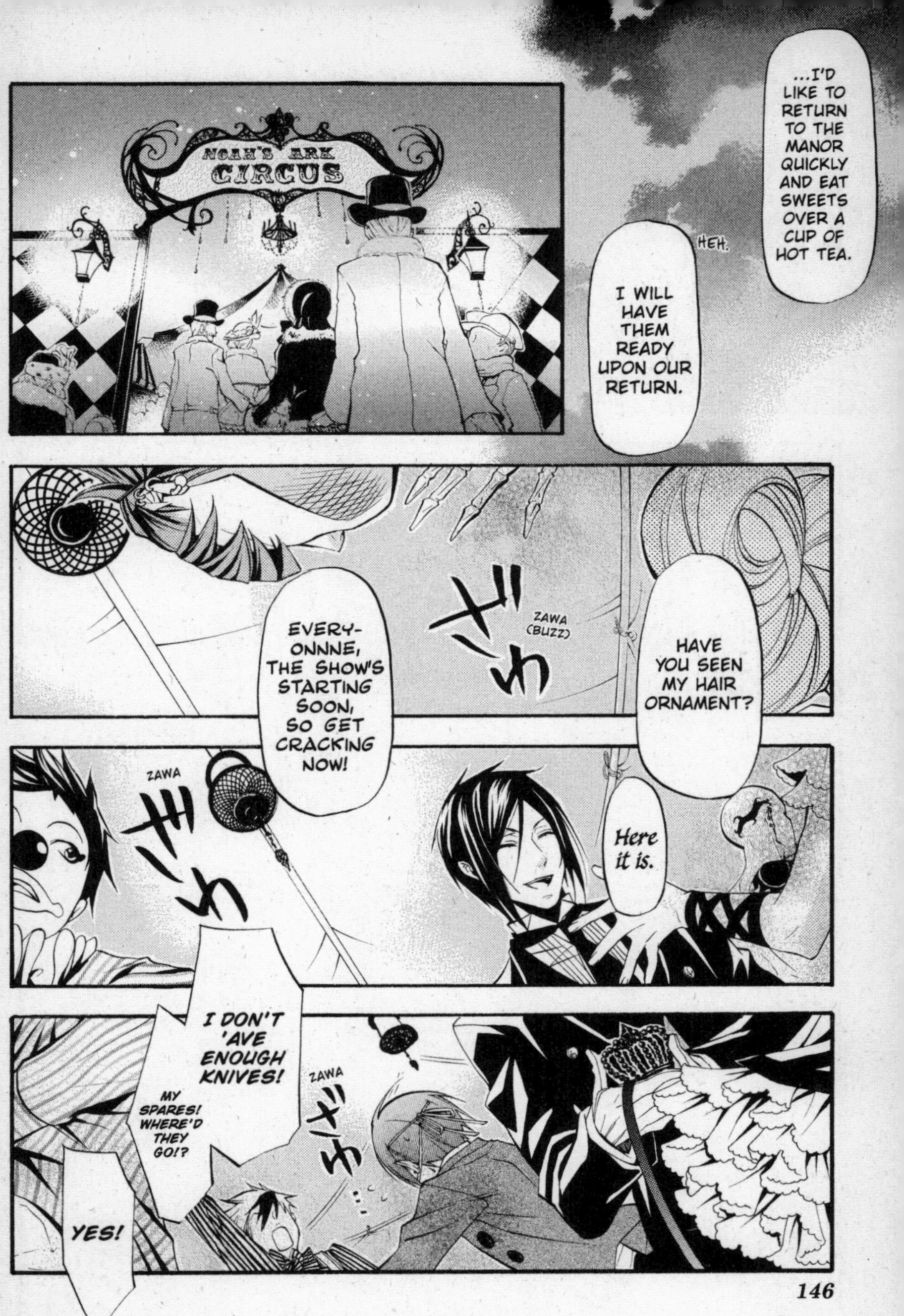
...I'D LIKE TO RETURN TO THE MANOR QUICKLY AND EAT SWEETS OVER A CUP OF HOT TEA.
HEH.
I WILL HAVE THEM READY UPON OUR RETURN.
NOAH'S ARK
CIRCUS
HAVE YOU SEEN MY HAIR ORNAMENT?
ZAWA (BUZZ)
EVERY-ONNNE, THE SHOW'S STARTING SOON, SO GET CRACKING NOW!
Here it is.
ZAWA
I DON'T 'AVE ENOUGH KNIVES!
ZAWA
MY SPARES! WHERE'D THEY GO!?
YES!

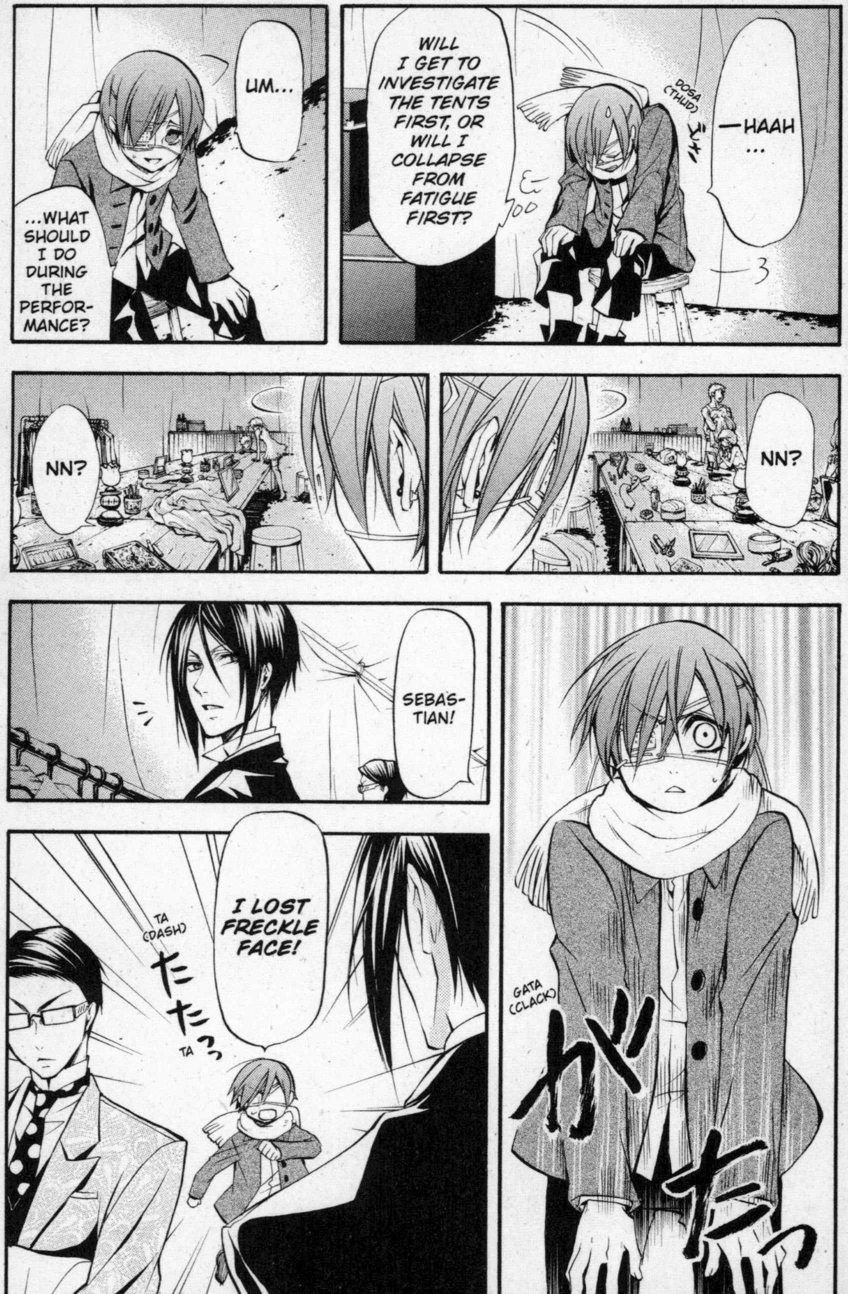
DOSA (THUD)
—HAAH ...
WILL I GET TO INVESTIGATE THE TENTS FIRST, OR WILL I COLLAPSE FROM FATIGUE FIRST?
UM...
...WHAT SHOULD I DO DURING THE PERFORMANCE?
NN?
NN?
GATA (CLACK)
SEBAS-TIAN!
I LOST FRECKLE FACE!
TA (DASH)
TA

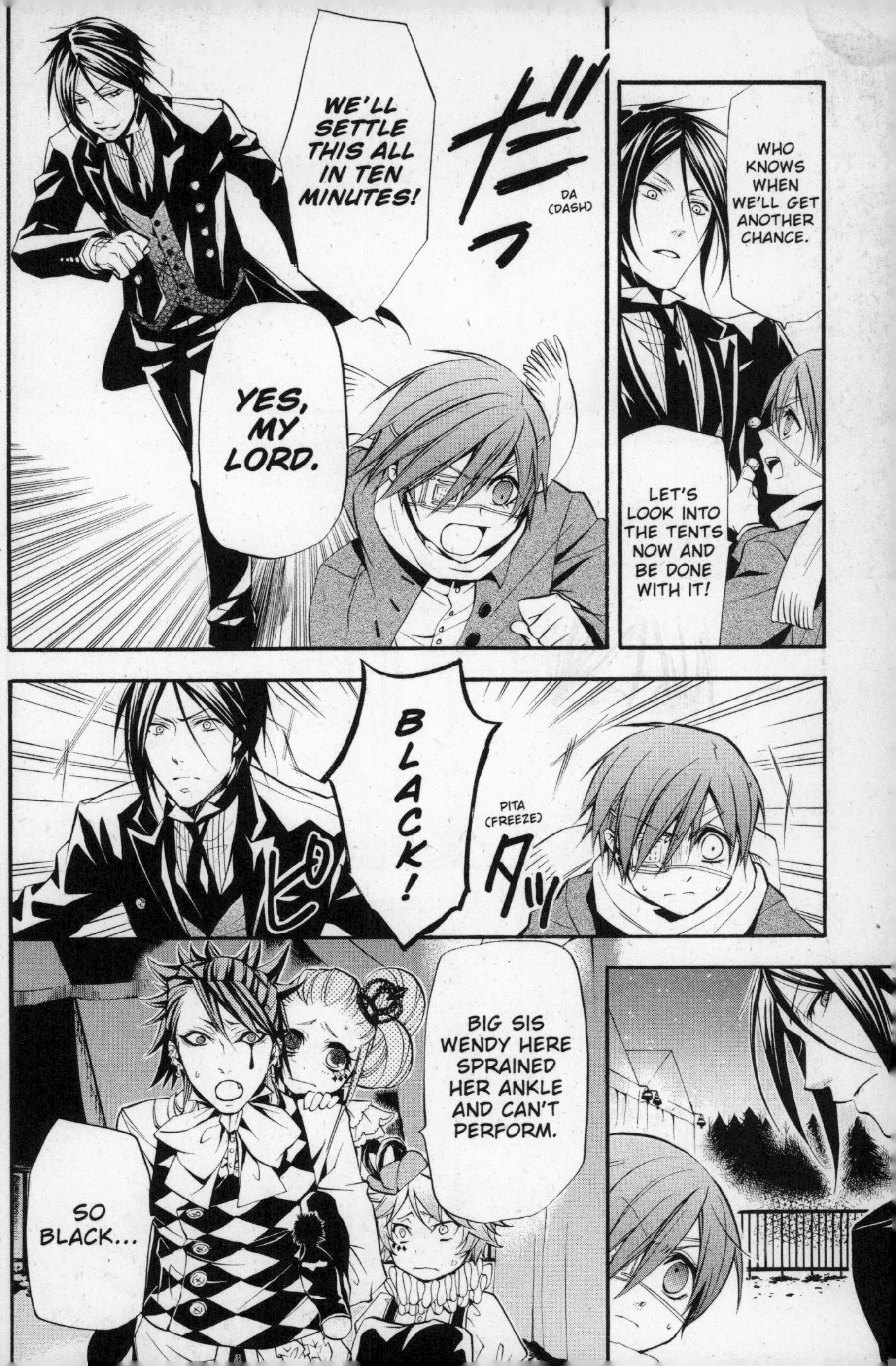
WHO KNOWS WHEN WE'LL GET ANOTHER CHANCE.
LET'S LOOK INTO THE TENTS NOW AND BE DONE WITH IT!
WE'LL SETTLE THIS ALL IN TEN MINUTES!
DA (DASH)
YES, MY LORD.
PITA (FREEZE)
BLACK!
BIG SIS WENDY HERE SPRAINED HER ANKLE AND CAN'T PERFORM.
SO BLACK...

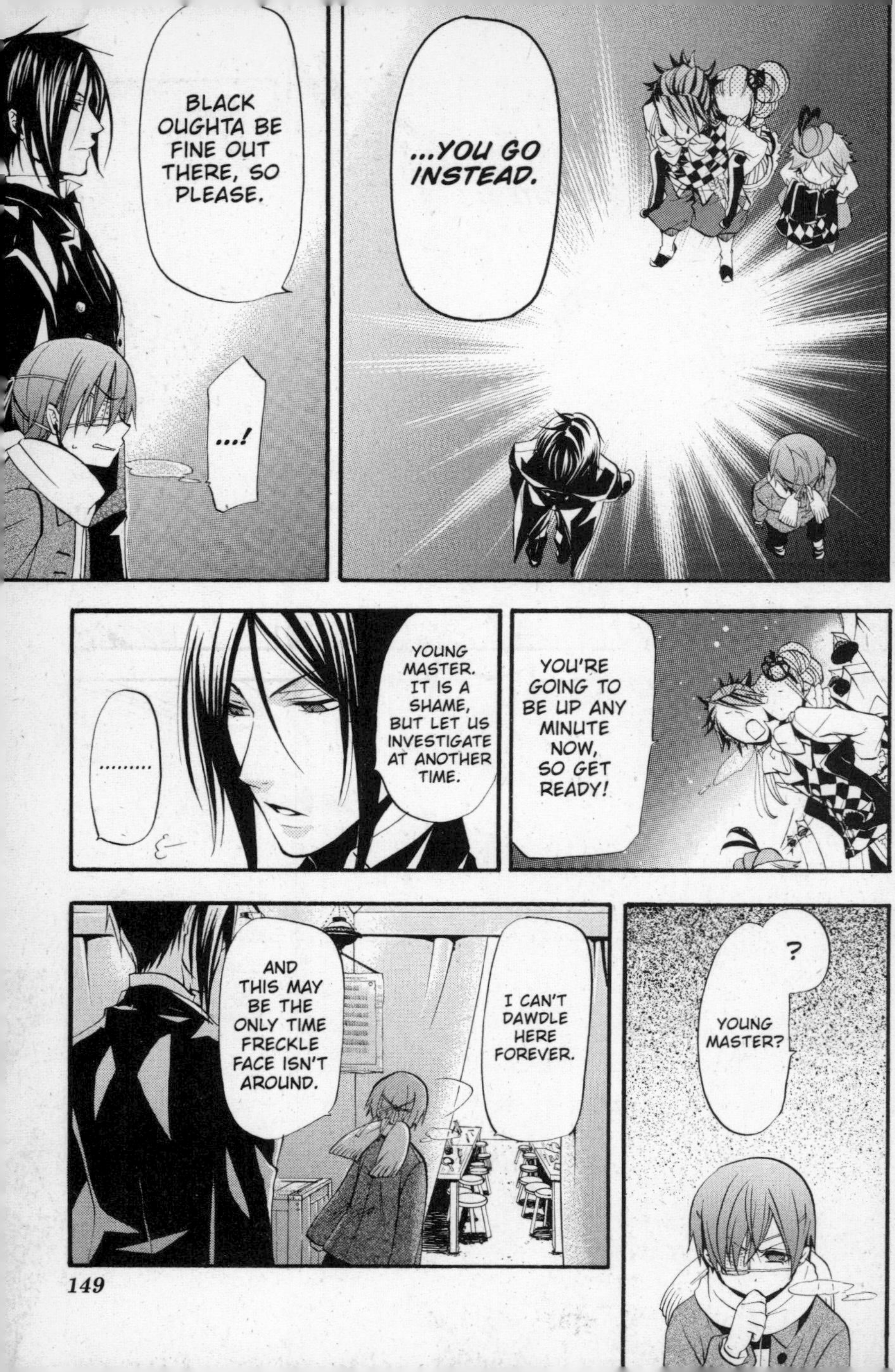
...YOU GO INSTEAD.
BLACK OUGHTA BE FINE OUT THERE, SO PLEASE.
...!
YOU'RE GOING TO BE UP ANY MINUTE NOW, SO GET READY!
YOUNG MASTER. IT IS A SHAME, BUT LET US INVESTIGATE AT ANOTHER TIME.
....
?
YOUNG MASTER?
I CAN'T DAWDLE HERE FOREVER.
AND THIS MAY BE THE ONLY TIME FRECKLE FACE ISN'T AROUND.

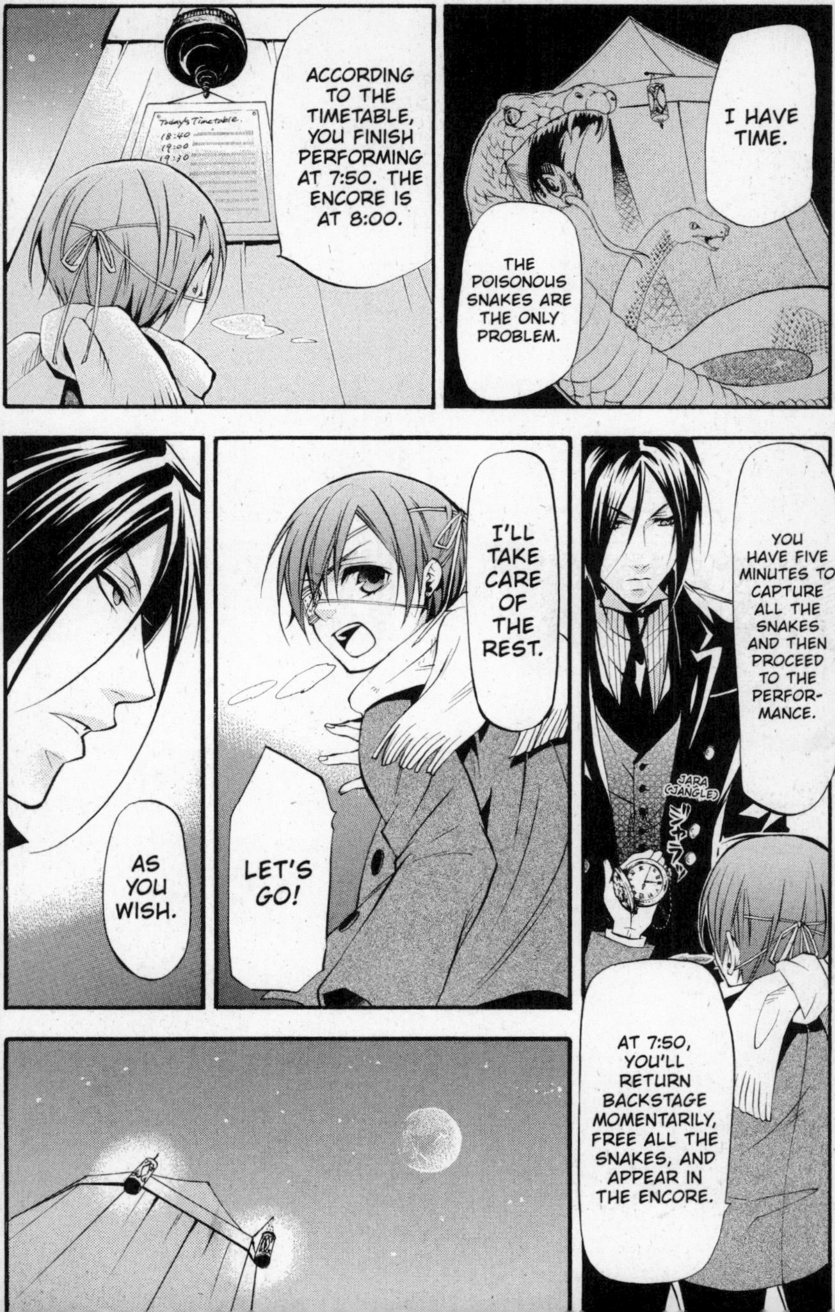
I HAVE TIME.
THE POISONOUS SNAKES ARE THE ONLY PROBLEM.
ACCORDING TO THE TIMETABLE, YOU FINISH PERFORMING AT 7:50. THE ENCORE IS AT 8:00.
Today's Timetable
18:40
19:00
19:30
YOU HAVE FIVE MINUTES TO CAPTURE ALL THE SNAKES AND THEN PROCEED TO THE PERFORMANCE.
JARA (JANGLE)
AT 7:50, YOU'LL RETURN BACKSTAGE MOMENTARILY, FREE ALL THE SNAKES, AND APPEAR IN THE ENCORE.
I'LL TAKE CARE OF THE REST.
LET'S GO!
AS YOU WISH.

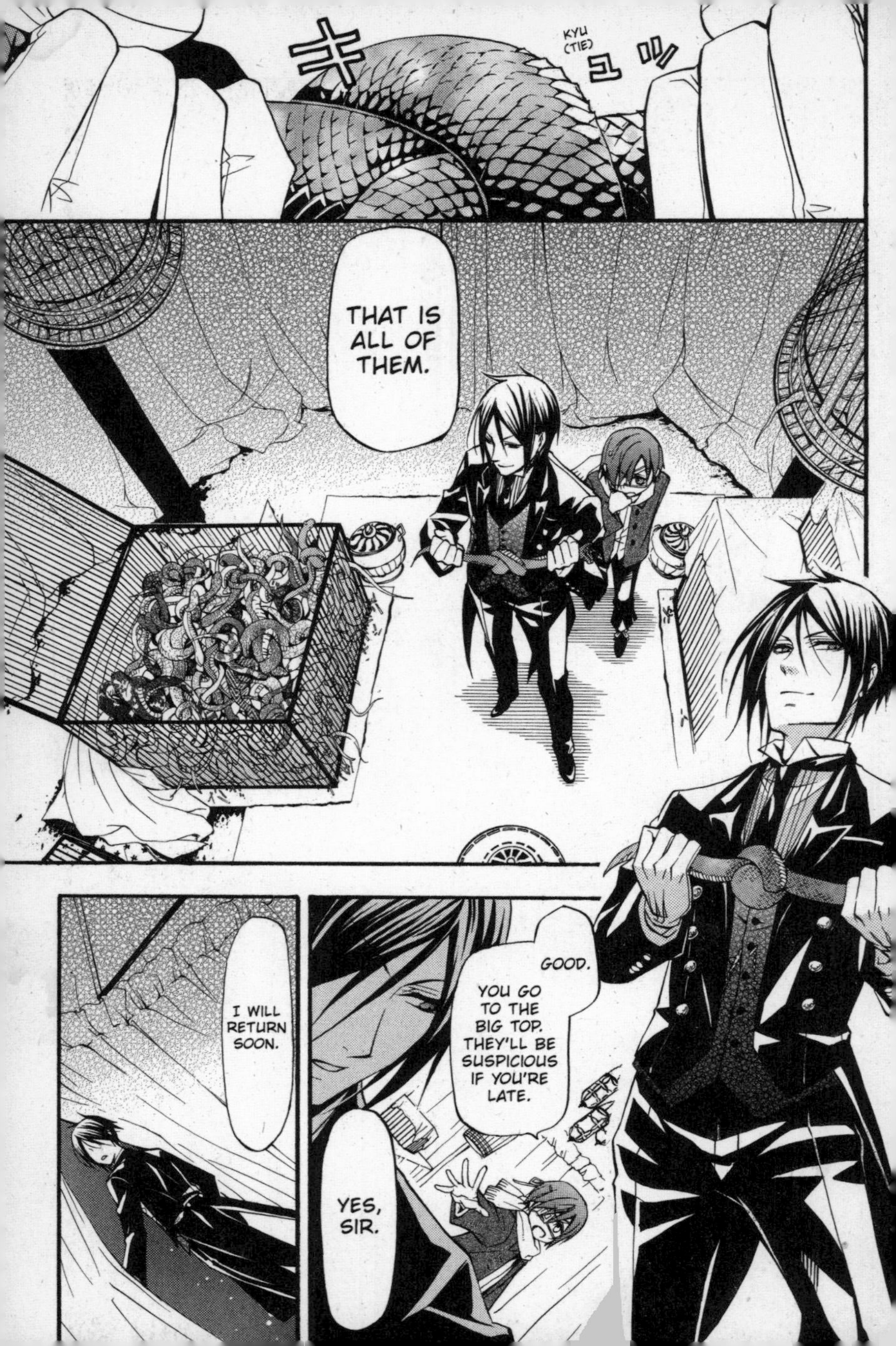
キュッ
KYU (TIE)
THAT IS ALL OF THEM.
GOOD.
YOU GO TO THE BIG TOP. THEY'LL BE SUSPICIOUS IF YOU'RE LATE.
YES, SIR.
I WILL RETURN SOON.

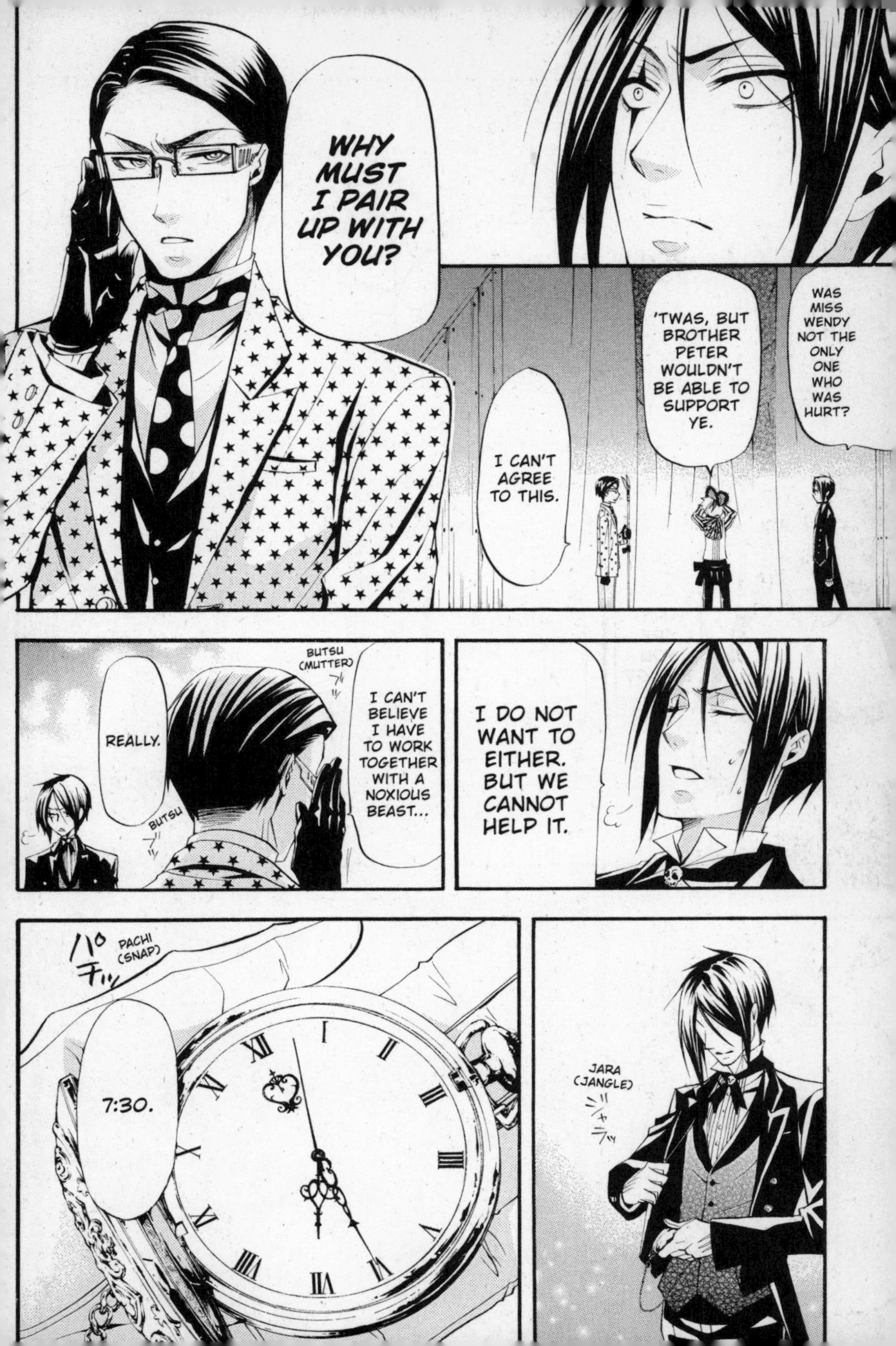
WAS MISS WENDY NOT THE ONLY ONE WHO WAS HURT?
'TWAS, BUT BROTHER PETER WOULDN'T BE ABLE TO SUPPORT YE.
I CAN'T AGREE TO THIS.
WHY MUST I PAIR UP WITH YOU?
I DO NOT WANT TO EITHER. BUT WE CANNOT HELP IT.
BUTSU (MUTTER)
I CAN'T BELIEVE I HAVE TO WORK TOGETHER WITH A NOXIOUS BEAST...
BUTSU
REALLY.
JARA (JANGLE)
PACHI (SNAP)
7:30.

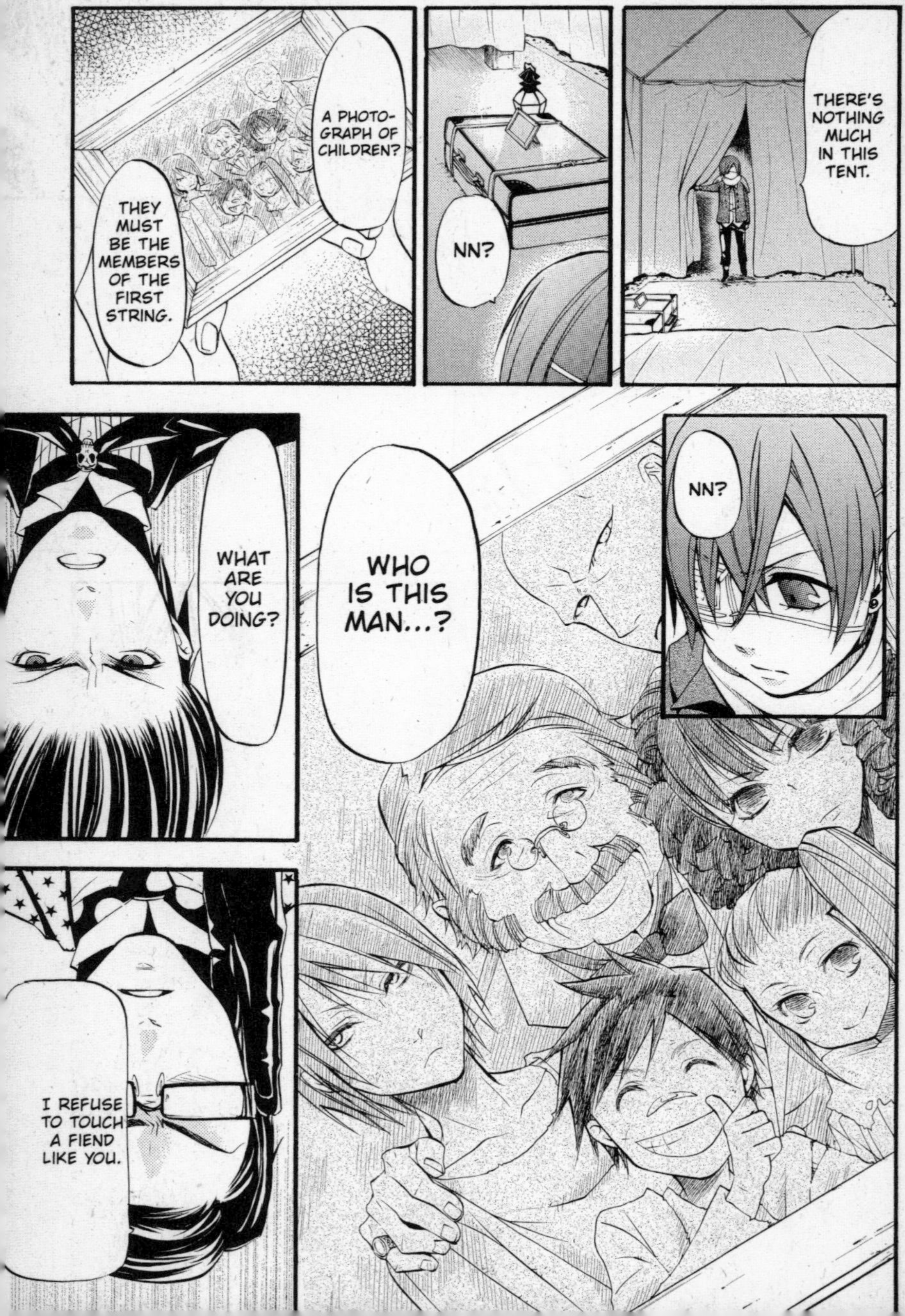
THERE'S NOTHING MUCH IN THIS TENT.
NN?
A PHOTOGRAPH OF CHILDREN?
THEY MUST BE THE MEMBERS OF THE FIRST STRING.
NN?
WHO IS THIS MAN...?
WHAT ARE YOU DOING?
I REFUSE TO TOUCH A FIEND LIKE YOU.

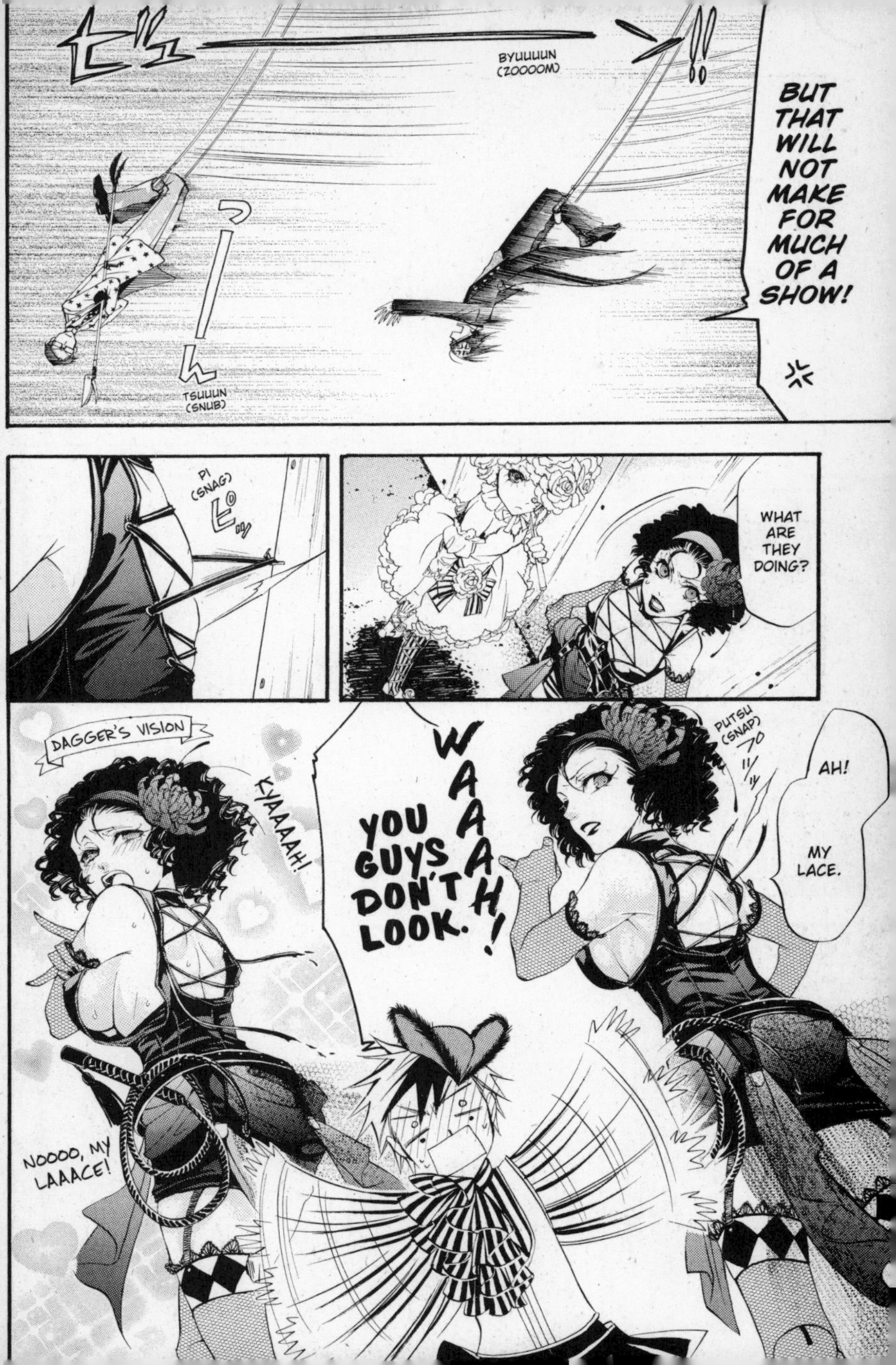
BUT THAT WILL NOT MAKE FOR MUCH OF A SHOW!
BYUUUUN (ZOOOOM)
TSUUUN (SNUB)
WHAT ARE THEY DOING?
PI (SNAG)
AH!
MY LACE.
PUTSU (SNAP)
WAAAAAH!
YOU GUYS DON'T LOOK.
KYAAAAH!
DAGGER'S VISION
NOOOO, MY LAAACE!

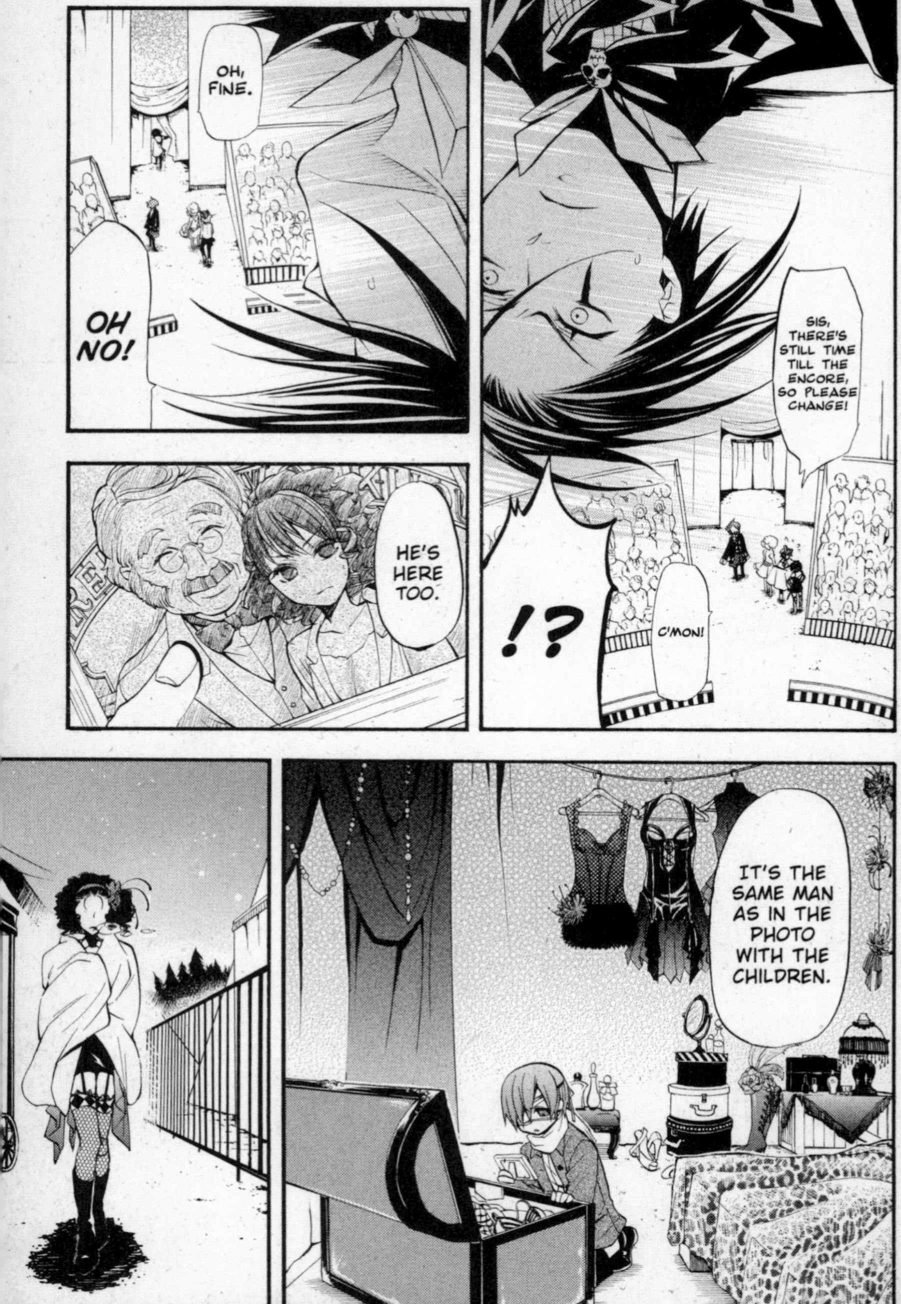
SIS, THERE'S STILL TIME TILL THE ENCORE, SO PLEASE CHANGE!
C'MON!
!?
OH, FINE.
OH NO!
HE'S HERE TOO.
IT'S THE SAME MAN AS IN THE PHOTO WITH THE CHILDREN.

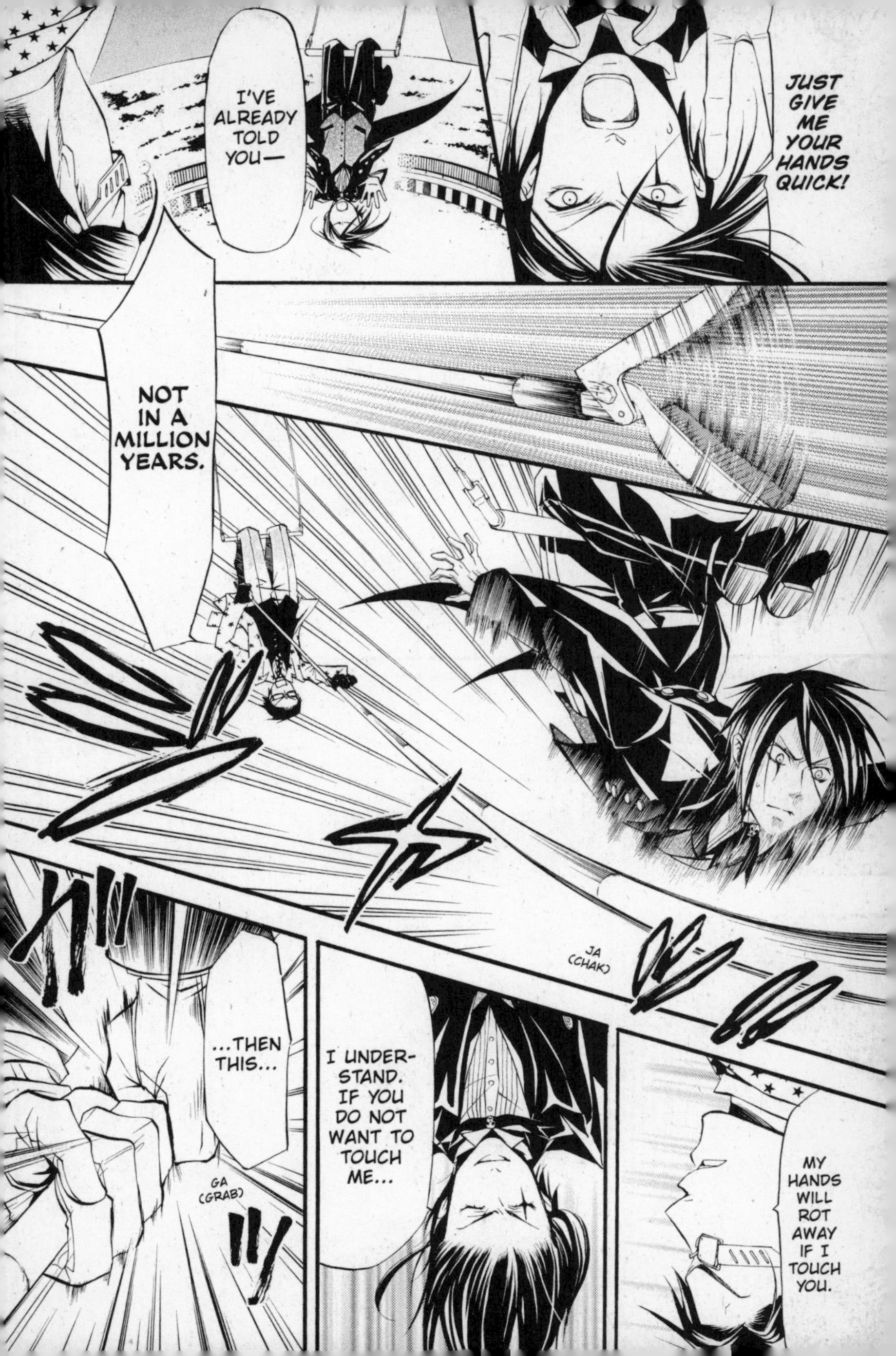

JUST GIVE ME YOUR HANDS QUICK!
I'VE ALREADY TOLD YOU—
NOT IN A MILLION YEARS.
JA (CHAK)
MY HANDS WILL ROT AWAY IF I TOUCH YOU.
I UNDER-STAND. IF YOU DO NOT WANT TO TOUCH ME...
...THEN THIS...
GA (GRAB)

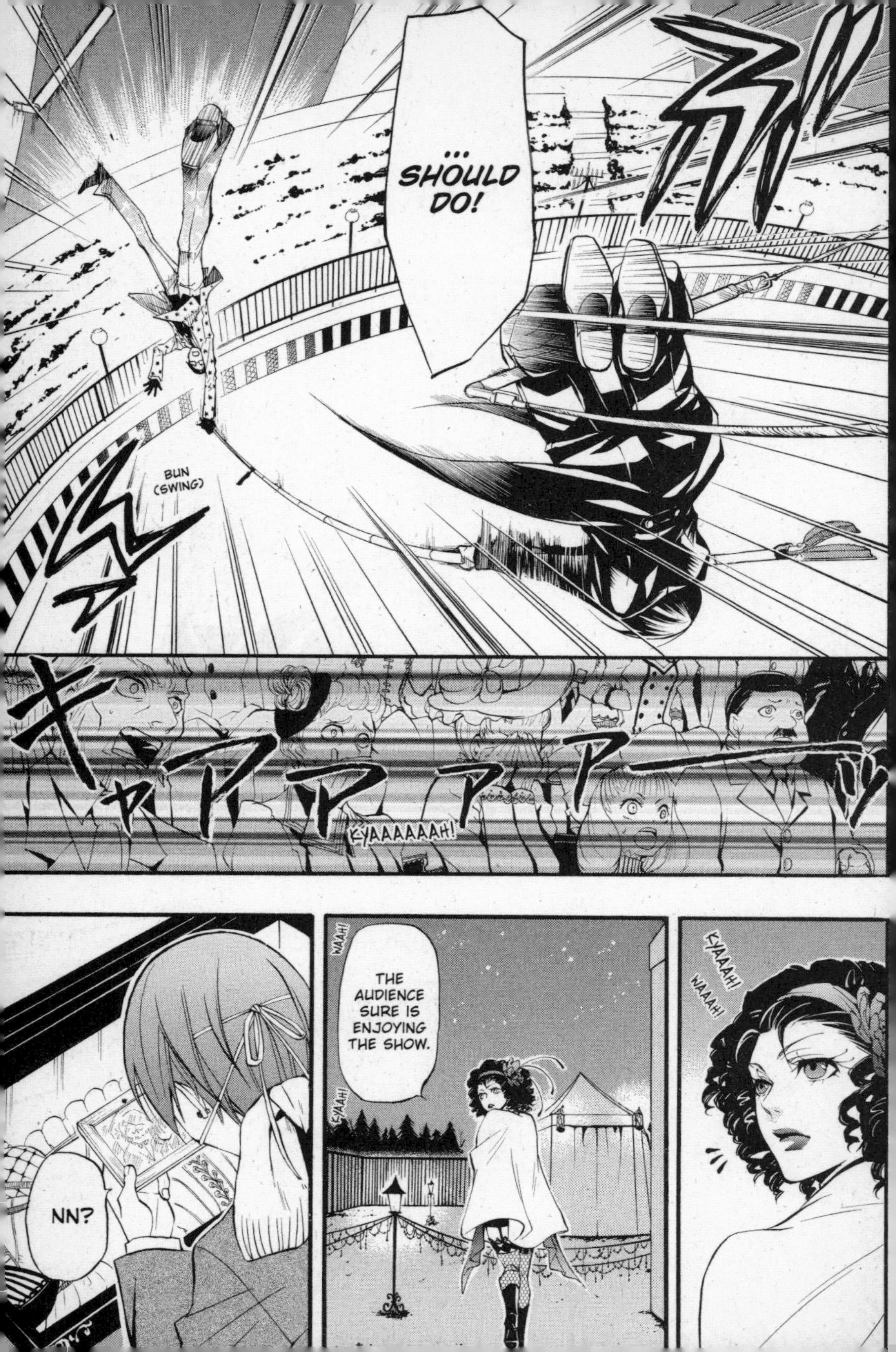

... SHOULD DO!
BUN (SWING)
KYAAAAAAH!
KYAAAH!
NAAAH!
WAAH!
THE AUDIENCE SURE IS ENJOYING THE SHOW.
KYAAH!
NN?

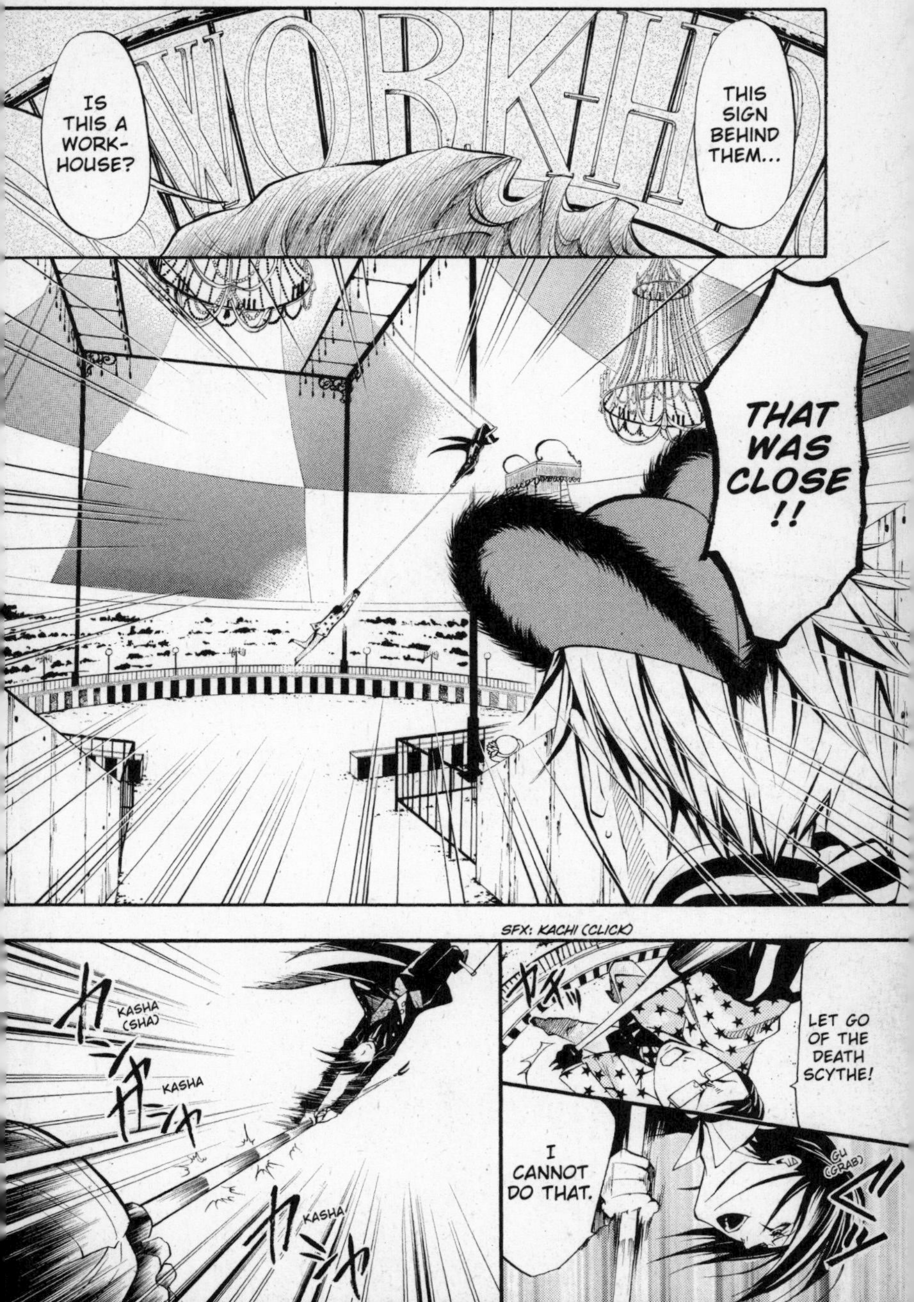
THIS SIGN BEHIND THEM...
IS THIS A WORK-HOUSE?
THAT WAS CLOSE !!
SFX: KACHI (CLICK)
LET GO OF THE DEATH SCYTHE!
I CANNOT DO THAT.
GU (GRAB)
KASHA (SHA)
KASHA
KASHA

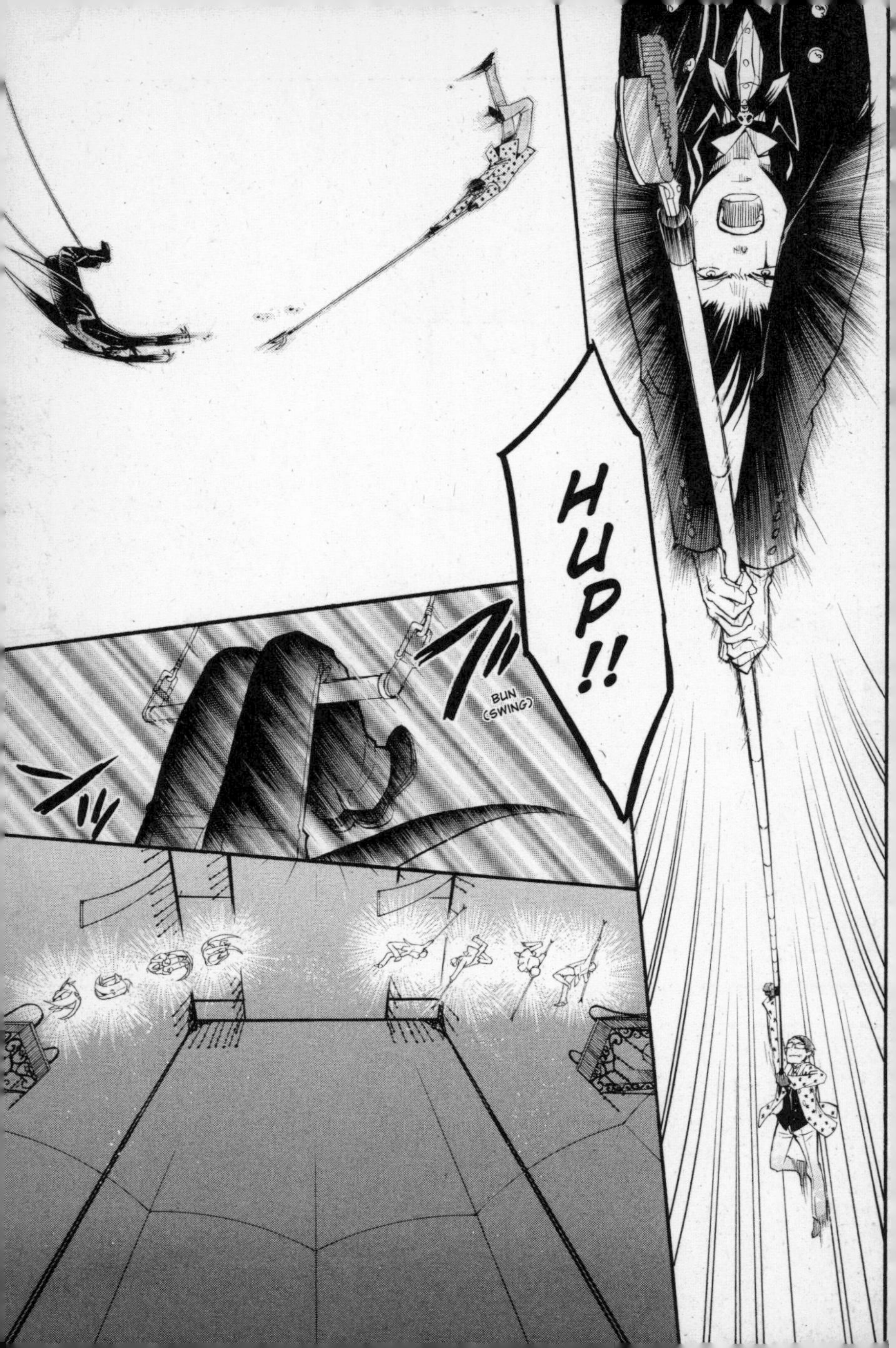
HUP!!
BUN (SWING)

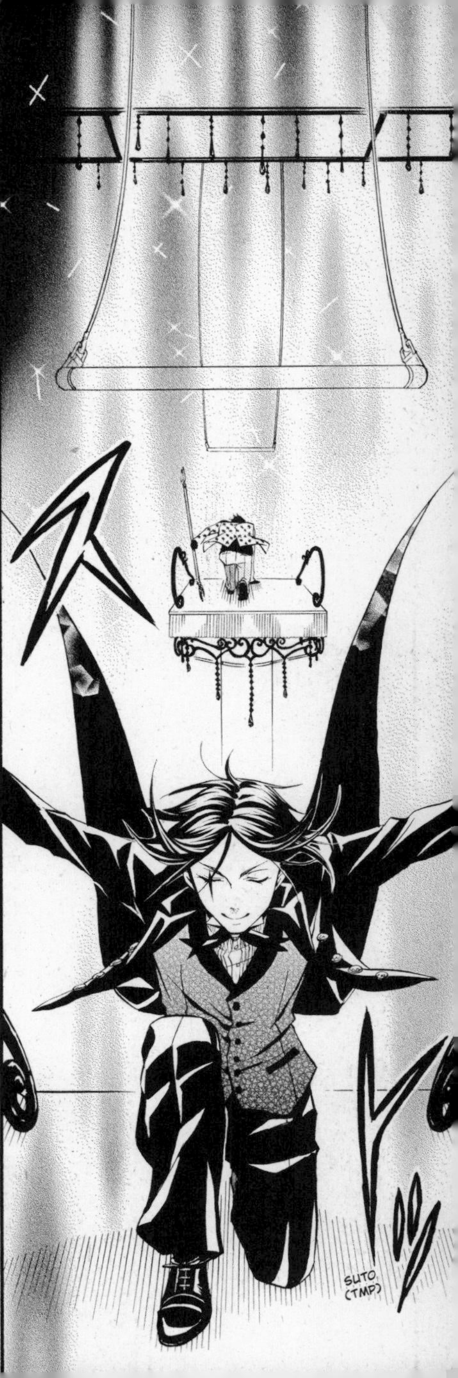
ス
トッ
SUTO (TMP)

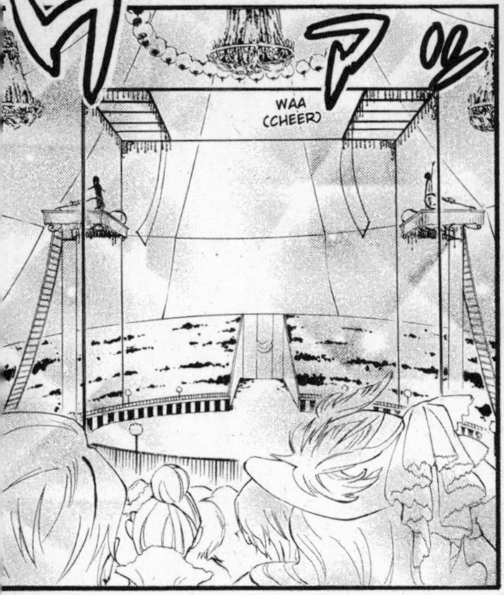
ワァッ
WAA (CHEER)

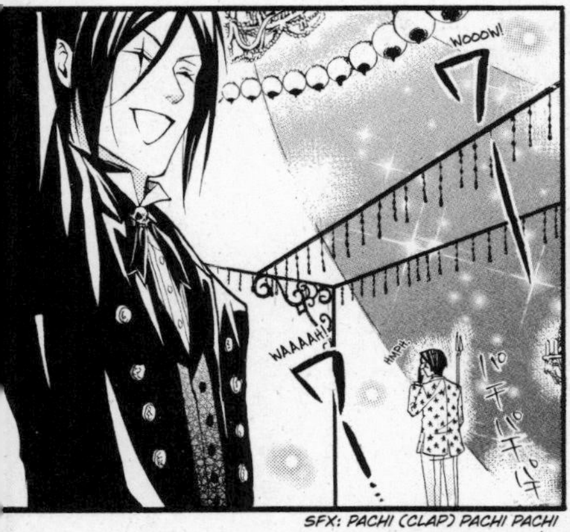
ワー
WOOOW!
ワー…
WAAAAH!
HMPH.
パチパチパチ

SFX: PACHI (CLAP) PACHI PACHI

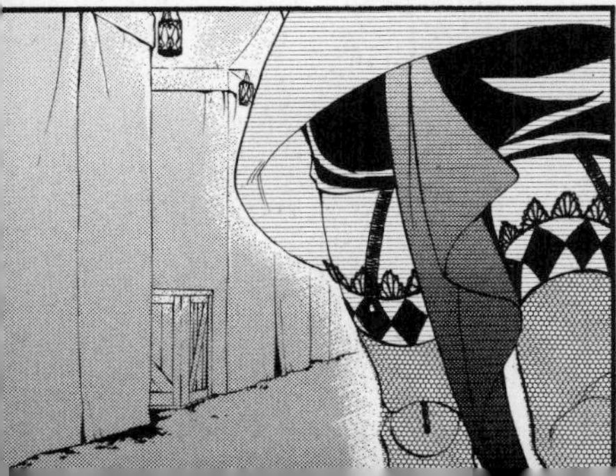

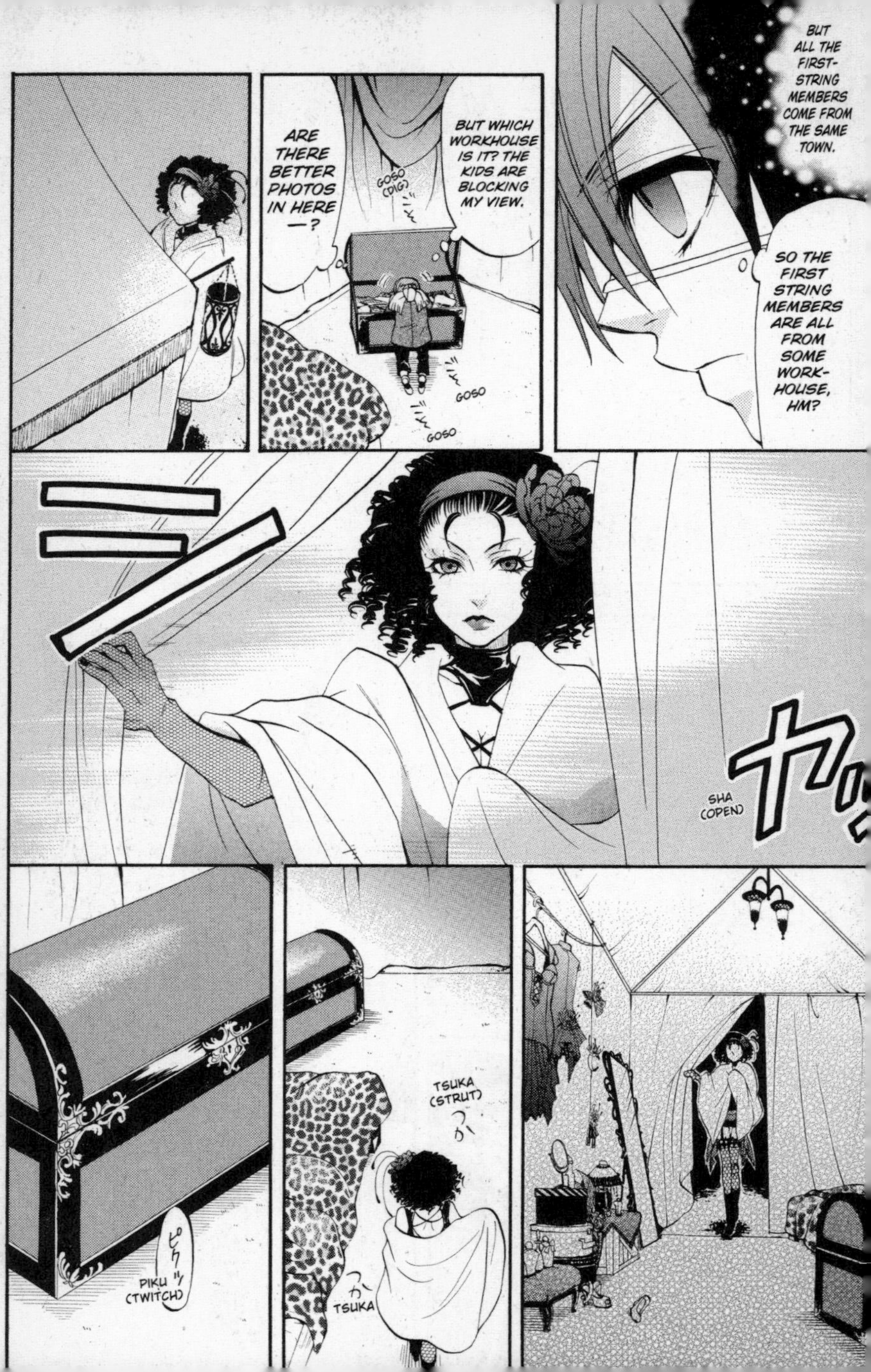
BUT ALL THE FIRST-STRING MEMBERS COME FROM THE SAME TOWN.
SO THE FIRST STRING MEMBERS ARE ALL FROM SOME WORK-HOUSE, HM?
BUT WHICH WORKHOUSE IS IT? THE KIDS ARE BLOCKING MY VIEW.
GOSO (DIG)
GOSO
GOSO
ARE THERE BETTER PHOTOS IN HERE—?
SHA (OPEN)
TSUKA (STRUT)
TSUKA
PIKU (TWITCH)

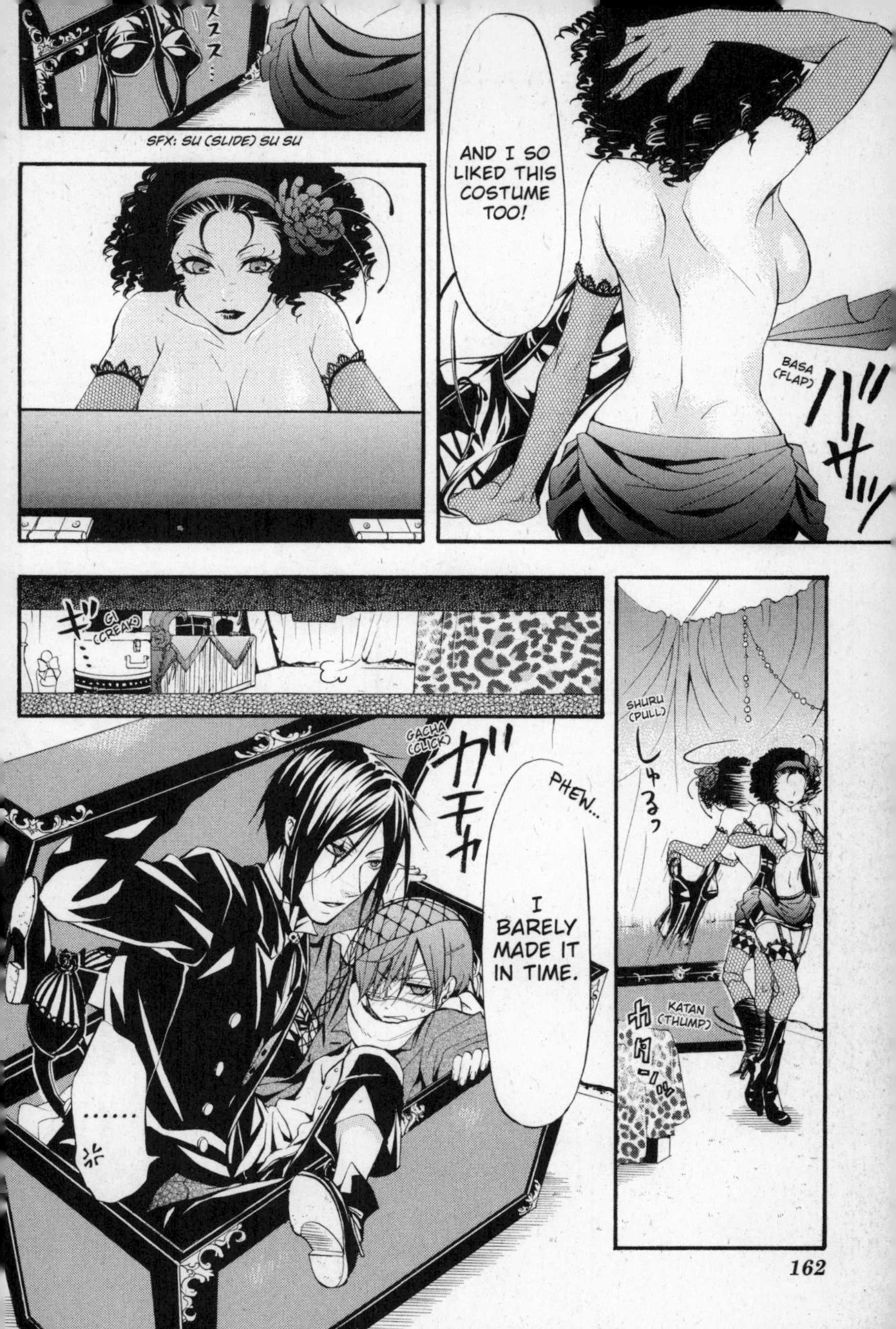
AND I SO LIKED THIS COSTUME TOO!
BASA (FLAP)
SFX: SU (SLIDE) SU SU
SHURU (PULL)
KATAN (THUMP)
GI (CREAK)
GACHA (CLICK)
PHEW...
I BARELY MADE IT IN TIME.
......

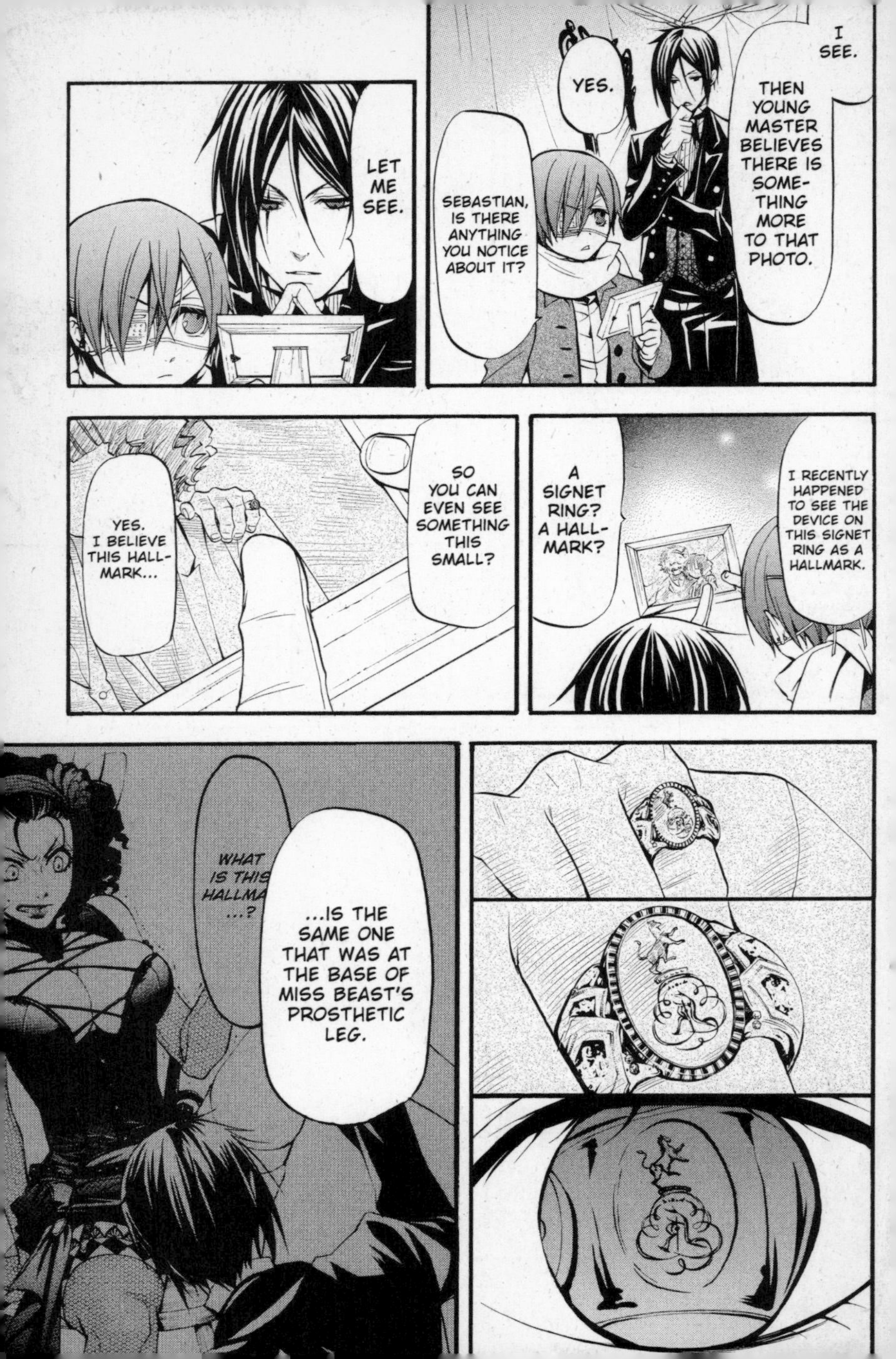
I SEE.
THEN YOUNG MASTER BELIEVES THERE IS SOME-THING MORE TO THAT PHOTO.
YES.
SEBASTIAN, IS THERE ANYTHING YOU NOTICE ABOUT IT?
LET ME SEE.
I RECENTLY HAPPENED TO SEE THE DEVICE ON THIS SIGNET RING AS A HALLMARK.
A SIGNET RING? A HALL-MARK?
SO YOU CAN EVEN SEE SOMETHING THIS SMALL?
YES. I BELIEVE THIS HALL-MARK...
...IS THE SAME ONE THAT WAS AT THE BASE OF MISS BEAST'S PROSTHETIC LEG.
WHAT IS THIS HALLMA ...?

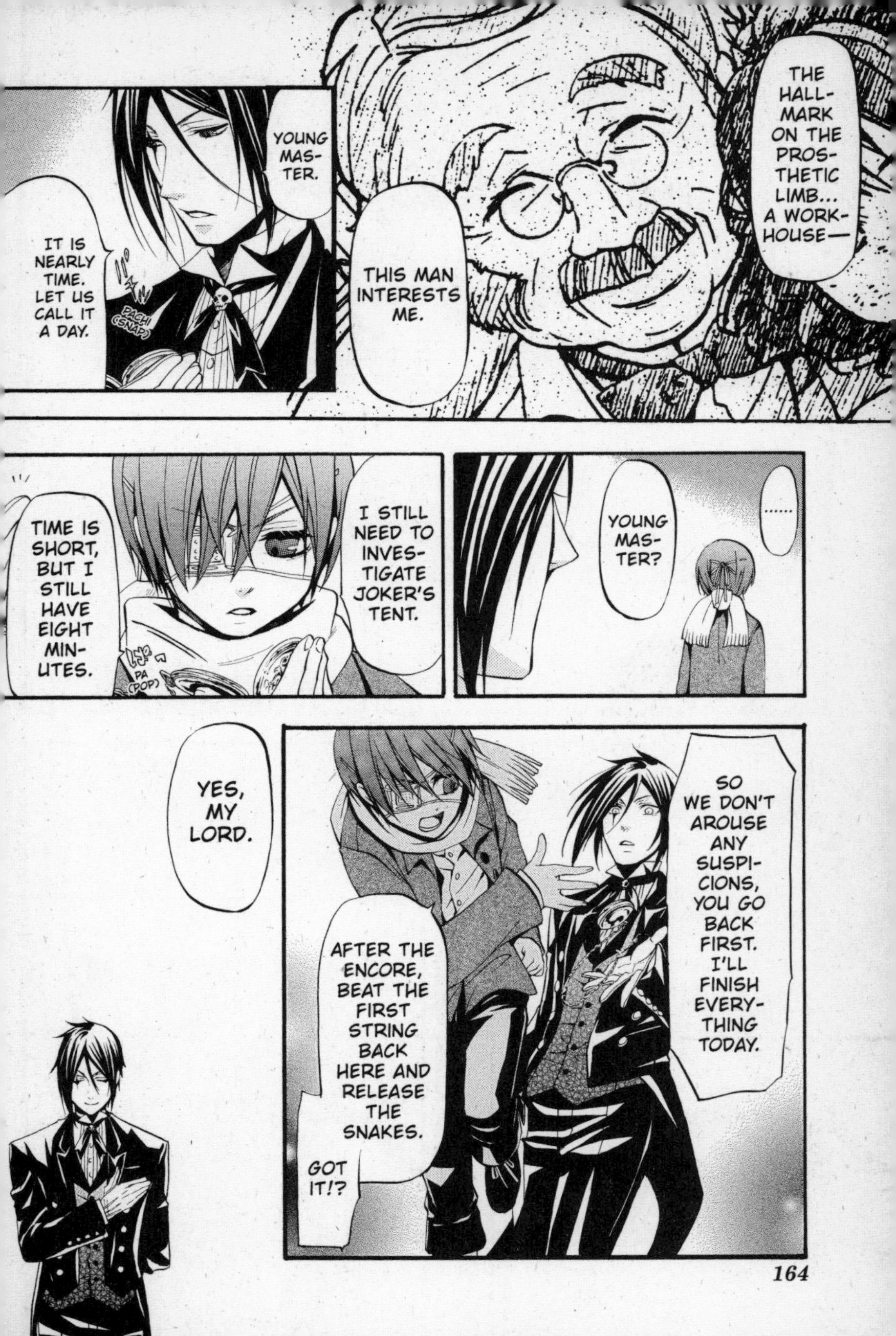
THE HALLMARK ON THE PROSTHETIC LIMB... A WORKHOUSE—
THIS MAN INTERESTS ME.
YOUNG MASTER.
IT IS NEARLY TIME. LET US CALL IT A DAY.
PACHI (SNAP)
......
YOUNG MASTER?
I STILL NEED TO INVESTIGATE JOKER'S TENT.
TIME IS SHORT, BUT I STILL HAVE EIGHT MINUTES.
PA (POP)
SO WE DON'T AROUSE ANY SUSPICIONS, YOU GO BACK FIRST. I'LL FINISH EVERYTHING TODAY.
AFTER THE ENCORE, BEAT THE FIRST STRING BACK HERE AND RELEASE THE SNAKES.
GOT IT!?
YES, MY LORD.

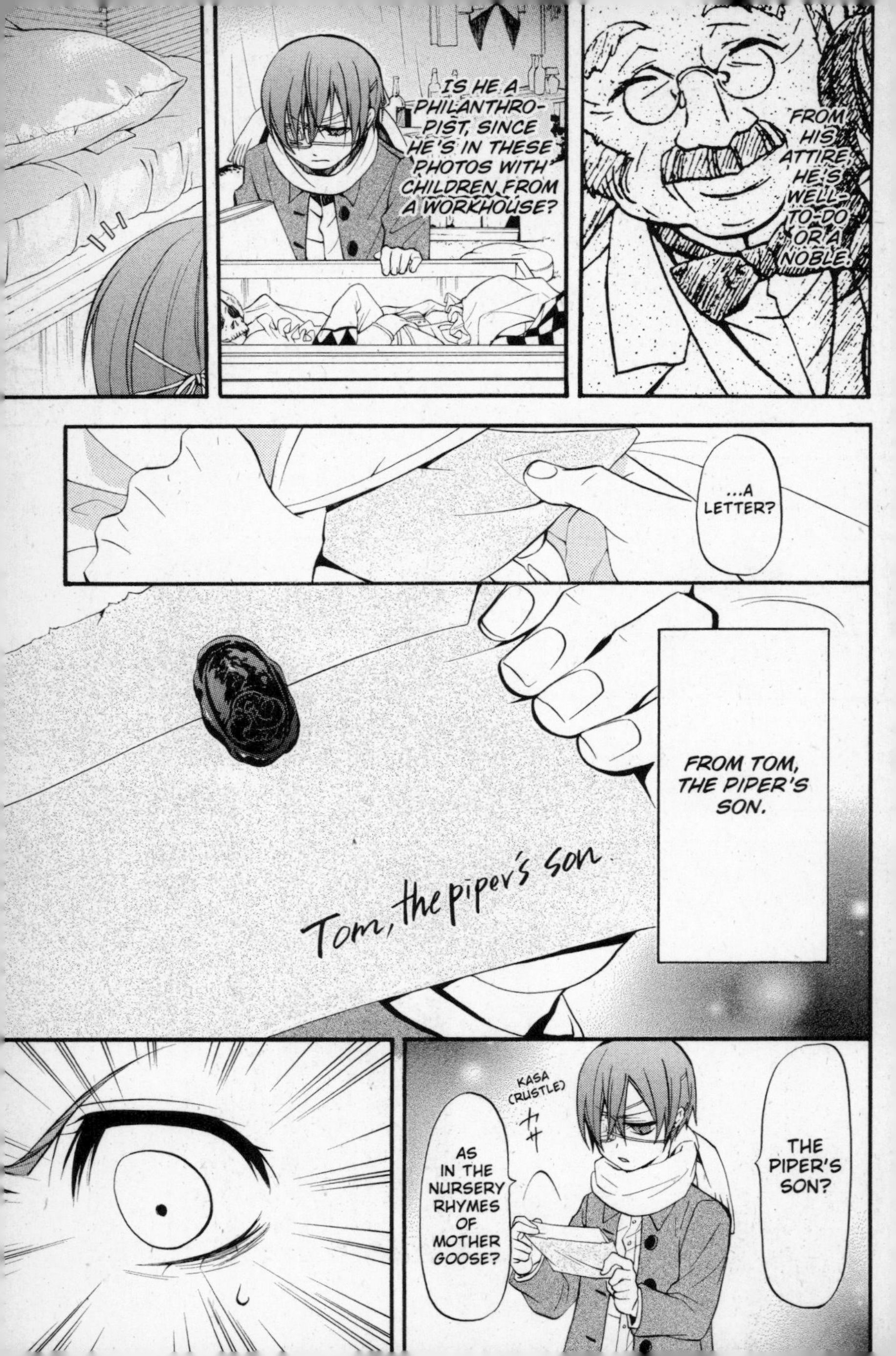
FROM HIS ATTIRE, HE'S WELL-TO-DO OR A NOBLE.
IS HE A PHILANTHROPIST, SINCE HE'S IN THESE PHOTOS WITH CHILDREN FROM A WORKHOUSE?
...A LETTER?
FROM TOM, THE PIPER'S SON.
Tom, the piper's son
THE PIPER'S SON?
KASA (RUSTLE)
カサ
AS IN THE NURSERY RHYMES OF MOTHER GOOSE?

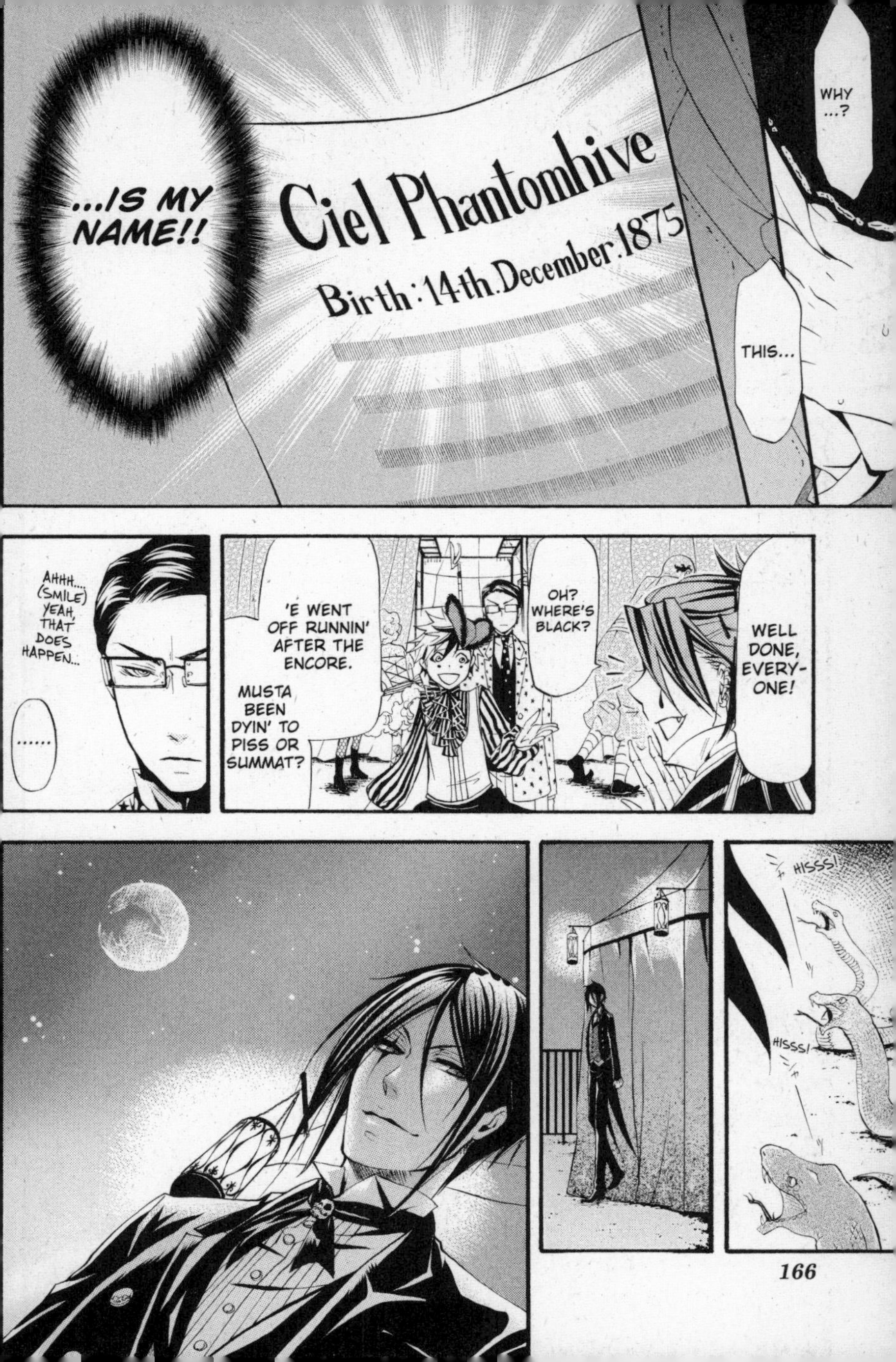
WHY ...?
THIS...
Ciel Phantomhive
Birth: 14th. December. 1875
...IS MY NAME!!
WELL DONE, EVERY-ONE!
OH? WHERE'S BLACK?
'E WENT OFF RUNNIN' AFTER THE ENCORE.
MUSTA BEEN DYIN' TO PISS OR SUMMAT?
AHHH.... (SMILE) YEAH, THAT DOES HAPPEN...
......
HISSS!
HISSS!

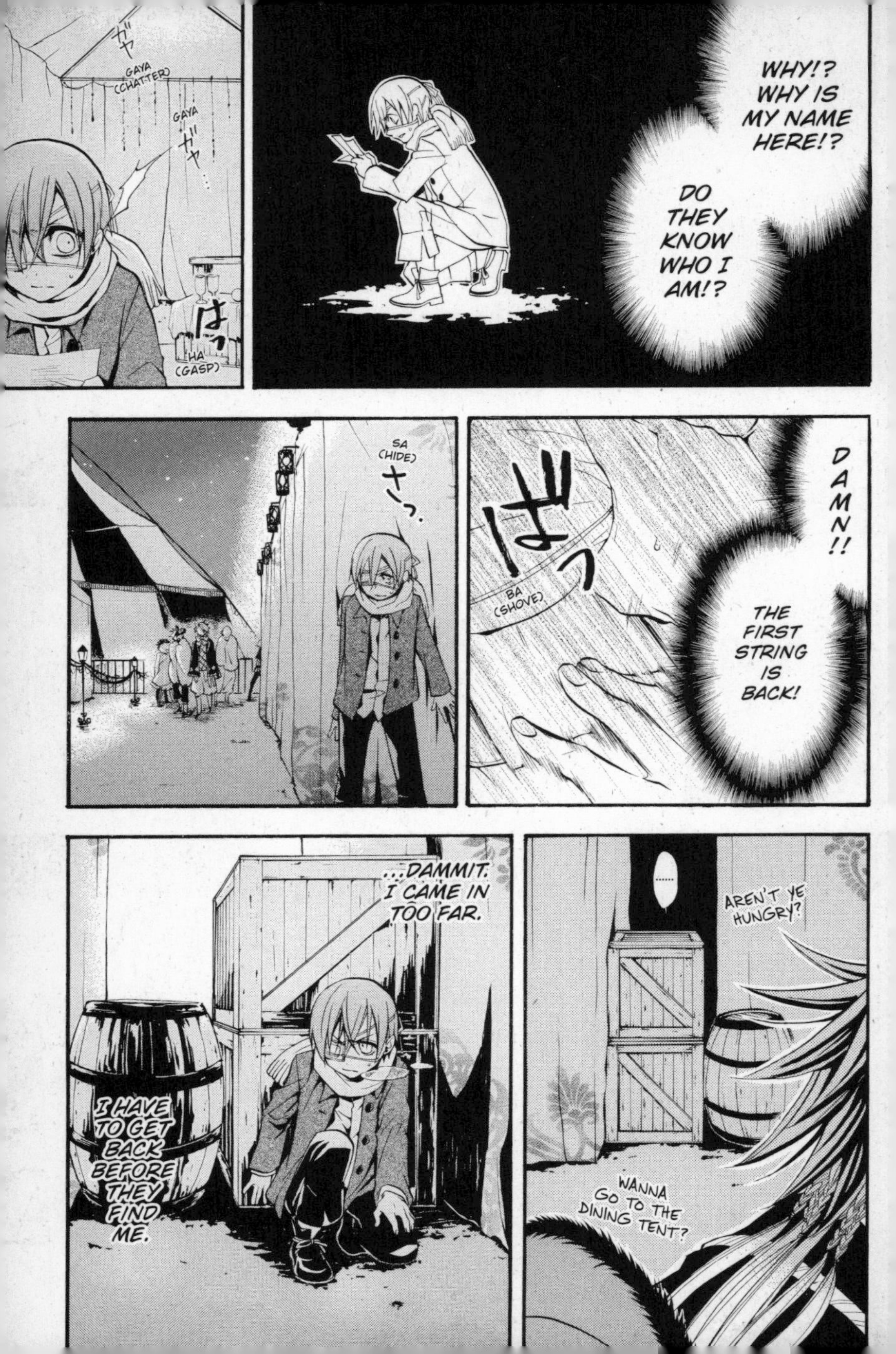
WHY!? WHY IS MY NAME HERE!?
DO THEY KNOW WHO I AM!?
ガヤ
GAYA (CHATTER)
GAYA
ガヤ…
はっ
HA (GASP)
DAMN!!
THE FIRST STRING IS BACK!
ばっ
BA (SHOVE)
SA (HIDE)
さっ.
......
AREN'T YE HUNGRY?
WANNA GO TO THE DINING TENT?
...DAMMIT. I CAME IN TOO FAR.
I HAVE TO GET BACK BEFORE THEY FIND ME.

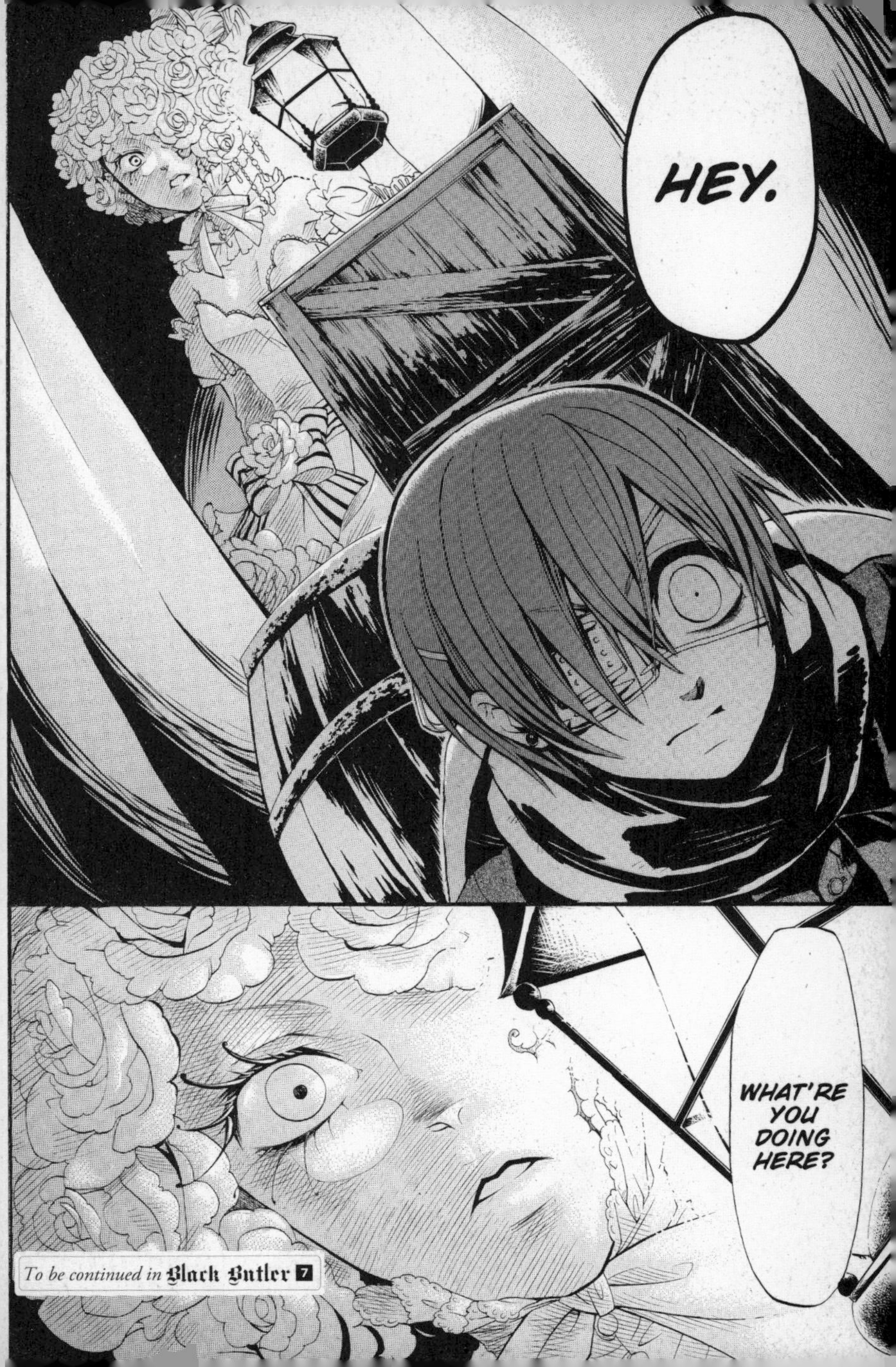
HEY.
WHAT'RE YOU DOING HERE?
To be continued in Black Butler 7

➤ Black Butler ➤

黒執事

✦ Downstairs

Wakana Haduki

Akiyo Satorigi

SuKe

Kiyo

7

Nobuko.M

*

Takeshi Kuma

*

Yana Toboso

✦

SpecialThanks

Yana's Mother

for You!

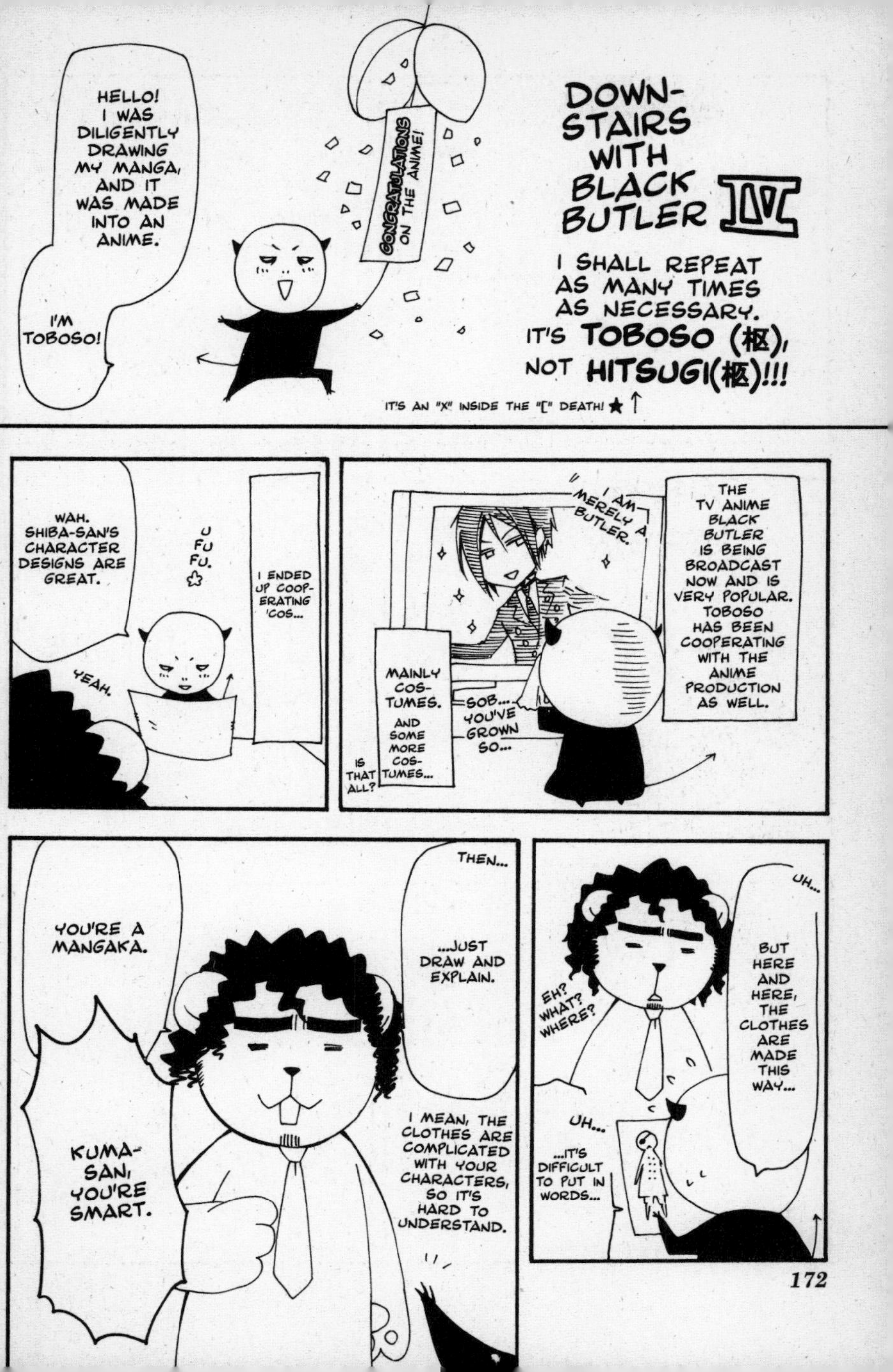
DOWN-STAIRS WITH BLACK BUTLER IV
I SHALL REPEAT AS MANY TIMES AS NECESSARY. IT'S TOBOSO (枢), NOT HITSUGI(柩)!!!
IT'S AN "X" INSIDE THE "[" DEATH! ★ ↑
CONGRATULATIONS ON THE ANIME!
HELLO! I WAS DILIGENTLY DRAWING MY MANGA, AND IT WAS MADE INTO AN ANIME.
I'M TOBOSO!
THE TV ANIME BLACK BUTLER IS BEING BROADCAST NOW AND IS VERY POPULAR. TOBOSO HAS BEEN COOPERATING WITH THE ANIME PRODUCTION AS WELL.
"I AM MERELY A BUTLER."
SOB... YOU'VE GROWN SO...
MAINLY COS-TUMES.
AND SOME MORE COS-TUMES...
IS THAT ALL?
I ENDED UP COOP-ERATING 'COS...
WAH. SHIBA-SAN'S CHARACTER DESIGNS ARE GREAT.
U FU FU.
YEAH.
UH...
BUT HERE AND HERE, THE CLOTHES ARE MADE THIS WAY...
EH? WHAT? WHERE?
UH...
...IT'S DIFFICULT TO PUT IN WORDS...
THEN...
...JUST DRAW AND EXPLAIN.
YOU'RE A MANGAKA.
KUMA-SAN, YOU'RE SMART.
I MEAN, THE CLOTHES ARE COMPLICATED WITH YOUR CHARACTERS, SO IT'S HARD TO UNDERSTAND.

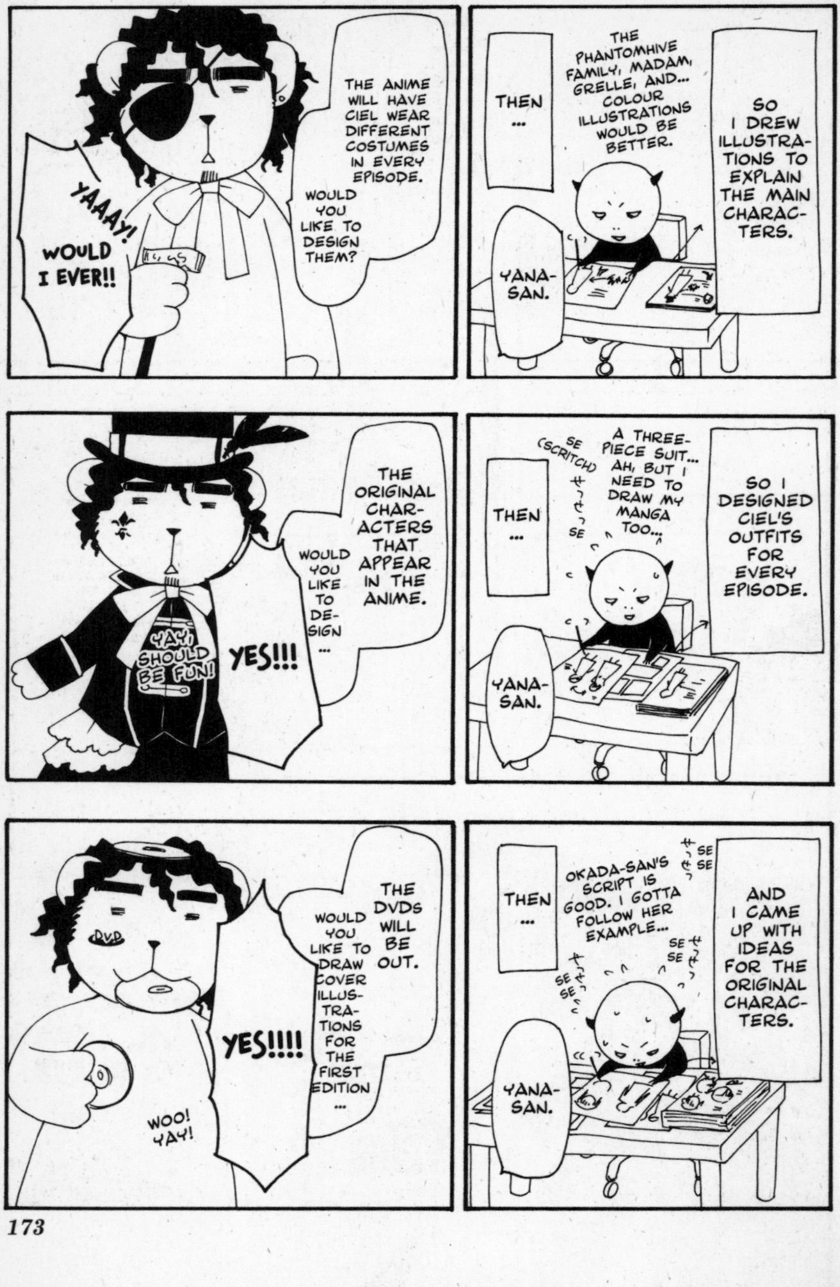
SO I DREW ILLUSTRATIONS TO EXPLAIN THE MAIN CHARACTERS.
THE PHANTOMHIVE FAMILY, MADAM, GRELLE, AND... COLOUR ILLUSTRATIONS WOULD BE BETTER.
THEN ...
YANA-SAN.
THE ANIME WILL HAVE CIEL WEAR DIFFERENT COSTUMES IN EVERY EPISODE.
WOULD YOU LIKE TO DESIGN THEM?
YAAAAY!
WOULD I EVER!!
SO I DESIGNED CIEL'S OUTFITS FOR EVERY EPISODE.
A THREE-PIECE SUIT... AH, BUT I NEED TO DRAW MY MANGA TOO...
SE (SCRITCH)
SE
THEN ...
YANA-SAN.
THE ORIGINAL CHARACTERS THAT APPEAR IN THE ANIME.
WOULD YOU LIKE TO DESIGN ...
YES!!!
YAY! SHOULD BE FUN!
AND I CAME UP WITH IDEAS FOR THE ORIGINAL CHARACTERS.
SE SE
OKADA-SAN'S SCRIPT IS GOOD. I GOTTA FOLLOW HER EXAMPLE...
SE SE
THEN ...
SE SE
YANA-SAN.
THE DVDS WILL BE OUT.
WOULD YOU LIKE TO DRAW COVER ILLUSTRATIONS FOR THE FIRST EDITION ...
YES!!!!
DVD
WOO! YAY!

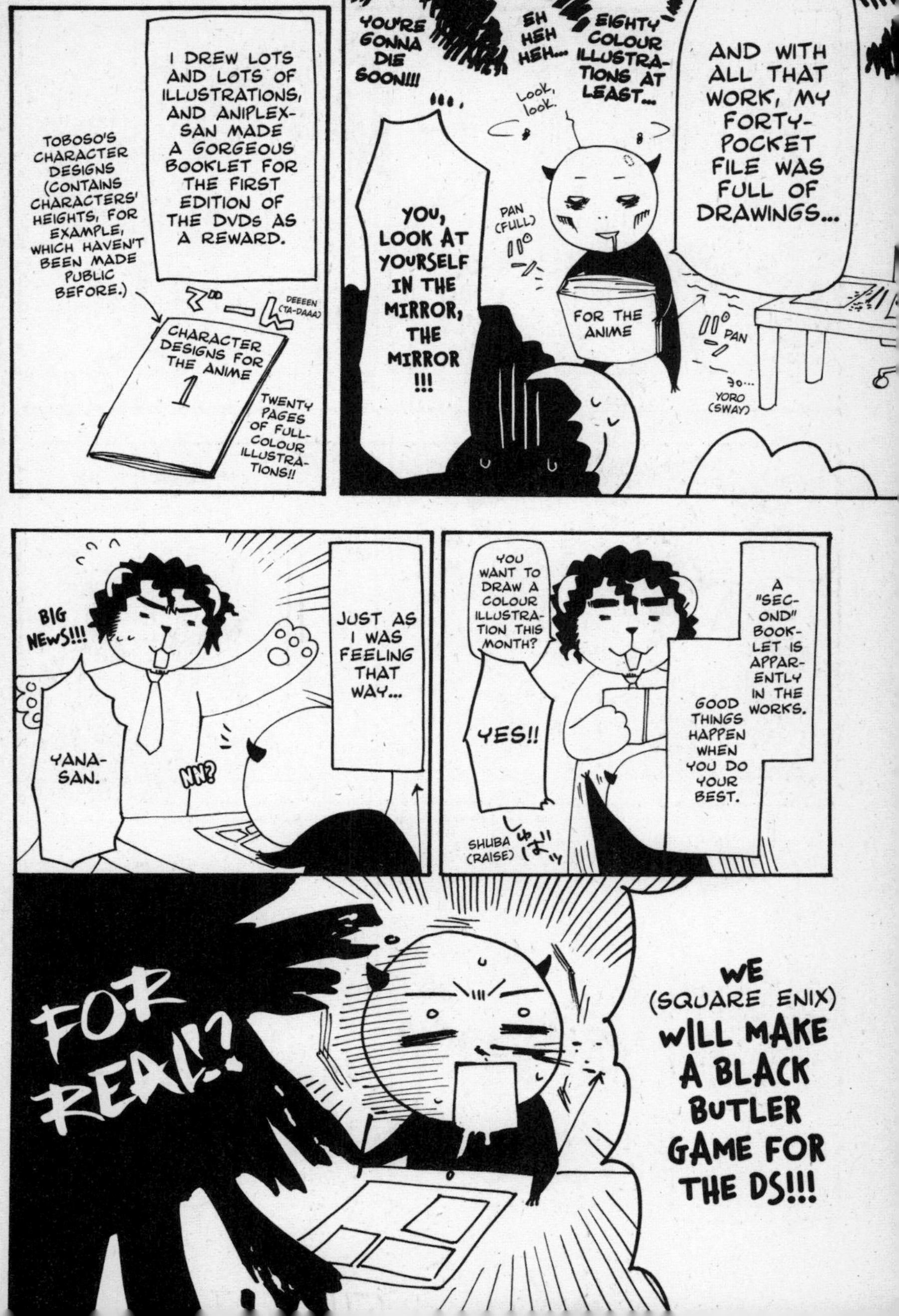
AND WITH ALL THAT WORK, MY FORTY-POCKET FILE WAS FULL OF DRAWINGS...
EIGHTY COLOUR ILLUSTRATIONS AT LEAST...
EH HEH HEH...
Look, look.
YOU'RE GONNA DIE SOON!!!
...
PAN
YORO (SWAY)
FOR THE ANIME
PAN (FULL)
YOU, LOOK AT YOURSELF IN THE MIRROR, THE MIRROR!!!
I DREW LOTS AND LOTS OF ILLUSTRATIONS, AND ANIPLEX-SAN MADE A GORGEOUS BOOKLET FOR THE FIRST EDITION OF THE DVDS AS A REWARD.
TOBOSO'S CHARACTER DESIGNS (CONTAINS CHARACTERS' HEIGHTS, FOR EXAMPLE, WHICH HAVEN'T BEEN MADE PUBLIC BEFORE.)
DEEEEN (TA-DAAA)
CHARACTER DESIGNS FOR THE ANIME 1
TWENTY PAGES OF FULL-COLOUR ILLUSTRATIONS!!
A "SECOND" BOOKLET IS APPARENTLY IN THE WORKS.
GOOD THINGS HAPPEN WHEN YOU DO YOUR BEST.
YOU WANT TO DRAW A COLOUR ILLUSTRATION THIS MONTH?
YES!!
SHUBA (RAISE)
JUST AS I WAS FEELING THAT WAY...
BIG NEWS!!!
YANA-SAN.
NN?
WE (SQUARE ENIX) WILL MAKE A BLACK BUTLER GAME FOR THE DS!!!
FOR REAL!?

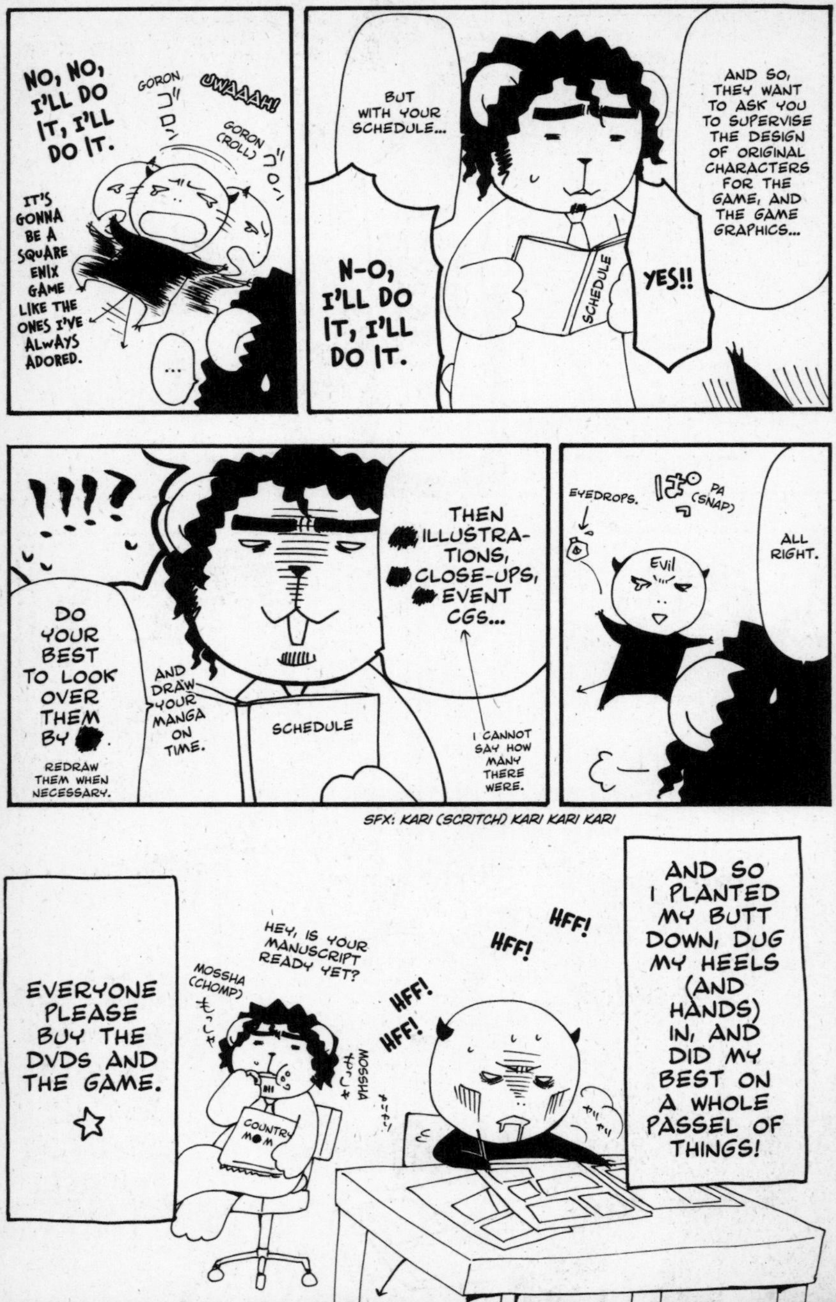
AND SO, THEY WANT TO ASK YOU TO SUPERVISE THE DESIGN OF ORIGINAL CHARACTERS FOR THE GAME, AND THE GAME GRAPHICS...
YES!!
SCHEDULE
BUT WITH YOUR SCHEDULE...
N-O, I'LL DO IT, I'LL DO IT.
UWAAAH!
GORON
GORON (ROLL)
NO, NO, I'LL DO IT, I'LL DO IT.
IT'S GONNA BE A SQUARE ENIX GAME LIKE THE ONES I'VE ALWAYS ADORED.
...
ALL RIGHT.
PA (SNAP)
EYEDROPS.
Evil
THEN [redacted] ILLUSTRATIONS, [redacted] CLOSE-UPS, [redacted] EVENT CGS...
I CANNOT SAY HOW MANY THERE WERE.
!!!?
SCHEDULE
AND DRAW YOUR MANGA ON TIME.
DO YOUR BEST TO LOOK OVER THEM BY [redacted].
REDRAW THEM WHEN NECESSARY.
SFX: KARI (SCRITCH) KARI KARI KARI
AND SO I PLANTED MY BUTT DOWN, DUG MY HEELS (AND HANDS) IN, AND DID MY BEST ON A WHOLE PASSEL OF THINGS!
HFF!
HFF!
HFF!
HFF!
HEY, IS YOUR MANUSCRIPT READY YET?
MOSSHA (CHOMP)
MOSSHA
COUNTRY MOM
EVERYONE PLEASE BUY THE DVDS AND THE GAME. ☆

Translation Notes

PAGE 6
Abberline
The real Frederick Abberline was a chief inspector with the nineteenth-century Metropolitan Police in London and is most famous for being tasked with catching Jack the Ripper, but failing to do so.

PAGE 9
Phillip, John, Grey
It is hard to say if these persons to whom Queen Victoria is referring have historical counterparts. Phillip may refer to the current Prince Phillip, Duke of Edinburgh, who is Queen Victoria's oldest living descendant and great-great-grandson. However, Phillip was born in 1921, while Victoria died in 1901. John may refer to her butler, who was introduced in Volume 5, while Grey may refer to General Charles Grey, a relation to many of the men who served as Earl Grey. Grey served in both the British army and in the British House of Commons, and would go on to serve Albert, the Queen Consort, as a personal secretary. After Albert's death, Grey became secretary to Queen Victoria herself.

PAGE 22
Joker's manner of speech
In the Japanese edition, Joker speaks in the Kyoto dialect (*ben*), which today is commonly associated with geisha (though not strictly used by females). Though this dialect is considered Kansai-*ben*, often thought of as being faster, livelier, and occasionally rough, Kyoto-*ben* is softer and more elegant. Much of this is due to the dialect being used in the imperial court during the Heian era, when modern Kyoto was the capital of Japan.

PAGE 47
Prosthetic
Prosthetics used during the Victorian era were likely made of wood and/or metal and disguised using clothing. They were also most commonly used by those who had suffered wounds in war, though the wealthy would have had relatively easy access to them as well.

PAGE 61
Wilde and Goethe
Snake's snakes are named after two of the most famous writers active in Europe around the approximate time of the events in this volume. Among these writers' most famous works are two stories that involve a familiar topic—the selling of souls. The German writer Johann Wolfgang von Goethe, who died in 1832, is most famous for *Faust*, a story about Mephistopheles, a devil who helps the knowledge-seeking Faust stray from the righteous path, all as part of a wager with God. Faust agrees to the devil's terms to serve him in Hell upon his death, while the devil agrees to serve Faust on Earth however long he lives. The writer Oscar Wilde, on the other hand, was active from 1854 to 1900 and is known for *The Picture of Dorian Grey*, whose titular character states off the cuff that he would sell his soul to stay youthful, while a portrait painted of him would age in his stead. His wish granted, Dorian's portrait grows more horrid with every hedonistic act in which he indulges, until it finally drives him to his death.

PAGE 154
Dagger's vision
In the original, the "vi" in "vision" is replaced by the character for "beauty," which is read "bi" and pronounced the same as "vi" in Japanese.

PAGE 173
Editor K's second costume
While the first and third costumes on this page are fairly obvious (the first being Ciel, the third being a DVD package of some kind), K's second costume is of Drossel, from the *Black Butler* anime (season 1). Drossel, most likely named after the character of Herr Drosselmeyer, the toymaker from *The Nutcracker*, is one of the anime-only characters designed by Yana Toboso.

PAGE 175
Country M●m
There is a Japanese brand of cookies called Country Ma'am.

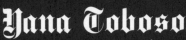

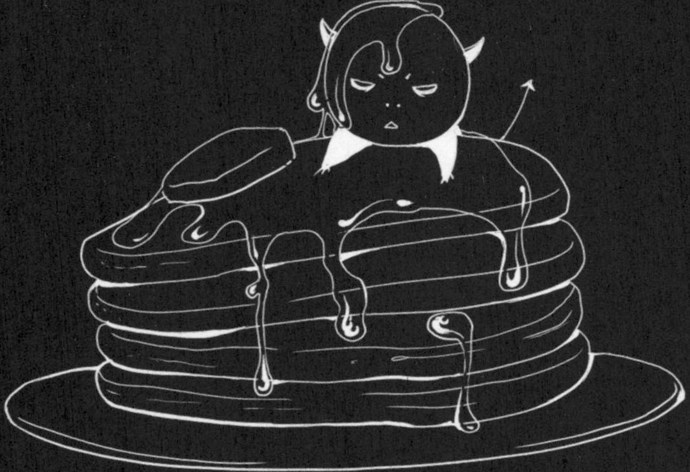

Yana Toboso

AUTHOR'S NOTE

I was simply aiming to draw an entertaining manga. And now an anime, which is the best form of entertainment, has been made from it.

Every day the creators of that other world give me new discoveries and inspiration.

I decided to give the cover a makeover to express my fresh new feelings.

And that's what I am feeling with Volume 6.

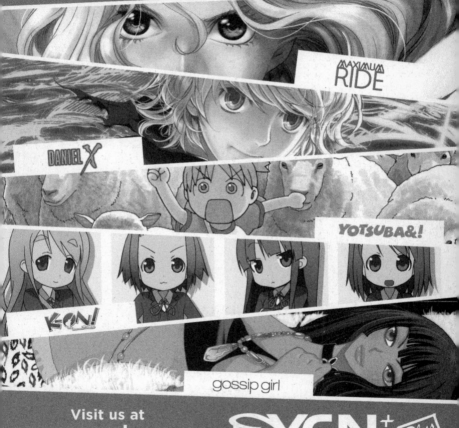
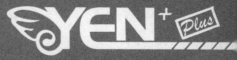

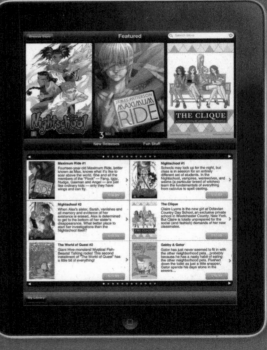

BLACK BUTLER

YANA TOBOSO

Translation: Tomo Kimura • Lettering: Alexis Eckerman

KUROSHITSUJI Vol. 6 © 2009 Yana Toboso / SQUARE ENIX CO., LTD. All
rights reserved. First published in Japan in 2009 by SQUARE ENIX CO.,
LTD. English translation rights arranged with SQUARE ENIX CO., LTD.
and Hachette Book Group through Tuttle-Mori Agency, Inc.

Translation © 2011 by SQUARE ENIX CO., LTD.

Yen Press
Hachette Book Group
237 Park Avenue, New York, NY 10017

www.HachetteBookGroup.com
www.YenPress.com

Yen Press is an imprint of Hachette Book Group, Inc. The Yen Press name
and logo are trademarks of Hachette Book Group, Inc.

First Yen Press Edition: July 2011

ISBN: 978-0-316-08430-7

10 9 8 7 6 5 4 3 2 1

BVG

Printed in the United States of America